DAVID WEIR was born in 1939 and educated at Bradford Grammar School and at Queen's College, Oxford. He subsequently held the post of research sociologist at Aberdeen University (1961-2) and from 1962 to 1963 was attached to the Extra-Mural Department of Leeds University. He then joined the Sociology Department of Hull University as research assistant and subsequently assistant lecturer (1963-5) and from 1966 to 1971 was lecturer in the Sociology Department of Manchester University. From 1971 to 1974 he was lecuturer and subsequently senior lecturer in Sociology at Manchester Business School. He is at present Professor of Organizational Behaviour at Glasgow University. Among his other publications are *Men and Work in Modern Britain* (1973) and *Social Problems of Modern Britain* (1972), which he co-edited with Eric Butterworth.

Edited by David Weir

Men and Work
in Modern Britain

Fontana/Collins

First published in Fontana Books 1973
Second impression September 1976

Made and printed in Great Britain by
William Collins Sons and Co Ltd Glasgow

Contents

Acknowledgments

Once again I wish to thank the many colleagues, friends and students with whom this book has been discussed. But above all I wish to acknowledge my great debt to Noreen Davey, whose role in the real labour of collecting material and dealing efficiently with the heavy administrative load that is inevitably entailed in this kind of enterprise, has been that of a colleague in the best sense of the word. Francis Bennett and Lydia Greeves of Fontana Books have supported and sustained us throughout with every kind of assistance whenever we have needed it. My wife, Mary, knows how much her love, encouragement and forbearance and that of Timothy, Belinda and Sophie has meant over the last few months.

David Weir
January 1973

The editors and publishers gratefully acknowledge John Murray Ltd for permission to include the extract from 'Summoned by Bells' by John Betjeman, Faber and Faber Ltd for the extracts from 'Toads Revisited' from *The Whitsun Wedding* by Philip Larkin and 'The Confidential Clerk' from *Collected Poems 1901-1962* by T. S. Eliot. The extract from 'Muckers' from *Chicago Poems* by Carl Sandburg, copyright 1916, by Holt, Rinehart and Winston, Inc., renewed, 1944, by Carl Sandburg, is reprinted by permission of Harcourt Brace Jovanovich, Inc. The extract from 'Psalm of Those Who Go Forth Before Daylight' from *Cornhuskers* by Carl Sandburg, copyright 1918 by Holt Rinehart and Winston, Inc.; renewed, 1946, by Carl Sandburg is reprinted by permission of Harcourt Brace Jovanovich, Inc.

'For the better things'

Introduction to the Modern Britain series

The main purpose of this series of readers is to introduce students to the study of their own society. Sociology provides a frame of reference, an approach, which allows us to make some sense of our society even where it would be impossible to consider more than a fraction of the mass of material which is being produced about it.

An increasing number of people are taking courses on 'British society' which have a bearing on their training or reflect their concern to understand social processes and social functions. For many, given the reading available, this may reflect a heavy diet of factual material (the number of households, rate of divorce, circulation of newspapers and the like) which becomes largely concerned with what *is* rather than with *how* or *why*. It tends to lose out on sociological perspective and relevance. For other students the diet is excessively rich in the esoteric ramifications of fashionable theories, and this presents problems of a different nature.

It is our view that the two approaches mentioned are equally unsatisfactory for the student who is a beginner. He may have had no previous intensive contact with the social sciences. However, he has lived in this society, or one similar to it, all his life. This, then, must constitute the teacher's starting point.

In the first place the teacher has to begin where the student happens to be, with a particular experience of life and a system of beliefs and attitudes which help him to explain that experience. He already has views about his society, although they may be misinformed or based on untenable assumptions about how things happen. In this situation, it seems to us he requires material which allows him to examine some of his preconceptions. As Walter Lippmann, the American writer, has said: 'For the most part we do not first see, and then define, we define first and then see. We are told about the world before we see it. We imagine most things before we experience them. And these preconceptions, unless education has made us acutely aware, govern deeply the whole process of perception.' Aneurin Bevan made a similar point when he wrote 'It is inherent in our intellectual activity that we seek to imprison reality in our description of it. Soon, long before we realize it, it is we who become the prisoners of the description. From that point on, our ideas degenerate into a kind of folklore which we pass to each other, fondly thinking we are still talking of the reality around us.' Of course, sociologists have their 'folklore' just as do any other group in society and we would not wish to claim any more for this series of books of readings than that they may stimulate the student to consider alternative perceptions and constructions of social reality to those which he brings to the study of his own society.

Our decision to compile the first book in this series – *The Sociology of Modern Britain* – arose from our experience in teaching a wide range of students, many of whom were adults, in university extra-mural and on undergraduate and postgraduate courses, on professional courses of many kinds, and in other educational institutions. We recognized a number of factors which made the courses on this theme less satisfactory than they might have been. Our series is an attempt to remedy some of these deficiencies.

This, like others in the series, is an introductory reader. An attempt has been made to introduce a range of topics and approaches, with a balance between what is descriptive and what is analytical and conceptual. Had we been trying to meet the needs of university students near the end of their courses our selection would have been quite different in a number of respects.

Every chapter has an introductory section which is designed to pose some of the important questions which arise in the particular context of our readings without providing a detailed commentary on *all* the relevant sociological concepts and issues. These introductory sections attempt also to link certain pertinent themes, which are not dealt with in specific extracts, to further reading. To some extent these issues arise in readings, but the book can be used profitably in conjunction with one of the text books in current use. The Textbook Reference section at the end contains detailed page references to the most relevant themes that any of the courses for which we are catering will wish to cover, irrespective of whether we have specific readings on all of them.

The readings follow the introductory section in each chapter. Because of the audience it was felt unnecessary to reproduce the detailed footnotes and references many of them contained. As far as possible references in the text to authors or books have either been included in the Further Reading at the end of the relevant chapter or omitted altogether. The common practice of numbering tables according to their place in the particular reading rather than the numbers to be found in the work from which they are taken has been followed. Most of the readings are, of course, edited or abbreviated versions of the original texts, which inevitably repay fuller and more detailed study if time permits.

As far as further reading is concerned, we concentrate on books which are reasonably easy to obtain. Many are in paperback, and using our source book it would be possible to obtain a wide range of material quite cheaply. Others will lead the student to utilize libraries.

Several criteria have guided us in the course of our selection of readings. Readability is one of these, and although the extracts vary in difficulty it is hoped that the most difficult can be tackled successfully with the help of the references provided. The variations in the level of the readings, and the different approaches to be found in them, are not fortuitous: they are designed to pose questions from which every student must start. Some are deliberately short, lending themselves to class discussion; others may be more properly studied independently. In some cases the readings deal with similar material from different points of view, and this is a deliberate policy to make links between themes which cut across the boundaries of chapters, and reinforce, for example, the sense of inter-relationships between social institutions and an awareness of the cumulative consequences of social change.

In our experience of introductory courses, much original and relevant work never finds its way to the student body, even though it may be mentioned in the reading lists. University libraries may have only single copies of a journal containing an article recommended to many students. The problems are much worse in other educational settings. Often these may be compounded by teachers who are not themselves trained in the subject and who feel equally in need of a frame of reference. Systematic teaching demands this. Too often, perhaps, subjects may be introduced to students as a series of disconnected episodes of merely intrinsic interest. We have chosen work which is not on the whole readily available to the student, often from journals and books to which he is unlikely to have access. We have tended to avoid choosing from paperbacks though in one or two cases books have reappeared in paperback after our original selection was made.

There are many personal elements which arise in making a choice of readings and we have tried to be explicit about some of them, but our focus throughout has been upon the specific needs and requirements of the students taking introductory courses, largely in non-university settings. The audience we have aimed at covers a wide range. There are members of the general public whose interest in the nature of their society may have been stimulated by television programmes, colour supplements and the like. These may or may not move on to adult classes, or courses of study, such as those provided by the Open University, Extra-Mural Departments, the WEA, and by local authorities. Many students at Colleges of Education, Technical Colleges and Colleges of Further Education undertake general introductory courses in sociology, much of the content of which relates to Britain, and these are beginning to develop in the sixth forms of some schools. Professional or pre-professional courses of training, in-service and refresher courses for such groups as hospital administrators, managers and social workers, are more and more common. As the amount of this provision in the social sciences increases, the problems of teaching it and gaining access to relevant material become, if anything, greater than they have been before.

It is hoped that this series of source books of readings will go some way to meeting some of the needs of students and teachers involved in the kinds of courses we have mentioned. Their value will depend on the extent to which they are used. They are above all intended to assist teachers and students in the process of mutually learning about the nature of their own society. They are not intended to promote any particular sectarian or theoretically purist position. In our experience of textbook and other one-sided approaches this is an unnecessary attempt to do the teacher's job for him and is anyway fairly rapidly seen through by students. We have been very much encouraged and helped by feedback from students and teachers about *The Sociology of Modern Britain* and *Social Problems of Modern Britain*. Above all we welcome comments and criticisms from those teaching and studying in this field.

Eric Butterworth
David Weir

Chapter One

Occupations and Organizations

There is nothing better for a man,
than that he should eat and drink,
and that he should make his soul enjoy good in his
labour. *Ecclesiastes 2:24*

Being one of the men
You meet of an afternoon,
. . . .
All dodging the toad work
By being stupid or weak.

Philip Larkin, Toads Revisited

'Work' is a vital and significant part of most people's everyday lives. For this reason alone it is not surprising that the study of work has been a central concern for many sociologists, both in Britain and elsewhere. Yet, in most institutions in which sociology is taught, 'work' as such is not directly studied. There are courses in 'industrial sociology', although everybody does not work in industry, courses in the 'sociology of occupations', although everybody who works does not necessarily pursue the same occupation throughout his working life, and courses on 'formal organizations', although everybody who follows an occupation does not do so within a complex, imperatively co-ordinated organization.

So this book of readings has not been compiled in order to slavishly pursue the requirements of a particular syllabus or to satisfy the demands of some tightly structured area of sociological theory. I believe that it will be useful for students engaged in the kind of courses I have just mentioned, but that it will not constrain them or their teachers to adopt any particular intellectual straitjacket.

But none the less the book as a whole does possess a

certain structure and the readings were selected in order to illustrate certain points rather than others. So in this introductory chapter I will try to briefly explain the principles on which the book is organized.

Firstly, it should be clear from the general introduction that this book forms part of a series, the separate parts of which are related by a common conception of what sociology is all about and how students can learn about their own society. So this book relates to Chapter 4 on 'Work' in *The Sociology of Modern Britain* and Chapter 10 on 'Problems of Work' in *Social Problems of Modern Britain.* In general, although there is a certain amount of cross-referencing and overlap I have tried to steer clear of specific topics which are directly covered in those more general books. Moreover, although there is a sense in which the comprehensive study of work in modern Britain could lead into consideration of many other topics, I have tried to stick fairly strictly to the job in hand. Thus, the ways in which the social relations of the workplace are influenced by family, class, political and cultural factors, are hinted at in many extracts but not thoroughly and systematically explored. Even such topics as unemployment and leisure are not accorded as much space as, ideally, one would like to do, and as some teachers and students may wish to. There are many loose ends, therefore, which I hope will be noticed and picked upon as points from which discussion can start and on which inter-relations between work and other aspects of society may be developed.

In the last section of this collection of readings I have attempted to indicate the kind of comparative coverage which is given by the major texts and readers in the field of 'work'. So to some extent students will be able to fill in the gaps themselves. But it may be helpful at this point to give an idea of the way in which the study of work may lead into a consideration of other significant aspects of the social structure as well as being important in its own right.

In his introductory textbook *The Sociology of Work* Caplow defines his subject matter as 'the study of those social roles which arise from the classification of men by the work they do'. This definition leads him into such areas as the way in which societies 'assign' work to individuals, members of families and inhabitants of particular locations and of how the population is distributed between one type of work and another. For instance, if we were to ask the simple question 'why are there miners in County Durham and what are they like?', there would seem to be a simple answer . . . 'because there is coal in Durham'.

But this answer is clearly inadequate on its own because there is coal in many areas and any comprehensive answer would have to tell us something about the historical development of mining as an industry, about miners as an occupational group and about the national and regional policies towards coal-mining in recent years. And this would only be a start towards answering the question.

We would need to ask questions about occupational choice and socialization to find out something about how people entered mining and what the typical career pattern of miners in Durham was. We might want to know what the relative social standing of mining in the area was. And answering this question might lead us to consider the ways in which miners were typical of or different from other people. Thus Caplow asks 'Why do we find variations among occupational groups in political attitudes, life expectancy, interests, intelligence, insanity, reading tastes, family size and standards of conduct? What consequences do these differences have for the community?'

In conducting our enquiries into the miners of County Durham we might well find that many were sons of miners, and came from a family background of mining. In general we would be interested to compare the rate of 'occupational inheritance' with that for other occupations. For instance, among doctors, lawyers and farmers the rate might be high, among businessmen and university lecturers it might be rather lower. We would want to ask why this should be, and whether the occupational structure was becoming more or less rigid in this way.

We should be bound to consider the strong tradition of trade unionism among the Durham miners, and to examine the crucial confrontations between miners and employers which had forged this militant unionism. We should find that certain patterns of behaviour, apparently arbitrary, irrational and unpredictable from *our* perspective, were in fact strongly sanctioned and supported by occupational values. Finally we should want to examine the ways in which mining as an occupation and miners as members of an occupational group related to other occupational groups in British society, and how the organizational structures which were typical of mining as an industry were supported by and impinged on other features of society. And working through these problems would lead to a consideration of some long-term trends, for instance of technological innovation and change, which were likely to affect the 'social structure of mining' which our analysis had illuminated.

It is appropriate at this point to say something very briefly about the labour force as a whole. At any one time, the labour force consists of three types of people: there are those who are actually employed, those who are not employed but are registered as available for employment and those who may be available for employment but are not registered as such. In Chapter 10 the paper by Phillips indicates some of the difficulties which we may get into through neglect of these simple distinctions.

At any one time about half of the adult population are members of the labour force. It is generally estimated that something in the order of 90 per cent of men and 30–40 per cent of women between 20 and 65 are either in employment, looking for employment or are potentially available for employment. Table 1, taken from a recently published compilation of statistical information relating to trends in British society during the past seventy years, indicates some important features of the labour force and the way it has changed occupationally since 1900. It is clear from looking at the right-hand column, which consists of indices of growth of major occupational groups (taking 1911 as the base year), that while the labour force has increased in size by 35 per cent, this increase has been very uneven as between one occupational group and another. The major increase has come in the white-collar sector; clerks, salesmen, technicians, managers, but above all the professions have increased in number and in significance to the economy as a whole over this period. And among these groups it is the scientifically and technically-based occupations which have increased most disproportionately. While, in the remainder of this book, we are not concerned very much with this kind of overall statistical analysis, as there are many good sources for such information, it is essential to bear in mind this background to our study.

Table 1. The occupied population of Great Britain by major occupational groups 1911–1966

Occupational groups	No of persons ('000)		Major groups as % of population		Growth indices of major groups*
	1911	1966	1911	1966	1966
1. Employers and proprietors	1,232	832	6·7	3·4	68
2. White-collar workers	3,433	9,461	18·7	38·3	276
1. Managers and administrators	631	1,514	3·4	6·1	240
2. Higher professionals	184	829	1·0	3·4	451
3. Technicians and lower professionals	560	1,604	3·1	6·5	286
4. Foreman and inspectors	237	736	1·3	3·0	311
5. Clerks	832	3,262	4·5	13·2	392
6. Salesmen	989	1,516	5·4	6·1	153
3. Manual workers	13,685	14,393	74·6	58·3	105
1. Skilled	5,608	5,857	30·5	23·7	104
2. Semi-skilled	6,310	6,437	34·4	26·1	102
3. Unskilled	1,767	2,099	9·6	8·5	119
4. All occupied	18,350	24,686	100·0	100·0	135

* 1911 = 100

Source: Based on Table 4.1 in G. S. Bain, R. Bacon, J. Pimlott, 'The Labour Force', in *Trends in British Society since 1900*, ed. A. H. Halsey, London, Macmillan, 1972.

Table 2, taken from the same source, shows how the proportion of women in the labour force has increased between 1911 and 1966. The table shows the extent to which women in various statistical categories 'participated' in the occupied labour force by giving the women engaged in paid work at the two dates as a percentage of all women in that age group. Clearly while it is true that the participation of *all* categories of women has increased, it is among married women of all ages that the increase has been most marked. But the *increase* itself is not as significant as is the indication these figures give of a change in the expectation on the part of many women that they *should* work, and *will* continue to work even after marriage, and will tend to come back to work after they have had children. Several of the pieces in this reader deal with some of the implications of these changes.

Table 2. The changes in the female labour force 1911–1966 – Female Participation Rate (%)

Age	1911				1966			
	Single	Married	Widowed and divorced	All	Single	Married	Widowed and divorced	All
School leaving age–24	73	12	58	65	74	44	58	64
25–34	74	10	65	34	89	34	66	41
35–44	66	10	61	24	86	49	74	53
45–54	55	10	46	23	82	50	72	55
55+	35	7	19	16	30	21	16	21
All	69	9	29	35	66	38	24	42

Source: Table 4.7 in Halsey, *op. cit.*

The major ways in which sociologists have attempted to structure the topic of work are in terms of the 'sociology of occupations' and the 'sociology of organizations'. Each has had its vogue for variable periods of time in syllabuses and on reading lists: each has certain conceptual and practical limitations which make it unsuitable as a universal matrix into which what we know about 'work' can be poured. Each has traditionally had a characteristic style and methods of approach, and each has had its band of devotees and enthusiasts who have had a heavy involvement in criticizing as non-kosher the efforts of protagonists of the rival camp.

The study of occupations has gone through a phase of micro-analysis with much concentration on certain specific occupations, sometimes apparently chosen for their news-value and general interest, or possibly because the researcher had a particular entrée into them. It would probably be fair to say that there have been relatively more studies of manual jobs which fall into the category of 'extreme occupations' than their intrinsic relevance to the study of occupations would warrant. This is not to deny the importance of such books as *Coal is Our Life*, *Coal and Conflict* or *The Fishermen*, which have contributed enormously to our understanding of what working conditions are like, and how the pattern of work relates to home and community life in areas in which jobs such as these are important. But it is important, too, to remember that only a comprehensive study of many other jobs not intrinsically so exciting or unusual to the middle-class sociologist can provide the basis for a typology of all jobs. It has often been suggested that the traditional interests of many sociologists were in the field of 'low-life' or in the study of the conditions of the life and work of the working classes with a view to their amelioration. As a result some quite significant and potentially rewarding middle-class occupations have been neglected. It is for reasons such as these that we have attempted as far as possible to steer a 'mainstream' course in this reader: to avoid the unusual for its own sake, and to concentrate on extracts which raise general questions for readers of this book about the role of work in their own lives and in areas in which they may have had personal experience.

However, we have not tried to 'cover the waterfront'. Many very important kinds of work have not been studied, and can therefore not figure in a collection of readings such as this. Some topics such as the role of women, or the assimilation of coloured workers, or the values of top managers in industry may seem to be worthy of more extended treatment and discussion than we have been able to give here. The criteria which we have tried to bear in mind in selecting material have been those of relevance to the point in hand, rather than of attempting a comprehensive, fair and 'balanced' description of all of the various kinds of activities we typically characterize as 'work'.

Books like this are clearly not meant to be read from cover to cover as if they were novels. They are meant to be *used*, and they are meant to serve as a basis for further reading. So the principles on which this book is organized will not seem suitable to all those who use it. As one way of resolving this difficulty we have provided an alternative table of contents (p. 435), organized possibly on more traditional lines, which may be useful to some readers whose timetables may be more tightly bound to examination requirements.

But the main organizing principles of this collection derive from the two major fields we mentioned earlier: occupations and organizations.

Occupations

In their important collection, *Men, Work and Society*, Nosow and Form make the claim that 'occupational sociology has become a new and vital subdiscipline within sociology'. They identify five broad themes which characteristically have been the concern of occupational sociology, as follows:

1. 'The Social nature of work and related phenomena . . . leisure, play recreation, retirement, . . . unemployment.'
2. 'The analysis of occupational structure . . .'
3. 'The study of individual occupations . . . recruitment and training, adjustment problems, interpersonal relations at work . . .'
4. 'The analysis of how the occupational structure and individual occupations articulate with other segments of society . . .'
5. 'The study of a particular occupation to highlight an important problem in the broader society.'

These are broad aims and we shall not attempt to deal adequately with all of them. We are probably most concerned at present with points 1, 3 and 5 though not necessarily in that order. But there are some important implications of the 'occupational' approach. One is that if we focus on individual occupations we become aware of the existence of a complex inter-relationship between the individual, who we may identify as occupying a particular position in the occupational structure, and the requirements which apparently derive from his occupying that position. Thus, to be more specific, when we call someone a 'doctor' or a 'docker', the term stands for something much more detailed and, to some extent, intangible.

Individuals are not simply 'doctors' in isolation, they *become* doctors; their being doctors has involved them in a *process* over a period of time, and marked by certain turning points, of emerging as doctors. Thus they learn to behave as doctors should, to treat others as members of *other* categories, as patients, perhaps as nurses or as colleagues. They have to

learn to become what they are and they are involved in a
continued exercise of behaving in specific ways which justify
their own and the community's expectation of what it is to be
a doctor. Typically we say of people in jobs like this that they
are involved in a *career*.

The concept of career is possibly a characteristic contribution
of the sociology of occupations to the field of sociology in
general. There are many types of career pattern. Some present
a picture of orderly movement in an upward direction. In
others there is a period, possibly fairly prolonged, of *enforced*
childishness and of being retained in a juvenile role, before
one suddenly emerges as a fully fledged capable and competent
worker. Some apprenticeships work like this. In some kinds of
work, movement is not regular at all, but individuals go from
job to job in an apparently patternless or intermittent form.
Among some kinds of manual work the first half of one's
working life is 'upward', the second is 'downward'. Others
may appear superficially patternless; random factors seem
important. The significance of these may have been under-rated
by sociologists, whose job it is to seek a structure in everything.
Likewise individuals often tend to over-estimate their own
perspicacity and ability when looking back over a 'successful'
life and to berate the inequity of fate or the antagonism of
the authorities when attempting to explain what they have
come to perceive as their own failure.

The most influential work in the study of occupations has
probably come from E. C. Hughes (whose approach, and
this is possibly significant, is best seen in what he and his
students did, rather than in his pre- or post-factum
explanations and justification of why he was right to do it and
why it was the only correct thing to do at that time). In a
short essay[1] he makes some important points.

He emphasizes the moral imperative that '. . . sociology has
much to gain from such studies, provided that those who
undertake them make and keep a sociological bargain with
those who support them and those who allow themselves
to be studied'. He points to the significance of occupational
categorizations in government, commerce and research, but
agrees to '. . . leave others the task of counting the occupations

[1] E. C. Hughes: 'The Study of Occupations', in *Sociology Today*,
eds. R. K. Merton, L. Broom and L. S. Cottrell, New York, Basic
Books, 1959.

in industrial economies and the changing numbers of people engaged in each of them, and the tiresome business of fitting the many occupations into a small enough number of categories to permit overcrowding them into tables'. It is salutory to be reminded that 'analysis by occupational status' is the most widely used method of presenting results from census, analyses of mortality and disease, voting habits, consumer demand, even of religious affiliation.

The object of the exercise – the 'occupation' – is defined by Hughes in terms of the division of labour. 'The essential is that the occupation is the place ordinarily filled by one person in an organization or complex of efforts and activities.' The specific type of organization is related to the differentiation of function in the division of labour – a poor title according to Hughes because it 'emphasizes the division and neglects the integration'. But an occupation is more than merely a position, for society *licenses* certain people to carry on specific activities. Moreover, the members of an occupational group commonly feel some solidarity and believe that they have been given a *mandate* 'to define proper conduct with respect to the matters concerned in their work'. Professions are occupational groups which are specifically licensed, generally in terms of a legal charter, and possess, in a strong degree, the belief in their mandate. 'Not only do the practitioners, by virtue of gaining admission to the charmed circle of the profession, individually exercise a license to do things others do not do, but collectively they presume to tell society what is good and right for it in a broad and crucial aspect of life. Indeed, they set the very terms of thinking about it. When such a presumption is granted as legitimate a profession in the full sense has come into being.'

We mentioned earlier the importance of the notion of a career to the analysis of occupations. Hughes defines a career very simply as '. . . the fate of a man running his life-cycle in a particular society at a particular time'. The study of a career involves consideration of the process of socialization into a career, of the capacity of occupational groups to act as reference groups, and of the way in which individuals come to accept the requirements of an occupational role as binding on them. It thus leads into many of the most central problems of sociology.

In his book, *The Sociology of Occupations*, Krause

distinguishes four major perspectives on occupations – the historical, the biographical and the division of labour in terms of both function and of conflict. It is mainly with the second of these that we are concerned at present, but Krause's book is recommended for those who wish to pursue the occupational approach more thoroughly.

Organizations

Another focus of the study of work is the 'organization'. As many definitions of this creature exist as there are hot dinners, but some salient features are common to all.

Over the last two decades, probably more time and effort has gone into sociological research into organizations than into any other substantive field of sociology. It would be an impossible task, and one that is much better performed in the standard texts and readers which deal specifically with this topic, to attempt to go over all of this ground. There are several excellent reviews of the literature on organizations. The books by Burns, Etzioni, March and Simon, Perrow and Silverman suggested for further reading offer guides of varying scope and difficulty to this field, and it is not our present aim to attempt to cover similar ground. In this collection of readings the major themes are related to the conception of organizations as bureaucracies, derived from the work of Max Weber.

But it is important to remember that there are many other conceptions of the organization than the bureaucratic one. One that is very commonly met with is that the organization represents in some sense a 'natural whole' or system. As a system it attempts to survive and maintain an equilibrium and these pressures may lead to the neglect or corruption of the organization's original goals. As Gouldner says, 'once established, organizations tend to generate new ends which constrain subsequent decisions and limit the manner in which the nominal group goals can be pursued'. Those who adopt this kind of strategy for analysing organizations and their activities tend to see them as systems which are to a certain extent self-generating. They also tend to see the separate parts of the organization as *necessarily* linked together in the same kind of way as the arms and legs of a living mammal are co-ordinated by an infra-structure of bones, tendons, muscles, nerves and the bloodstream. Few sociologists adhere slavishly to this kind of view but it is none the less an important element in many analyses.

Some research in Britain by Burns and Stalker distinguishes between the organismic type of organization structure and the mechanistic. The latter, which approximates fairly closely to the Weberian type, is appropriate, according to Burns and Stalker, when the environment is relatively stable, the organization has an assured 'market', and the human raw material, the labour power which is acted on and generated by the organization, enters with relatively fixed and predictable expectations of what behaviour is expected of it. The organismic type is more suitable for a changing situation in which the environment poses a succession of difficult problems for the organization which its previously learnt and rehearsed routines are incapable of adapting too quickly. But, as a corollary of course, the people who work in the organismic type of situation will tend to develop different expectations of how they may be expected to behave as well. They may be less committed to the organization, more mobile, and less disposed to accept the organization's word as binding law for them. Some studies of computer programmers and systems analysts tend to show that their view of the organization and their position in it does tend to be on organismic lines.

For writers such as Woodward the major characteristic determining organizational structure and hence organizational behaviour is the underlying technology on which the organization is based. Woodward classified business firms according to their method of production and was able to show that technology was a major determinant of managerial structure. The actual production technology employed in a plant tended to be associated with the number of levels of management authority. The ratio of managers and supervisors to other workers directly employed on production is less in unit production, somewhat higher in mass production and highest of all in continuous process industries, which would conventionally be regarded as illustrating a 'more advanced' type of technology.

A relative newcomer to the repertory of organizational analysis is that of 'contingency theory'. The structure of an organization may depend on the environment in which it exists. Moreover, one kind of structure may be well adapted and 'successful' in meeting one kind of goal, but not another. Thus there may be a more or less good 'fit' between an organization's structure and its capacity to achieve its goals. At present the contingency approach has informed and generated a good deal of empirical research but has possibly not succeeded in offering a viable alternative to the prevailing orthodoxies. In a recent paper Bowey suggests that it may now be helpful to integrate the contingency approach with the 'systems' and 'action' theories to interpret empirical data 'from the perspective of a more accurate model of human interaction'.

Other writers, such as Silverman, have argued that analyses of organizations based on the idea of the organization as some kind of system have been deficient. He criticizes many writers in this tradition for tending to begin from the questions asked by those in positions of authority. To a great extent this criticism of Silverman's is justified: it is also true, however, as we pointed out in *Social Problems of Modern Britain*, of most other areas of research in which sociologists have worked. Again, it is probably fair comment to say that most writers on organizations have tended to ignore or to pay little attention to the environmental context in which organizations function, and this is likewise true of work in, for instance, the sociology of the family. But it is the systems frame of reference itself which is the principal target of Silverman's criticism. He argues that the systems approach to organizational analysis has become a 'paradigm' which defines the nature of the social reality it purports to describe. Thus, while no sociologist would ever seriously hold that organizations really *are* hydraulic or mechanical, or electrical or organic entities, many would tend to use analogies drawn from hydraulic, mechanical, electrical or organic models of the organization, as if organizations possessed similar kinds of properties.

Silverman argues that it is time for the systems paradigm to be supplanted by a new kind of paradigm based on a different view of social reality as something perpetually in flux and perennially being recreated in terms of the way human beings engaged in social interaction define their own goals and purposes. Social action is thus not a fixed and given aspect of some stable structure – the 'social system' – it is the process by which individuals attempt to make sense of and succeed in accomplishing definitions of reality which 'work' for themselves and those with whom they are involved.

The 'action' perspective proposed by Silverman involves a careful consideration of the ways in which members of 'social systems' like organizations define reality and come to accept certain definitions as legitimate. This approach derives from the work of such writers as Weber, Schutz and more recently Goffman and Garfinkel. Weber pointed out that 'every artefact . . . can be understood only in terms of the meaning which its production and use have had or will have for human action . . . that which is intelligible or understandable about it is thus its relation to human action in the role either of means or of end . . . only in terms of such categories is it possible to "understand" objects of this kind'.

Action takes place in characteristic patterns, and the patterns recur within a relatively stable social structure in which certain relations between means and ends appear 'rational' to those involved in them. This 'rationality' can also typify the social structure as a whole. According to Weber the characteristic type of social organization in Western capitalist industrial society was the *bureaucracy*. In such a society organized on rational principles, social relations were predominantly characterized by the rule of law. Such a view presupposes that it is possible for an organization to define certain goals, to recognize certain means of attaining these goals as more efficient than others, and that such organizations will select the most efficient means and institutionalize and codify them in a set of written procedures (Table 3). The people who work in such organizations would tend to behave in certain ways which would reinforce their institutionalized positions (Table 4). Such organizations would be technically superior to other forms of organization in the same kind of way as machine production was superior to the non-machine methods which it superseded (Table 5).

The increasing demands of society for more order and regulation, and the progression of the division of labour would, according to Weber, tend to produce more and more bureaucratization.

But other writers saw bureaucracy in a rather less positive light. Michels argued that, far from being the ideal and technically efficient solution, bureaucracy tended to develop in response to demands made by the educated élite for more

Table 3. Weber's definition of bureaucracy

A bureaucracy is an organization with the following attributes:

1. Official business is conducted continuously, in accordance with stipulated rules.
2. Each official's work is delimited in terms of impersonal criteria.
3. Authority is delegated to the extent necessary to carry out the precise work of each position.
4. The official in any position has only limited means of compulsion.
5. Each official's responsibilities and authority are part of a hierarchy of authority.
6. No official has property rights in his job.
7. Official business is conducted on the basis of written documents.

Table 4. The role of the bureaucrat

---

1. He is personally free and appointed to his position on the basis of contact.
2. He exercises authority impersonally.
3. He is faithfully involved in the organization.
4. He is appointed and placed in his job on the basis o f technical qualifications.
5. He has a full time involvement in administrative work.
6. His career rewards largely consist of regular salary and prospects of regular advancement.

Table 5. The attributes of bureaucracy

---

1. It is technically superior because of its precision, speed, lack of equivocation, continuity, uniformity of operation and calculability.
2. It concentrates the means o f administration.
3. It tends to level socio-economic differences.
4. It produces an indestructible system of authority relationships.
5. It maintains all bureaucratic decisions under the Rule of Law.

---

responsible, powerful and secure positions. And the aims of the bureaucracy would not necessarily be those of society as a whole: indeed they would very commonly conflict with the goals and aspirations of working people.

Mosca made a similar point when he contrasted the feudal type of political organization with the bureaucratic. In the bureaucratic state the direction of society is mostly in the hands of salaried officials, whose largely middle-class social origins make them unlikely to pursue the interests of the mass of the population. Later, Burnham argued that the bureaucratization of business and industry had tended to create a new ruling class consisting of men who did not own the means of production, but controlled their application in what Dahrendorf later described as 'imperatively co-ordinated associations'.

Other writers on bureaucracy have concentrated on its empirical shortcomings. Thus, Merton developed the idea that bureaucracies would tend to produce in their employees a state of 'trained incapacity'. The very training which promoted the capacity to work methodically and rigorously by applying general principles to specific cases made it difficult for them to adapt successfully to a changing situation. Another dysfunctional aspect of bureaucracy is the 'displacement of goals' in which the *means* to the bureacratic *end* become ends in their own right. Bureaucrats tend to act rigidly and to become obsessive and ritualistic in their devotion to the form rather than to the substance of the administrative procedures.

Gouldner attacked the trend in some writing which concentrates only on the inevitability of bureaucratization and the loss of individual freedom that this entails. He pointed out that not all relationships within an organization have to be impersonalized: the degree of impersonality tends to vary according to status level within the organizational structure and is not necessarily characteristic of all relations between bureaucrats and the clients of the bureaucracy. He pointed out that we need to have a much more clearly specified conception of the environment in which the organization operates. The nature of ownership and control, the increasing tendency towards a monopoly structure in capitalist industry, a growth in overhead costs, and trends in social mobility were among the factors which he drew attention to.

In his own analysis of 'patterns of industrial bureaucracy', Gouldner defined three types of rules. These were punishment rules, representative rules and mock rules. The first were enforced and legitimized without the agreement of all parties. The second were supported by both management and workers. The last category, that of mock bureaucracy, occurred when an agency outside of the organization imposed the rules and neither management or workers could reciprocate them as legitimate. He suggested that conflict would tend to be avoided in bureaucratic organizations in which representative rules predominated.

Another important development in the study of bureaucracy was the work of Selznick. He accepted the view of Chester Barnard that the organizational necessity of getting people to work together and co-operate required a delegation of functions. But in every case it seemed that a dichotomy of interests would develop between the functionary who initiated action and his subordinate who had to carry it out. The crucial issues in bureaucracy, then, according to Selznick, are those of control; the crucial problems for the organization are the problems of officials who need to maintain their control over others. One of the ways in which the problem of control can be solved is by officials creating informal groups. These groups develop an ideology of their own which becomes in time the ideology of the organization. Some of the work which writers like Skolnick have undertaken on the police indicates how this process may occur. Although the policeman works within a bureaucracy that is clearly subordinated and governed by rule of law in labour's terms, the training, formal education and informal group structures in which a policeman is involved tend to encourage a view of himself as a craftsman coupled with what Skolnick calls 'a guild-like affirmation of worker autonomy'.

Another important development in the tradition of the study of organizations and bureaucracy is that of Etzioni. In an attempt to clarify the differences between organizations he produced a typology in which the important elements are the kind of power applied by the organization and the kind of involvement of participants in it.

There are basically three types of power which an organization may apply to its lower participants – those who work in and for an organization but do not share in its decision-making processes. They may be coerced by physical or other sanctions, they may be induced to strike a bargain for monetary rewards, or they may be persuaded that the organization has something of value to offer them which is consonant with their own personal goals. These three types of power are described as 'coercive', 'remunerative' and 'normative'. Correspondingly, there are three kinds of ways in which the lower participants may be involved in the organization – they may be alienated from it, expect financial returns from it or derive moral satisfaction from playing the part the organization wishes them to.

Table 6. The compliance relationship as a basis for organizational classification

		Involvement of lower participants		
		Alienative	Calculative	Moral
Power applied by the organization	Coercive	1 (prison)	2	3
	Remunerative	4	5 (business)	6
	Normative	7	8	9 (church)

1, 5, 9 = Congruent organizational types

Source: A. Etzioni, *A Comparative Analysis of Complex Organizations.*

For each kind of organization there is a 'modal' type of power – the power which is most characteristically applied. And for each group of participants there is a 'modal' pattern of involvement, based on the expectations which these 'lower participants' have about the kind of rewards and satisfaction they hope to derive from work. When the modal power and involvement match up, a compliance pattern occurs which is in Etzioni's terminology 'congruent' (Table 6). Not only are congruent organizations most efficient, they are also more commonly found than are 'incongruent' types. Moreover there is likely to be some pressure on incongruent organizations to move towards a position of congruency. Thus, it could be argued that a prison which had previously functioned on the basis of a compliance pattern consisting of coercive power applied to an alienated population, might get into difficulties if it started to operate on the basis of trying to generate calculative involvement if no attempt was made to simultaneously change the coercive power structure. Etzioni's analysis of organizations has been criticized but it none the less may provide a useful framework for looking at some of the problems and dilemmas of organizational life raised in this book of readings.

The structure of this book

The structure of this book is very simple. In the next chapter we look at some of the classical statements about the division of labour and the role of work in modern society. In Chapter 3 we take up some of these themes and relate them to empirical studies undertaken in specific work settings in British society. Chapters 4, 5 and 6 are concerned with the occupational way of looking at work. In them we look at the way in which people enter work, become socialized in particular patterns of behaviour, experience certain characteristic kinds of conflict between their work roles and other roles and tend to adopt certain specific types of value and attitude which are in one way or another appropriate for their occupational role.

In Chapters 7, 8 and 9 we turn our attention to the organizational aspect of work. But here again we are not so much concerned with examining the structures themselves as considering the effect of those structures on the people who work within them. We have made a very crude and possibly rather arbitrary distinction between two types of work situations. In the first the individual is quite closely constrained for a variety of reasons by the precise requirements of his organizational role. He is what the organization requires him to be. In Chapter 8, however, we look at some kinds of work situation in which individuals may be perceived as striving towards a degree of self-fulfilment and self-development in their work. In Chapter 9, we look at another kind of organization, that of the organized collectivities of employees, and raise some questions about the role of trade unions and occupational associations in contemporary society. Finally, in Chapter 10, we revert back to some of the major themes which were raised in the first two chapters. I am attempting here to suggest some of the points of linkage between the slice of social life which I have, for the purposes of this particular book, abstracted, taken out, dusted and put into Sunday best clothes for the purposes of analysis, and the

Figure 1. How this book is organized

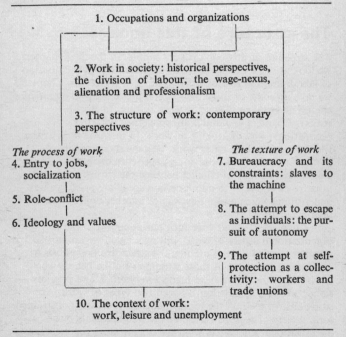

1. Occupations and organizations

2. Work in society: historical perspectives, the division of labour, the wage-nexus, alienation and professionalism

3. The structure of work: contemporary perspectives

The process of work
4. Entry to jobs, socialization

5. Role-conflict

6. Ideology and values

The texture of work
7. Bureaucracy and its constraints: slaves to the machine

8. The attempt to escape as individuals: the pursuit of autonomy

9. The attempt at self-protection as a collectivity: workers and trade unions

10. The context of work: work, leisure and unemployment

rest of society. In this section, as indeed throughout this collection as a whole, I am hopefully raising more questions than I feel capable of providing specific answers to. Hopefully, too, I shall have provided a basic structure which will enable the interested student to use the suggestions for further reading to carry on asking appropriate questions about work in modern Britain.

Further Reading: Occupations and Organizations

R. BENDIX, *Work and Authority in Industry*, New York, Wiley, 1956.

A. M. BOWEY, 'Approaches to Organization Theory', *Social Science Information 116*, 1973, pp. 109–28.

*J. BURNHAM, *The Managerial Revolution*, New York, John Day, 1941 (since reprinted in Penguin).

*T. BURNS AND G. M. STALKER, *The Management of Innovation*, London, Tavistock, 1961.

*T. BURNS, *Industrial Man*, London, Penguin, 1969.

*T. CAPLOW, *The Sociology of Work*, London, McGraw-Hill, 1954.

*J. CHILD, *The Business Enterprise in Modern Industrial Society*, London, Collier-Macmillan, 1969.

*L. COSER AND B. ROSENBERG, *Sociological Theory*, New York, Macmillan, 1968.

*A. ETZIONI, *Readings on Modern Organizations*, Englewood Cliffs, New Jersey, Prentice-Hall, 1962.

*W. A. FAUNCE, *Readings in Industrial Sociology*, New York, Appleton-Century Crofts, 1967.

*A. FOX, *A Sociology of Work in Industry*, London, Collier-Macmillan, 1971.

*A. W. GOULDNER, *Patterns of Industrial Bureaucracy*, Glencoe, Illinois, The Free Press, 1954.

E. C. HUGHES, *Men and their Work*, Glencoe, The Free Press, 1958.

E. A. KRAUSE, *The Sociology of Occupations*, Boston, Little Brown, 1971.

J. G. MARCH AND H. A. SIMON, *Organizations*, London, Wiley, 1958.

R. K. MERTON *et al.*, *Reader in Bureaucracy*, Glencoe, Illinois, The Free Press, 1952.

R. W. E. MICHELS, *Political Parties*, New York, Dover, 1959.

G. MOSCA, *The Ruling Class*, New York, McGraw-Hill, 1939.

*N. MOUZELIS, *Organization and Bureaucracy*, London, Routledge and Kegan Paul, 1967.

S. NOSOW AND W. H. FORM, *Man, Work and Society*, New York, Basic Books, 1962.

*S. R. PARKER, R. K. BROWN, J. CHILD and M. A. SMITH, *The Sociology of Industry*, London, Allen and Unwin, 1968.

*C. PERROW, *Organizational Analysis*, London, Tavistock, 1971.

D. SILVERMAN, *The Theory of Organizations*, London, Heinemann, 1970.

J. SKOLNICK, *Justice without Trial: Law Enforcement in a Democratic Society*, New York, Wiley, 1966.

J. D. THOMPSON, *Organizations in Action*, New York, McGraw-Hill, 1967.

M. WEBER, *The Theory of Social and Economic Organization*, New York, Free Press, 1964.

W. F. WHYTE, *Men at Work*, Homewood, Illinois, Irwin-Dorsey, 1961.

J. WOODWARD, *Industrial Organization*, London, Oxford University Press, 1965.

* Available in paperback

Chapter Two

Work and Society

Twenty men stand watching the muckers
. . . .
of the twenty men looking on
Ten murmur, 'O, its a hell of a job'
Ten others, 'Jesus, I wish I had the job'
                              Carl Sandburg, Muckers

This chapter illustrates a few, but only a very few, of the
themes which have engaged the interests of sociologists
studying the position of work in modern society. In *The World
We Have Lost*, Peter Laslett describes the structure of British
society before the long drawn out trauma of the first
'Industrial Revolution'. Looking at Britain during the Stuart
period, he attempts to reconstruct the texture of a society
which was in certain important ways 'one-class'. That is not to
say that there was no inequality in pre-industrial Britain for
there were quite gross differences relating to every facet of
individual's life-chances. Nor does Laslett mean that there
were no differences between people. But there was only one
class in the sense of a body of people who were linked by a
distinctive consciousness which set them apart from others in
society, and who were capable of concerted action on a
nationwide basis in terms of their own class interest. Thus
there were no *classes*, based on relations to the means of
production in the Marxist sense.

But if there were no classes, there was economic oppression
and exploitation. Laslett argues that the patriarchal
domestic-centred organization of production which formed
the basis of English social life '. . . abused and enslaved
people quite as remorselessly as the economic arrangements
which replaced them . . .'. The short expectancy of life – no
more than thirty years – and the stringent constraints of the
apprenticeship system meant that many workers must have
spent most if not all of their life working for *subsistence* in

someone else's family. For 'apprentices . . . were workers who were also children . . . clothed and educated as well as fed, obliged to obedience and forbidden to marry, unpaid and absolutely dependent until the age of twenty-one'. But there was a reciprocity about these role arrangements; for if 'workers' were 'sons', then 'sons' were also 'workers'. Laslett claims that as 'everything physical was on the human scale', so social arrangements were based on small groups to which everyone in practice belonged. Relationships might be based on love or on hatred but even conflict was between individuals; it was on a personal scale.

This, then, was not merely a world in which factories, office blocks and housing estates did not predominate, it was a world in which all social arrangements were in a sense *familial*. Working groups were not normally composed of large numbers of workers all of whom were of the same sex and age, but were complex in a different way. Men worked with boys, women with girls, as parents with their children, or as craftsmen with their apprentices. The inexorable rhythm of the seasons meant that social life in the country was more rigorously prescriptive than in the towns, where more occupational choice was available. But it was in the country too that the need for large groups of workers to come together regularly at hay-time and for harvesting meant that the inherently small scale organization of working life was more frequently transcended. Otherwise only wars and pestilence disturbed the basic structure of work.

To a degree, Laslett's picture is an idealized one, and not accepted by all historians. But it is an essential starting point because to the nineteenth-century commentators and critics of the social consequences of the division of labour it represented, even if in an exaggerated and similarly idealized form, the essential ingredients of the 'world we have lost'.

For some, such as Adam Smith, the loss had been to society's advantage. It represented the liberation of the 'productive powers of labour'. It was for Smith an undeniable and generally applicable truth that 'the division of labour, however, so far as it can be introduced, occasions in every art, a proportionable increase of the productive powers of labour'. The specialization of production and the concentration of similar activities were the foundation of the generation of profit from labour; for without the division of labour *value* could not be created.

Many features of Smith's account and that of the exponents of the newly discovered 'dismal science' of economics were accepted by Marx. But Marx saw an obverse side to the division of labour. The concentration of ownership and control of the means of production in the hands of the few provided the basis for the exploitation of the many. Regardless of the personal, biographical origins of the factory owners, they represented a new *class*, whose existence was based on the exploitation of the surplus value accruing to the product of the labour of others. The continued existence of a 'reserve army' of potential employees enabled the capitalist to maintain wages merely at the level of subsistence. Only the generation of a common consciousness of the fact of their exploitation and the creation of a political organization, both of which would be facilitated in the long run by the factory organization of production, would enable the workers to derive their rightful entitlement to the value created by their own labour. The fundamental nexus, the social relationship which provides the type or matrix of social relationships in capitalist society, is that between employer and worker. 'Upon this relation . . . between the employing capitalist and the wages labourer the whole wages system and the whole present system of production hinge.'

The objective facts of exploitation were matched by the subjective experiences of alienation. The workers in the new industrial system were alienated in several ways from essential aspects of their own human nature. They were alienated from the process of production, and being unable to control or command the resources to construct more than a small part of the final product, they were thus alienated from the product of their own labour. The artefacts they produced, then, existed as something alien and apart from them – something objectified. In creating objects, they became, to employing capitalist and to their fellow-workers alike, objects themselves.

Weber extended Marx's analysis of the foundations of social class differentiation and of exploitation in the factory system by showing that similar types of relationship would be produced in any situation in which a market for a good or service existed. There would thus be, in a complex, differentiated society, as many bases for class-interest group formation and class conflict as there were major markets. There would, of course, be points of articulation between these markets. Marx had already revealed the relationship between the class of landowners and that of factory owners and controllers. But there would not, *necessarily*, be a coalescence between these groups, who were powerful in different sections, to produce a monolithic class structure. More recently Dahrendorf has argued that there are many bases of conflict deriving from the differential distribution of power within what he refers to as imperatively co-ordinated associations. It is only when there is a systematic and consistent overlap between class interests and points of conflict in more than one sector that a revolutionary situation of the kind ultimately envisaged by Marx is likely to emerge.

Durkheim's view of the division of labour was more complex again. For him, the division of labour was a moral phenomenon and was related to the ways in which contemporary society was co-ordinated. For Durkheim the division of labour was '. . . more and more filling the role that was once filled by the "conscience collective" . . . ' by which he meant the attitudes, beliefs and values held in common by all members of simpler, less differentiated societies. The division of labour was associated also with the classic dilemma of western society, that of reconciling social needs with the individual's aspirations and interests. It was '. . . the sole process which enables the necessities of social cohesion to be reconciled with the principle of individuation . . .'. It was the underlying feature of the *organic solidarity* which Durkheim saw as characteristic of western society in which individuals as occupants of specific positions within the division of labour were linked to others by relations of functional interdependence. The breakdown of this functional interdependence because of the increased pace of economic change, unaccompanied by changes in moral regulation, constituted the situation of *anomie*.

In the extract from his work, Fromm argues that the abstraction and impersonality of social relationships which can occur in an anomic situation is a general feature of modern social life, deriving from the universality of the types of social relation based on the market. In the society based on the exchange value of commodities, personality itself becomes a commodity. Interpersonal relationships become trivialized and degraded: the 'successful' doctor is the heart-surgeon with the winning ways, the beautiful blonde wife, the acceptable liberal persona, but whose most 'successful' patients show a rather minimal capacity for survival, rather than the medical officer of health whose routine organization of inspection and certification prevents mass outbreaks of infection due to poisoned food or inadequate disposal of sewage effluent. The 'marketing orientation' affects the texture of human relationships in general for '. . . its very nature is that no specific and permanent kind of relatedness is developed, but that the very changeability of attitudes is the only permanent quality of such orientation. In this orientation those qualities are developed which can best be sold.'

The paper by Faunce brings these themes together. He not merely relates the breakdown of the 'world we have lost' to the growth of alienation and to the 'fear of freedom' but shows its positive aspects also in asking 'Whether man has, since the mediaeval period, achieved increasing freedom from small group controls . . . and has escaped from the fixed self-identity characteristics of a stable and rigid social order?' The loss of security was counterbalanced by an increase in freedom. But a new threat to the possibilities of individual self-determination arises from the increasing complexity and specialization of contemporary western society. The complex interdependence of an advanced industrial system demands a high level of social control, possibly centralized, in order to promote integration. Once again, shades of the prison-house re-emerge, this time in the shape of 'impersonal, rationalized controls'. And Faunce concludes that for a substantial segment of the population today, 'there is very little control over the important events that shape their lives'.

Many writers, in attempting to analyse the fundamental differences between contemporary society and that of 'the world we have lost', have hit on the notion of 'professionalization'. Harold Wilensky's analysis of occupational associations leads him to predict the 'professionalization of everyone'.

But perhaps the most succinct and biting comment on the divisiveness of professionalization was offered by Herbert Spencer in *The Study of Sociology*, thus: 'Many years ago a solicitor sitting by me at dinner, complained bitterly of the injury which the then lately established county courts, were doing his profession. He enlarged on the topic in a way implying that he expected me to agree with him in therefore condemning them. So incapable was he of getting beyond the professional point of view, that what he regarded as a grievance he thought I also ought to regard as a grievance: oblivious of the fact that the more economical administration of justice of which his lamentation gave me proof, was to me, not being a lawyer, matter for rejoicing.'

Reader's analysis of the development of the professions in Victorian England is interesting for several reasons. It illuminates the continuing strength of the traditional power centres of British society which inhibited the growth of institutions designed to promote *La carriere ouverte aux talents* such as were contemporarily being set up on the continent. The 'professionalism' and concern for technical expertise demonstrated by the English professional man was matched by his obsessive concern for his 'professional status'. The imperial myth and the muscular Christian ethic of the public school system provoked a general misapprehension of the real bases of national strength. As Reader says: '. . . the fundamental antipathy induced by public school education to everything commercial made it fatally easy for men from public schools to miss the central fact of England's power – that without her own industrial strength, let her empire be never so large, she was nothing more than an over-populated island off the coast of north-west Europe.'

The Division of Labour

A. Smith

Reprinted with permission from *The Wealth of Nations*, Methuen, 1961, pp. 7–16

The greatest improvement in the productive powers of labour, and the greater part of the skill, dexterity, and judgment with which it is any where directed, or applied, seem to have been the effects of the division of labour.

The effects of the division of labour, in the general business of society, will be more easily understood, by considering in what manner it operates in some particular manufactures. It is commonly supposed to be carried furthest in some very trifling ones; not perhaps that it really is carried further in them than in others of more importance: but in those trifling manufactures which are destined to supply the small wants of but a small number of people, the whole number of workmen must necessarily be small; and those employed in every different branch of the work can often be collected into the same workhouse, and placed at once under the view of the spectator. In those great manufactures, on the contrary, which are destined to supply the great wants of the great body of the people, every different branch of the work employs so great a number of workmen, that it is impossible to collect them all into the same workhouse. We can seldom see more, at one time, than those employed in one single branch. Though in such manufactures, therefore, the work may really be divided into a much greater number of parts, than in those of a more trifling nature, the division is not near so obvious, and has accordingly been much less observed.

To take an example, therefore, from a very trifling manufacture; but one in which the division of labour has been very often taken notice of, the trade of the pin-maker; a workman not educated to this business (which the division of labour has rendered a distinct trade), nor acquainted with the use of the machinery employed in it (to the invention of which the same division of labour has probably given occasion), could scarce, perhaps, with his utmost industry, make one pin in a day, and certainly could not make twenty. But in the way in which this business is now carried on, not only the whole work is a peculiar trade, but it is divided into a number of branches, of which the greater part are likewise peculiar trades. One man draws out the wire, another straights it, a third cuts it, a fourth points it, a fifth grinds it at the top for receiving the head; to make the head requires two or three distinct operations; to put it on, is a peculiar business, to whiten the pins is another; it is even a trade by itself to put them into the paper; and the important business of making a pin is, in this manner, divided into about eighteen distinct operations, which, in some manufactories, are all performed by distinct hands, though in others the same man will sometimes perform two or three of them. I have seen a small manufactory of this kind where ten men only were employed, and where some of them consequently performed two or three distinct operations. But though they were very poor, and therefore but indifferently accommodated with the necessary machinery, they could, when they exerted themselves, make among them about twelve pounds of pins in a day. There are in a pound upwards of four thousand pins of a middling size. Those ten persons, there-fore, could make among them upwards of forty-eight thousand pins in a day. Each person, therefore, making a tenth part of forty-eight thousand pins, might be considered as making four thousand eight hundred pins in a day. But if they had all wrought separately and independently, and without any of them having been educated to this peculiar business, they certainly could not each of them have made twenty, perhaps not one pin in a day; that is, certainly, not the two hundred and fortieth, perhaps not the four thousand eight hundredth part of what they are at present capable of performing, in consequence of a proper division and combination of their different operations.

In every other art and manufacture, the effects of the division of labour are similar to what they are in this very trifling one; though, in many of them, the labour can neither be so much subdivided, nor reduced to so great a simplicity of operation. The division of labour, however, so far as it can be introduced, occasions, in every art, a proportionable increase of the pro-ductive powers of labour. The separation of different trades and employments from one another, seems to have taken place, in consequence of this advantage. This separation too is generally carried furthest in those countries which enjoy the highest degree of industry and improvement; what is the work of one man in a rude state of society, being generally that of several in an im-proved one. In every improved society, the farmer is generally

nothing but a farmer; the manufacturer, nothing but a manufacturer. The labour too which is necessary to produce any one
complete manufacture, is almost always divided among a great
number of hands. How many different trades are employed in
each branch of the linen and woollen manufactures, from the
growers of the flax and the wool, to the bleachers and smoothers
of the linen, or to the dyers and dressers of the cloth! The nature
of agriculture, indeed, does not admit of so many subdivisions
of labour, nor of so complete a separation of one business from
another, as manufactures. It is impossible to separate so entirely,
the business of the grazier from that of the corn-farmer, as the
trade of the carpenter is commonly separated from that of the
smith. The spinner is almost always a distinct person from the
weaver; but the ploughman, the harrower, the sower of the seed,
and the reaper of the corn, are often the same. The occasions for
those differing sorts of labour returning with the different seasons
of the year, it is impossible that one man should be constantly
employed in any one of them. This impossibility of making so
complete and entire a separation of all the different branches of
labour employed in agriculture, is perhaps the reason why the
improvement of the productive powers of labour in this art, does
not always keep pace with their improvement in manufactures.
The most opulent nations, indeed, generally excel all their
neighbours in agriculture as well as in manufactures; but they
are commonly more distinguished by their superiority in the
latter than in the former. Their lands are in general better cultivated, and having more labour and expense bestowed upon them,
produce more in proportion to the extent and natural fertility
of the ground. But this superiority of produce is seldom much
more than in proportion to the superiority of labour and expense.
In agriculture, the labour of the rich country is not always much
more productive than that of the poor; or, at least, it is never so
much more productive, as it commonly is in manufactures. The
corn of the rich country, therefore, will not always, in the same
degrees of goodness, come cheaper to market than that of the
poor. The corn of Poland, in the same degree of goodness, is as
cheap as that of France, notwithstanding the superior opulence
and improvement of the latter country. The corn of France is,
in the corn provinces, fully as good, and in most years nearly
about the same price with the corn of England, though, in
opulence and improvement, France is perhaps inferior to England.
The corn-lands of England, however, are better cultivated than

those of France, and the corn-lands of France are said to be much better cultivated than those of Poland. But though the poor country, notwithstanding the inferiority of its cultivation, can, in some measure, rival the rich in the cheapness and goodness of its corn, it can pretend to no such competition in its manufactures; at least if those manufactures suit the soil, climate, and situation of the rich country. The silks of France are better and cheaper than those of England, because the silk manufacture, at least under the present high duties upon the importation of raw silk, does not so well suit the climate of England as that of France. But the hard-ware and the coarse woollens of England are beyond all comparison superior to those of France, and much cheaper too in the same degree of goodness. In Poland there are said to be scarce any manufactures of any kind, a few of those coarser household manufactures excepted, without which no country can well subsist.

This great increase of the quantity of work which, in consequence of the division of labour, the same number of people are capable of performing, is owing to three different circumstances; first to the increase of dexterity in every particular workman; secondly, to the saving of the time which is commonly lost in passing from one species of work to another; and lastly, to the invention of a great number of machines which facilitate and abridge labour, and enable one man to do the work of many.

First, the improvement of the dexterity of the workman necessarily increases the quantity of the work he can perform; and the division of labour, by reducing every man's business to some one simple operation, and by making this operation the sole employment of his life, necessarily increases very much the dexterity of the workman. A common smith, who, though accustomed to handle the hammer, has never been used to make nails, if upon some particular occasion he is obliged to attempt it, will scarce, I am assured, be able to make above two or three hundred nails in a day, and those too very bad ones. A smith who has been accustomed to make nails, but whose sole or principal business has not been that of a nailer, can seldom with his utmost diligence make more than eight hundred or a thousand nails in a day. I have seen several boys under twenty years of age who had never exercised any other trade but that of making nails, and who, when they exerted themselves, could make, each of them, upwards of two thousand three hundred nails in a day. The making of a nail, however, is by no means one of the simplest operations. The same person blows the bellows, stirs or mends the fire as there is occasion, heats the iron, and forges every part of the nail: In forging the head too he is obliged to change his tools. The different operations into which the making of a pin, or of a metal button, is subdivided, are all of them much more simple, and the dexterity of the person, of whose life it has been the sole business to perform them, is usually much greater. The rapidity with which some of the operations of those manufactures are performed, exceeds what the human hand could, by those who had never seen them, be supposed capable of acquiring.

Secondly, the advantage which is gained by saving the time commonly lost in passing from one sort of work to another, is much greater than we should at first view be apt to imagine it. It is impossible to pass very quickly from one kind of work to another; that is carried on in a different place, and with quite different tools. A country weaver, who cultivates a small farm, must lose a good deal of time in passing from his loom to the field, and from the field to his loom. When the two trades can be carried on in the same workhouse, the loss of time is no doubt much less. It is even in this case, however, very considerable. A man commonly saunters a little in turning his hand from one sort of employment to another. When he first begins the new work he is seldom very keen and hearty; his mind, as they say, does not go to it, and for some time he rather trifles than applies to good purpose. The habit of sauntering and of indolent careless application, which is naturally, or rather necessarily acquired by every country workman who is obliged to change his work and his tools every half hour, and to apply his hand in twenty different ways almost every day of his life; renders him almost always slothful and lazy, and incapable of any vigorous application even on the most pressing occasions. Independent, therefore, of his deficiency in point of dexterity this cause alone must always reduce considerably the quantity of work which he is capable of performing.

Thirdly, and lastly, every body must be sensible how much labour is facilitated and abridged by the application of proper machinery. It is unnecessary to give any example. I shall only observe, therefore, that the invention of all those machines by which labour is so much facilitated and abridged, seems to have been originally owing to the division of labour. Men are much more likely to discover easier and readier methods of attaining any object, when the whole attention of their minds is directed towards that single object, than when it is dissipated among a great variety of things. But in consequence of the division of labour, the whole of every man's attention comes naturally to be directed towards some one very simple object. It is naturally to be expected, therefore, that some one or other of those who are employed in each particular branch of labour should soon find out easier and readier methods of performing their own particular work, wherever the nature of it admits of such improvement. A great part of the machines made use of in those manufactures in which labour is most subdivided, were originally the inventions of common workmen, who, being each of them employed in some very simple operation, naturally turned their thoughts towards finding out easier and readier methods of performing it. Whoever has been much accustomed to visit such manufactures, must frequently have been shown very pretty machines, which were the inventions of such workmen, in order to facilitate and quicken their own particular part of the work. In the first fire-engines, a boy was constantly employed to open and shut alternately the communication between the boiler and the cylinder, according as the piston either ascended or descended. One of those boys, who loved to play with his companions, observed that, by tying a string from the handle of the valve which opened this communication to another part of the machine, the valve would open and shut without his assistance, and leave him at liberty to divert himself with his play-fellows. One of the greatest improvements that has been made upon this machine, since it was first invented, was in this manner the discovery of a boy who wanted to save his own labour.

All the improvements in machinery, however, have by no means been the inventions of those who had occasion to use the machines. Many improvements have been made by the ingenuity of the makers of the machines, when to make them became the business of a peculiar trade; and some by that of those who are called philosophers or men of speculation, whose trade it is not to do any thing, but to observe every thing; and who, upon that account, are often capable of combining together the powers of the most distant and dissimilar objects. In the progress of society, philosophy or speculation becomes, like every other employment, the principal or sole trade and occupation of a particular class of citizens. Like every other employment too, it is subdivided into a great number of different branches, each of which affords occupation to a peculiar tribe or class of philosophers; and this subdivision of employment in philosophy, as well as in every other business, improves dexterity, and saves time. Each individual becomes more expert in his own peculiar branch, more work is done upon the whole, and the quantity of science is considerably increased by it.

It is the great multiplication of the productions of all the different arts, in consequence of the division of labour, which occasions, in a well-governed society, that universal opulence which extends itself to the lowest ranks of the people. Every workman has a great quantity of his own work to dispose of beyond what he himself has occasion for; and every other workman being exactly in the same situation, he is enabled to exchange a great quantity of his own goods for a great quantity, or, what comes to the same thing, for the price of a great quantity of theirs. He supplies them abundantly with what they have occasion for, and they accommodate him as amply with what he has occasion for, and a general plenty diffuses itself through all the different ranks of the society.

Observe the accommodation of the most common artificer or day-labourer in a civilized and thriving country, and you will perceive that the number of people of whose industry a part, though but a small part, has been employed in procuring him this accommodation, exceeds all computation. The woollen coat, for example, which covers the day-labourer, as coarse and rough as it may appear, is the produce of the joint labour of a great multitude of workmen. The shepherd, the sorter of the wool, the wool-comber or carder, the dyer, the scribbler, the spinner, the weaver, the fuller, the dresser, with many others, must all join their different arts in order to complete even this homely production. How many merchants and carriers, besides, must have been employed in transporting the materials from some of those workmen to others who often live in a very distant part of the country! how much commerce and navigation in particular, how many ship-builders, sailors, sail-makers, rope-makers, must have been employed in order to bring together the different drugs made use of by the dyer, which often come from the remotest corners of the world! What a variety of labour too is necessary in order to produce the tools of the meanest of those workmen! To say nothing of such complicated machines as the ship of the sailor, the mill of the fuller, or even the loom of the weaver, let us consider only what a variety of labour is requisite in order to form that very simple machine, the shears with which the shepherd clips the wool. The miner, the builder of the furnace for smelting the ore, the feller of the timber, the burner of the charcoal to be made use of in the smelting-house, the brick-maker, the brick-layer, the workmen who attend the furnace, the mill-wright, the forger, the smith, must all of them join their different arts in order to produce them. Were we to examine, in the same manner, all the different parts of his dress and house-hold furniture, the coarse linen shirt which he wears next his skin, the shoes which cover his feet, the bed which he lies on, and all the different parts which compose it, the kitchen-grate at which he prepares his victuals, the coals which he makes use of for that purpose, dug from the bowels of the earth, and brought to him perhaps by a long sea and a long land carriage, all the other utensils of his kitchen, all the furniture of his table, the knives and forks, the earthen or pewter plates upon which he serves up and divides his victuals, the different hands employed in preparing his bread and his beer, the glass window which lets in the heat and the light, and keeps out the wind and the rain, with all the knowledge and art requisite for preparing that beauti-ful and happy invention, without which these northern parts of the world could scarce have afforded a very comfortable habita-tion, together with the tools of all the different workmen employed in producing those different conveniences; if we examine, I say, all these things, and consider what a variety of labour is em-ployed about each of them, we shall be sensible that without the assistance and co-operation of many thousands, the very meanest person in a civilized country could not be provided, even accord-ing to what we very falsely imagine, the easy and simple manner in which he is commonly accommodated. Compared, indeed, with the more extravagant luxury of the great, his accommodation must no doubt appear extremely simple and easy; and yet it may be true, perhaps, that the accommodation of an European prince does not always so much exceed that of an industrious and frugal peasant, as the accommodation of the latter exceeds that of many an African king, the absolute master of the lives and liberties of ten thousand naked savages.

Value, Labour and Labouring Power

K. Marx

Reprinted with permission from Marx and Engels: *Selected Works*, Lawrence and Wishart, 1958, pp. 416–24, 424–33.

The first question we have to put is: What is the *value* of a commodity? How is it determined?

At first sight it would seem that the value of a commodity is a thing quite *relative*, and not to be settled without considering one commodity in its relations to all other commodities. In fact, in speaking of the value, the value in exchange of a commodity, we mean the proportional quantities in which it exchanges with all other commodities. But then arises the question: How are the proportions in which commodities exchange with each other regulated?

We know from experience that these proportions vary infinitely. Taking one single commodity, wheat, for instance, we shall find that a quarter of wheat exchanges in almost countless variations of proportion with different commodities. Yet, *its value remaining always the same*, whether expressed in silk, gold, or any other commodity, it must be something distinct from, and independent of, these *different rates of exchange* with different articles. It must be possible to express, in a very different form, these various equations with various commodities.

Besides, if I say a quarter of wheat exchanges with iron in a certain proportion, or the value of a quarter of wheat is expressed in a certain amount of iron, I say that the value of wheat and its equivalent in iron are equal *to some third thing*, which is neither wheat nor iron, because I suppose them to express the same magnitude in two different shapes. Either of them, the wheat or the iron, must, therefore, independently of the other, be reducible to this third thing which is their common measure.

To elucidate this point I shall recur to a very simple geometrical illustration. In comparing the areas of triangles of all possible forms and magnitudes, or comparing triangles with rectangles, or any other rectilinear figure, how do we proceed? We reduce the area of any triangle whatever to an expression quite different from its visible form. Having found from the nature of the triangle that its area is equal to half the product of its base by its height, we can then compare the different values of all sorts of triangles, and of all rectilinear figures whatever, because all of them may be resolved into a certain number of triangles.

The same mode of procedure must obtain with the values of commodities. We must be able to reduce all of them to an expression common to all, distinguishing them only by the proportions in which they contain that identical measure.

As the *exchangeable values* of commodities are only *social functions* of those things, and have nothing at all to do with their *natural* qualities, we must first ask, What is the common *social substance* of all commodities? It is *Labour*. To produce a commodity a certain amount of labour must be bestowed upon it, or worked up in it. And I say not only *Labour*, but *social Labour*. A man who produces an article for his own immediate use, to consume it himself, creates a *product*, but not a commodity. As a self-sustaining producer he has nothing to do with society. But to produce a *commodity*, a man must not only produce an article satisfying some *social* want, but his labour itself must form part and parcel of the total sum of labour expended by society. It must be subordinate to the *Division of Labour within Society*. It is nothing without the other divisions of labour, and on its part is required to *integrate* them.

If we consider *commodities as values*, we consider them exclusively under the single aspect of *realized, fixed,* or, if you like, *crystallized social labour*. In this respect they can *differ* only by representing greater or smaller quantities of labour, as, for example, a greater amount of labour may be worked up in a silken handkerchief than in a brick. But how does one measure *quantities of labour*? By the *time the labour lasts*, in measuring the labour by the hour, the day, etc. Of course, to apply this measure, all sorts of labour are reduced to average or simple labour as their unit.

We arrive, therefore, at this conclusion. A commodity has a *value*, because it is a *crystallization of social labour*. The *greatness* of its value, of its *relative* value, depends upon the greater or less amount of that social substance contained in it; that is to say, on the relative mass of labour necessary for its production. The *relative values of commodities* are, therefore, determined by the *respective quantities or amounts of labour, worked up, realized, fixed in them*. The *correlative* quantities of commodities which can be produced in the *same time of labour* are *equal*. Or the value of one commodity is to the value of another commodity as the quantity of labour fixed in the one is to the quantity of labour fixed in the other.

*　　*　　*

Having now, as far as it could be done in such a cursory manner, analysed the nature of *Value*, of the *Value of any commodity whatever*, we must turn our attention to the specific *Value of Labour*. And here, again, I must startle you by a seeming paradox. All of you feel sure that what they daily sell is their Labour; that, therefore, Labour has a Price, and that, the price of a commodity being only the monetary expression of its value, there must certainly exist such a thing as the *Value of Labour*. However, there exists no such thing as the *Value of Labour* in the common acceptance of the word. We have seen that the amount of necessary labour crystallized in a commodity constitutes its value. Now, applying this notion of value, how could we define, say, the value of a ten hours' working day? How much labour is contained in that day? Ten hours' labour. To say that the value of a ten hours' working day is equal to ten hours' labour, or the quantity of labour contained in it, would be a tautological and, moroever, a nonsensical expression. Of course, having once found out the true but hidden sense of the expression '*Value of Labour*', we shall be able to interpret this irrational, and seemingly impossible application of value, in the same way that, having once made sure of the real movement of the celestial bodies, we shall be able to explain their apparent or merely phenomenal movements.

What the working man sells is not directly his *Labour*, but his *Labouring Power*, the temporary disposal of which he makes over to the capitalist. This is so much the case that I do not know whether by the English laws, but certainly by some Continental Laws, the *maximum time* is fixed for which a man is allowed to sell his labouring power. If allowed to do so for any indefinite period whatever, slavery would be immediately restored. Such a sale, if it comprised his lifetime, for example, would make him at once the lifelong slave of his employer.

One of the oldest economists and most original philosophers of England – Thomas Hobbes – has already, in his *Leviathan*, instinctively hit upon this point overlooked by all his successors. He says: '*The value or worth of a man* is, as in all other things, his *price*: that is, so much as would be given for the *Use of his Power*.'

Proceeding from this basis, we shall be able to determine the *Value of Labour* as that of all other commodities.

But before doing so, we might ask, how does this strange phenomenon arise, that we find on the market a set of buyers, possessed of land, machinery, raw material, and the means of subsistence, all of them, save land in its crude state, the *products of labour*, and on the other hand, a set of sellers who have nothing to sell except their labouring power, their working arms and brains? That the one set buys continually in order to make a profit and enrich themselves, while the other set continually sells in order to earn their livelihood? The enquiry into this question would be an enquiry into what the economists call '*Previous, or Original Accumulation*', but which ought to be called *Original Expropriation*. We should find that this so-called *Original Accumulation* means nothing but a series of historical processes, resulting in a *Decomposition of the Original Union* existing between the Labouring Man and his Instruments of Labour. Such an enquiry, however, lies beyond the pale of my present subject. The *Separation* between the Man of Labour and the Instruments of Labour once established, such a state of things will maintain itself and reproduce itself upon a constantly increasing scale, until a new and fundamental revolution in the mode of production should again overturn it, and restore the original union in a new historical form.

What, then, is the *Value of Labouring Power*?

Like that of every other commodity, its value is determined by the quantity of labour necessary to produce it. The labouring power of a man exists only in his living individuality. A certain mass of necessaries must be consumed by a man to grow up and maintain his life. But the man, like the machine, will wear out, and must be replaced by another man. Beside the mass of necessaries required for *his own* maintenance, he wants another amount of necessaries to bring up a certain quota of children that are to replace him on the labour market and to perpetuate the race of labourers. Moreover, to develop his labouring power, and acquire a given skill, another amount of values must be spent. For our purpose it suffices to consider only *average* labour, the costs of whose education and development are vanishing magnitudes. Still I must seize upon this occasion to state that, as the costs of producing labouring powers of different quality differ, so must differ the values of the labouring powers employed in different trades. The cry for an *equality of wages* rests, therefore, upon a mistake, is an *insane* wish never to be fulfilled. It is an offspring of that false and superficial radicalism that accepts premises and tries to evade conclusions. Upon the basis of the wages system the value of labouring power is settled like that of every other commodity; and as different kinds of labouring power have different values, or require different quantities of labour for their production, they *must* fetch different prices in the labour market. To clamour for *equal or even equitable retribution* on the basis of the wages system is the same as to clamour for *freedom* on the basis of the slavery system. What you think just or equitable is out of the question. The question is: What is necessary and unavoidable with a given system of production?

After what has been said, it will be seen that the *value of labouring power* is determined by the *value of the necessaries* required to produce, develop, maintain, and perpetuate the labouring power.

Production of surplus value

Now suppose that the average amount of the daily necessaries of a labouring man require *six hours of average labour* for their production. Suppose, moreover, six hours of average labour to be also realized in a quantity of gold equal to 3*s*. Then 3*s* would be the *Price*, or the monetary expression of the *Daily Value* of that man's *Labouring Power*. If he worked daily six hours he would daily produce a value sufficient to buy the average amount of his daily necessaries, or to maintain himself as a labouring man.

But our man is a wages labourer. He must, therefore, sell his labouring power to a capitalist. If he sells it at 3*s* daily, or 18*s* weekly, he sells it at its value. Suppose him to be a spinner. If he works six hours daily he will add to the cotton a value of 3*s* daily. This value, daily added by him, would be an exact equivalent for the wages, or the price of his labouring power, received daily. But in that case *no surplus value or surplus produce* whatever would go to the capitalist. Here, then, we come to the rub.

In buying the labouring power of the workman, and paying its value, the capitalist, like every other purchaser, has acquired the right to consume or use the commodity bought. You consume or use the labouring power of a man by making him work, as you consume or use a machine by making it run. By paying the daily or weekly value of the labouring power of the workman, the capitalist has, therefore, acquired the right to use or make that labouring power work during the *whole day or week*. The working day or the working week has, of course, certain limits, but those we shall afterwards look more closely at.

For the present I want to turn your attention to one decisive point.

The *value* of the labouring power is determined by the quantity of labour necessary to maintain or reproduce it, but the *use* of that labouring power is only limited by the active energies and physical strength of the labourer. The daily or weekly *value* of the labouring power is quite distinct from the daily or weekly exercise of that power, the same as the food a horse wants and the time it can carry the horseman are quite distinct. The quantity of labour by which the *value* of the workman's labouring power is limited forms by no means a limit to the quantity of labour which his labouring power is apt to perform. Take the example of our spinner. We have seen that, to daily reproduce his labouring power, he must daily reproduce a value of three shillings, which he will do by working six hours daily. But this does not disable him from working ten or twelve or more hours a day. But by paying the daily or weekly *value* of the spinner's labouring power, the capitalist has acquired the right of using that labouring power during *the whole day or week*. He will, therefore, make him work say, daily, *twelve* hours. *Over and above* the six hours required to replace his wages, or the value of his labouring power, he will, therefore, have to work *six other hours*, which I shall call hours of *surplus labour*, which surplus labour will realize itself in a *surplus value* and a *surplus produce*. If our spinner, for example, by his daily labour of six hours, added three shillings' value to the cotton, a value forming an exact equivalent to his wages, he will, in twelve hours, add six shillings' worth to the cotton, and produce *a proportional surplus of yarn*. As he has sold his labouring power to the capitalist, the whole value or produce created by him belongs to the capitalist, the owner *pro tem* of his labouring power. By advancing three shillings, the capitalist will, therefore, realize a value of six shillings, because, advancing a value in which six hours of labour are crystallized, he will receive in return a value in which twelve hours of labour are crystallized. By repeating this same process daily, the capitalist will daily advance three shillings and daily pocket six shillings, one-half of which will go to pay wages anew, and the other half of which will form *surplus value*, for which the capitalist pays no equivalent. It is this *sort of exchange between capital and labour* upon which capitalistic production, or the wages system, is founded, and which must constantly result in reproducing the working man as a working man, and the capitalist as a capitalist.

The rate of surplus value, all other circumstances remaining the same, will depend on the proportion between that part of the working day necessary to reproduce the value of the labouring power and the *surplus time* or *surplus labour* performed for the capitalist. It will, therefore, depend on the *ratio in which the working day is prolonged over and above that extent*, by working which the working man would only reproduce the value of his labouring power, or replace his wages.

*   *   *

The different parts into which surplus value is decomposed

The *surplus value*, or that part of the total value of the commodity in which the *surplus labour* or *unpaid labour* of the working man is realized, I call *Profit*. The whole of that profit is not pocketed by the employing capitalist. The monopoly of land enables the landlord to take one part of that *surplus value*, under the name of *rent*, whether the land is used for agriculture, buildings or railways, or for any other productive purpose. On the other hand, the very fact that the possession of the *instruments of labour* enables the employing capitalist to produce a *surplus value*, or, what comes to the same, to *appropriate to himself a certain amount of unpaid labour*, enables the owner of the means of labour, which he lends wholly or partly to the employing capitalist – enables, in one word, the money-lending capitalist to claim for himself under the name of *interest* another part of that surplus value, so that there remains to the employing capitalist *as such* only what is called *industrial* or *commercial profit*.

By what laws this division of the total amount of surplus value among the three categories of people is regulated is a question quite foreign to our subject. This much, however, results from what has been stated.

Rent, Interest, and Industrial Profit are only *different names for different parts* of the *surplus value* of the commodity, or the *unpaid labour enclosed in it*, and they are *equally derived from this source, and from this source alone*. They are not derived from *land* as such or from *capital* as such, but land and capital enable their owners to get their respective shares out of the surplus value extracted by the employing capitalist from the labourer. For the labourer himself it is a matter of subordinate importance whether that surplus value, the result of his surplus labour, or unpaid labour, is altogether pocketed by the employing capitalist, or whether the latter is obliged to pay portions of it, under the name of rent and interest, away to third parties. Suppose the employing capitalist to use only his own capital and to be his own landlord, then the whole surplus value would go into his pocket.

It is the employing capitalist who immediately extracts from the labourer this surplus value, whatever part of it he may ultimately be able to keep for himself. Upon this relation, therefore, between the employing capitalist and the wages labourer the whole wages system and the whole present system of production hinge.

Personality and the Market Place
E. Fromm

Reprinted with permission from *Man for Himself*,
Holt, Reinhart and Winston, 1947, pp. 67–78.

The marketing orientation developed as a dominant one only in the modern era. In order to understand its nature one must consider the economic function of the market in modern society as being not only analogous to this character orientation but as the basis and the main condition for its development in modern man.

Barter is one of the oldest economic mechanisms. The traditional local market, however, is essentially different from the market as it has developed in modern capitalism. Bartering on a local market offered an opportunity to meet for the purpose of exchanging commodities. Producers and customers became acquainted; they were relatively small groups; the demand was more or less known, so that the producer could produce for this specific demand.

The modern market is no longer a meeting place but a mechanism characterized by abstract and impersonal demand. One produces for this market, not for a known circle of customers; its verdict is based on laws of supply and demand; and it determines whether the commodity can be sold and at what price. No matter what the use value of a pair of shoes may be, for instance, if the supply is greater than the demand, some shoes will be sentenced to economic death; they might as well not have been produced at all. The market day is the 'day of judgment' as far as the exchange value of commodities is concerned.

The reader may object that this description of the market is oversimplified. The producer does try to judge the demand in advance, and under monopoly conditions even obtains a certain degree of control over it. Nevertheless, the regulatory function of the market has been, and still is, predominant enough to have a profound influence on the character formation of the urban middle class and, through the latter's social and cultural influence, on the whole population. The market concept of value, the emphasis on exchange value rather than on use value, has led to a similar concept of value with regard to people and particularly to oneself. The character orientation which is rooted in the experience of oneself as a commodity and of one's value as exchange value I call the marketing orientation.

In our time the marketing orientation has been growing rapidly, together with the development of a new market that is a phenomenon of the last decade – the 'personality market'. Clerks and salesmen, business executives and doctors, lawyers and artists all appear on this market. It is true that their legal status and economic positions are different: some are independent, charging for their services; others are employed, receiving salaries. But all are dependent for their material success on a personal acceptance by those who need their services or who employ them.

The principle of evaluation is the same on both the personality and the commodity market: on the one, personalities are offered for sale; on the other, commodities. Value in both cases is their exchange value, for which use value is a necessary but not a sufficient condition. It is true, our economic system could not function if people were not skilled in the particular work they have to perform and were gifted only with a pleasant personality. Even the best bedside manner and the most beautifully equipped office on Park Avenue would not make a New York doctor successful if he did not have a minimum of medical knowledge and skill. Even the most winning personality would not prevent a secretary from losing her job unless she could type reasonably fast. However, if we ask what the respective weight of skill and personality as a condition for success is, we find that only in exceptional cases is success predominantly the result of skill and of certain other human qualities like honesty, decency, and integrity. Although the proportion between skill and human qualities on the one hand and 'personality' on the other hand as prerequisites for success varies, the 'personality factor' always plays a decisive role. Success depends largely on how well a person sells himself on the market, how well he gets his personality across, how nice a 'package' he is; whether he is 'cheerful', 'sound', 'aggressive', 'reliable', 'ambitious'; furthermore what his family background is, what clubs he belongs to, and whether he knows the right people. The type of personality required depends to some degree on the special field in which a person works. A stockbroker, a salesman, a secretary, a railroad executive, a college professor, or a hotel manager must each offer different kinds of personality that, regardless of their differences, must fulfill one condition to be in demand.

The fact that in order to have success it is not sufficient to have the skill and equipment for performing a given task but that one must be able to 'put across' one's personality in competition with many others shapes the attitude towards oneself. If it were enough for the purpose of making a living to rely on what one knows and what one can do, one's self-esteem would be in proportion to one's capacities, that is, to one's use value; but since success depends largely on how one sells one's personality, one experiences oneself as a commodity or rather simultaneously as the seller and the commodity to be sold. A person is not concerned with his life and happiness, but with becoming salable. This feeling might be compared to that of a commodity, of handbags on a counter, for instance, could they feel and think. Each handbag would try to make itself as 'attractive' as possible in order to attract customers and to look as expensive as possible in order to obtain a higher price than its rivals. The handbag sold for the highest price would feel elated, since that would mean it was the most 'valuable' one; the one which was not sold would feel sad and convinced of its own worthlessness. This fate might befall a bag which, though excellent in appearance and usefulness, had the bad luck to be out of date because of a change in fashion.

* * *

Since modern man experiences himself both as the seller and as the commodity to be sold on the market, his self-esteem depends on conditions beyond his control. If he is 'successful', he is valuable; if he is not, he is worthless. The degree of insecurity which results from this orientation can hardly be overestimated. If one feels that one's own value is not constituted primarily by the human qualities one possesses, but by one's success on a competitive market with ever-changing conditions, one's self-esteem is bound to be shaky and in constant need of confirmation by others. Hence one is driven to strive relentlessly for success, and any setback is a severe threat to one's self-esteem; helplessness, insecurity, and inferiority feelings are the result. If the vicissitudes of the market are the judges of one's value, the sense of dignity and pride is destroyed.

But the problem is not only that of self-evaluation and self-esteem but of one's experience of oneself as an independent entity, of one's identity with oneself. As we shall see later, the mature and productive individual derives his feeling of identity from the experience of himself as the agent who is one with his powers; this feeling of self can be briefly expressed as meaning 'I am what I do'. In the marketing orientation man encounters his own powers as commodities alienated from him. He is not one with them but they are masked from him because what matters is not his self-realization in the process of using them but his success in the process of selling them. Both his powers and what they create become estranged, something different from himself, something for others to judge and to use; thus his feeling of identity becomes as shaky as his self-esteem; it is constituted by the sum total of roles one can play: 'I am as you desire me.'

Ibsen has expressed this state of selfhood in Peer Gynt: Peer Gynt tries to discover his self and he finds that he is like an onion – one layer after the other can be peeled off and there is no core to be found. Since man cannot live doubting his identity, he must, in the marketing orientation, find the conviction of identity not in reference to himself and his powers but in the opinion of others about him. His prestige, status, success, the fact that he is known to others as being a certain person are a substitute for the genuine feeling of identity. This situation makes him utterly dependent on the way others look at him and forces him to keep up the role in which he once had become successful. If I and my powers are separated from each other then, indeed, is my self constituted by the price I fetch.

Industrialization and Alienation
W. A. Faunce

Reprinted with permission from *Problems of an Industrial Society*, McGraw Hill, 1968, pp. 100–15.

One of the ways in which we are different, according to Fromm, is that we are free from the constraints of a small group society and a fixed economic and political order. The member of a small-group society is never fully an individual in the sense of having independence of action but is only the sum of the stable set of roles that he enacts. Under these circumstances, self image does not develop as an important component of personality and as a determinant of behaviour because the answer to the question, 'Who am I?' is so apparent that the question need not be asked. Fromm describes individuation, or the emergence of the individual in human history, as being similar in some ways to the developmental process in childhood and adolescence. The process of social maturation involves the severing of primary ties with parents and the development of freedom and independence of action. As the child matures he develops an image of self that serves as an internal guide to behaviour substituting for the external constraints administered by his parents. Although the analogy is an imperfect one, Western man has, since the medieval period, achieved increasing freedom from small group controls, or what has been described as the 'tyranny of the genos', and has escaped from the fixed self-identity characteristic of a stable and rigid social order.

There was a price for this new-found freedom. There is a form of security in having a fixed identity in a stable social order that is rarely experienced today. When all one's social experience occurs within the framework of small-group controls, many of the problems afflicting modern man – insecurity, powerlessness, doubt, aloneness, or anxiety – are less likely to occur. In the following passage Fromm describes both the loss of security and the increase in freedom that accompany the process of individuation:

'The breakdown of the medieval system of feudal society had

one main significance for all classes of society: the individual was left alone and isolated. He was free. This freedom had a twofold result. Man was deprived of the security he had enjoyed, of the unquestionable feeling of belonging, and he was torn loose from the world which had satisfied his quest for security both economically and spiritually. He felt alone and anxious. But he was also free to act and to think independently, to become his own master and do with his life as he could – not as he was told to do.'

The significance of Fromm's analysis for our purpose is that alienation becomes a social problem only after the process of an individual's social experience began to encompass a much wider range than a small circle of family and friends that the disjuncture between self-esteem maintenance and status assignment became common. It is only in rapidly changing and highly differentiated societies that people are *frequently* exposed to sets of values at variance with their own. In *Escape from Freedom*, Fromm describes in detail how freedom and insecurity were products of changes occurring during the Renaissance and Reformation. Although the seeds of alienation were sown at that time, it is during the period since the Industrial Revolution that they have come to fruition.

Most of the expressions that have been used to describe the alienated industrial man can be seen as being related to the disjuncture between the status-assignment and self-esteem-maintenance processes. If industrial man is lonely, it is clearly not because he is physically isolated – urbanization has accompanied industrialization almost everywhere it has occurred. However, loneliness and anonymity can also be products of the generally shallow quality of interpersonal relationships in highly differentiated, industrial societies. Close or intimate social relations are always based upon a system of shared values in which each person is evaluated by others with the same criteria he uses in evaluating himself.

Apathy, indifference, a feeling of emptiness, or a lack of a sense of purpose in life all represent a second set of terms describing the experience of alienation. These experiences are products of a lack of identification with, or commitment to, *shared* goals and beliefs. In social psychological terms, the processes of identification and commitment involve self-evaluation in terms of the values on which social status is based. When we speak of a person being committed to a shared goal or identified with an organization within which the goal is shared, we mean that he is motivated to achieve the objectives of the organization. And it is through the achievement of organizational objectives that social status is acquired and self-assessments are confirmed.

A third way in which the consequences of alienation have been described is overconformity. Overconformity, along with loneliness and apathy, is a major issue in the social criticism of industrial society. And overconformity, along with loneliness and apathy, is produced, at least in part, by the disjuncture between self-esteem-maintenance and status-assignment processes: apathy and indifference discourage innovativeness, and ambiguities in complex urban–industrial status structures make conformity the path of least resistance.

The pervasiveness of alienation in industrial societies results from its relationship to characteristics inherent in the social structure of these societies. The major thesis in this chapter can be summarized as follows: rapid social change, increased structural differentiation, decreased structural integration, and rationalization of social organization have produced widespread feelings of powerlessness, normlessness, or meaninglessness; this pattern of social experience reduces the correspondence between the criteria used in maintaining self-esteem and those used in assigning social status, which results in loneliness, apathy, or overconformity. Not everyone in industrial societies experiences alienation; and among those who do, some are more alienated than others. Difficulty in maintaining an adequate level of self-esteem is sufficiently widespread, however, to justify viewing alienation as an important problem of industrial society. . . . We shall consider first the ways in which the structure of industrial society gives rise to feelings of powerlessness, normlessness, and meaninglessness and then the ways in which these feelings are related to alienation.

The complexity of industrial societies alone is sufficient to induce a sense of powerlessness. If power implies the ability to effectively control, even for the power elite there is objectively some degree of powerlessness. Only relative power is possible in an industrial society and not absolute power of the sort that could be wielded, for example, in a feudal society. The *experience* of power or of powerlessness is a matter of *relative* advantage or deprivation; and despite the difficulties of exercising effective control over complex social systems, there is an elite group in industrial societies, which can accurately be described as powerful.

What is unique to industrial societies is, first of all, the extent to which the *sense* of powerlessness pervades our experience and, second, the impersonality of the forces which produce it. . . . Pre-industrial societies are characterized by a high level of group control of behaviour. These constraints are unlikely to be perceived as being external to the individual or imposed upon him. Where norms and values are widely shared and enforced through informal social processes, the individual member of the group is less likely to *feel* powerless, although objectively speaking, he may be so. With the process of individuation and the imposition of external controls such as laws or bureaucratic regulations by a power elite, having power or not having power may be seen as genuine alternatives. It is under these circumstances that powerlessness is apt to be *experienced* as a form of deprivation. The amount of rationalization required by the complexity of industrial societies means that there are few areas of our experience that are unaffected either directly or indirectly by some form of external regulation.

The impersonality of these constraints in industrial societies contributes in an important way to the sense of powerlessness. If the only source of oppressive control is a totalitarian leader, he can be overthrown. If the source is an entire way of life, revolution is a less effective response. The idea that 'you can't beat the system' expresses the impotence of people confronted by a rationalized and impersonal system of social control. Even where the controls are administered personally, as in a foreman-worker relationship, the basis of the control is recognized as being within the system rather than the person. When a foreman gives an unpopular order, it is generally understood that he is simply doing his job. A common response to the sense of powerlessness resulting from pervasive impersonal controls is apathy. And apathy, as we shall see presently, is a symptom of alienation as defined above.

One reflection of the difficulty in dealing with the complex control structure of industrial societies is the creation of the *ombudsman* role. *Ombudsman* is a Swedish word meaning, literally, 'one who represents someone'. The position was developed in the Scandinavian countries to serve as an appeal mechanism circumventing the usual channels through which the complaints of private citizens are heard. The system has spread to other countries, and in fact, an *ombudsman* was recently appointed at Michigan State University with the responsibility to 'assist students in accomplishing the expeditious settlement of their problems'. The *ombudsman's* function reflects not only the complexity of control systems but also the unequal distribution of ability to cope with these systems: the *ombudsman's* clientele are private citizens who are most likely to experience powerlessness when faced with the structural and procedural complexity of bureaucratic organizations. Ability to deal with and 'beat' the system is most directly in proportion to experience in large, formal organizations, particularly at higher administrative levels, and to the amount of formal education. For this reason, a sense of powerlessness and resulting apathy are more common among people in lower- and in higher-status occupations. People likely to experience powerlessness, however, represent a substantial majority of the population in industrial societies.

With the breakup of the medieval social order, men achieved freedom from personalized small-group controls. The deterioraration of *any* established social order is followed by a period in which social controls are at a minimum. The experience of new African nations as they develop from tribal societies today is a case in point. An industrial society, however, requires a high level of social control in order to achieve sufficient integration of its complex interdependent structure. Impersonal, rationalized controls are the only possible means to achieve this integration. In mature industrial societies there is much less of the kind of freedom that Fromm described as having developed with the Renaissance. For a substantial segment of the population today, there is very little control over the important events that shape their lives.

Professionalism in Victorian England
W. J. Reader

Reprinted with permission from *Professional Men*, Weidenfeld and Nicolson, 1966, pp. 183–211.

At any time before 1914, £1,000 a year represented considerable worldly success, though not great wealth, and placed a man, economically speaking, well towards the top of the middle classes. On an income of £500 a year, soon after 1900, the editors of *Mrs*

Beeton's Every Day Cookery allowed 'two women servants only' for a family of four, 'but a family living in the country . . . would probably require a gardener or useful man.' A professional man, with decent luck and ability, might expect an income comfortably above the middle-class average: perhaps a long way above it. The letters after his name, apart from any social prestige they might confer, had a hard cash value too.

But it cannot have been easy for the majority to find the money to launch sons into professional life. How did the parsons do it in such numbers? Some parsons were rich and many public schools made allowances for the sons of those who were not. One major school – Marlborough – was founded for their benefit. Similarly there were awards at Oxford and Cambridge colleges reserved for them. But in many clerical families the strain must have been heavy: as, also, in the families of officers without private means, though for them, too, allowances were made at some schools and one major one – Wellington – was intended especially for them. In general, as a late Victorian ICS man remarked: 'Money for younger sons was scarce, and it was not easy to be independent.'

This is one more reason for surprise that the mid-Victorian movement for the reform of secondary and higher education petered out. Why was no system established, like the system in Germany, for providing excellent professional and technical education at a very low cost to those who wanted it? Why was the very expensive system of late Victorian England not only acquiesced in, but actively connived at, by the professional classes? They were the very people who had forced through drastic schemes of qualifying and competitive examinations, requiring a curriculum totally different from that of the traditional 'liberal education' which in the public schools they had to pay so heavily for. They more than most people, it might have been thought, would appreciate the danger to England from persistent neglect of professional education and education in science and technology. And yet nothing was done: nothing, after at one time it had seemed that everything was possible.

Perhaps the explanation lies in the dual character of the professional man's ambition. On the one hand he cared deeply about purely professional matters. He took a pride in his work; he wanted to see skill developed by education and recognized by a regular process of qualification. And he certainly took seriously the obligation to observe at least a minimum standard of ethical behaviour, which even at its minimum was above the standard commonly expected and observed in contemporary 'trade'. And by caring for these matters the professional man, as he progressively asserted himself during the early and middle years of the century, permanently enriched and purified the life of the nation.

But there was another thing the professional man cared deeply about, and that was his social standing. Sir Astley Cooper, early in the century, considered that the only true basis for a professional man's social standing was his scientific understanding of his profession, but then Sir Astley in his young days had been a radical and a democrat. By Escott's time not many professional men were like that. Their idea of social standing was to get as close as they could to the pattern set by the landed gentry, or what they imagined the pattern to be.

In this they followed the example set by successful Englishmen in every age before them. Nor is their aim to be wondered at, considering how extremely attractive the life of the landed gentry could be, with their unassailable social position, their independence, their authority, their influence, and their wealth. It was unfortunate, though, that the leaders of an industrial nation threatened by foreign competition should have chosen to emulate a class whose whole cast of mind and scale of values was anticommercial. It hardened yet one more division – the division between 'professions' and 'trade' – in an already deeply divided society. It put a formidable obstacle in the way of those who could feel the foundations of England's prosperity cracking under their feet, and wanted to repair them.

It was doubly unfortunate that, as the competitive situation grew worse, English attention was distracted by the heady vision of Empire. The early Victorians had paid very little attention to their possessions overseas, except periodically to wonder whether they would not certainly lose them, and whether things might not be better if they did. They had got on with their own affairs with conspicuous success, and England's strength in the forties and fifties was firmly based on her own industrial supremacy.

The later Victorians, on the other hand, increasingly found it easy – and comforting – to believe that England, beset by industrial competitors, drew strength from her empire, and their belief was widely shared, not least in Germany and America. How much reality there was in it may be questioned. The 'white dominions' were no doubt profitable enough, with food supplies moving one way and manufactured goods the other. Even then, it may be supposed that the trade would have gone on without the existence of any British connection except the British fleet and that, after all, protected America as well. It is much more doubtful whether India and the African and Asian dependencies were ever really worth their keep, when the expense of administration and defence is taken into account, especially when it is considered that in some parts of the empire, notably West Africa, the ruling power, acting, as was sincerely believed, in the interests of the ruled, prevented the exploitation of agricultural resources by forbidding the alienation of land to Europeans.

Whatever may be the economic truth of the matter, and it is certainly highly debatable, it nevertheless seems incontestable that expanding imperial glory, in the last twenty years or so of the nineteenth century and during the first part of the twentieth, drew attention away from England's competitive position in the world and tempted people to underestimate the seriousness of it. Empire-building and empire-holding were congenial activities: much more congenial, to the mind of the ruling classes, than running an industrial economy. Imperialism, late in the day, was grafted on to the public school tradition and took its place among the public school boy's set of neatly packaged received ideas.

British rule did a great deal of good for most of those who came under it: that need not be doubted. Nor need it be doubted that the pursuit of empire gave British public life a spaciousness and a sense of purpose which it subsequently lost and has not yet found again. And there was much that was good in the public school boy's outlook, especially when it was illuminated by intelligence and culture. The public school boy was brought up to a sense of duty. He was expected to sacrifice himself unquestioningly for what was regarded as his country's good. He had a strong sense of personal loyalty, not least to those – of any race – who came under his authority. These excellent qualities make it all the sadder that the fundamental antipathy induced by public school education to everything commercial made it fatally easy for men from public schools to miss the central fact of England's power – that without her own industrial strength, let her empire be never so large, she was nothing more than an over-populated island off the coast of north-west Europe. Late Victorian and post-Victorian imperialism, seen from this point of view, looks like nothing so much as a large and gaudy Union Jack hiding the facts of life from the British ruling class.

It would not be true to suggest that the danger was entirely ignored, especially after the Boer War in which, in Kipling's inelegant words, 'We have had no end of a lesson. It will do us no end of good.' Once again, as in the sixties, foreign technical education was anxiously inspected and reported on: once again the air was astir with good intentions.

Between 1903 and 1905, for instance, the *Architectural Review* published the results of an elaborate comparative survey of foreign and English methods of training architects. The German Technical High Schools were reported on, with their four-year full-time courses, their severe entrance requirements and qualifying examinations, and their State subsidies. The social mixture in them was duly noted – at Berlin 'the students are drawn, to a far larger extent than . . . in England or France, from all classes'. They were uncomfortably compared with 'the old-fashioned system of articles' – 'relics of a medieval system of training stripped of its severe sanctions'. The courses of instruction, most of them part-time, provided by various authorities, including the Architectural Association, Liverpool University, and the London County Council, were anxiously examined. It was plain that they did not look very well against the elaborate long-established German system.

There were stirrings in the provincial universities. Imperial College of Science and Technology came into massive existence in 1907. A few public school boys began to go to the 'new' universities. But there was nothing like a radical change of attitude. So far as the really prosperous classes were concerned, these developments were for other people's children. The public schools, increasingly criticized, went on their way practically unaffected, and the central citadels of English education, with all their authority, wealth and social prestige, remained divorced from the growing realities of power in the modern world. The waves of change beat all around them: they could not break in. And they were more than ever the accepted nursery of the professional class. Even the *Architectural Review*, the organ of a profession generally considered artistic and therefore eccentric, assumed as a matter of course that a young man looking for architectural training would have come from a public school.

Thus, as the professional men had a hand in the rise of Victorian England, so they must bear some responsibility for its decline. Look at Sir Astley Cooper, especially in his early days. Look at those quarrelsome doctors who fought for the due recognition of good qualifications and high professional standards. Listen to the attorneys of the fifties, insisting that it was the business of a barrister to know the law and never mind his social standing. Surely they had a firm grip on the essentials of professional life, and indeed on the practical essentials of life generally. It is impossible to feel so confident of those who were perfectly well aware that Germany was putting all her formidable strength and organizing powers into first-rate technical and professional training, and yet were content to muddle along, reserving all their real enthusiasm for a system of education openly contemptuous of anything with a practical bent to it, and biased very heavily towards the social and sporting side of life. Their awakening, from 1914 on, was slow, and bitter, and perhaps it is not quite completed even yet.

Further Reading: Work and Society

R. DAHRENDORF, *Class and Class Conflict in Industrial Society*, London, Routledge and Kegan Paul, 1959.

J. A. BANKS, *Marxist Sociology in Action*, London, Faber and Faber, 1970.

*E. DURKHEIM, *The Division of Labour in Society*, New York, The Free Press, 1964.

*W. A. FAUNCE and W. H. FORM, *Comparative Perspectives on Industrial Society*, Boston, Little Brown, 1969.

*P. LASLETT, *The World We Have Lost*, London, Methuen, 1965.

S. LUKES, *Emile Durkheim: His Life and Work*, London, Allen Lane, The Penguin Press, 1973.

K. MARX, *Capital*, London, Lawrence and Wishart, 1961.

W. G. RUNCIMAN, *Relative Deprivation and Social Justice*, London, Routledge and Kegan Paul, 1966.

*R. H. TAWNEY, *The Acquisitive Society*, London, Fontana, 1961.

E. P. THOMPSON, 'Time, Work Discipline and Industrial Capitalism', in *Past and Present*, Vol. 38, 1967.

H. L. WILENSKY, 'Work as a Social Problem' in H. S. Becker (ed.), *Social Problems: a Modern Approach*, New York, Wiley, 1966.

* Available in paperback

Chapter Three

The Structure
of Work

Cash payment is not the sole nexus of man with man.
T. Carlyle

The previous chapter identified certain topics with which, in
one way or another, the rest of the book deals. The division of
labour, the wage-nexus, alienation, satisfaction from work and
professionalization form common themes in most of the
extracts which form the chapters that follow. The purpose of
this chapter is to offer some guidance to the reader in using
the rest of the book, by indicating how these themes may
combine to form a structure to the study of work in modern
Britain.

Baldamus deals with a rather basic issue which anyone who
has worked for any period on boring, monotonous tasks, as are
likely to occur under such conditions as assembly line
production, will readily recognize. The question is simply 'why
do people stick it?' To some extent the answer is a simple one:
it relates to the cash nexus and to the structure of
administrative procedures through which the organization of
work is controlled. People work because they are buying time
or opportunities to do things they *really* want to do – their
real *projets de vivre*, and because they are told to do so, helped
to do so, and conditioned to believe that it is necessary to
work. Of course, they are pretty clear indications that it is
imperative to work in most societies. It is not only leader-
writers on Conservative newspapers who see the withdrawal of
labour by a trade union, or worse by an 'unrecognized group',
as an act which somehow threatens the fabric of society.
Sociologists such as Davis and Moore, who give crucial
importance to the integrative role of the division of labour,
often seem to make the same sort of assumptions, even if
implicitly.

But if there can, in any society, be little doubt about the answer to the question 'should we work?', there must be, plainly are, a multiplicity of answers to the question 'how should work be organized?' All we can do in this section is start to structure the answers in possibly fruitful ways.

Baldamus makes a cogent, and not always heeded, point when he says of the concept of 'boredom' – '. . . to be able to ask fruitful questions, the investigator himself must first have some idea of what is specific to *industrial* boredom; to use an introspective notion derived from his own professional work is obviously not very helpful, and may indeed falsify the whole approach from the start'. While Baldamus accepts that much light industrial work is inherently *tedious*, he is puzzled that the conditions of severe distress sometimes produced by exposing people to similar types of work under experimental conditions, do not typically seem to occur among factory workers. Why do they stick it? One answer is that the work itself may provide a secondary or substitute kind of satisfaction, deriving from the nature of the work itself, which he calls 'traction'. This is '. . . . a feeling of being pulled along by the nertia inherent in a particular activity'. The experience of 'traction' may be one of rhythm, it may be subjectively pleasurable, and it may be associated with a sensation of reduced rather than of increased effort. Baldamus distinguishes several different types of traction, and the concept obviously has a wide potential utility. But it is vital not to forget the sting in the tail of this analysis. Traction, as a relief from a situation that is 'fundamentally disliked', that may be alienating or exploitative, is none the less a *relative* satisfaction only. Moreover the semi-skilled worker 'will also tend, normally, to take the external situation for granted: the need to take a dissatisfying job at all'. Or as H. L. Mencken put it 'I go on working for the same reason that a hen goes on laying eggs.'

Cunnison's study is less often quoted than is that of her co-worker, Lupton, whose *On the Shop Floor* contains an attempt to identify aspects of the internal and external structure of the organization which tend to be associated with specific wage-payment systems. This interest is carried on by the papers by Gowler and Legge in the collection edited by Robinson. But Cunnison's analysis of the debt relationship of 'dead horse' in the garment industry provides a clear illustration of the way in which the wage-nexus is central to the complex web of interdependencies and interactions which constitute the raw material of the shop-floor social structure.

One widely promoted nostrum for increasing the meaning which people derive from work is that of workers' participation. Cotgrove, Vamplew and Dunham studied the effects of introducing a participative type of management in which there is 'a high level of group participation in decision-making, with high levels of communication'. Most emphasis was put on grass-roots communication which it was believed would have more 'immediacy' and 'relevance' in terms of 'more immediate translation of decisions into action'.

Within the working groups there had been a high degree of interaction, prior to the change, and there was evidence that workers derived some quite major satisfaction from the maintenance of effective relations with workmates and supervisors. All of these facets of work experience were improved by the introduction of a more participative style of management, as also were relations with management itself. The authors conclude that 'participation does more than provide a therapeutic outlet for grievances, important as this may be'.

The structure of work in the work situation of any particular individual or group of workers is affected by wider issues also, as the article by Richardson makes clear. The organizational structures on British and American ships differ not merely because of functional requirements, but for reasons related to the structure of social relations which obtained in British and American society at large. The experience of being 'British' or 'American' implied different expectations, rooted in a culture which made certain ways of behaving appear 'normal' and 'natural' and therefore non-problematical.

So, in the final extract in this chapter we enter another realm again, another way of exploring and of developing tools to analyse the work experience of individuals. To some extent, Turner is advocating, in a rather loose way, the approach which has been more traditionally adopted by cultural anthropologists: the rather strong tendencies towards the analysis of *social* structure in a way rather divorced from the *cultural* has possibly been typical of British anthropology and sociology as a whole. (Though perhaps the ethnoscience approach recently advocated by such writers as Garfinkel and Cicourel may help to redress this balance.) For to Turner the essential fact is that industry itself constitutes a 'meaning system' with its own private tribal memories and its own relative impermeability to the outsider, whether he is a journalist, politician or sociologist.

Tedium and Traction in Industrial Work

W. Baldamus

Reprinted with permission from *Efficiency and Effort*,
Tavistock Publications, 1961, pp. 57–65.

Under modern conditions of mass production, the most pertinent
work reality is the high degree of repetitiveness of light work.
What is usually described as 'boredom' is more conspicuous here
than impairment. A few observations are fairly well established,
particularly with regard to individual differences in susceptibility
to boredom. But many questions remain as baffling as they were
some forty years ago when Münsterberg first started to distinguish boredom from fatigue (impairment). Above all, there is no
answer to the question, admittedly not a simple one, as to what
the nature of boredom is. As T. A. Ryan sums up the problem:
'the only method of gauging the tendency to boredom in a given
worker is to question him as carefully as possible.' But to be able
to ask fruitful questions, the investigator himself must first have
some idea of what is specific to *industrial* boredom; to use an
introspective notion derived from his own professional work is
obviously not very helpful, and may indeed falsify the whole
approach from the start. For it is possible that the repetition
worker's experience of boredom is of quite a different nature
from that connected with professional work. The academic
person, for instance, is bored by a technical book if its subject-
matter has no connection with his particular sphere of interests.
This has nothing to do with repetition. I therefore suggest that
the term 'boredom' be reserved for professional occupations and
'tedium' for the corresponding sentiment in repetition work.

In describing the feeling of tedium on the basis of what is
generally known from published reports, the most important
feature seems to me to be its instability. Unlike impairment, it is
not a condition that appears in a fairly predictable manner after
a certain time and increases its intensity with increased activity.
Moreover, it cannot easily be separated from other causes of
discomfort. Nor has it been possible to find a definite relationship
between the degree of repetition measured by the time normally
taken by a trained worker to complete one work cycle, and the

intensity of the feeling. This is largely due to the impossibility of isolating the degree of repetition from other characteristics of the activity. If, to accentuate the phenomenon, operations with greatly differing length of cycle are compared, these will be jobs which are qualitatively so different that sentiments and feelings other than tedium are bound to interfere. By comparing very similar activities with but a slight variation in cycle time, the matter becomes so subtle that no noticeable difference in intensity of tedium is felt.

There is one point, however, which does lead us a little further. In operations such as press-operating, simple inspection, assembling, labelling, machine-feeding, etc., which are intermittent, so that each cycle appears as a separate act, it appears that the discomfort of tedium is noticeably greater between two cycles than in the course of the cycle operation. More effort seems to be required to start a new cycle than to conclude one already in process. This suggests that tedium is primarily connected with the mental effort required to join two consecutive cycles. It would follow that the shorter the unit cycle, the greater (per day or hour) is the number of inter-cycle decisions required for a continuous performance, and hence, probably, the greater the tedium. But the word 'decision' should not be taken too literally, for in any routine operation the whole thing is semi-automatic.

The impression that it is more tedious to join than to complete separate cycles has some support from the experiments on satiation carried out by Anitra Karsten. They consisted, briefly, of asking various subjects to cover pieces of paper with pencil strokes in certain patterns. After a period, when a stage of satiation was reached, several subjects found that it was relatively more painful to start a new page than to complete one already started. Although they are not sufficiently comparable with industrial conditions, these experiments are illuminating for another reason. They indicated that satiation is strongly dependent on motivational projections; with subjects who thought the experiment served some important purpose, the onset of satiation was delayed, whereas those who interpreted the experiments as meaningless from the start, experienced greater discomfort. The crucial role of motivation emerged also in the fact that the feelings expressed were highly unstable.

Returning to industrial repetitive tasks, there is no doubt that workers do associate a feeling of tedium with highly monotonous operations, although on the whole it is only a feeling of a mild discomfort which has no apparent relationship with the degree of repetition. The surprising absence of severe distress (such as has occurred in experimental situations) has often been commented upon. It will therefore be our main task to look out for all those relative satisfactions which are likely to overlay, postpone, or remove any very acute experience of tedium. This means that the specific work reality, repetitiveness, would produce the severely painful experience of satiation only if there were no concurrent satisfactions.

The strongest and most frequent of these relative satisfactions is what, in an earlier study, I have called 'traction' because, in a sense, it is the opposite of 'dis-traction'. It is a feeling of being pulled along by the inertia inherent in a particular activity. The experience is pleasant and may therefore function as a relief from tedium. It usually appears to be associated, though not always, with a feeling of reduced effort, relative to actual or imagined situations where it is difficult to maintain continuity of performance.

Traction seems closely related to 'rhythm' which is a better-known phenomenon because it is familiar from common experience. Rhythm in work was first extensively described by the historian Karl Bücher, who was fully aware of the effort-reducing character of rhythm. But his observations were only descriptive and based chiefly on non-industrial work. The importance of rhythm as an effort-reducing factor also occurs in specific industrial activities; this is indicated by numerous chance observations, particularly in some of the reports by the Industrial Health Research Board. In studies on variety in work it was found that frequent changes from one operation to another reduced the rate of output owing to the interference with the 'swing of work'. A comparison of the work curves of handkerchief folding and ironing in a laundry showed a regular fall of the curve in the case of folding but a remarkable rise throughout the spell for ironing; this was tentatively explained by a 'natural rhythm' inherent in ironing. Wyatt repeatedly refers to similar observations in a number of studies on repetitive work. For instance, a lathe, 'when running, exerts a pull which impels the operative to keep going even when fatigued : . .'

However, most of these observations were interpreted by reference to the concept of capacity to work. It was, therefore, an important change of orientation when attention was first directed to the fact that emotional attitudes to work may be a crucial factor in the relation between output and effort. This step was taken in the course of a study by Wyatt on Incentives in Repetitive Work. If it is true that such phenomena as 'rhythm', 'swing', and 'pull' affect effort at work, different types of work must produce different reactions on the part of the worker. The study compares (under controlled conditions) five repetitive, outwardly very similar, operations connected with the packing of toffees and chocolates: wrapping, unwrapping, packing (into tins), weighing, and weighing combined with wrapping, It was found that the various types of work produced marked differences in the worker's attitudes and patterns of behaviour. This was closely related to variations in the rate of improvement during the learning period. During this period, which lasted altogether 35 weeks, the external incentive pressure was twice stepped up, from daywork to bonus rate and then to piece-rate. Of the five operations, wrapping showed the greatest improvement, while there was practically no change in the output rate of unwrapping. The other operations took an intermediate position both in order of preference and relative improvement.

Much of the explanation offered to account for the differences in emotional attitude and performance is clearly relevant to the elements of traction inherent in the various operations, or alternatively to interferences with traction. Unwrapping was disliked by the workers partly because of 'the tendency of the paper to stick to the toffee'. Of weighing, which was disliked almost as much as unwrapping, it was said that 'the short but frequent interruptions caused by inserting paper slips in the tins and the packing of the tins in cartons was annoying because they interfered with the main operation'. Wrapping was performed with 'rapidity and ease' and was 'free from interruptions and variations so that the operatives were able to adopt a rhythmical method of work'.

Similarly, 'the statements of the operatives contained many references to minor features of the work which were regarded as annoying interruptions because they interfered with the continuity of the processes and impeded progress'; or 'the annoyance caused whenever the cycles of movement were interrupted or impaired was intensified by occasional defects in the material'. So numerous are such references that one wonders whether a common source for these irritations may not be found in specific elements of the external working situation. The answer is, I think, that they stem from imperfections in the routine pattern of production, imperfections that interfere with the expectation of traction.

It will help further analysis if we obtain a mental image of traction that is sufficiently meaningful to permit the comparison of different situations. The following types of traction may be distinguished.

Object traction. This kind of traction is also experienced in many non-industrial activities and is therefore more easily recognized by those who are not familiar with manual industrial work. The experience derives mainly from visualizing an object or its parts which one feels urged to reproduce or complete. It is found in many hobby activities such as modelling, carpentry, painting. In industrial work its most powerful form exists in crafts that are concerned with making things. A single press-tool may occupy the toolmaker for a period of 4 to 6 weeks. During this time the object is mentally, and to some extent actually, divided up into separate stages and parts, and it is first of all the desired shape of a part that exercises traction on the worker. A picture of the whole product is, however, also present in his mind, and this added element of traction increases in intensity as the job nears completion. In labelling cartons, though object traction is present, it is very weak indeed. The object is one labelled carton, and traction is experienced during each work cycle. Its effect becomes noticeable when irritating obstacles interfere with the smooth run of the cycle. The comparison between tool-making and labelling shows that the two jobs do not differ only in tedium. The chief difference derives from the different intensity of object traction, apart from the contrast in respect of tedium.

Batch traction. Many operations in industry are subject to a type of traction that is connected with a desire to complete a batch of articles. This too is well illustrated by the case of labelling. The feeling of traction is stronger when the completion of the batch is approaching. It is known from various studies on repetitive work that subdividing a large number of articles or components into smaller groups helps to diminish the feeling of tedium. This phenomenon is also related to observations on the beneficial influence of 'knowledge of results'.

Process traction. This is experienced in operations where the tempo and sequence of the motions are determined by the chemical or physical nature of the production process, as is the case in melting, casting, glass-blowing, soldering, welding, painting, chocolate-dipping, forging, spraying, etc. However, it should not be thought that the movements of the operator are simply forced on him. There is usually a distinctly pleasant sensation in being guided or pulled along by the process in completing a given work cycle. Frequently, process traction is combined with object traction, for example, in glass-blowing.

Machine traction. Operations on machines which are constantly running produce in the operator the feeling of being drawn along. To isolate machine traction, care must be taken to put object traction out of one's mind, as this usually occurs simultaneously. For instance, in turning a steel bar along a given distance, there is a pull towards completing each run in one movement, even before the desired thickness is approached; although in the first stages of the operation the worker could, if he wanted, interrupt the action without damage to the finished product, there is a tendency to extend the continuous operation as long as possible. Thus, he feels inclined to keep going with repeated cycles while the machine is running.

Line traction. Modern methods of flow production are characterized by the same object passing through a series of operations which are carried out by different workers, with or without the help of a conveyor belt. Usually a strong movement of traction is inherent in such methods of production. But it is not easily recognized because most outside observers associate work on a conveyor belt with a feeling of coercion.

Further distinctions between types of traction may be possible but they are not needed for our purpose. There is, however, one experience that is akin to traction, though not necessarily associated with specific characteristics of the job. That is the well-known observation that workers are stimulated in their effort by the knowledge that output is expanding and that there is a pressure of work. Similarly, rumours about shortage of orders are known to have a depressing effect on activity. The classical example is that of the mica splitting girls in the Hawthorne studies, whose output generally declined when the work schedules had to be reduced in view of the 1930 depression. Although the overall psychological effect of production is difficult to isolate as a separate factor in motivation, the similarity to traction effects helps us to understand such situations. Line traction in particular acts as a psychological multiplier of the external output situation. The operator feels himself as a particle in the ceaseless flow of activity. Any step towards increased flow production intensifies that feeling. Similarly, if there is in the factory an all-round atmosphere of speed and pressure of production, no one can escape being affected by it. The similarity between line traction and general production traction also follows from the fact that it makes little difference whether line production is based on mechanical conveyors or human chains, whereby the manufactured article passes through a consecutive series of operations by being handed on from one operator to the next.

I have described traction at some length, and with more emphasis than I gave to tedium, its counterpart, for a good reason. Traction is probably the most important, in any case the most specific, example in the industrial context of relative satisfactions. These are, as I mentioned before, feelings that arise as a relief from fundamentally disliked situations, and they are very difficult to understand. The operator need not be conscious of the relativity of traction. It is quite possible that he usually, if not always, has the definite impression that traction is a genuine satisfaction inherent in particular operations. The ordinary worker has few opportunities to compare experiences from widely differing occupations. If he is a semi-skilled repetition worker, he can compare only a limited range of similar operations, and therefore, taking it for granted that his job is bound to be fundamentally tedious, he will then strive to obtain a job where traction is relatively strong and interferences to traction small. He will also tend, normally, to take the external situation for granted: the need to have a dissatisfying job at all, the necessity to 'keep going', to follow the line of least resistance. Thus, only at the particular moment when there are special imperfections, irritations, and interferences with the usual type of traction, only then does he become aware, vaguely and reluctantly, of the deprivation fundamentally inherent in the work realities of tedium. In other words, traction (or any other relative satisfaction) tends to become a normal expectation; a feeling that is projected into the currently accepted definition of routine operations.

Dead Horse, Debt, and the Wage Nexus in the Garment Industry
Sheila Cunnison

Reprinted with permission from *Wages and Work Allocation*, Tavistock, 1966, pp. 55–7.

Calculating wages

The weekly wage was calculated from the piece-rate prices paid to makers and machiners. The style slip issued with a bundle of work included the total piece-rate price for the maker and for the machiner. The prices for each item were not listed, and a worker could check only by consulting the price list issued to each member by the union. Slips were not given out with all work; workers were often told to refer to slips they had received earlier.

The work given to a maker was entered in a book, usually by the supervisor, sometimes by the manager. This book consisted of a set of loose-leaf cards (see Table 1), each carrying a worker's name and clock number. A maker receiving work had the order number, the quantity of coats, the machiner's name, and the date entered on his card. Later, the date of return was entered. Although machiners had separate cards, the Makers' Work which they sewed was recorded only on the makers' cards.

The book of cards was used in making up wages at the end of the week. In theory, the firm worked four days in hand, books being made up on Monday for Friday's wages. In slack times books were sometimes not made up until Tuesday or even Wednesday. But in fact workers were seldom in front with their work. The practice known as the dead-horse system operated throughout the waterproof and rainwear trades. Under this system, the worker is paid at the end of the week for a quantity of work which may include work completed, work in progress, and work booked out to the worker but not yet started. This last was known as the worker's dead horse. It brought the worker into a debt relationship with the firm which, in a sense, tied him to the firm.

At Dee, the production system fitted in naturally with the way in which wages were calculated each week. On the day 'the books

Table 1. Example of a maker's work card for five seleted weeks

No. 85	Name: Brown					
	Order No.	Style No.	Machiner No.	Quantity	Date issued	Date returned
Week 1	s29	L63	35	10	14/4	30/4
	s29	L63	35	6	19/4	24/4
	s22	L68	35	1	19/4	20/4
	s20	L68	35	8	23/4	30/4
	s29	L63	35	6	23/4	30/4
	[Books made up on] Monday 23/4/56					
Week 2	s29	L63	35	3	26/4	30/4
	s29	L63	35	4	26/4	30/4
	s29	L63	35	2	26/4	30/4
	s29	L26	35	2	26/4	30/4
	x7	G42	35	12	30/4	4/5
	[Books made up on] Monday 30/4/56					
Week 3	s27	L63	35	9	3/5	9/5
	s27	L63	35	8	3/5	9/5
	x11	G42	35	7	8/5	14/5
	[Books made up on] Tuesday 8/5/56					
Week 4	x15	G32	35	6	14/5	17/5
	x15	G32	35	6	14/5	18/5
	[Books made up on] Monday 14/5/56					
Week 5	x15	G32	35	6	17·5	24·5
	x15	G422	35	10	23/5	not ret'd
	[Books made up on] Wednesday 23/5/56					
Week 6 (beginning)	F25	G438	35	6	23/5	not ret'd
	[Books not yet made up]					

Notes: L was used to denote a ladies' coat, G a gents'.
All work returned after the books were made up was, according to management usage of lhe term, dead horse.

were made up' (as it was put), the manager went through the makers' cards. He could tell whether work booked out had been completed; from the order number he could tell the style of the coats, and from the style he knew the price; the order number also told him whether the work was 'wanted' or not. From long experience he could tell, at a glance, the money value of the work booked to each worker. Lines ruled across the card at intervals marked off the amount of work that had been paid for in previous weeks. The manager accordingly drew a line to show how much of the work currently booked out was to be paid for as the next Friday's wages.

The position of the line thus determined the amount of the week's wage. Frequently it was drawn only after a conference between worker and manager. On the day the books were made up, makers often went in turn, as they were sent for, into the manager's office; and there they might ask to have more work booked out to them. Sometimes they were not consulted at all. At other times, when the work was plentiful, the manager would come round the workshop with the book of cards, stopping by each maker to tell him the value of the work booked out and how much he intended to pay that week. Usually, workers were paid for all the work booked out the day that wages were made up. Wage slips were given out on the Thursday stating what the next day's wages would be. Workers who had not been consulted and who now discovered that they were not going to get enough on the Friday would go to the manager's office to complain.

*   *   *

The debt relationship of dead horse

Dead horse was once described to me as 'the pieceworker's privilege'. This referred to its use to even out fluctuations in wages from one week to another. But it had other uses and other consequences as well. Another worker called it 'the boss's weapon and the curse of the trade'. 'Dead horse is used in this firm to keep workers,' he went on, 'it gives them a hold over you. Dee has always had a bad reputation for keeping its workers.' This was the opinion of a worker who had recently come to Dee and wanted to avoid getting indebted, so that he could leave easily when trade picked up. A big dead horse tied workers to the firm because they felt morally obliged to finish work for which they had been paid. There was no legal obligation to do so, and since the union did not recognize the practice, the management could expect no help from that source if a worker made off without finishing his work. The feeling of obligation no doubt rested largely on self-interest: 'You never know in this trade when you may want to come back to a shop,' workers told me. They spoke with a touch of envy about the old days when the dead horse was disposed of by cutting it up into small pieces and throwing it in the canal.

Like Dee, many firms work a week in hand, but, unlike Dee, most firms outside the trade have no highly developed system of dead horse. Many Dee workers were indebted up to the value of one week's wage. Anyone thinking of leaving, particularly of moving out of the trade, thus faced a week without any wages. Moving within the trade usually involved a loss of wages because new workers were generally allowed only a small dead horse of up to one or two days' wages. A worker who stayed at Dee, however, hoped to be able to work off his dead horse gradually through allocations of good work, thus losing no wages. In all probability he would be forced to get straight through a series of wage cuts, but this at least would spread the loss.

Dead horse was not the only debt at Dee. The firm regularly lent interest-free cash sums of £1 to £2 to certain workers, to be paid off through weekly wage deductions of two to five shillings. The loans were usually offered to new workers to tide them over the first week; this was in addition to a small dead horse. Most loans to new workers were not renewed, but some long-service workers who were permanently about a week behind were also in a permanent money debt of amounts from £3 to £4; as soon as one loan was paid off, they asked for another. Loans were also made to help workers who were in financial difficulties, caused perhaps by absence. Some workers preferred a small loan (if the manager would grant it) and a small dead horse to a big dead horse. Bernie said on this subject: 'It makes you sick when you have £10 of dead horse to work off. You don't feel like working at all. It's different when you have a sub; you feel like working then.' Others hated the idea of yet a further debt, thinking that the manager deliberately tried to tie them in this way: He gives you bad work and waits till you've got a big dead horse; then he comes around with his sub.' The manager said he lent money to workers who needed it: 'They would have to borrow from somebody, so why not from me?'

The dead-horse system had two main effects on the struggle over the wage: it put power into the hands of management, the creditor in the debt relation; and it was a source of cleavage between workers and of a further particularization and strengthening of the tie between individual worker and manager.

There was a good reason for calling dead horse the boss's weapon: the manager could grant or withhold it as he thought fit; he thus had the power to cut wages at his discretion. When trade was slack and there was not enough work to go round it was inevitable that some people should have their wages cut. The decision as to whose it should be rested with the manager; and it was then that he found the cutting down of dead horse a useful means of cutting wages.

Faced with a prospective wage cut, a worker could protest, argue, and beg. Legally his position was weak unless the manager proposed cutting his wages to less than the agreed or statutory time-rates; and this was unlikely because these rates were far below pieceworkers' normal earnings. But the distribution of wage cuts was a matter for the manager to decide and so, in any particular instance, he might be persuaded to change his mind.

The personal element in the manager-worker relation was important on such occasions. Another factor that might influence the manager's decision on whether to reconsider a wage cut was the indebtedness of the petitioning worker. A heavily indebted worker protesting against a wage cut was, in effect, asking to continue or even increase his debt. And this the manager was easily able to refuse, when other factors in the situation indicated such a refusal.

A worker with a small dead horse was perhaps in a better position to escape a cut. I recorded two instances when the manager was persuaded to change his mind. First, Audrey: 'I came in this morning and went to Pat for work. But she said I'd had my quota and I had been "crossed off". ["Crossing off" refers to the line drawn across the maker's card to show the amount of work to be paid for in a particular week.] I decided to go and see Jones and I told him that my wages were going down because the prices are no good. He said that the prices aren't his fault. I told him that I didn't mind my wages going down one week, but I didn't like to see them going down week after week. Then he talked to me about the girls who work on the back table; he said that he had to make their wages up. But I said I didn't care about their wages, and so we went on. Anyhow, he let me have more work.'

Similarly with Margie: halfway through the study period Jones had asked her to take a cut. 'Can you manage with what you've got?' he asked, referring to the amount of work already booked out to her. Trade was going off, he explained, and work was short. Margie told me: 'I said no, I couldn't. A couple of weeks ago he cut my wages down to £4, and I told him it was someone else's turn. He gave me some more work; it's not good work but at least it's wages.'

A worker who had no debt was in a stronger position, but such a case was unusual. Audrey, after suffering a wage cut one week, managed by making a special effort to get herself out of debt. She hoped to avoid another cut: 'Last week I asked Ted Jones if I could have six extra coats booked. He looked at me and just said, "You'll be lucky!", and I didn't get them. But he's not going to get the better of me. He'll have a shock when he finds out how much work I've got booked out this week, and he'd better not try to do me out of it!'

But the personal element and the degree of indebtedness were only two factors influencing the manager's decision. Important also were the labour requirements of the firm and the financia l needs of the workers themselves. During periods when work shortage was only slight, the manager favoured the slower workers. He allowed them to be about a week behind with their work, whereas fast workers were permitted to be only one or two days behind. The fast workers were kept in this position by being refused fresh work until they had completed work in hand, and they were even kept waiting. In any week, therefore, the slower workers were making up coats that they had been paid for the previous Friday, and coats that were to be paid for on the Friday of the current week were in unopened bundles of dead horse on their tables. On the day that the books were made up, slower workers were allocated work equal to about a week's earnings; thus they were assured of their wages at the end of the week. If all the workers had been refused work until they completed what they already had in hand, the slower ones would have fared very badly. They would have been forced to leave Dee and look for better-paying jobs. As it was the manager was able to keep them, ready for the upswing.

The discrimination between fast and slow workers caused a great deal of ill-feeling in the workshop. Fast workers who were waiting looked at the unopened bundles lying on the tables of the slower workers, and were jealous. They regularly went in to complain to the manager, and they regularly got the same answer: 'They have to make their wages too. They don't get as much as you and they have children to keep. So I have to give them work.'

Two of the fastest workers were married women without children. 'I can see that he can't let them go home without any wages,' said one of them, 'but I don't see why they should have unopened bundles on their table while I'm waiting.' She never saw the logic of this.

Dead horse also enabled the manager to discriminate beween workers as regards type of work. Workers with a big dead horse were, in a sense, tied to the firm; and the manager was believed to exploit this by giving them bad work, thus creating a vicious circle of debt. For example, there was Joe: he was a highly skilled long-service maker, but he had a big dead horse and a permanent sub. He had been given an intricate coat which he disliked; it was new and difficult, and put him further behind with his work. He complained, and Jones said that he would give the next lot to Ellen, the alteration maker. But he gave them to Joe again. 'If I refuse to make them' Joe said, 'it will mean another quarrel with Ted Jones. We already had words last week and you can't afford to quarrel with him every week.' Indeed, with a large dead horse and a permanent sub, it did not seem advisable. Joe made the coats without protest. In this case the manager probably gave the work to Joe because he was one of the few workers who could do it properly. Ellen had been a good maker too, but her sight was failing, and because she would not wear glasses the standard of her work had fallen.

The personal element carried weight here also. It sometimes seemed that, tired of continual complaints, the manager off-loaded bad work like odd coats of different sizes and colours onto slow and indebted workers who were unlikely to protest. Betty thought that this was what happened to her. One day Elsie looked at Betty's work, eleven coats and nearly all different. 'You've got liquorice allsorts again,' she said. Betty, who would never speak up to the manager, replied rather peevishly, 'Yes, he didn't give them to you because he knows you'd have thrown them back in his face.' 'These are days when you don't throw anything back in his face; you're thankful for what you've got,' snapped Elsie. Elsie had a big dead horse and was in desperate need of money to support her sick husband and small son.

At times, the manager seemed to have been irritated to the point where he deliberately, and for no good market reason, exacerbated conflict between workers. Towards the end of the fieldwork period some good work, navy capes, came into the shop. Word spread around quickly and Herb, a long-service maker, one of those people who always stand up for themselves, and a thorn in the manager's flesh, went and asked for some. He had been nearly £2 down in his wages the week before, not from working any less hard than usual – he was one of the most consistent workers in the shop – but from having his dead horse reduced after a run of bad work. Here was an opportunity to get straight. 'I can't give them to you,' Jones said, 'you're too far behind. If people see you with work on your table and they are standing waiting, they'll go down to the union.' This refusal to share the good work would seem calculated to foment discord between workers. But apparently the manager reconsidered his decision, for later in the day Herb received a bundle of the capes.

By and large, however, allocations of both type and quantity of work were made with the interests of the firm foremost, and the interests of the workers running a good second. This was shown at each of the two-day holidays that occurred during the six months of fieldwork. Then the manager cut the dead horse of practically everyone, thus making the available work go further without cutting anyone's take-home pay. The pay for each day's holiday was calculated on the previous year's earnings and, since 1955 had been a year of brisk trade, the rate was far above the rate that workers were currently earning. The workers however did not look at the manager's action in this light; they felt cheated of their high holiday pay, and attributed other motives to him. Said Elsie, on receiving a large allocation of dead horse a week or two before the Whitsun holiday: 'He wouldn't have sent me my knacker if it was Whitsun. He's afraid you'll die over the holiday and he'll have it to finish off. Old Joseph [the waterproof director] doesn't care about our wages. He might cut them out of spite. He doesn't care about anything except keeping his old factory going.'

*   *   *

The five most important variables determining a man's wage at Dee were: piece-rate prices; the quantity and type of work booked out to him; the quality of work he produced; the effort he put in; and the hours he worked.

Of these, effort and hours worked were the only ones over which he had anything approaching unilateral control. Yet, although there was no machine-pacing and no set work target, his control was not entirely complete. The pace of work was by no means purely a matter of individual choice. The whole system of social relations at Dee contributed to a fast pace of work – one that many felt was too fast. In addition, pressure was put on workers to produce more at certain times, for example when an order was wanted very quickly by a valuable customer. Within these limits, however, the pace of work was controlled by workers themselves. Similarly, hours of work were a matter of choice unless an order was urgently needed or workers feared for their jobs. Over other matters there was a running battle between worker and manager. These emphases on individual choice and individual struggle affected the way in which workers regarded their wages and their relations as they co-operated in production.

Organizational Contrasts on British and American Ships

S. A. Richardson

Reprinted with permission from *Administrative Science Quarterly*, September 1956, pp. 189–207.

To be effective, an organization must have a structure appropriate for the particular purpose and the resulting necessary tasks. At the same time, the form of organization and the values and needs of its members must be adapted to one another. Variations in organization, then, can be expected to follow from variations of the cultures from which members of an organization are drawn. The effects of cultural factors can be seen in comparing organizations which function in a wide variety of countries and have identical purposes and similar environments.

The social organization on British and United States merchant ships was selected for study because cargo ships have identical purposes, closely comparable environments, and a set of conditions as near to the research ideal as is likely to be found in a natural setting without experimental manipulation. Cargo ships or freighters of approximately seven thousand tons, carrying crews of forty men, were selected for study.

We will first describe the purpose and environment which are common to foreign-going cargo ships of all nationalities. Then we will describe how British and United States seamen arrange their shipboard lives to meet these common conditions. For the purposes of this paper the description will be limited to some differences found between the two nationalities in training, social control, and stratification.

*   *   *

Common purpose and environment

A merchant ship's purpose is to transport cargo and passengers. This demands three main focuses of work for the crew: (1) aiding and facilitating the loading and discharging of cargo and passengers; (2) bringing the ship and her contents safely to her appointed destination, and (3) throughout the life of the ship, maintaining and repairing her so that she will give efficient service.

A ship and her contents are a large capital investment. She is exposed frequently to such hazards as storms, collision, fire, and shipwreck. The safety of the ship depends in large measure upon the quick judgments and actions of experienced and skillful seamen. The social organization of the crew must therefore have a clearly designated hierarchy of responsibility and must make provision for rapid communication and execution of orders. Because potential hazards to the ship exist at all times, the organization must function continuously.

A ship's movements impose limitations as to when a member of the crew may form and sever connection with the ship. A seaman joins a ship when it is in his country and reasonably close to his home. With few exceptions, he must remain with the ship until it returns to his home country. This period may be from a month to two years. During the voyage, the crew therefore has a smaller turnover than any comparable organization ashore.

Members of the crew spend their working hours and leisure time at sea, isolated from other people. In foreign ports the friendships they can form ashore are limited by the brief duration of the ship's stay and by the limited channels that may be used to establish social contacts. Life at sea has in most cases been found unsuitable for families. Members of the crew must therefore be separated from their families for the duration of the voyage.

The social system of merchant ship crews

To fulfill the purpose of a ship and to adapt the seaman to the environment which has been described, a clearly defined social system has been evolved through centuries of experience. This system must be sufficiently clear so that a new crew made up of men who have never before met can immediately co-ordinate the complex task of running a ship.

Effects of social stratification on patterns of behaviour

If the social structure of the crew is conceived as occupying a vertical scale with the captain at the top and a first-voyage ordinary seaman at the bottom, it should be possible to place all crew members on this scale and to determine the range within which groups form. This grouping may be called social stratification, and the distance along the scale may be called social distance. There are a number of indicators of social stratification and distance which are recognized implicitly or explicitly by members of British and American crews. These include wages, qualifications formally required for holding an office (such as examinations and length of sea service), number of persons supervised, food and living conditions, and such behaviour as the use of titles in addressing people. Together these indicators influence the behaviour of every member of the crew with respect to every other member, providing pressures towards maintaining approved patterns of behaviour.

Comparison of British and American crews on indicators of social stratification and distance showed that American seamen consistently play down behavioural and physical symbols that strengthen status and social distance. Some examples of the differences will now be given.

Food and the division of the crew at meals

The value of the eating arrangements aboard ship as a measure of social stratification was recognized by Herman Melville in *White Jacket* when he observed that 'the dinner table is the criterion of rank in our man-of-war world'.

The British crews have more divisions than the American. The British bosun and carpenter eat with the engine-room supervisory men; this group is often called the petty officers. The American bosun and carpenter and other petty officers eat with the able-bodied seamen and ordinary seamen, but generally at a separate table. Interviews showed a close positive relationship between status and the quality of food on British ships. The same was true of American ships in an earlier period, until unions won the right of equal food for all. This right is carefully guarded by unlicensed personnel, whose delegates compare the quality of food being served officers and men. The British able-bodied seamen and ordinary seamen collect their meals from the cook, carry food to their messroom, and after eating do their own cleaning up. American able-bodied seamen and ordinary seamen are provided with a steward, who takes orders from the men, acts as waiter, and afterwards cleans up the utensils and messroom. Both British and American officers are served at meals. Whereas on British ships only officers have tablecloths at meals, on American ships tablecloths are provided for all hands.

Although union membership has had little effect on status on British ships, the American union organization among unlicensed personnel at sea has tended to decrease social distance between fellow union members of different status, because the union teachings of brotherhood and equality are in contradiction to the official social hierarchy. Social pressures are applied to the bosun, chief steward, and carpenter to make them work in close co-operation with, and give their loyalty to, the able-bodied and ordinary seamen rather than form a separate petty-officer group. Through union efforts, the pay differential and differences in living conditions have been reduced between bosun, carpenter, chief steward, and the able-bodied and ordinary seamen.

On American ships the consistent playing down of symbols that strengthen status and social distance as compared with British practice appears to be closely related to the sentiments the men have toward social distance and authority. While interviewing, I found a consistent difference between British and American seamen in the degree of awareness and acceptance of social distance between statuses. On American ships, early in the interviews, I met such expressions as:

'The bosun, he's one of the boys. He's just another fellow.' (Able-bodied seaman)

'The mates, they just act big because they don't do no lousy jobs, and walk up and down the bridge doing nothing. I'm as good a man as any of them.' (Able-bodied seaman)

As the interviews developed, seamen did give various reasons why there was a need for social distance, and these explanations would often be accompanied by surprise, as if these were ideas they had never before explicitly recognized.

On British ships, in contrast, social distance was accepted as a matter of course, and it was stressed among the men that one of the reasons that officers and men for the most part kept separate was that the men had no wish to mix with the officers and preferred companions from their own or a similar status.

Conclusion

The description of the purpose and environment of a ship showed that it was necessary to have a clearly designated hierarchy of authority to meet the hazards and emergencies which the ship may encounter at any time. During non-emergency activities which account for most of the routine aboard ships, the full measure of vested authority remains latent, and a form of authority more suited to non-emergency routine work and living is manifest. There is always the possibility, however, that the powers necessary for emergency action may be misused by the captain and officers for dealing with non-emergency issues. Comparison of British and American crews suggests that the British realize and accept the authority of competent persons and are not as fearful of the misuse of authority as Americans. This acceptance of authority is closely related to acceptance of social stratification and the symbols of these differences. Status symbols function as cues for self-regulation, in conformity with the status and role requirements of the ship. British seamen are conditioned before coming to sea to accept authority, and consequently the change in attitudes required when a man becomes a seaman is slight. Acceptance of authority, by trainees, facilitates training and a willingness to rely largely on informal and traditional practices for dealing with behaviour of the captains and officers which they consider deviant.

Among American crews a far greater fear and suspicion of authority appears to exist. Social stratification is not widely accepted and is often denied. Many symbols of social stratification and authority have been removed, and, because they are suspect, the remaining symbols do little to enhance self-regulation of the men in conformity with the status and role demands of the ship's social organization. If the symbols of social stratification are ineffective, alternative procedures are necessary for training Americans for the requirements of life at sea and for maintaining the necessary social system. The alternative procedure has been a far greater formalization of the social system than the British. Greater formalization is evident in training men for the system, in maintaining the expected patterns of behaviour, and especially in placing constraints upon authority.

Examples given have included the formalization of working conditions through a detailed union contract, formalizing the system of handling complaints, and the training of officers and men to a far greater degree than the British through specialized shore-based training institutions. The unions have played an important part in this process of formalization. The cultural differences between the British and Americans operating through their beliefs and attitudes have, then, important effects in the operation and maintenance of a social system developed to meet an identical purpose and similar environment.

Industrial Meaning Systems
B. A. Turner

Reprinted with permission from *Exploring the Industrial Subculture*, Macmillan, 1971, pp. 106–14.

The industrial subculture is a complex aggregation of norms, job-roles, social definitions, explanatory frameworks and moral injunctions, the existence of which is crucial to the preservation of a continuity of human activities within the industrial sector. But the cultural tradition is not a single or a unified one: the precise content of the systems of meaning which are transmitted by groups of individuals to their successors varies from company to company, from factory to factory, and from department to department. There are different strains of tradition which conflict or compete, or which separate out into their own 'segregated meaning systems'.

Within this varied cultural pattern, there are differences in the degree to which given individuals are exposed to the range of meaning systems, and there are differences in the extent to which they are able to accept the subcultural meaning patterns which they are offered. Similarly, there are differences in the contributions which they make to their own portion of the tradition, leading to the development and change of the whole.

A consideration of the processes by which meaning is attached to objects, people and events is central to an examination of subcultural phenomena; and these processes not only play a part in the transmission of existing cultural patterns, but they also enable individuals to contribute in varying degrees to the alteration and modification of these patterns. When an individual in an industrial environment is dealing with his colleagues, he is constantly having to attribute meaning to them and their actions. And, provided that he has passed the early stage of 'egocentricity', he also comes to wonder what he would see if he could look at his own actions through their eyes.

As an instance, consider the remarks of a manager of a company which had recently taken over a second company, on meeting the managers of this second company: 'I felt what it was like to be in the role of an axe-man . . . because you know that the jobs of the people sitting opposite you hang on a thread.' He saw at the meeting that an unpleasant meaning was being ascribed to the part which he was playing in the takeover process. Although he offered, by way of self-excuse, his regrets about this, he recognized that the unpleasant meaning was true, adding: 'But you just had to get used to it, and get on collecting information.'

In other cases, individuals may see their actions being endowed with a meaning which they do not intend, as when a manager in charge of a section manufacturing special equipment tries to explain the reasons why his section needs special attention in various forms; although he has a genuine point to make, he sees his attempts to explain it regarded by his colleagues as the setting-up of a 'mystique' around his department, as a preliminary to some empire-building on his part. When it is realized that actions may be misinterpreted, attempts may be made to use this property deliberately to encourage the reading or the mis-reading of the meaning of one's actions in a certain way.

The chief executive of any organization or portion of an organization possesses, by virtue of his position, a combination of power and relative autonomy. Because of this, he holds a peculiar significance relative to the culture of his own organization, a significance which has repercussions upon the kinds of meaning attributed to the events which surround him. Any chief executive is in a position which gives him considerable leverage in the dis-semination of his own views about the way in which his own portion of the organization should function. And even when he is removed, the extent to which he has committed the organization during his time in office will be likely to persist. For this reason, he is the person who has the peculiar responsibility of setting the style of the organization: or, as Selznick puts it, he is the person who must create the 'myth' of the organization.

In the twenty concerns which they studied, Burns and Stalker noted that: 'The one constant element . . . was the extraordinary importance ascribed to the personal qualities of the managing director, or general manager of the plant. In many firms, almost every interview would contain reference to the "outstanding personality", the "flair", the "wisdom", the "tremendous personal courage", even the "genius" of the managing director, and the all-important part he had played in the success of the firm.'

And they concluded that: 'The head of the concern stands for the concern and its relative successes – he symbolizes or personifies it.'

Of course, even if the chief executive of an organization or a portion of an organization chooses not to make use of his position to impose his own personal manner of operation on the organization; or if he is self-effacing; or if he conveys contradictory impressions to those under him; he may still be regarded as setting the ethos of the organization by default. Under conditions such as these, it is easier than would normally be the case for other top managers to seize the initiative and to shape the organization in their own way. It therefore becomes particularly important for members of an organization to know the actions and intentions of the chief executive, to know his attitudes, and the priorities which he places upon the issues of the day. This is not to suggest that every executive is surrounded by 'yes-men' – but, unless his authority is completely discredited, even the most uncompliant of subordinates needs to know what meaning he should attribute to his chief executive's words or actions, in order to prepare his own challenge to them.'

A chief executive or an organizational leader at any level sets limits to the behaviour and operations which occur within his portion of the organization. In consequence, he is particularly likely to have his words and actions, perhaps even his friendships and his leisure pursuits, subjected to minute and searching examination by his subordinates. In spite of the apparent clarity of any remarks or pronouncements which he may make, these will be ransacked for latent meanings.

Additionally, any aspect of his behaviour may be treated *as if it contained messages* for others in the organization, and examined accordingly. An instance is provided by the following interpretation of the choice of office made by a new Chairman of the Governors of the BBC:

'Coming from the enemy lines into a Byzantine bureaucracy he knew to be hostile to him, he took some elementary steps to safeguard his own communications. Previous chairmen had occupied the small panelled office with a communicating door into the Director-General's room on the third floor at Broadcasting House, and had shared the same secretary. Lord Hill moved into a separate office on the fourth floor and brought in the secretary who has been with him for 23 years.'

'Long-serving Corporation men steeped in the high-minded traditions of their priestcraft, marked this as symbolic of Hill's devilish intentions. As one of them, looking back from the experience of these turbulent days to that first act of the new Chairman, says: "Hill's action has meant that there have been two centres of power within the BBC. Hill seemed to set out from the beginning to break what has been the secret of healthy administration in the BBC, the really close alliance between the Chairman and the Director-General." '

The Chief executive ' "defines the work situation", displaying in his own actions and expecting in others (a) the span of considerations, technical, commercial, humane, politic, sentimental, and so forth which are admissible to decisions within the working organization; and (b) the demands of the working organization for commitment, effort, and self-involvement which the individual should regard as feasible, and should attempt to meet'.

Therefore, when a communication is received from the chief executive, the overt meaning of it is first noted; and subsequently the communication is examined for its hidden connotations at a different level. Then, if a covert as well as an overt response is felt to be necessary, these must both be contained in the reply, even though it is often difficult to achieve this without ambiguity. To take a simple example, at a time of financial stringency, a works manager applied to his managing director for £500 to be spent on capital improvements. The managing director's response was to return the application with a request for details of how the money was to be spent. The manager interpreted this as a threatened encroachment on his area of autonomy, and decided that he was not willing to accept such an encroachment. Translating this back to the overt level, he therefore withdrew his request, and resolved to find the money from elsewhere within his works budget. Clearly, there is here the possibility of ambiguity both in the interpretation of the managing director's response, and in the meaning of the works manager's withdrawal.

The overt meaning content of a message cannot normally be ignored, and the most skilful practitioners of this sort of manoeuvring are those who are able to link both the hidden and the apparent meanings. A successful manager can be expected to present cases that are both accurate *and* calculated to advance his own cause. There are a few occasions, however, when the overt meaning of a message can be ignored, and a response made on another level. Firstly, when the overt message is inadequate in some way: if, for example, because of a personal feud, a person is being constantly harried by trivial and inconsequential requests, he might consider it reasonable to ignore the content of the latent message and to attack with an accusation of persecution. Secondly, when the overt message is unpleasant, or contains an argument which cannot be countered directly, it may be felt more appropriate to make a response by shifting the level. This sort of sequence, which often involves a resort to an *argumentum ad hominem*, is a common tactic in the political arena, but it also occurs in organizational politics.

Because he is able to define much of the framework within which debate is carried on within his portion of the organization, the chief executive usually sets limits to interchanges of this kind. Burns and Stalker mention a foremen's meeting at which the foremen wanted to raise questions about the adequacy of the rate-fixing and bonus system used within the factory. However, they were unable to do so because the chairman of the meeting consistently limited the discussion by joking about these matters when the foremen raised them, or by overruling the foremen's attempts at discussion. Burns and Stalker comment that 'the bounds of admissible considerations in any decision-making situation [are usually] set by superiors. The span of such considerations for normal use throughout the concern tends to be set by the managing director. The effect is to specify the terms in which questions can be discussed. . . .'

In many cases, subjection to a constant and searching analysis by his subordinates creates difficulties for the chief executive. For this means that not only is he, alone, responsible for his portion of the organization, but all of his relationships with subordinates are pervaded by the knowledge that he has the power significantly to affect their lives and careers. This difficulty is likely to increase as one moves up the hierarchy, for as the power becomes greater, so the scrutiny becomes more careful, and the analysis becomes deeper. Further, the higher up the hierarchy an executive is placed, the fewer are the opportunities for balancing his relationships with subordinates with different kinds of relationships with his peers.

The chief executive, then, makes an impact upon his portion of the industrial subculture in several ways: he takes decisions which commit his subordinates to act in a certain context, and to deal with a range of issues arising from this context; he also acts as exemplar of a particular management style, and he sets the bounds to the special form of 'bounded rationality' which is to be employed in his area of command. But he also contributes to the subculture in a slightly different way, for those people who come into contact with him will talk about aspects of their experiences with him, using language to 'detach' these experiences from their own consciousness, in order to make them available to others. In this way, certain meanings which are attributed to the actions of the chief executive are externalized, and may then be incorporated into the transmitted tradition of the organization.

This incorporation takes the form of anecdotes and aphorisms about contacts which have been made with the chief executive. The interesting thing about very many of these anecdotes is their lack of any point *as anecdotes*: they are often concerned with what appear to be trivial and inconsequential aspects of inter-action with the chief executive. Thus, for example, when a pro-duction manager, Johnson, had opened a conversation with a chief inspector about some spots of paint on the inspector's tie, the inspector replied: 'I always remember the works manager saying to you one day when you came in wearing a bright blue knitted cardigan: "Cover it up, Johnson." ' Or again, in another factory, the production controller recalled a former works manager in the following way: 'I'd sit there at meetings sighing, and he'd yell, "For f— sake stop sighing," and a bit later on he'd say, "Ah, but I can see what you're sighing about though." '

These individually inconsequential examples, which could be matched with many others, seem to suggest parallels with the way in which the minor remarks of visiting royalty are preserved and recollected. And in spite of their apparent triviality, they are listened to by other members of the organization because these trivia have the same importance to them as they have to those telling the anecdotes: they offer clues about the behaviour and the meaning of someone who occupies a position of some significance in their lives.

This process, in turn, reflects upon the position of the executive, for the fact that those below him spend time debating and mulling over the trivia of his existence serves to emphasize his position of power, and acts as one of the ways in which the nature of the hierarchy is made evident to those within it. As Duncan says:

'Vestments, like relics under glass, must be made part of intense and frequent dramatization of their power, in order to retain their glamour and mystery.' In this sense, the anecdotes serve as minor but frequent 'dramatizations' of the power of the chief executive.

The precise form of the anecdotes circulating will clearly vary widely, according to the form of the organization, the nature of the leader, and the characteristics of those recounting and those listening to them. They may range from the crudest use of stereotype, through pointed caricature, to quite sophisticated and subtle personal analyses. It is particularly noticeable that sets of anecdotes circulate when a new manager is appointed; and these anecdotes serve to describe and 'package' the characterization of the new manager, often bringing him into relief by comparisons with certain aspects of his predecessor:

Foreman A: I was in a meeting when [the previous works manager] slammed the minutes shut, and said he was leaving if we couldn't agree, and stamped out, slamming the door.

Foreman B: Well, this manager will never slam a door, *he's always got his hands in his pockets*!

Another member of the same organization added a further dimension to the comparison: '[The previous works manager] had the technical know-how, coming from that department, and this helped. He could say have you tried this? – no – Well bloody well try it. Whereas at the moment, with the greatest respect, you could say that the "meganut" was slipping on the "woofler", and [the present works manager] would have to accept it.'

In addition to the information which they convey about a new chief executive, such anecdotes also give meaning to the change which he brings to the lives of others in the organization, for these anecdotes form part of the 'explanations' of the changes, which can be incorporated into individual biographies within the organization, and thence into the 'collective biography'.

In this way, experiences with both present and former chief executives are built into the patterns of meaning, and fitted into the transmitted tradition. As time passes, those anecdotes that survive, together with tales about other notable personalities, serve to convey to those who did not experience it something of the flavour and atmosphere of the organization in the past. Of course, with the further passage of time, the initial significance of the anecdotes fades, for much of their meaning lies in their immediacy as a description of what happened yesterday, or last week, next door, or in the next department. After this immediacy has disappeared, they survive only because of their relevance to individual organizational biographies; because of their merit as good stories; or because of their interest to the amateur historian, to the collectors of bric-à-brac, or to industrial sociologists. Also, in a situation of rapid change, where traditional survivals are subjected to rational scrutiny, the symbolic content of the anecdotes will decrease over time, and they will tend to disappear, just as rituals do under similar circumstances.

Further Reading: The Structure of Work

N. ANDERSON, *Dimensions of Work*, New York, McKay, 1964.

E. W. BAKKE, *Bonds of Organization*, New York, Archon Books, 1966.

O. BANKS, *The Attitudes of Steelworkers to Technical Change*, Liverpool, Liverpool University Press, 1960.

J. A. BANKS, *Industrial Participation: Theory and Practice*, Liverpool, Liverpool University Press, 1963.

*R. BENDIX, *Work and Authority in Industry*, New York, Harper and Row, 1963.

A. V. CICOUREL, *Method and Measurement in Sociology*, New York, Free Press, 1954.

S. COTGROVE, J. DUNHAM and C. VAMPLEW, *The Nylon Spinners*, London, Allen and Unwin, 1971.

K. DAVIS and W. E. MOORE, 'Some Principles of Stratification', *American Sociological Review*, 1945, pp. 242–9, and often reprinted.

*P. FILMER, M. PHILLIPSON, D. SILVERMAN and D. WALSH, *New Directions in Sociological Theory*, London, Collier-Macmillan, 1972.

T. LUPTON, *On the Shop Floor*, London, Pergamon Press, 1963.

D. ROBINSON, *Local Labour Markets and Wage Structures*, London, Gower, 1970.

* Available in paperback

Chapter Four

The Process of Work 1: Commitment and Career

The young apprentices old custom called,
Indentures done, to passing out parade
Down a long alley formed among the men
Beating on bits of metal

John Betjeman, Summoned by Bells

Becker's study of the moral career of the marijuana user utilizes the idea of commitment to illuminate the way in which individuals tend to identify progressively with the requirements of a particular role. Being a marijuana user is not normally conceived of in occupational terms. Pot smoking is not a job (at least, not yet). But the concepts of commitment and identification with a role can be helpful in tracing out the development of what, looked at retrospectively, we may regard as a 'career'.

Tausky and Dubin remind us that it is important, when talking about a 'career', to bear in mind the perspective from which we are regarding it. Are we looking back or forward? In either case we almost certainly have some sort of reference point in mind. Looking forward, we could describe this reference point in terms of some goal we might expect or hope to achieve at some time in the future. At age five this might be the pilot of a lunar module; at age twelve to match up to our parents' expectations by making the top set at both maths and english in our unstreamed comprehensive; at age twenty-one to complete a PhD within the statutory two years plus; at age forty to make board level by the end of the year; and so on.

This tendency to mark one's progress by reference to a fixed point which one *should* attain – many other things being equal – at some point in the future is called by Tausky and Dubin 'upward career anchorage'.

But individuals also have a need to make sense of their lives retrospectively. They wish to look back and see 'how it happened', why such and such an event was significant, why 'being in the right place at the right time' really led to the opening up of a range of possibilities that at one time had seemed out of the question. More sadly, perhaps, people also need to make sense of their own apparent or subjectively experienced feeling of failure. They look back and compare themselves with parents, close kin, school or college contemporaries, neighbours and early acquaintances. It is noteworthy that when reunions of such groups take place there is generally a good deal of discussion about members of the group who are unable or unwilling to be present, perhaps because they have 'done' especially well or especially badly. Perhaps it would make sense in a multiplex, constantly changing society, to regard such attempts to revitalize and reanimate a basis for association which ceased to have any important meaning in the distant past as themselves 'deviant' and requiring some sort of explanation. Why are 'old school' and 'old college', even 'old family', reunions normal or inevitable? Possibly because they are small ceremonials intended to mark the significance of what, retrospectively, may be regarded as a downward career anchorage point.

The first extract in this chapter examines one particular kind of job – that of the nurse – which it is common to discuss in terms of a 'vocation'. McGuire summarizes and reports on the results of a great many studies on the pattern of recruitment to nursing. She is able to show that, regardless of the existence or not of 'vocation', structural factors are important too. There are clear differences in class and education background which go some way to explaining the differential 'success' rates of the members of different cohorts of entrants to the nursing profession.

Thus it is important not to take the notion of 'commitment' for granted. It may be that it is only with the benefit of hindsight that we can make the decision that at such and such a point and not at some other a degree of commitment to the values, ethos, and structures of a specific occupation or organization had occurred. Cotgrove and Box point out that individuals tend to '. . . answer the question "who am I?" in terms of the names and categories current in the groups in which they participate'. But this gives rise to a chicken and egg sort of difficulty, because it is not clear how we can separate occupational socialization from occupational choice.

Given that 'occupational choice' is really a summary term used for a process extending over a long period of time, Cotgrove and Box argue that the mechanisms which account for the commitment of one group of science students to a particular view of what science *is*, what their training has *fitted them for*, and what their *role* is to be, are different from those which account for others. For the student from a working-class background the commitment to science appeared to represent a solution to some problems of marginality and a crisis of identity. Among the middle-class students who had experienced childhood isolation and had been unable to develop social skills they observed a tendency to seek out situations which did not demand the successful utilization of interpersonal skills, but could permit success by operating in the world of 'things', of artefacts rather than of people. Thus an analysis of the institutional careers of university science students and a straightforward comparison of the 'successful' with the 'unsuccessful' can only go a small way towards explaining why some students commit themselves to academic values, others to the values exemplified in the work of the scientist in industry.

If we can use the concept of 'career' to look either forwards or backwards – if it relates to an anchorage point in the future or in the past – it also conveys the notion of a *process* – of a movement towards or away from something. And this progress is marked by stages divided, at least hypothetically, by some kind of ceremonial or ritual. Many jobs are entered by way of some kind of initiation ceremony. There are many such rituals in social life, but perhaps the ones best known to most people who have been through the educational system are those which mark crucial educational 'events'. In this category would be such ceremonials as passing examinations, degree days, school prize giving.

These ceremonials symbolize the transition of an individual from one type of status to another, such as from undergraduate to graduate, or from apprentice to craftsman. And ceremonials of this sort are often referred to as *rites de passage*.

As Mansfield points out '. . . status transitions can have a considerable effect on the development and stabilization of the individual's sense of personal identity. Following upon a change of status the individual must typically learn to live his new role, and in doing so he is likely to change his conception of himself and of his social world.' But such a transition is not without its dangers for the individual, for two reasons. Firstly, he must himself come to terms with the new role, and the new self-conceptions that go with it. Perhaps he has been prepared for it, or has attempted to prepare himself for it by what Merton, among others, refers to as 'anticipatory socialization'. Possibly he is able to subconsciously reorder and make sense of his past career when some crucial turning point occurs.

But if the individual can reconcile and make sense of his past and future identities, there still remains another source of problems for him. For his new identity has to be 'ratified' by significant others. The combination of pressures from both these sources may result in stress and anxiety.

One of the most important transitions for the graduate who wishes to make a success of industrial or commercial management is the very first of all – his entry to the alien world and culture of industry. Mansfield traces some of the relations between the resolution of this particular identity-stress and the successful 'unfreezing of the old identity' and the reaction of the neophyte to various aspects of his work situation, including his capacity to derive satisfaction from work.

Banton shows how strictly the professional roles are defined in twentieth-century Britain. In examining the role-relationships within the legal profession, Banton argues that '. . . the separation of the advocate's role from incompatible personal relationships facilitates his performance of professional tasks'. For it is the solicitor, not the barrister, who has all the dealings with the client, collects information, prepares files and 'briefs' for a Counsel whose only contact with the individual whose case he is representing to the Court may be actually on the day of the hearing.

Banton's analysis is illuminating, although in some respects already rather dated, as the principle that solicitors may plead in courts without detriment to their dual duties, to the client, and to the system of justice represented by the court, has already been accepted.

But the lawyer is still fairly free to create an area of his life within which he can relate to others as a person rather than merely as the incumbent of a particular type of role. An exception to this is the rule that he may not consort with known criminals. A similar dilemma is faced in an even more invidious form in the role of the police detective who is technically banned from consorting with criminals, but may be utterly reliant on such people as sources of information. In such a case continued success at apprehending law-breakers of a type that the public believes should be caught is probably of more value to the policeman in relation to his chances of promotion, than would be strict adherence to the rule book. Yet, if something goes wrong, it is 'down to him' not to the system which puts him into this equivocal situation.

Another example of the same kind of problem is that faced by the minister's wives discussed by Banton. Thus: the wives of ministers and policeman – like their husbands – are both a little sacred and a little dangerous, for many people do not speak so freely in their presence. One wife felt this so strongly that she wrote: 'Once I'd been looked over I became that "not quite human object, the minister's wife".' Banton discusses the ways in which these problems in role relations can be minimized. For example, if a doctor's wife falls ill he may solve his role-dilemma by calling in another doctor, possibly one of higher status so that the potential for conflict between his relations with her as patient and as wife may be decreased.

When we talk of a 'nurse', a 'scientist', a 'minister' we may fall into the trap of investing these shorthand designations with a life of their own. We feel we know what is meant by a 'nurse' – she is noble, self-sacrificing, devoted to the interests of her patients, and even in the saccharine world of *Doctor in the House*, never supposed to actually partake of sensual pleasure. At any rate, like the archetypal lady she 'doesn't move'. Therefore the cataclysmic and publicly audible seduction of Nurse Hotlips in *Mash* represents a symbolic subversion of a ritualized role-expectation.

But it is salutory to be reminded, as Clements does, of the widely differing ways in which people come to be what they are. Clements' managers, all operating in one part of the country, may be 'crown princes', 'technical experts', 'ex-trainees' or have come from the ranks by various different routes. In a specific situation, their reactions may differ because their reflexes and expertise are drawn from different life experiences.

One such salient and significant experience is the role of luck. The study of managers and their wives by the Pahls throws a certain amount of doubt on the way the idea of 'career' has been used by many sociologists. In practice many of their respondents hardly seemed to be conscious of occupying a particular position in the middle of a life-long process at all. They had been 'in the right place at the right time', been 'taken under somebody's wing', or quite simply 'lucky'. These themes cast echoes in other professions too. Gowling's paper deals with the role of luck in the life of the professional footballer.

Significantly also much of the interest in the last volume of C. P. Snow's saga *Strangers and Brothers*, entitled *Last Things*, lies in the relative failure of Lewis Elliot and his wife, Margaret, themselves incontrovertibly (if inconspicuously) successful in terms of their own expectations, to exert any influence on the career choices of the children. The one breaks with the establishment to marry a working-class girl and adopt a life of religious fanaticism, the other leaves England, upper middle-class home and beauty in the form of a liaison with a cool, rich and well-connected left-wing divorcee (surely every sociologist's dream) to achieve fame before thirty among Middle-Eastern guerrillas.

As the Pahls point out 'many of our couples might have agreed with Mr and Mrs Newington when they said "the most important decisions we have to make are those concerning the children and their future – to bring them up in a certain way, to have the right job and the right home, etc.". All the other things, such as home and job are relatively unimportant decisions.' Chapter 5 examines some of these potential areas of conflict.

Why Girls go into Nursing
J. McGuire

Reprinted with permission from *Threshold to Nursing*,
G. Bell and Sons Ltd., 1969, pp. 37–45.

The standing of nursing

Some indication of the comparative standing of nursing is to be gained from the NOP study of attitudes to nurses among the general population. Respondents were put in a forced choice position of evaluating nursing in comparison with secretarial work, teaching and working as a bank clerk. Secretarial work gained the highest proportion of endorsements as a suitable 'first choice' for young girls leaving school. Teaching came second. Nursing came third with about one in four of the respondents putting nursing first. The fact that respondents put nursing third out of the four possible jobs suggested to them says very little about the relative status of nursing in the whole range of job/training opportunities open to girls leaving school. It is interesting that the NOP schedule should have characterized both nursing and teaching as 'job' options rather than training or educational options. Nursing was rated less highly by men than by women. It was rated more highly by older people, by those in lower social classes, by those who had left school early and by those living in the Midland and West Regions. Nursing is seen by the general population as conferring high status in the community as a whole and being a worthwhile and rewarding occupation. At the same time the pay and conditions of work are seen as being less good than in other kinds of employment. Knowledge about nursing was not accurate among substantial proportions of the sample. Three in five adults knew what SRN stood for and two in five knew what SEN stood for. Respondents from lower social class groupings tended to be less accurate and few respondents from the lowest socio-economic group knew the meaning of the letters SEN. Two out of three adults would encourage a daughter to enter nursing. As Marsh and Willcocks have pointed out the very success with which the image of nursing has been promoted among the general population has brought certain difficulties in its wake. Nursing is seen as conferring high social standing in the commmunity yet it involves a lot of menial work. Nursing is a worthwhile job yet it is underpaid. Nurses are competent and self-possessed yet they have no free time for social engagements outside the hospital. Nurses need to be intelligent but do not need to be highly educated. The image is composed of so many sets of contrary elements, so many negative as well as positive attributes that it appears to polarize around two extremes and reactions to nursing as a whole seem to depend upon which of the two extremes happen to be salient in any particular context. Paradoxically part of the disenchantment with nursing which affects some entrants to training may come from finding that the working conditions are more congenial than they had imagined while the programme of training is much less rigorous.

The general population is not normally regarded as being synonymous with the field of potential recruits to nursing. It is well known that the majority of entrants to student nurse training are female, unmarried and within the age range of eighteen (seventeen-and-a-half in Scotland) and twenty-four. Married women and women in the older age ranges are drawn into pupil nurse training but the precise characteristics of this population are not known. Most studies of potential entrants to nursing have concerned themselves primarily with unmarried women in the age range 15–30 and with girls still at school. The potential of the same age range among boys and the potential of married and older women has scarcely received any consideration in studies of this kind. Nursing already takes a high proportion of available eighteen year olds and it is unlikely that this proportion can be greatly stepped-up given the expanding opportunities which are available to women both in employment and in higher education. If further increases in the initial input to nurse training are considered necessary this expansion will have to come from groups other than the one which has been so extensively tapped in the past. It therefore becomes more and more important to identify other groups with potential for nursing even if the training has to be modified to meet their special needs.

Interest in nursing

About 10 per cent of recruits to student nurse training are male so it is not, perhaps, a surprising finding that the proportion of girls who are interested in nursing is much higher than that for boys. Indeed interest among girls in nursing is widespread. It is estimated that about a third of all girls develop an interest in nursing at some time. The findings of one survey suggest an even higher level of interest. As Pomeranz has pointed out, it is difficult to know what girls mean when they say they are 'interested' in nursing. In the same way as all children have some understanding of the role of the teacher because thay have been to school, so, many girls and boys will have some idea of the role of the nurse because they themselves or their close relatives have had some experience of hospitals. It is suggested that only a very small proportion of boys have a strong interest in nursing while about one in six of girls of school age have an interest amounting to a career intention. The peak period of interest in nursing among girls is in the 13–16 age range and after this interest begins to decline. One author has suggested that nursing loses to other occupations which are open to girls before their eighteenth birthday. Another author suggests that at least part of the reason lies in the failure of hospitals to develop a close liaison with the local schools and to capitalize on the interest which is evident at the fifth form stage. That 13–16 is the peak age is given further support by the finding that a large proportion of actual entrants to schools of nursing state that they beceme interested in nursing or made their final decision to nurse before the age of sixteen.

The appeal of nursing

The appeal of nursing appears to be undifferentiated. Potential recruits are interested in 'nursing' in general. They do not appear to be interested in particular types of nursing. Knowledge of specific types of nursing or specific types of training does not appear to be widespread. It is not possible to say whether lack of interest is a product of lack of information about different kinds of course or whether those who are not interested do not seek information about courses other than general ones. It i s likely that this is a circular process and that information reinforces interest. More information is now available from various sources about particular types of nursing courses and the findings of the two more recent studies do suggest that some potential recruits are able to state preferences for different types of basic training. The Marsh and Willcocks study in which the fieldwork took place in 1961–2 suggested that only a very small proportion of girls in the relevant age groups can differentiate correctly between training for the register and training for the roll. The National Opinion Poll study (1966) found that some 20 per cent of the respondents could differentiate correctly between the two forms of training. The higher proportion found in this study is likely to be due partly to the composition of the sample and partly to a change in the real level of information subsequent on the most recent campaign conducted by the Department of Health to change the image of nursing. The sub-samples of the latter study still show very clearly that girls from the lower social class groups and those with low levels of educational attainment are not able to differentiate between the two forms of training.

The principal attraction of nursing is undoubtedly the opportunity which it offers for service to others. Linked with this is the intrinsic interest of the work and the opportunity to advance the education of the entrant herself. This latter aspect does not show up so clearly in the later studies. This may simply reflect differences in the questionnaires but could indicate a shift in the image of nursing among potential recruits. If the latter were in fact the case this could have serious implications for the recruitment of girls who seek intellectual satisfaction and further education in their choice of career. There is little doubt that nurse training, like teacher training, was viewed as an opportunity for the acquisition of further qualifications which would otherwise not have been available. In the pre-grant era nursing combined a training with a cash allowance which made it an attractive proposition. The vast expansion of LEA grants for studies of various kinds and at various levels means that nursing training is in a much less competitive position than formerly.

In general the hours of work and conditions of service are seen as deterrents to nursing. Pay is seen as a disincentive also. The 1943 survey found that potential recruits tended to underestimate the changes that had taken place in pay and conditions and the Mansfield study and the NOP study showed that potential recruits had inaccurate information about nursing. They tended to underestimate the pay and overestimate the hours worked by nurses. At the same time, the Mansfield respondents overestimated the pay which they would be able to get in other kinds of employment which were, in fact, open to them in the area. The lack of free time and the circumscribed social life of the nurse are also viewed as negative aspects of nursing. Girls from working-class backgrounds are more likely to see this as a disincentive than are those from middle-class/grammar-school backgrounds.

Findings in three of the studies suggest that those who express no interest in nursing reject nursing on the basis of their self-assessed unsuitability rather than on the basis of pay or conditions of service. Girls who are not interested tend to be put off by the uniform and by the idea of leaving home to train. Tentative findings suggest that bright boys are less likely to be interested in nursing than are bright girls. The author suggests that the reason for this difference lies in the career expectations of the bright boys who 'demand' a higher salary in their first jobs than do girls. The bright girls are more likely to consider the career prospects in nursing to be good. The image of nursing held by boys and girls is different, their ordering of preferences for different types of training differs and those who are not interested in nursing have different modes of rationalizing their lack of interest. The NOP study findings indicate that there are at least two major dimensions in the acceptance or rejection of the idea of nursing. One dimension has already been identified in other studies and is the dimension of 'self-assessed' suitability. The other dimension is concerned with the perceived conditions of nursing service and training. This would tie up with the 'double-image' perception of nursing already referred to and is probably related in a rather complex manner to socio-economic and educational background.

The 1943 study found no differences in attitudes to nursing among potential recruits in different areas of the country. There appeared to be no differences between those living in rural or urban areas. These findings have not been replicated in any of the later studies since each of these has concentrated on a specific locality. The NOP survey shows some slight regional differences but it is likely that inter-regional differences are less than intra-regional ones. The socio-economic characteristics of populations in specific localities are likely to be closely related to attitudes and interest in nursing so that area studies would show up greater differences than regional studies.

The Mansfield study found no evidence to suggest that family size or position in the family were in any way related to recruitment. It has frequently been suggested that nursing might be more attractive to girls from large families and that they would make better recruits because they are used to dealing with younger brothers and sisters. There is no hard evidence to suggest that girls from large families are any more interested in nursing than are girls from small families. This is not to say that at the point of actual recruitment into training there may be not a systematic difference between large and small families in their propensity to produce would-be nurses. Family contact with hospital work slightly modified the views of respondents. Girls with family contacts tended to have a more accurate picture of the job content of nursing and their image of nursing tended to be more negative. The NOP study found that respondents who claimed to know a nurse well were slightly better informed about nursing than those who had no such contacts.

The image of nursing

The image of nursing differs between those who are still at school and those who have some work experience. The image held by those with work experience tends to be more negative than that of girls still at school. In the Mansfield study, girls working in the locality tended to see the jobs they were in as having better pay and conditions of service than nursing. The information on which such judgments were made was frequently wrong. The few nurses included in the sample tended to be even more negative in their view of nursing than other girls in employment. The NOP findings suggest that the population of unmarried working girls is far from homogeneous in relation to nursing. The girls in the age group 16–17 are less interested in nursing and hold more negative views than those in the older age groups. This may be simply a reflection of the fact that girls working in this age group are more likely to be from working-class backgrounds and to have low levels of educational attainment. They are not a cross-section of the age group. The findings, taken together with those of the survey of all adults, did show a marked tendency for those in the 'recruitment' age bracket to be less enthusiastic about nursing than either the schoolchild or the older adult. These findings lend some support to the view that once a girl has entered some other occupation she is lost to nursing. This is not simply because of her unwillingness to change jobs but because her conception of nursing has been modified by her experience in the world of work. This finding again has important implications for the structure of nurse training particularly in relation to the age of entry and the educational qualifications demanded of entrants.

Girls who have experience as patients in hospital do not have markedly different views from the rest. Their knowledge of the job content of nursing tends to be more accurate than that of those without such experience. While those with hospital experience have more information it is doubtful if their experience predisposes them to select nursing as a career.

The mobilization of interest

Interest in nursing does not appear to be related to socio-economic background. This is a surprising finding in view of the socio-economic background of actual entrants. A high proportion of entrants to nursing tend to come from lower middle and middle-class backgrounds. Girls from lower working-class backgrounds are severely under-represented among entrants to nursing. These two findings taken together would suggest that the loss of potential recruits to nursing varies with social class. The proportion of girls from lower working class backgrounds whose 'interest' culminates in 'entry' to training is very small, while the girl from an upper middle-class family, if she is interested in nursing, is much more likely to mobilize her interest to the point of actual entry into a school of nursing.

There are a number of reasons why this should be so. The first, and most obvious, reason lies in the structure of secondary education in the United Kingdom. It is likely that the majority of the 'interested' girls will leave school without the minimum educational attainments which will enable them to gain ready acceptance in a school of nursing. The interested population will in the last years of their educational experience become two distinct and separate populations in respect of educational attainments. In general the girl whose secondary education has been in a grammar school will be more likely to have at least the basic requirements for nurse training than her counterpart in the modern school. She will have left school at an older age and is much less likely to go straight into work. Her occupational horizons will be wider than those of the girl leaving from the modern school and she will be much more willing and able to move away from home to acquire any training she may decide on. Because of the relationship between socio-economic background, selective education, staying on beyond the minimum school-leaving age and the attainment of formal educational qualifications more girls from the middle and upper socio-economic groups will be in a position to opt for nursing. The introduction of a comprehensive structure of secondary education may bring about significant changes in this situation as may the raising of the school-leaving age to sixteen. If the age of entry to nursing is then lowered to seventeen it would be likely that a much higher proportion of potential entrants would not be in employment before the age at which they could start training. Both the proposed changes in the general educational system would help to cut down the rate of attrition among interested girls from working-class backgrounds.

The second reason for the differential loss of interested girls from working-class backgrounds stems indirectly from the situation described above. This has to do not so much with the objective factors which make nursing out of reach for some school-leavers but with their subjective self-assessment of suitability in relation to the picture which they have of what nursing and hospitals are like. The image held of nursing is different for girls from different kinds of educational background. The level of formal educational attainment currently required of entrants to student nurse training tends to be overestimated and the girl from the secondary modern school tends, therefore, to consider herself as unsuitable for nurse training on educational grounds. The girl from the grammar school is more likely to consider herself suitable on educational grounds. The 'positive' half of the image of nursing is likely to be dominant for the middle-class girl and the 'negative' half of the image to be dominant for the girl from the working-class/secondary modern background.

The third reason for the differential loss of potential recruits from working-class backgrounds lies in the sub-cultural differences which surround job choice. In general, school-leavers from middle-class and grammar school backgrounds have more knowledge about career opportunities and receive more help from the school in making their decision. This is borne out by the pattern of responses of the 16–24 age group interviewed in the NOP study. The girl from the middle-class grammar school background is more likely to make her career choice on instrumental grounds than on the basis of the people she will work with. She is more willing to move away from home and is more concerned with long-term career prospects than with immediate pay and conditions of service. The grammar school girl who is 'interested' in nursing is likely to see it as a vocation and is therefore likely to accept the negative aspects of the image. The girl from the working-class/secondary modern background is likely to see nursing as a job rather worse than most open to her without deriving any compensation from the idea of long-term career prospects or from the vocational element. In a predominantly working-class area, such as Mansfield, job choices tended to be made on the basis of informal contacts. The formal channels of communication, of careers guidance and the rational assessment of opportunities seemed to play a small part. There was, in fact, little vocational preparation of any kind and the link between the local hospitals and schools was tenuous. The West Riding study suggested that 'significant others' even among girls preparing to take GCE were more important in determining an interest in nursing than was any careers guidance. The NOP survey indicated the girls in the age range 16–24 from middle-class/grammar school backgrounds were more likely to have access to people who were nurses than were those from working-class/secondary modern school backgrounds. The Leicestershire study confirmed the lack of contact between hospitals and secondary schools. Given the socio-economic composition of the Mansfield area it is not surprising that the proportion of girls in the age group 18–20 working in hospitals is below the national average.

The Initiation of Graduates in Industry
R. Mansfield

Reprinted with permission from *Human Relations*, Vol. 25, No. 1, pp. 77–86.

A number of writers have noted the critical impact of passages of status on the working out of individual careers. In particular, it has been argued and shown empirically that status transitions can have a considerable effect on the development and stabilization of the individual's sense of personal identity. Following upon a change of status the individual must typically learn to live his new role, and in doing so he is likely to change his conception of himself and of his social world. This process of identity development may be seen as one of identification. Foote has stated that the meaning of identification is the 'appreciation of and commitment to a particular identity or series of identities. As a process it proceeds by naming; its products are ever-evolving self-conceptions – with the emphasis on the *con* – that is upon ratification by significant others.'

This process of identity change following upon a passage of status may be analytically divided into two parts. The first part involves the individual in deciding upon a possible new identity; the second requires the ratification of this identity by significant others. There is considerable evidence to suggest that where an individual is exposed to pressures which cause him to modify his attitudes, this pressure is likely to provoke anxiety or stress. Where the attitudes involved are fundamental to the individual's conception of himself and of his position in the world, then the anxiety or stress experienced is liable to be considerable. A number of research studies have shown that adoption of a new occupational status can involve considerable identity-stress for the individuals concerned.

Coincident with or following upon a change of status, there are likely to be certain devices or systems for admitting the individual to 'full-membership' of his new status. One of the functions served by such initiations is to signal to the individual and significant others that his status is really changed, thus easing the process of identity change. Initiations provide the recruit with visible evidence that he is not what he was, and at the same time allow established others to show their ratification of his entry into the new status. Where this initiation process continues over a considerable period of time (weeks or months), then the individual has time to adjust himself to the adoption of a new identity congruent with the status he is to take. Where the recruit perceives no great uncertainty in the outcome of this initiation process, then it would seem likely that he will experience a minimum of identity-stress, that is, stress arising for the individual from difficulties in establishing or maintaining an identity. However, where the recruit is uncertain as to the outcome of this initiation process, he is likely to experience considerable identity-stress, particularly where he has made a personal decision as to the outcome he would like and feels that this may be repudiated by established others.

In the remainder of this paper consideration is focused on graduate recruits entering a large industrial company in the United Kingdom. The passage of the recruits through the company's training (initiation) scheme is examined to determine the implications of the uncertainties implicit in the scheme for the recruits' identity development and the effect of this on the recruits' attitudes to various aspects of their work situation.

Recruits in an industrial company

The results reported here are based on a series of interviews with the whole of one year's graduate intake in one company. The population studied was defined as all those (97) that joined the company between the end of the 1966–7 academic year and the

end of the 1967 calendar year who were designated graduate
recruits by the company's personnel department. The recruits
were interviewed after they had been in the company between two
and three months. The interviews were conducted on company
premises and in company time and lasted just over an hour on
average. They were conducted using a schedule of questions, the
majority of which were open-ended. The topics covered in the
interviews included the recruits' reasons for joining the company,
their experiences since joining, their work at the time of the
interviews, their plans for the future, and the place work held in
their lives at that time.

In this company, the recruits entered in four groups – one in
each month following the end of the previous academic year. The
groups varied in size from 15 to 40. The majority of the graduate
recruits had taken degrees which did not provide them with any
specialized training which was readily transferable to industry.
(The exceptions to this were 17 engineers.) None of them were
recruited for any particular department; they entered rather as
company recruits. Each group started with a four-week formal
induction course. These courses basically comprised three parts: a
week of lectures and demonstrations, designed to give recruits
some knowledge of the company's products; a week of lectures
and visits to various of the company's manufacturing plants,
designed to familiarize recruits with the main manufacturing
areas of the company; and two weeks of lectures and discussions,
designed to instruct recruits in the way the company was organized, the work of the various functions, and the career opportunities available in each function. Just over half the recruits had
reservations about the induction courses. Mostly, their criticisms
implied that they felt too much time was spent listening to
lectures. This may be partly considered as reaction to treatment
better suited to their former identity of student than to the identity
of industrial employee they were trying to adopt.

After the formal induction course, recruits started a pre-
placement training scheme of indefinite length. Typically, recruits
went individually to a series of departments for periods of a
fortnight in each. These pre-placements were arranged by the
company's graduate training officers after consultation with the
individual involved about the functions in which he was interested
in working. The programmes of pre-placements arranged for each
recruit could be changed on the request of the recruit, or for
other contingencies. However, a number of recruits claimed that

the programmes were not flexible enough. The graduate recruitment officer described the purpose of these pre-placements as to give the recruits, many of whom had little experience of industry, a chance to look at a number of departments before deciding on the sort of work they wanted to do. The pre-placements would enable them to find out more about the company and to see for themselves what work in the various functions involved. This pre-placement training continued until the recruit was placed in an established job.

When a suitable vacancy occurred in a department, graduates interested in working there were interviewed by a panel consisting of the relevant managers and a member of the personnel department. As a result of the interviews one of the graduates would be offered the job, which he was free to accept or refuse. In fact, few placement offers were refused. Sometimes this process was short-circuited when a manager made a direct offer to a graduate who was pre-placed in his section, and the graduate accepted.

The pre-placement training of the 17 engineers was slightly different from that of the others. Their training was designed to satisfy the requirements of the relevant professional institution and was, therefore, expected to extend over a rather longer period. For the engineers, each pre-placement typically lasted rather more than two weeks. However, as this training was flexible and could be terminated at any time by a placement in the same manner as for other recruits, it seemed reasonable to consider both categories together in the results.

In this context, the formal induction course and the series of pre-placements correspond to the initiation process. While the recruit is passing through this initiation phase he is an employee of the company, but he is 'not like other employees'. Unlike them, he has not established duties to perform or expectations to meet. Other than in the most general sense, he has not 'got a job'. Only when he is placed can the recruit consider himself fully to belong. Thus, during this stage the recruit is likely to experience difficulty in integrating his new occupational status into his identity. He cannot easily decide what he is and where he is going. This uncertainty in establishing a new identity caused the recruits to experience a considerable amount of identity-stress. As one recruit who had just been placed described it: 'I got fed up in my early pre-placements. I felt unsettled – didn't know where I was going.' Comments by other recruits who were still unplaced indicated the same difficulties:

'I want to get a definite job . . . so I can settle down.'

'I expect to get more involved when I stay in one place and can identify with it.'

'It [the work] consumes a good half of my life – till I get a job I feel is mine and find something satisfying to do, I resent this.'

The general status of company employee they had assumed did not seem sufficiently specific to allow the recruits to identify with it and alleviate their identity-stress. As one recruit remarked: 'The individual can't associate himself with the finished product, only with the department. The company doesn't seem to have an identity as a whole.' Not surprisingly, the recruits found it almost impossible to identify with a department they were only in for two weeks.

The uncertainty involved in the position of those recruits who had not decided where they wanted to work and those who anticipated delays or difficulties in securing the placement they wanted, prevented them having anything but a very short time perspective. Mainly, they only knew where they were going to be working for a week or two ahead. When asked about any plans they might have for their future careers, many replied that they would only be able to plan ahead when they had decided on what they wanted to do and were placed. This was an additional source of identity-stress coming from this form of initiation process.

These stresses were increased by the tight company restrictions on the manpower used in each department, which limited the number of vacancies open to graduates for placements. Many of the recruits criticized the company over this policy, and some of them said that they had been misled in this respect at the recruitment stage. A number of the recruits felt that it might be a long time before they would be able to obtain a placement, and this added to their worries. Some of them reported being told that there were not likely to be any vacancies in the function they wished to join, and that this involved them in having to re-think the decision they had just made. In addition, the company was undergoing a major reorganization at the time the recruits joined. This reorganization added still more to the uncertainty inherent in the initiation process.

However, it must be emphasized that at the time of the interviews, 75 per cent of the recruits rated the company better than average for firms in Britain on the way it treated graduate recruits.

One of the defences the recruits found against the stresses of the initiation process was to form small groups which met at lunch in the canteen, or in the evening for a drink. These groups were mainly formed during the formal induction courses, when numbers of recruits were together for the whole four weeks. This aspect of the company's induction scheme was praised by many of the recruits. These groups provided the recruits with some point of orientation prior to placement. However, the groups also aggravated the stress for some of their members when other members were placed before them.

In this situation, identity-stress was created for the recruits by the difficulties they experienced in both processes of identity development, that is in deciding upon the new role they wished to take and thus incorporate into their self-concept, and in gaining ratification of this decision. In terms of these two processes, a sixfold classification of the recruits was made, based on their interview responses. The six categories can be summarized as follows:

1. Recruits who were placed or had definite offers of a placement which they intended to accept ('Placed').

2. Recruits who had decided on the function they intended to follow and who did not mention any consequential difficulty they expected to meet in securing a placement in that function ('Decided-optimistic').

3. Recruits who had decided on the function they intended to follow, but foresaw considerable difficulty or delay before getting a placement to that function, and those who had been placed but who felt they should change, thus expecting a delay before getting a placement they wanted ('Decided-pessimistic').

4. Recruits who were still undecided about the function they intended to follow, but mentioned no consequential difficulty they expected to meet in securing the placement they wanted when they decided ('Undecided-optimistic').

5. Recruits who were still undecided about the function they intended to follow and mentioned major difficulties or worries about getting placed ('Undecided-pessimistic').

6. Recruits who had decided on the function they wanted to follow, but who reported that there would be no vacancies in which they could be placed in the function of their choice ('Impeded').

The recruits in Categories 1, 2, 3 and 6 have gone some way in the process of identity change by deciding on the function in which they wanted to be placed. That is, they have explicitly or implicitly stated: 'This is what I am – that is where I am going.' Where this statement has been ratified by established others ('placed') or the recruit fully expects it to be ratified ('decided-optimistic'), then the recruit should experience little identity-stress. However, where the statement has been refuted by significant others ('impeded') or where the recruit has not yet made the decision but feels that when he does it may be refuted ('undecided-pessimistic'), then he is likely to experience a high level of identity-stress. Where the statement is expected to be ratified only after a significant delay ('decided-pessimistic') or where the recruit has not yet made a decision but expects it to be ratified when he does, then the period of identity-stress is prolonged. However, inasmuch as the recruit does not anticipate refutation of his statement of what he is and where he is going, the stress should not be acute. Therefore, these two categories should experience a medium level of identity-stress.

The distribution of the recruits by this categorization is shown in Table 1.

Table 1. Distribution of sample by degree of identity-stress

Low identity-stress		Medium identity-stress		High identity-stress	
Category 1 'Placed'	Category 2 'Decided-optimistic'	Category 3 'Decided-pessimistic'	Category 4 'Undecided-optimistic'	Category 5 'Undecided-pessimistic'	Category 6 'Impeded'
16	14	24	23	12	8
30		47		20	

Correlates of identity-stress

If, during this initiation phase, the development of a sense of personal identity congruent with the newly acquired status of company employee is critical to the recruits' evaluations of their position, then there should be a high negative correlation between the recruits' propensity to identity-stress and their level of overall job satisfaction, their views on the company, and their reflections on their choice in deciding to join it.

The measure of overall job satisfaction used to test this hypothesis was obtained from the answers to the question: 'Overall at the present time how satisfied are you with your job – highly satisfied, reasonably satisfied, or dissatisfied?' In fact, some of the recruits (14) chose to answer between the categories suggested. In these cases, their answers were classified highly satisfied if they answered between highly and reasonably satisfied, and dissatisfied if they answered between reasonably satisfied and dissatisfied. The justification for this is that, although the naming of the categories may conjure different ideas for different respondents, the wording of the question suggests a medium state which the respondent may rate himself in or above, or below.

Respondents were asked to compare their company overall with other companies operating in Britain and to rate it better, average or worse. However, as 92 of the 96 respondents answering this question rated the company better, this did not provide a very useful indicator. Therefore, answers to the question: 'Have your overall impressions of the company improved or worsened since you joined?' are used as an indicator of opinions on the company. As only 10 respondents reported that their opinions of the company had improved since joining, these are grouped with those who reported that their opinions had stayed about the same.

The indicator of recruits' feelings on their decision to join was obtained from answers to the question: 'Are you happy with the choice of job you made in joining the company?' The answers 'no', 'only reasonably' and 'not sure yet' are grouped together as the numbers are so small.

The relationships of each of these measures with the measure of identity-stress are shown in Tables 2, 3 and 4.

Table 2. Relationship of identity-stress to overall satisfaction

	Low identity-stress	Medium identity-stress	High identity-stress
Highly satisfied	27	2	0
Reasonably satisfied	3	42	3
Dissatisfied	0	3	16

N = 96 (no measure of satisfaction was obtained from one respondent).
Goodman and Kruskal's gamma = 0·99.

As predicted, there is a significant negative correlation between identity-stress and overall satisfaction, non-negative changes in opinions of the employing company, and satisfaction with choice of job in joining the company. Table 2 suggests that the propensity to identity-stress is almost completely decisive in this initiation period in determining the recruits' overall level of satisfaction in his new job.

Table 3. Relationship of identity-stress to changes in opinions of the company since joining

	Low identity-stress	Medium identity-stress	High identity-stress
Opinions of company improved or stayed the same	19	23	4
Opinions of company worsened	10	24	15

N = 95 (two respondents said they had no real opinion when they joined).
Goodman and Kruskal's gamma = 0·49.

Table 4. Relationship of identity-stress to satisfaction with choice of job in the company

	Low identity-stress	Medium identity-stress	High identity-stress
Happy with choice of job in joining company	29	35	11
Not altogether happy with choice of job in joining company	1	12	9

N = 97.
Goodman and Kruskal's gamma = 0·68.

Conclusions

It seems clear that during this sort of initiation period recruits are likely to experience identity-stress. During the period, this stress is likely to exercise a determining influence on the recruit's level of satisfaction and outlook on his employing company. The recruits were able to find some defence against this stress by forming friendships with others in the same position. The induction policy causing the recruits to enter in groups facilitated this defence. Resolution of this stress depended on the adoption of a new occupational identity and the ratification of this identity by established others. The friendships formed as a defence against the stressful situation served to emphasize the satisfaction of those who were placed or could see their way ahead, and the dissatisfaction of those who felt themselves impeded or very uncertain, as each provided a comparison group for the other. This relative satisfaction or dissatisfaction almost certainly caused the very high degree of correlation between identity-stress and overall satisfaction.

The consequences of this period of identity-stress and dissatisfaction are not necessarily negative. There is considerable evidence from studies of more extreme socialization settings that an initiation period of high stress can 'unfreeze' the old identity by providing both the recruit and others with decisive evidence that he is not what he was. This unfreezing facilitates the change process as the individual is forced to search for a new identity congruent with his new position. Ratification of this new identity by significant others then results in the refreezing of the recruit's identity. Schein, who put forward this paradigm of the adult socialization process, has suggested that it may also be applicable to the industrial setting. This study tends to support his contention. However, the question of whether the change that occurs is a functional one is a subject for further research.

The Professional Role
M. Banton

Reprinted with permission from *Roles*, Tavistock, 1965, pp. 152–71.

Barristers and solicitors

One of the most striking features of the liberal professions as they have developed in Western industrial societies is the strictness with which the professional roles are defined. Etiquette and custom stipulate the behaviour required of a member of the profession in many contexts and prevent him assuming roles which would compromise what is seen as a prior obligation. An industrial concern can be run on the principle that whatever legally produces maximum profit is the desirable policy, but professions must regulate self-aggrandizement if they are to preserve the role that the professional man presents to his client. In old Icelandic judicial practice, as it is represented in *Njal's Saga*, advocates used their technical knowledge of procedure to win their clients' cases without any regard for justice. If judges are to see that justice is done, such unscrupulousness prevents them trusting the advocates, slowing up the process and making its outcome more uncertain. The British and American judicial systems minimize tension between bench and bar by making the advocate an officer of the court as well as the representative of a client: one role combination is forced upon him, certain others – as will be seen later – are prohibited. But formal requirements are not sufficient unless the people in question accept them as being desirable and binding; this is sometimes facilitated by the inculcation of particular values or by the administration of an oath, such as that taken by a Massachusetts attorney. It reads:

'I solemnly swear that I will do no falsehood, nor consent to the doing of any in court; I will not wittingly or willingly promote or sue any false, groundless or unlawful suit, nor give aid or consent to the same; I will delay no man for lucre or malice; but I will conduct myself in the office of attorney within the courts according to the best of my knowledge and discretion and with all good fidelity as well to the courts as [to] my clients.'

In England no oath is taken, but the Inns of Courts and the characteristic life of the Temple help to instil in the newcomer the

norms he must observe. The barrister (to use the English terminology; in Scotland he is called an advocate) is required to bring
to the attention of the court any and every relevant statute or
decided case of which he has knowledge, whether or not it is in his
favour. He is not obliged to reveal anything to the discredit of his
client, but he must avoid any deception of the court. In 1960 a
case against a police inspector alleging assault and false imprisonment was heard. Shortly beforehand the policeman had appeared
before a police disciplinary board and had been reduced to the
rank of sergeant. Did the barrister representing him have to
notify the court of this? He allowed the policeman to give evidence in plain clothes as if he was still an inspector, and said
nothing about the disciplinary proceedings. Afterwards this aspect
of the matter came to light: a new trial was ordered and the
barrister was told that his duty to the court had been unwarrant-
ably subordinated to his duty to his client; though a leading
Queen's Counsel, he was suspended for twelve months. Standards
of integrity are maintained at a high level, so that what counsel
assert as truth, the court accepts without question. It is what
counsel argue that the court judges.

In England and Scotland the advocate's role as an officer of the
court is shielded by the existence of a separate profession – that of
solicitors – who prepare a counsel's brief and are responsible for
relations with the client. Indeed, with a few special exceptions, a
barrister must never accept instructions direct from a private
person, and when he does present a case often his only contact
with the client is a short conversation when the hearing is over. If
the barrister were in close relation with the litigant this would
strengthen his loyalty to him at the expense of his obligation to
the court. This isolation of the advocate from social pressures is
maintained while the case is proceeding. A juryman recently was
dismissed because he spoke during his lunch hour to a barrister
appearing in a case on which his jury was sitting; the juryman had
only asked the barrister if he would come and give a talk to a local
society unconnected with the law, but even so his action was
strongly reprehended when the barrister reported it to the court.

The interposition of the solicitor between client and counsel has
the effect of reinforcing the social distance between them and of
permitting the advocate to be a more highly specialized pleader of
cases. He is, in the words of Lord Macmillan, 'on the cab rank for
hire'. Every man is entitled to be represented in a court of law
and unless he has a prior commitment no barrister may refuse a

brief to appear in any class of case within his competence. Success in a particular field of law may well lead to an advocate's receiving more briefs of a particular kind, but it will also mean that he is engaged sometimes by plaintiffs and on other occasions by defendants. If he acquires a reputation when dealing with highway accident cases he will find himself appearing for claimants as well as insurance companies, for insurance companies as well as claimants. Similarly, a barrister may not reject a brief because he does not like the client; it is his advocacy that is wanted, not his moral approbation. Thus it comes about that a Conservative MP may represent a Labour city council in court, or a barrister of unbending personal rectitude may be found defending a drug merchant or a blackmailer. Says R. E. Megarry, QC, 'The dissociation between the man and the advocate is nearly complete, even in the public eye'. A further illustration of this was provided in Scotland when an advocate appeared for one party in an action which was later appealed to a higher court. In the interval between hearings the advocate 'took silk', becoming a Queen's Counsel entitled to lead cases in the higher courts. Later he was approached by a solicitor acting for the opposite party to represent his clients in the appeal. His clerk consulted the two solicitors, neither of whom thought this acceptance of the brief would be improper. Thus the separation of the advocate's role from incompatible personal relationships facilitates his performance of professional tasks. Under an inquisitorial judicial process in which the magistrate does the examining, a client without an advocate is not at a disadvantage; but where cases are heard on the accusatory principle with two sides arguing it out before a judge, a litigant must have the same access to skilled assistance as his adversary if he is to be equally represented. The British definition of the advocate's role seems an admirable social adaptation to such a judicial system.

A further function of the barrister-solicitor division is that both professions can concentrate upon distinctive tasks. Whenever a barrister appears in court he will be watched and assessed by at least two solicitors, and even if he loses his case his performance may well persuade the solicitors on both sides to send him briefs on future occasions. Solicitors are better able than laymen to evaluate the legal skills of advocates, so competent advocates will not lose clients on account of an unprepossessing manner. Solicitors, too, can always consult counsel when they need specialist advice without any fear that they may lose their clients to counsel.

The division is, however, drawn in a way that is open to criticism. It is strange that in England a solicitor may plead before a high-court judge sitting in private but not in the public court, and that he may present a claim in court only if the sum involved is less than £400. But in day-to-day affairs this sort of illogicality rarely arises; there are, after all, some 22,000 solicitors in England and Wales doing the great bulk of legal work, compared with fewer than 2,000 practising barristers who have specialized far more narrowly. In at least one respect the division also works to the disadvantage of the barrister. He comes into court with a duty to the public as well as to his client, and he could not perform his task if he were exposed to the threat that a disgruntled client might bring an action against him for incompetence were he to lose the case. So there is no contract between a solicitor or a client and a barrister; the fee that is given is regarded as an honorarium; therefore the barrister in turn cannot sue for payment. In England, writes Richard Du Cann, the barrister often waits months or even years to be paid.

Though the interposition of the solicitor shields the advocate from public importunities, it is not a sufficient protection, and the advocate must not do anything in a private capacity which suggests that he is under a personal obligation to any litigant. A lawyer may not be seen in the company of criminals except in circumstances – such as a consultation at the courts – that legitimize the association. One widely publicized case of a solicitor's improper associations was investigated in London in 1962 and the man was struck off the rolls for unprofessional conduct. Nor may a barrister do anything which might appear as personal advertisement. Mr Du Cann summarizes the position:

'He may describe himself as "barrister-at-law" in the telephone directory for his professional address, but not for his home even though the two entries may appear next to one another. He may describe himself as "barrister-at-law" if he stands for Parliament . . . but not on his stationery or visiting card. If he writes for the Press or takes part in a broadcast he may be described as a barrister but must not allow his name to be given. . . .'

Outside a barrister's chambers his name will be listed – only his name, without even QC or other mark of professional distinction. This custom also has the effect of stressing the equality of advocates in their professional role: a young advocate newly called may have to oppose a much senior man and no feelings of inequality should hamper his obligations to the court or to his client. So it is that from the moment he is called to the bar he addresses other members of the bar simply by their surnames. Barristers do not shake hands with each other; this is defended on the grounds that all are brothers at the bar and brothers do not shake hands!

The 'cab rank' principle also makes the advocate an individualist. Partnerships are prohibited, and are not wanted by the bar. A barrister is essentially a courtroom lawyer. Says Megarry:

'Apart from his personal affairs, he has a very small mail, and rarely writes a letter on professional matters. His telephone is not altogether idle, yet not much penetrates beyond his clerk; certainly the telephone is but a ghost of the tyrant that it is to solicitors . . . He is far less a "man of affairs" than a brain and a tongue and a character.'

A barrister is forbidden to discuss any question of fees with a solicitor or solicitor's clerk. A brief is priced by the barrister's clerk according to fairly standard criteria, though if a client is poor but deserving the solicitor may mention this to the barrister's clerk who may offer to mark it down. If a barrister has too much work coming in, his clerk may cut down the flow by raising the general level of his fees, but in any event the barrister himself is spared such discussions. A barrister's clerk with a staff of two or three normally serves a number of independent barristers occupying one set of chambers. His role, too, is an example of how conflicting interests may be contained within an institution regulated by interpersonal conventions. For the one barrister's Advice on Evidence for the plaintiff, with his suggestions as to how it should be exploited, may be typed by the same hands as his colleague's Advice on Evidence for the defendant, outlining the ways of meeting the plaintiff's various lines of attack. Yet, says Megarry, everyone in the clerk's room will be as scrupulous as the two counsel themselves in keeping apart all that should be kept apart. A leakage is unthinkable.

Ministers, doctors, and teachers

The example of the barrister shows how the performance of a role may be assisted by its isolation from other roles that could interfere with it. This segregation of roles is the easiest way of dealing with the problem of conflict but it is not always a fully effective solution. For example, the role of priest or minister of religion sets its incumbent apart from the mass of people who constitute his congregation or his public. If his preaching is to be effective, and if his contribution to ceremonial is to have the right quality, then he must be perceived primarily as a priest or minister. In the sense in which the term has been introduced, his relation with parishioners must be relatively impersonal, suppressing any individual features which might derogate from his occupational role. It may be considered undesirable for him to assume a subordinate role in an occupational hierarchy, like that of worker in a factory (as the French experience with worker-priests showed). Furthermore, any obligations a priest or minister assumes as husband or father (in other than an ecclesiastical sense) may conflict with his religious duties, while his family life may emphasize that he is a man like other men and show him in a role that is not compatible with his occupational claims. (It is no coincidence that 'familiarity' as describing the opposite to impersonality derives from the same root as the word 'family'.) This sense of possible incongruity underlies the Roman Catholic practice dating from the eleventh or twelfth century by which clerical marriages were declared void. The Pope retains a right to allow a cleric to marry by dispensation, though he rarely exercises it. The Eastern Orthodox Church permits clergy married before ordination to continue to live as married men. The Church of England abrogated the earlier law at the Reformation, as it well could, seeing that clerical celibacy was admitted by the canon law to be no part of divine law.

But if the clergy are permitted to marry they still have the problem of seeing that their family life causes no embarrassment to their calling. They, their wives, and their children have to overcome this problem by conducting their public roles in an exemplary manner. Indeed, the difficulties are sometimes more acute for the wife than for her husband. A Church of Scotland Training Centre questioned some fifty ministers' wives about what life in the manse had meant to their social relations. The outstanding feature of the responses was the emphasis upon how her husband's office put the minister's wife in an isolated position. She was expected to be friendly with all members of the congregation; this was an obligation of her role and it could conflict with her personal desire and need for purely individual friendships. If she were suspected of picking and choosing whom she would visit this could arouse jealousy of her associates, whose own lives – in a small parish – might be made the more difficult because of it.

One wrote:

'A minister's wife must have no favourites. This is one of the difficulties, for if she is too friendly with some it is apt to inspire jealousy in others. But, as a woman must have friends, the closest should be from other ministers' wives or *even outside the Church*' (italics added).

Another observed: 'Some ministers and their wives ask friends in the congregation to call them by their Christian names. This may be a help towards fellowship, but in my opinion it tends to lead to over-familiarity.'

A minister's wife is expected to 'take her place' at the head of parish concerns: 'I have been in three charges, town, city, and now, country, but so far as congregations are concerned, there is not much to choose between them. All of them have expected a lead from the minister's wife and in each I have been president of the Woman's Guild during all the time of my husband's ministry. When we were married over twenty years ago that was expected, though nowadays I think there is greater resistance among ministers' wives. . . .'

Another advised the new minister's wife: 'Do not be distressed if you are treated as "different" because you are married to a minister. A roomful of chattering women may fall silent as you enter, but do not take it as personal, it is really respect for your position.'

The wives of ministers and policemen – like their husbands – are both a little sacred and a little dangerous, for many people do not speak so freely in their presence. One wife felt this so strongly that she wrote: 'Once I'd been looked over I became that "not quite human object, the minister's wife".'

Another recurrent theme is the conflict between family responsibilities and church activities. Several wives insisted that the family must come first, for 'somebody else can chair a meeting; nobody else can be a mother to your children'.

A minister normally has to be both his wife's husband and her pastor. She knows him as a man with all his foibles and may find it hard fully to respect what he says in his ministerial capacity. Their children may experience a similar difficulty:

'A lady who had been a daughter of the manse said that for a long time she had a feeling of resentment when in her father's church, and it wasn't until she left home and worshipped in another church where she wasn't known that she experienced the refreshment and uplift of spirit that she was sure was the portion of her father's congregation. Her own observation was that, in spite of her parents' affection and care, she just "didn't like sharing them with a congregation".'

Manse children sometimes find they are regarded almost as parish mascots; they are expected to be better behaved than other children – though people are often relieved to discover that they can be just as naughty as other youngsters. Some boys take delight in involving the minister's son or the policeman's son in improper pursuits and the boy often feels obliged to take up such challenges to show that he is not afraid. But, apparently, one thing that manse children resent more than almost anything else is being used as illustrations in their father's sermons! Whenever the minister refers to some unidentified child his youthful hearers assume that it must be his own son or daughter and will want to joke about it afterwards. Thus the minister's role has important implications for all members of his family.

Some of the difficulties experienced by the minister's family are felt in varying degree by the wives and children of other professional men. The lawyer's wife may be expected to help her husband by entertaining and making friends with the right people. The doctor's wife has often to answer the telephone and to act as a buffer between her husband and his more demanding patients. There is also a parallel in the incompatibility between performance of the ministerial or medical role and a relation of familiarity. A doctor must be psychologically and socially a little aloof if he is to preserve the detachment necessary to his task, and not get personally agitated about whether he has prescribed the right treatment. Because a doctor cannot maintain this distance with members of his own family he usually prefers to call in a colleague to treat any serious illness under his own roof. Social distance also helps the patient to maintain confidence in his adviser and to take treatment because it is 'doctor's orders'. An unconscious recognition of this is contained in the tendency of people to consult doctors of somewhat higher social status than themselves; the difference in status discourages familiarity from the patient and enables the doctor to be more impersonal and 'professional'. Like the minister, though to a lesser degree, the doctor has to conceal any of his private roles which might reduce public confidence in his occupational skill. Even if unmarried, he should not be seen too much in the company of a female patient, lest it be thought that his masculine role takes precedence over his professional role; doctors have been disciplined for such conduct.

The extent to which a doctor has to maintain social distance from his patients may depend upon their individual qualities, such as their need for authoritative advice or the possibility of their taking advantage of any more affable demeanour on his part. In the case of the teacher, impersonality varies with pupils' age. With young children, the teacher can assume a quasi-parental role because he or she can preserve his or her superiority in nearly all the relationships with a child, which can be a basis for relations between them. Later on, relations have to become more impersonal because the teacher needs to take thought about maintaining his position; the pupil comes more and more to interpret relations between them as direct to the single end of transmitting knowledge and to resent any attempt on the teacher's part to comment on his private affairs – such as his dress, for example. If there is a big status difference the superior party (as the teacher to the young pupil or the plantation owner to his slave) can be familiar without exposing himself to reciprocal pressures, but as the status difference declines he has to make relations more impersonal to prevent this sort of counter pressure.

*   *   *

In some societies a woman cannot become a doctor because it is felt to be inappropriate. But there are other role combinations, like jockey and bookmaker, or importer and tax official, which would cause friction in any circumstances. We have examined some of the professional roles, showing how they can be maintained only because there are established rules to prevent their incumbents being compromised or compromising themselves. These rules fall into three categories: (i) regulations or conventions which segregate professional roles by stipulating that they may not be combined with certain other roles; (ii) customs which require a high level of personal commitment to the ideals of the role, such as the taking of an oath; (iii) the management of social relations in such a way as to indicate to others that any other than a particular kind of behaviour would be improper; the high social status of a professional man also helps him to be more impersonal in his dealings with clients.

Professions differ in the extent to which their members' activities are exposed to the judgment of outsiders; this, and the varying character of professional–client relations, influence the culture of occupational groups. Professions resemble one another in their response to common problems, such as: the use of a fixed scale of fees to prevent bargaining and to underline the norm of personal service independent of personal judgments; because professional service is often facilitated by stable client relations, so 'shopping around' is deprecated and 'poaching' by fellow professionals strongly condemned; to ensure that members of the profession observe common standards, the group establishes its own disciplinary bodies; however, in present-day circumstances, secular standards of efficiency and bureaucratic controls are pressing upon inherited social patterns so that the professions face important problems of public relations.

The Place of Luck in the Professional Footballer's Life
Alan Gowling

This extract was especially written for this volume and has not previously been published in this form.

Listening to the conversations of professional footballers off the field, and their expletives on the field, one cannot but notice the emphasis that is placed on 'luck'. 'We did not get the run of the ball today', or 'They were getting all the breaks', or 'Keep working and the breaks will come', are common phrases to be heard at half-time or after a game. On the field, during the match, there is no time for conversation, but verbal exchanges are short and common, and are not so sweet: 'You lucky b——d', or 'You lucky b——r' are commonly exchanged among the 'f's' and the 'b's', that is the language of a hard physical game.

It has often been said by people in the game that football is a game of luck; that skill, fitness and luck are the vital elements of football. However, in the above context they are using luck in a comprehensive manner, for luck in relation to the footballer has a number of elements. These elements can be categorized as follows: luck as an explanation, luck as an excuse, luck as a superstition.

Luck is often used as an explanation of those things that

appear to have no causal explanation. For example, why a perfectly struck ball hits a post and comes out into the field of play. Or why a ball seemingly going wide of the post strikes a defender and goes into the goal. Logically, we all know why these things happen because they are visible to us, but the footballer has to know more than what is seen. He wants to know why the ball hit the post and did not go into the goal. He wants to know why the ball hit the defender and did not go harmlessly wide, or back into play. He is looking for a deeper causal explanation. If he were an Azande, he might very well turn to witchcraft for his answer and consult the poison oracle. As E. Evans-Pritchard points out:

'The concept of witchcraft . . . provides them with a natural philosophy by which relations between men and unfortunate events are explained and a ready and stereotyped means of reacting to such events.' (*Witchcraft Oracles and Magic Among the Azande*, p. 63.)

In a similar way the footballer looking for the causal explanation chooses to use luck as the answer to this problem. If he were religious he might say it was 'the will of God', but he tends to be agnostic and simply use luck as the explanation.

Luck in this sense can be used to explain both good fortune and ill fortune. At the same time as footballers recognize the fact that they have the breaks against them, so they realize that they have luck, but not so readily. They would rather put the latter down to their own good play. In the sober moments, however, they will acknowledge that 'everything is going for us'.

Footballers will often explain their careers in the above way. They realize that to get to the top in the game necessitates a considerable degree of luck in some stage of their career. To a certain degree, to be 'spotted' by a scout requires a train of events the causal explanation of which would be put down to luck by the footballer. For example, not only does one have to play reasonably well, showing skill and application, but the scout has to be there to see it, and usually more than once!

Similarly, to keep free of serious injury would require luck in the terminology of the pro. In the reverse, they say that to receive a serious injury is 'just bad luck'. Injuries are something footballers live with every match. They accept that that particular game might be their last, but that's as far as thoughts go. They never dwell on such thoughts. If it happens then their fatalistic attitude puts it down to luck. (Tunstall illustrates a similar belief in luck and fate in his chapter on 'The World View of the Fishermen' in his book, *The Fishermen*.)

Not only is luck used as an explanation of events of which footballers have no real understanding (has anyone?), it is also used by footballers as an excuse for their own failures and errors. It would be fair to say that few people like criticism and footballers are no exception. Indeed, confidence is at such a high premium in the game that they possibly more than others dislike criticisms. To avoid apportionment of the blame they will often use luck, or ill-luck, as an excuse. In making a half-hearted tackle the ball bounces off the opponent's leg and goes behind the defender and he runs in to score. The defender will probably put this down to 'bloody bad luck', but in fact he is excusing himself for his half-hearted tackle. A ball which bounces between two defenders and runs to an opponent who scores will be put down to 'run of the ball', but it is essentially bad defensive play that is being excused.

Football is a team game and it is important not to upset the team or any member of it, or the whole does not function properly. Rather than criticize a player on the field, one will often hear the call 'bad luck . . . keep going', or 'hard luck'. This is encouragement, but knowing full well that they are excusing a mistake, perhaps a missed goal opportunity. In order not to upset the person who has made the mistake, who will be feeling it anyway, luck is used to explain the incident and to encourage the player, and excuse him.

Replacing the intangible element of luck as an excuse for error the person of the referee often comes in for criticism. Once again the referee provides the 'stereotyped means of reacting to such events'. The referee provides the human factor, the tangible element. Invariably, the referee can do no right. He is good for one side and consequently bad for another. He is human, he makes mistakes. He is a causal explanation in himself. The fact that he can be seen to make mistakes gives the footballer the perfect alibi for his own errors or those of his team. (This is not to whitewash referees. There are times when pros have a valid argument. For example when the referee gave a goal and the ball actually hit the stanchion outside the goal net! The fact that they do not appear to know what to look for and where to look for it, and their inconsistencies, create a lot of ill feeling.)

Luck as an explanation and an excuse are elements of the use of 'luck' in general and are quite common, but the most common element, and in many ways the most vital, is luck *vis-à-vis* superstition.

Linked to luck as an explanation, superstition precedes the former. Footballers resort to luck as an explanation of ill-luck that hits them, but to attempt to avoid ill-luck they create this belief in superstition. Superstition applies both personally and collectively. It is so important because mental application is an important factor in football – the mental application of the individual and the team through each person.

A League coach used to say, 'If you're right in mind then you're right in everything else.' In other words, if you are confident of your ability then you will do well on the field. In order to develop this confidence and to maintain it (the hardest part) players develop routines. These are often personalized and would have no consequence for any other player. Others are developed by the team and affect the psyche of the whole.

Personal superstitions may be simple. For example, re-tying boot laces on the field before the kick-off (Nobby Stiles), going out last in line on the field (Jack Charlton), putting on a certain boot before the other, etc. These superstitions are followed in order to keep luck on that particular person's side. Following the routines keeps peace of mind and gives confidence. It may seem silly that little things might have so great an effect on some people. But indeed they do. Jack Charlton gave up the Captaincy of Leeds because he had to go out first rather than last. This change of routine upset him, his mind was unsettled because he was not following the superstition he believed in, and which, for him, brought him luck.

Similarly, the team as a whole can take on superstitions to keep their confidence high and to bring them luck. The successful England World Cup team developed such a superstition; Sir Alf was not allowed to go to matches with his tracksuit on. He kept to this in order not to upset the mental rhythm of his side. Manchester United had a routine during their run of 1971 which took them five points clear at the top of the table. As the run of results built up, a good number of the team came to every game with the same clothes. It became a ritual: a ceremony to luck, to keep it with the team.

The latter did not succeed, and was rapidly ditched when its validity and credit were no longer 'seen' to be working. Other routines go the same way too once they have lost credibility. Footballers are all the time searching for good fortune and the answer to it. They are in search of success, and who or what brings success to some and not to others they do not know, but they attribute it to luck. They must have luck on their side. They must feel lucky.

At the same time as a team or person must feel lucky, so a team can be affected by a feeling of ill-luck, or 'jinxed'. A string of poor results, more often than not due to bad play, but attributed to bad luck (as an excuse), can set a team thinking that it is 'jinxed'. Their confidence goes and the results with it. There may be genuine misfortune, but this can rapidly develop into using luck as an excuse when bad results occur due to loss of confidence.

Confidence, superstition, explanation and excuse, are, therefore, all components that make up an important element of the professional footballer's life and make up. His aim is physical fitness and psychological fitness. The former is achieved through a training or physiological routine. The latter is achieved through a training or routine designed to keep the mind confident; this is seen by many pros to be the harder aspect of preparation. Confidence and superstition inextricably entwined provide the ritual for luck. Luck provides the causal explanation of events. It also provides the excuse. Such is the place of luck in a professional footballer's life.

Further Reading: Commitment and Career

H. BECKER, *Outsiders*, New York, Free Press, 1964.

R. V. CLEMENTS, *Managers*, London, Allen and Unwin, 1958.

S. COTGROVE and S. BOX, *Science, Industry and Society*, London, Allen and Unwin, 1970.

J. DOUGLAS, *Understanding Everyday Life*, London, Routledge and Kegan Paul, 1971.

H. GARFINKEL, *Studies in Ethnomethodology*, Englewood-Cliffs, New Jersey, Prentice-Hall, 1967.

K. PRANDY, *Professional Employees*, London, Faber and Faber, 1965.

C. P. SNOW, *Last Things*, London, Penguin, 1972.

C. M. TAUSKY and R. DUBIN, 'Career Anchorage: Managerial Mobility Aspirations, in *American Sociological Review*, Vol. XXX, 1965.

Chapter Five

The Process of Work 2: Community and Role Conflict

The policeman buys shoes slow and careful;
the teamster buys gloves slow and careful;
they take care of their feet and hands;
they live on their feet and hands.
*Carl Sandburg, The Psalm of those
who go forth before Daylight*

In the previous chapter we started with the concepts of
'commitment' and 'career' and ended by casting a certain
amount of doubt on the utility of concepts such as these in
explaining what actually happens during people's working
lives and why the crucial turning points are really so
significant.

Another concept that has enjoyed a long career of active
service among sociologists writing about men and their work
is that of the 'occupational community'. This was probably
first formalized by Lipset, Trow and Coleman in their study of
trade union bureaucracy, and the role of occupational
associations among groups such as printers.

Salaman identifies the occupational community as a
situation 'in which work relationships, activities, interests and
values permeate people's out of work lives'. He compares the
involvement in occupational communities of a sample of
London architects and Cambridge railwaymen with a view to
establishing whether the concepts of the 'local' and the
'cosmopolitan' help to illuminate the differences between these
two groups. It was hypothesized that 'a local community
would consist of people who actually work together in the
same organization or workplace and the cosmopolitan would
consist of the profession or occupation as a whole'. He argues
that the major determinants of occupational communities are
'. . . involvement in work and work tasks, marginality, and
restrictive factors'.

An organization which is very often referred to as a 'community' is the university. Yet Startup shows how systematic misconceptions and failure to match the expectations of significant others can bedevil the apparently quite clearly defined role of the university lecturer. The student gives prominence to the competence and capacity of the lecturer as a teacher, while recognizing that other professional activities are also significant. But the lecturer is caught in a knowledge nexus of a different kind. He knows that the maintenance of a high level of output based on 'original' research, coupled with visible though not necessarily time-consuming involvement in 'administration', will be more beneficial to him in successfully playing the promotion game than the mere opinions of 'ill-informed' students. Thus, many specific proposals for the extension of student involvement and control over university decision-making which have been put forward from the hierarchy in recent years have specifically excluded staff promotions as an area over which students can, or should have, 'competence'. Startup's analysis helps us to understand why these dilemmas should arise and are not satisfactorily resolved by bland references to 'student militance' or 'academic conservatism'.

Weir's paper looks at another basis for conflict of expectations – that deriving from the system of promotion which obtains in the organization. The clerks in private firms are committed to the ideology of individual achievement and are employed in structures which superficially permit a good deal of scope for the exercise of personal flexibility and latitude in determining their career patterns. Their counterparts in the public sector, by contrast, operate in a context of rigidly-defined rules about promotion and promotability, which apparently serve to limit any individual's chances of using the structure opportunistically.

But it is the members of the latter group, paradoxically, who feel less constrained and whose capacity to evolve personal strategies for playing the organizations' promotion game are enhanced by the fact that they operate within a structure which tells them what they need to know in order to achieve their personal goals. Failure may none the less occur, but it is failure which may be less stressful and less damaging to the individual's self image.

But the area in which the most violent and comprehensive

disagreements about occupational roles and their relation to the wider social structure have recently occurred is that of the position of women in the system of work. For some this topic is easily disposed of by a joke as are other disagreeable and threatening topics. But these 'jokes' owe their crispness and pungency to the very real and generalized threat which they contain. If women claim to enter one arena of male domination – the occupational system – this may be seen as a complementary attack to that on men's personal and sexual identity buttressed by the myth of man the all-conquering hunter and provider for the domestic nest watched over by his devoted helpmate – *the wife*.

While Nancy Seear's analysis in the next chapter starts out from and concentrates on the need of the labour market for the skills and competencies of women *as workers* she draws attention to the culture and structure of prejudice and misinformation which make the topic of women at work a joke in many circles. It is an understatement of enormous implication to say, as she does, that 'men's opposition to women in responsible posts is not however solely based on rational considerations of the labour market'. Seear's analysis concentrates on changes in attitude which might be induced by the intervention of the authorities. Fogarty and the Rapoports outline the ways in which 'dual-career families' (which are, as they point out, 'a statistically minor variant') attempt to cope with the dilemmas confronting *families* who are attempting as a partnership to pursue life-strategies which appear to be largely unsupported by societal provision. They pay particular attention to what they call 'overload dilemmas'.

Allen's description of the way of life of top women administrators in the Civil Service concludes that 'For the most part married women administrators seem to maintain their involvement in work and family at the cost of other involvements'. Their leisure is less, compared with that of their male colleagues, and their allocation of time as between domestic and professional activities leaves them fewer 'expendable' areas. It is possible that there is an inherent tendency for them to become highly specialized and segmented *as people*, lacking the basis of 'free floating' time for the development of new activities.

Throughout this chapter we have tried to indicate some of the ways in which, as a member of an occupational group, individuals relate in the wider society in which they play other roles. In the process of becoming socialized into a particular role and of coming to accept society's definition of that role they come to hold characteristic perspectives on themselves, their role, and on society as a whole. And these typical attitudes may be related to fundamental values – such as that men 'should' work and women 'should' mind the house and the children.

Two Occupational Communities

G. Salaman

Reprinted with permission from *Sociological Review*,
Vol. 19, 1971, pp. 389–99.

Although in general terms there is a close relationship between
men's work and out-of-work life, the exact nature of this relationship varies enormously. A number of possible work/leisure
relationships have been suggested and described. One recently
described case occurs where people attempt to enforce a thorough
separation of their work and leisure lives. These people view their
work in such a way that they are not prepared to allow their
work relationships, activities or interests to affect their leisure
lives, which are 'compartmentalized' from their work experience,
and which very often centre around their home and family. This
sort of pattern was displayed by some of the affluent workers
studied by Goldthorpe. It is closely connected to an instrumental
orientation towards work. Clearly when work is perceived
primarily as an activity devoid of any intrinsic meaning, as a
means of making money and living outside, it is unlikely to form
the basis for out-of-work activities, interests or relationships.

An entirely different type of work/leisure relationship is represented by the occupational community, in which work relationships, activities, interests and values permeate people's out-of-
work lives. Instead of separating their work and leisure friends and
activities, members of occupational communities display a remarkable fusion of their work and leisure lives. A close study of a
number of available accounts of occupational communities
suggests that this type of work/leisure convergence involves three
inter-related elements: self-image or identity, values, and relationships. Three factors seem to be causally responsible: involvement
in work and work tasks, marginality, and restrictive factors. An
earlier article spells out this view of the components and determinants of occupational communities in greater detail.

Community is a key sociological idea, and historically it has
played an important part in sociological thinking. But it is also a
notoriously open-ended concept, absorbing a variety of different
interpretations and uses, many of them with obvious evaluative
undertones. There have been some recent attempts to demystify
and operationalize the idea of community and to use it to apply to

situations where there is some degree of shared social living, but not necessarily any geographical propinquity. This shared element may be associational or normative. Used in this sense, 'community' need not involve people living together: a profession may be seen as a non-residential community based on a shared occupational value system and culture. Also it is now possible to talk of *degree of communitiness*, rather than a community/non-community dichotomy.

The material set out below was gathered in the course of an investigation into the determinants and components of occupational communities. The investigation was designed to investigate the possibility that occupational communities might be of two types: the local and the cosmopolitan. It was suggested that these two types would differ with regard to the constitution of the reference groups and the networks of associates. More specifically it was felt that the local community would consist of people who actually work together in the same *organization* or *work-place* and the cosmopolitan would consist of the *profession* or *occupation* as a whole.

Because of limitations of time and finance it was not possible in the research to test rigorously the propositions set out in the earlier article. Rather the investigation should be seen as a large-scale pilot study into one type of work/leisure relationship. Two occupational samples were selected for investigation: London architects and Cambridge railwaymen. These occupations were selected because there was good *a priori* evidence that they had occupational communities, and in order to gather data on communities which might be of different types.

The data on the components of these two communities will be set out under the three headings: self-image, values and associations.

Self-image: identification with occupational role

All but eight (16 per cent) of the architects saw themselves in terms of their occupational role. Most of them could remember the occasion when they first made this identification: it was usually when they had first accomplished what they considered to be the basic tasks of the professional architect, i.e. when they were first responsible for the entire design process. The architects' professional identification was contingent upon their being able to claim, with confidence, the professional autonomy which is the most important element in their professional value system.

Most of the architects were strongly 'attached' to their occupational role, in the sense that it was, as Goffman has said: 'One of which he may become effectively and cognitively enamoured, desiring and expecting to see himself in terms of the enactment of the role and the self-identity emerging from this enactment.' Most of the architects remembered the occasion of their first complete occupational identification as a moment of satisfaction and pride. Some typical comments were:

'I remember the occasion well, it was when I first designed and built – when I was responsible for the whole process. It was a marvellous moment.'

'I was so proud that I took off like a jet.'

'It was like becoming a father.'

It is clear that to see oneself as an architect carried a certain conception of oneself and others in the occupation as people with specific qualities and attributes. The architects felt that certain qualities were necessary to carry out the work tasks satisfactorily and that it was the possession of these qualities which differentiated the architect from members of other occupations. Over three-quarters (77 per cent) of the architects felt that members of their profession differed from outsiders by virtue of their interest and capacity for design. Whatever their criteria of good design – and these varied considerably – the architects stressed their interest in the way things are designed, and they mentioned how this interest was not restricted to their work alone, but permeated their perception of things generally.

Like architects, the vast majority of the railwaymen (96 per cent) said that they saw themselves as railwaymen and that this self-identification was a source of pride and satisfaction. Most of the railwaymen said that they first saw themselves in this way when they gained the support and approval of their work-mates. They too were strongly 'attached' to their occupational role. One railwayman said of the first occasion of this self-identification:

'Oh, it was when I first got my uniform, after twelve months service. I remember blacking my face so that people would think I was a fireman. I was that proud to be a railwayman.'

A number of the railwaymen described what this self-identification meant by listing the qualities, interests and abilities which they felt were attached to the title 'railwayman'. Most of the qualities and characteristics were concerned either with the relationships between railwaymen or with the way that they saw their work. In the first category were such characteristics as being helpful to one's work-mates and dealing fairly with them. Nearly a third of the sample (31 per cent) felt that railwaymen differed from outsiders by virtue of the nature of the relationships which existed between members of their occupation. They mentioned the close, solidaristic relationships that existed within the occupation and the separation of railwaymen from the rest of society. One common remark was:

'We're a race apart, a different breed. We stick together you know.'

Many of the railwaymen felt that members of their occupation differed from other people in their attitudes towards their work; conscientiousness, responsibility and taking a pride in one's work were frequently mentioned. They felt that members of their occupation were distinctive for their ability to accept responsibility. Many of them felt that this was directly due to the relatively dangerous and demanding nature of their work. One typical comment was:

'Railwaymen take a pride in their job, they've got to do it properly because lives depend on it.'

There can be little doubt that these remarks had a normative significance as well as a descriptive one: i.e. they state how railwaymen felt members of their occupation *should* feel about their work, as well as describing how they *did* feel about it.

Obviously the occupational identifications of architects and railwaymen are closely related to the value systems and cultures of the occupations. Members of both occupations tended to see themselves as people with certain characteristics – abilities or personality elements – which they believed were the necessary attributes of members of that occupation; necessary if they were to be able to do what they felt they ought to be doing in their work. Similarly they ascribed to themselves and others, as architects or as railwaymen, attitudes towards their work and their colleagues which they considered desirable.

Values: occupational reference groups

The architects shared a distinctive occupational culture consisting of values (how architects ought to behave, what they ought to do), attitudes about their work and their colleagues, and beliefs about the importance of their work and how it affected the lives of their clients. These elements are closely inter-related. They define and evaluate architects' reactions to their social reality. All but four of the architects felt that members of their profession shared attitudes and values. The most important element in this shared value system was the emphasis they placed on design or artistic autonomy. The architects seemed to regard it as axiomatic that since their job was to design buildings, and since this was an artistic activity, they must if they were to be good architects be as free as possible from any restrictions or interferences in their design autonomy. Many of the architects mentioned that they experienced considerable difficulty in giving their artistic impulses free rein; like jazz musicians and other creative people, they frequently found that their desire for artistic autonomy clashed with economic survival. The type of restriction that they mentioned most frequently occurred when the client attempted to interfere with the architect's design. Because he paid, the client was able to bring considerable pressure to bear on the architect, but because he usually lacked the architect's artistic sensibility this interference was much resented.

Architects also shared a very positive orientation towards their work. When asked what it was that they liked about their work they all mentioned 'intrinsic' factors, i.e. such things as the creativity of the work, the opportunity to use their design skills, or the problem-solving aspects. Most of their work dissatisfaction was directed towards features of the job which restricted their opportunities to derive these sorts of satisfactions. It was clear that the architects' involvement was in their *work* tasks and skills, and not necessarily in their jobs, which might or might not supply the sorts of professional opportunities they desired. A number of the architects were frustrated not by any interference in their design autonomy, but by lack of any opportunity to design at all. These architects worked in offices where they were unable to do any designing on the scale they wished.

The majority of the architects also felt that members of their occupation shared a particular approach to the world or a world-view. Some typical remarks illustrate this:

'Architects just have their own way of looking at things.'

'Architects, unlike other people, are really aware of their environment; they really see things around them.'

'We are interested in how things work and what they look like; that's what architecture is all about; architects notice the way things are designed and made.'

Although, generally speaking, architects see their professional role as supplying functional works of art, many of them stressed the social side of their work and used this as a claim for higher professional status. These architects felt that when they designed buildings they had an opportunity to affect and mould the lives of the people who live within them. Some of them spoke of producing structures which would permit and encourage the full development of the inhabitants' personalities. This aspect of the architects' belief system has recently been critically discussed by Alan Lipman.

Because the architects shared these and other attitudes and values, they tended to identify with other members of their occupation and to refer to themselves as 'we'. One interesting consequence of this identification was that many of the architects thought that they would be able to identify other members of their profession even though they were personally unknown to them. One architect said:

'Oh yes I could spot an architect anywhere. There's just something about them. It's impossible to explain; somehow one just knows.'

The railwaymen, like the architects, had a well developed occupational culture. Three-quarters of the sample thought that members of their occupation shared values and attitudes; and not surprisingly the subject on which they displayed the greatest degree of consensus was their work. Among other things, railwaymen stressed the skills that their work required, the proper orientation that it demanded and the sorts of personality characteristics that were necessary to do the job well.

The railwaymen stressed the skill that their job demanded. One man said:

'Being a railwayman is a lifelong job – you're always learning, the job demands it.'

The respondents were extremely proud of their work skills and accorded high prestige to those colleagues who were particularly skilled or knowledgeable technically. Like the architects, the railwaymen displayed a strong positive orientation towards their work skills and tasks. Only one mentioned money as a source of satisfaction or dissatisfaction. Various features of their work were considered to be sources of satisfaction; many said quite simply that they enjoyed doing it. Some typical remarks were:

'I just enjoy driving, I always have done. I love being on the road.'

'I like the work because it's always different and there's always more to learn; it's never the same.'

Associations: convergence of work and non-work activities, interests and relationships

The most striking thing about the architects was the extent to which they carried work activities, interests and relationships into their leisure-time lives. Two-thirds of the architects (66 per cent) had two or more architects among their five best friends and only nine of the architects (19 per cent) said that they had no architect friends at all. The incidence of work-based friendships among the architects was extremely high, even for a high status occupation. It is by no means unusual for members of high status or professional occupations to have friends who do the same work, and the architects not only had a large number of colleague friends, but many of them also have friends from 'related' occupations such as town planning, engineering, interior design, etc.

Many of the architects made a distinction between 'associates' and 'best friends'. A best friend was not necessarily a frequent associate or vice versa. Over three-quarters of the architects (82 per cent) met colleague associates other than their best friends regularly or frequently. It seems that the vast majority of the architects preferred their informal friendships and social relationships to be with their colleagues. There are two main reasons for this: their shared commitment to their work and work tasks, and the fact that they had attitudes and values in common. As one architect put it:

'I have architect friends because we belong to the same world. When you come down to it they have the same priorities; they know what you're talking about. We have so much in common.'

Another one said:

'The important thing is that my architect friends and I share the same backlog of experience and interests, we talk the same language.'

The most remarkable thing about the architects' friendship patterns was that unlike members of other occupational communities – and especially the working class ones – the architects' colleague friends were rarely people they currently worked with; most of their colleague friends were people they had met during their training period or with whom they had worked at some earlier time. The architects did not have architect friends merely because they were forced into their company at work; they had architect friends because they chose to, and because they felt most at ease with members of their own occupation.

Having a number of occupational colleagues among one's friends and associates was but one aspect – and the most important one – of a general fusion of the worlds of work and leisure. The architects carried work activities and interests as well as relationships into their leisure lives. Over three-quarters of the architects (76 per cent) said that they were neither able nor willing to forget their work in their free time. One said:

'I can't stop thinking about work. This is not a nine to five job, you just can't cut it off, it's with you all the time.'

Another remarked:

'If something is important to you and you are totally involved in it, how can you possibly forget about it merely because you leave the office?'

Not only did the architects think – and talk – about their work during their free time, many of them were also members of societies, clubs and associations which were in some way connected with their work. Nearly half the sample (44 per cent) were members of such associations as the Town Planning Association, the Architectural Association, the Architects in Industry Group, etc. A further indication of the extent to which architects' work infiltrates their leisure lives can be gathered from the fact that sixty per cent of the architects had a hobby which was in some way connected with their work, in as much as their interest in the hobby derived from, or was closely related to, their work activity. Ten (19 per cent) of the architects said simply that their work was their hobby: by this they meant both that they regarded their work as very much more than just a means of earning a livelihood, and that they spent some of their free time in architectural work of some sort, or in studying architecture and looking at buildings. Another fourteen architects (27 per cent) said they had artistic hobbies such as painting, sketching, sculpting or designing. These hobbies are of course closely related to architects' central interests – design and aesthetics. A further eight architects (16 per cent) had hobbies such as building or doing alterations to old houses, and these hobbies are related to the practical aspects of the architects' work. Finally over three-quarters of the architects (83 per cent) said that they spend at least two hours a week in some sort of reading connected with their work.

All in all then, it is clear that the architects' leisure lives were closely related to their work lives. Their leisure time activities, interests, values, attitudes and relationships were derived from their work, and indeed for some of the architects the very separation itself of work and leisure was not a meaningful one. For the architects work was a total experience, not a compartmentalized, restricted activity. This situation is rare among manual occupations and not common – at least to this extent – among professions, although there are other occupations which involve a similar fusion of work and leisure.

Seventy per cent of the railwaymen had two or more best friends from their occupation. They also displayed a high incidence of casual association with colleagues: forty (78 per cent) said that they met their work colleagues 'regularly' or 'occasionally'. This was undoubtedly partly due to the fact that the Cambridge railwaymen tended to live within a certain area of the town and that, as one remarked:

'You can't walk down the street without meeting another railwayman.'

But the railwaymen's concentration in one area was undoubtedly as much the result of the enjoyment they derived from this sort of contact as from any other factors.

The railwaymen's colleague friends were nearly always their workmates and in all but one case they were from the same department as the respondent. In this respect the railwaymen differed markedly from the architects. This difference reflected the different bases of the two occupational communities: the railwaymen's community was local in as much as it was composed of their Cambridge work-mates. The railwaymen rarely made any general occupational reference; their interests, affiliations and loyalties were predominantly local. This of course is not surprising in view of the fact that apart from time in the services, only five (10 per cent) had ever worked outside Cambridge.

The architects, on the other hand, were subject to very much greater occupational and geographical mobility: only fifty-two per cent had always been in the sort of work they were doing when interviewed and twenty-five per cent had spent at least some time in architectural work outside London. The architects' colleague friends were rarely their current work colleagues (23 per cent), more usually they were people with whom they had once worked (46 per cent), or people with whom they had trained (43 per cent). The architects did not restrict their friendship choices to any particular group within the occupation but displayed a more cosmopolitan orientation towards the profession as a whole. Unlike the railwaymen, the architects were constantly making reference to 'The Profession', and their answers to a question on occupational identification clearly showed that for most of them (60 per cent) their 'we' references referred to *all* members of their occupation. The opposite was true of the railwaymen, whose 'we' statements in most cases (94 per cent) referred to members of their particular department who shared their work situation (i.e. their work-mates). It is on the basis of these differences in identification and friendship choice that we regard these two communities as local and cosmopolitan.

For the railwaymen work was, quite clearly, a dominant central life interest. Like the architects, they carried work activities and interests – as well as relationships – into their non-work lives. One very noticeable feature of the railwaymen was their willingness to talk about their work outside of working hours. One railwayman's wife said:

'It's railways, railways, railways with him. All railwaymen are like it, they just want to get together and talk railways. As though they didn't have enough. If you want to find out about the railways ask the wives. We're the ones who have had the railways all these years.'

Forty per cent of the sample were members of the Railways Social Club or the Labour Club. The former was actually organized and run by the British Railways Board; the latter was not work-connected in this sense but was well known as a railwaymen's meeting place.

Few of the railwaymen had hobbies that could be described as work-connected in the sense that their interest in the activity derived from their interest in their work skills or that the actual activity was similar to their work tasks. But seventy-six per cent of the railwaymen shared an interest in gardening, which could usefully be regarded as a *community-connected* hobby, i.e. although it bore no relationship to their work it was an activity that attracted a great deal of enthusiasm and interest within the community. It was an activity which was particularly well suited to the nature of railwaymen's work. All the railwaymen worked shifts and this affected their choice of leisure-time activity in two ways. In the first place, due to the irregularity of the shifts they found it difficult to engage in any group activities or activities that required the presence of even one other person; secondly, it meant that they had more daylight hours at home than many people and so gardening particularly was an appropriate hobby for them. The links between railwaymen's work and the rest of their lives was admirably summed up by one of the respondents, a driver. He said:

'This is no job you know, it's a way of life. The railways are in the blood with us. You can't get away from it; my whole life has been railways.'

How Students see the Role of the University Lecturer

R. Startup

Reprinted with permission from *Sociology*, Vol. 16, No. 2, May 1972, pp. 237–53.

Introduction

In universities, as Peter Marris has said, 'learning is communicated by means of a complex interaction of personal relationships, and upon the quality of these relationships the success of higher education is seen to depend'. The central *relationship* is between teacher and pupil, yet our understanding is limited as to how each party to this relationship sees the other and what criteria each uses to judge whether the relationship is a useful and valuable one, or not. We know that students are to some extent aware of the many and various activities of university staff, but which of these activities do they consider most integral to the role of lecturer? In addition, it is a familiar observation that students evaluate the attitudes of members of staff positively or negatively – but how do they arrive at this assessment? It is the purpose of this article to report research findings which throw new light on the expectations which students have of university teachers and the way in which they make judgments of the academic services which the teachers provide.

The study is based on information collected in a survey of students at a provincial university ('the University') conducted in the early summer of 1969. The University had at that time approximately 3,300 students. In the previous ten years student numbers had increased by 180 per cent. The University had therefore, like most other institutions of its type, expanded considerably in the 1960s. The survey was designed to assess students' attitudes to different aspects of their experience of higher education. It was thought desirable that the sample studied should be drawn from students who had spent sufficient time at the university to have a reasonably informed opinion about the extent to which it lived up to their expectations. For this reason first-year students were not included in the sample. It was also considered important to study students who were maximally orientated towards the university world. For this reason, third-year students, who could be expected to be already thinking about 'finals' and future careers, were also excluded. The sample therefore was taken from second-year students.

A 50 per cent interval sample of students was selected and 321, just under 70 per cent of those chosen, returned a completed questionnaire. The response rate was high for a survey of this kind, and the sample can be shown to be reasonably representative, along certain important dimensions for which information for second-year students as a whole is available from University records. Table 1 shows the distribution of the sample between the two sexes and in the four faculties which make up the University. The expected distribution based on all second-year students is also indicated.

Table 1. Distribution over sex and faculty

Sex	Arts expected	Arts actual	Pure sciences expected	Pure sciences actual	Applied sciences expected	Applied sciences actual	Social studies expected	Social studies actual	All expected	All actual	Total N
					(percentages)						
Male	51	52	66	62	96	97	62	57	66	65	207
Female	49	48	34	38	4	3	38	43	34	35	114
Total	37	37	30	28	20	20	13	15	100	100	
N		117		91		64		49		321	

As many as 65 per cent of the sample were students whose fathers were in non-manual occupations. A further 27 per cent had fathers in skilled manual occupations, while only 8 per cent had fathers in partly-skilled or unskilled occupations. Thus the sample is a predominantly 'middle-class' one.

The students were asked to record on the questionnaire certain personal information such as that referring to place of birth, age, schooling and the subjects at that moment being studied. In addition, in that part of the survey being reported here, they were asked a large number of questions relating to the activities and attitudes of lecturers and the academic services which they provide. They were also asked to indicate any radical changes they would like to see taking place in the University. In the answers to this latter section of the questionnaire, the numerous references to various aspects of teachers and teaching provide a valuable supplement to the answers to the structured questions. They provide a clearer understanding about the sort of changes in the relationship between staff and students which some students wish to see come about.

The activities of members of staff

One must never assume that students have a clear idea about the various activities of members of staff, or the proportion of time devoted to these various activities. As one student said after filling in the questionnaire, 'I had never thought before about the sort of things lecturers have to do.'

In order that the importance they give to the various activities of members of staff could be assessed, the students were instructed as follows: 'Given below is a list of the things that some university teaching staff actually do. Opposite each are five numbers, which have the following meanings:

5   of greatest importance
4   of great importance
3   of some importance
2   of little importance
1   of least importance

Opposite each, ring the number which reflects the importance you give to that activity. Add other things you think they ought to do, giving a number for each to show their importance.'

There followed, in a random order, a list of 24 activities of members of staff. These activities can now be displayed, re-ordered, according to the pattern of the students' responses as a whole. This re-ordering was achieved in the following way. First those activities were placed earlier in the order which obtained a higher median score from the respondents. All of those activities with the same median score were then considered in pairs. The number of students who scored higher on each activity of the pair was then noted, as was the number who scored the same on both activities. One activity was placed earlier than the other in the order if a greater number of students gave it a higher score.

The 24 activities can also be placed in six categories, partly on the basis of the different sets of people with whom the member of staff has to relate in the performance of the activity, but also according to the objectives of the activity and the kind of skill employed. The six categories are:

A   Activities involving contact with undergraduates (four activities)
B   Activities associated with teaching (eight activities)
C   Research (one activity)
D   Postgraduate supervision (one activity)
E   Professional activities (five activities)
F   Administrative activities (five activities)

Table 2 indicates the order of importance of the activities, together with the median score for each activity and the category into which it falls.

Included in the top eight items, all of which have median scores of four, are the activities involving contact with undergraduates. Not surprisingly, tutorial work and lecturing are particularly stressed. These activities are generally considered to be of great importance. The activities associated with teaching (category B) vary considerably in the importance attributed to them. However, what is clear is that it is those activities in this category which are means to improving the quality of teaching which are most emphasized. Thus, preparing for lectures, learning most up to date teaching methods, and designing new courses are included in the top eight items. Activities which are generally seen as having little or no relationship with improving the standard of teaching (e.g. keeping student work and progress records) obtain much more lowly positions.

The other item in the top eight is the professional activity of increasing through study the lecturer's own knowledge of his subject. Clearly this is of fundamental importance to the work of the academic. It is also necessarily a means to improving the quality of undergraduate teaching.

Research and post-graduate supervision come about halfway down the order of importance. The only administrative activity to come higher is the job of ordering books for the library. This item presumably gets its relatively high position because of the

Table 2. Activities of members of staff

	Median Score	Category
1. Holding small group tutorials/supervising lab work	4	A
2. Increasing through study his own knowledge of his subject	4	E
3. Preparing for lectures	4	B
4. *Lecturing	4	A
5. Holding individual tutorials	4	A
6. Holding seminars	4	A
7. Learning most up to date teaching methods	4	B
8. Designing new courses	4	B
9. *Ordering books for the library	3	F
10. Setting and marking examinations	3	B
11. *Reading for, getting money for, organizing and carrying out, research	3	C
12. *Supervising post-graduate students	3	D
13. Writing student references	3	B
14. Marking	3	B
15. Giving specialist advice to outside bodies	3	E
16. Keeping student work and progress records	3	B
17. Writing textbooks and articles	3	E
18. Ordering equipment	3	F
19. Dealing with admissions	3	F
20. Sitting on faculty or other administrative committees	3	F
21. Dealing with students' personal problems	3	B
22. †Lecturing to outside bodies	3	E
23. Arranging timetables	2	F
24. Sitting on local committees in his professional capacity	2	E

* The difference between the pattern of responses for this item and the one immediately following it is significant at the 5 per cent level.
† The difference between the pattern of responses for this item and the one immediately following it is significant at the 1 per cent level.

great strategic importance of the library in relation to the academic work of the undergraduate (and indeed of the whole university). Research and post-graduate supervision are also placed ahead of the professional activities which involve the member of staff relating to outside bodies.

Given this pattern, the activities can be grouped into three classes, which differ significantly in their importance:

A	*B*	*C*
Student contact	Research	Activities associated with student contact which are not means to effective teaching
Activities associated with student contact which are means to effective teaching	Post-graduate supervision	
		Professional activities relating to outside bodies
		Administrative activities

We are entitled to say that the activities in A are judged most important, those in B are less important, and those in C are considered least important of all.

*　　　*　　　*

The conclusion from the evidence presented in this section is that the normative expectations which students have of staff are centred on the undergraduate teaching aspects of the staff role. Nevertheless, the other activities of staff are seen to differ in importance. It seems likely that research and post-graduate teaching are genuinely valued activities, though they are seen as having to take second place to undergraduate teaching in their claim on staff time. Many of the other activities which are considered less important may be seen as means by which staff are able to perform their main functions, but they are not necessarily valued in their own right. It is only when they are immediately geared to the undergraduate teaching function (as with lecture preparation) that they are given the same importance as the generally accepted main functions of university staff. Generally, one can say that he who wills the end, also wills the means – but with less enthusiasm! It can be suggested why the enthusiasm is less: though an activity may be viewed as a necessary preliminary to, or adjunct of, another valued activity, it can still be a competitor with the latter for scarce time and resources. Thus, keeping student work and progress records takes time which cannot be devoted to teaching or research.

The administrative activities and some of the professional activities get their lowly position because, though they may be viewed as necessary, they are somewhat remote from teaching activities. Some, at least, are time-consuming chores (e.g. time-tabling). These chores may be seen as hardly deserving of the time and energy of academic staff. Indeed the very notion of an 'academic' task could be said to be one which does not encompass administrative activity. Some comments reflect this conception: 'Professors and the senior lecturing staff should have all their purely administrative duties done by some official so they can concentrate on their various academic works.'

Some of the professional and administrative activities have the character of 'back-stage' activities, at least from the point of view of the students. This being so, when they are performed by staff, they cannot directly be seen to conform to the expectations which students may have of them. To take an example: the students probably realize that certain activities must be carried on at a Faculty level. Nevertheless, they may reasonably doubt whether in practice these activities are carried on expeditiously and efficiently. It is being suggested that the judgment of the importance of an activity (even when one is considering ideally how it should be performed) is influenced by the extent to which it is observable and by whom.

Some of the professional activities involve the lecturer relating to groups outside university. These are seen as being entitled to the last claim on staff time. The general emphasis the undergraduates give to the teaching function of staff is not unreasonable, given the way in which staff are labelled. Names may not always mean what they say, but 'lecturers' who do not lecture are few and far between.

A student ranking of the importance of the various activities of members of staff has been described. This is, in part at least, an indication of the *knowledge* which students have of what lecturers do. This knowledge is essentially limited. Students know lecturers 'do research' – but what exactly does this involve? Students may know that their teachers give specialist advice to outside bodies – but how time-consuming is this activity and how does it link up with the other things lecturers do? Much information needs to be conveyed if students are to come to have a better understanding of the activities of members of staff. It is difficult for them to assess the importance of things of which they are ignorant.

The attitudes of members of staff

Students were asked to indicate in how many cases members of staff known to them had 'poor' attitudes. In all, just over 30 per cent considered this was so in half or more cases. The proportion giving this response varies from faculty to faculty, being as low as a quarter in Social Studies and nearer 40 per cent in the Arts faculty.

Subsequent questions probed the dimensions of these 'poor' attitudes. Respondents were asked whether those with poor attitudes could be described as 'mostly remote, superior and patronizing'. Overall about two-thirds thought that this was at least partly true. In every faculty (other than the virtually all-male Applied Science faculty), this aspect of a 'poor' attitude was emphasized more by men than by women.

The students were asked whether those with poor attitudes were 'more interested in research than teaching'. About 60 per cent thought that this was at least partly true. As one might expect, this was more emphasized by science students than by those in Arts and Social Studies. A similar proportion at least partly agreed with the proposition that those with poor attitudes 'treat you as if you were still at school'.

The most popular interpretation of poor attitudes, however, was 'taking too little trouble and devoting too little time to individual students'. Almost three-quarters thought that this was at least partly true.

Earlier it was stated that of all staff duties, teaching activities are judged to be most important by students. Thus it is natural that a member of staff whose attitude is considered to be 'poor' should be judged deficient in this teaching area. However, there is evidence that an awareness of status differences by a member of staff can be a component in his 'poor' attitude. This is an interpretation which is somewhat more stressed by men than by women. There are also some complaints which conceive of the 'poor attitude' as being peculiarly local:

'There is a particular section of lecturers (not all older ones) who have been brought up in this locality and still seem to believe that either you work yourselves so hard to get a degree that you end up with a nervous breakdown *or* you find yourselves working in some sort of sweat shop. . . . They also had the idea that university education is only to cram, cram all you can into the brain – it seems to be unheard of that you should also try to develop your personality.'

*　　*　　*

Individual and informal contact

Role expectations associated with different positions vary in the degree of their generality or specificity. At one end of the continuum, role expectations specify precisely how and where the

behaviour should be executed. The role of soldier has this character. The role of lecturer tends towards the other end of the
continuum – here the individual role occupant is given the opportunity to enact the role in the particular way he prefers within a
wide range of acceptable behaviours. True, the times and places
of lectures and tutorials are laid down. Yet there is a wide scope
for different ways of conducting these formal sessions. In addition, there is considerable individual discretion as to the amount
of staff–student contact which takes place on an extra-curricular
basis.

Questions were asked about the student's degree of satisfaction
with the individual help and instruction he received from staff
and the amount of informal contact he had with members of
staff. The survey shows that slightly more students are dissatisfied with the amount of individual help and attention they
receive from staff (25 per cent), than are dissatisfied with the
quality of help they receive (18 per cent). The largest proportions
dissatisfied with the amount of help received (30 per cent) are
found in the faculties of Arts and Social Studies.

Though there is pressure for more individual contact, there is
also recognition of what may be necessary if this is to be achieved:
'Student numbers should be cut drastically until sufficient staff
and facilities are available for the degree of personal supervision
which is essential to such a relatively high level of education.'

The greatest dissatisfaction was found to be felt in relation to
the amount of informal contact which students had with members
of staff. Fully two-fifths expressed themselves dissatisfied on this
score. Those who are dissatisfied with the amount of informal
contact are fairly evenly spread over all faculty and sex groups.
One student put the problem thus: 'Although I know that staff
have their own lives to lead, I believe they could make more of an
effort to join in the social life of the university . . . much good
would be done, I think, if the staff could at least make an effort to
join in the socials etc. which are, after all, only held about three
times a year.'

There is a desire both for more frequent tutorials and seminars,
but also for more interaction outside the formal teaching arena.
There is an underlying search for a community of staff and
students, going beyond the academic sphere. Involved in this is a
wish to see a greater degree of equality in the relationship. This
desire for equality is stronger outside the academic sphere than it
is in it. This is because the students are often aware of the depen-

dency element in their academic relationships with staff. By the
nature of things the teaching relationship is asymmetrical. Yet
why should this asymmetry be extended into the university bars,
halls of residence and the social sphere generally?

The students feel that they are entitled to more informal contact with staff. However, the staff are subject to competing claims
from their wives, children and others, as well as needing time for
reading and research. Here there is manifestly *a conflict of substantive interests* between members of staff and students. The
conflicting expectations centre around what has been termed 'the
pre-emptiveness of the role'. This has been defined as 'the amount
of time a person spends in one role relative to the amount of time
he spends in other roles' (Sarbin and Allen 1968: 496). Just where
are the limits of the students' claim on staff time and energy to be
fixed and where do the claims of wives and children take over?
The extent to which inter-role conflict is experienced by a particular member of staff will depend upon the other roles enacted by
him. Whereas attendance at student socials may be looked upon
as a tiresome chore by a senior married member of staff, a young
bachelor may see things differently.

Conclusion

Undergraduate teaching is seen as, far and away, the most important part of the job of a university lecturer. Given its importance,
it is natural that considerable emphasis is also placed on necessary preliminaries to it (e.g. lecture preparation) and adjuncts of
it (e.g. setting and marking examinations). In addition to undergraduate teaching, research and post-graduate teaching are valued
activities of lecturers. Administrative activities and professional
activities (e.g. giving specialist advice to outside bodies), students
judge to be least in their importance. One can order various
groups according to the priority of their claim on staff time.
Those who have first claim are undergraduates, then come post-
graduates, and finally groups outside the university. The order in
which students rank the importance of the activities of members of
staff is partly an indication of the knowledge which they have of
these activities. Where their knowledge is limited, they tend to
attach a lower degree of importance to the activity.

Before coming to the university, most students have only a
rough idea what lecturers do. Therefore their expectations are
developed to a considerable extent *within* the particular university itself. Their experience is largely limited to one institution.

Thus the staff in that university essentially define for them what lecturers do. It does not follow from this that a particular lecturer cannot be judged deficient or incompetent. It does, however, suggest that he will tend to be judged deficient by reference to norms which get their sense from student observation of what other lecturers in that particular university do. The position of university lecturer occupies an intermediate position in the society between those positions about which there exists widespread public knowledge and those positions known only to a small coterie.

Student ideas about what constitutes a 'poor attitude' of a member of staff are influenced by the importance which they attach to the teaching function. When offered various descriptions of the behaviour of a lecturer with a 'poor' attitude, the most favoured was, that he 'took too little trouble and devoted too little time to individual students'. However, other interpretations of a 'poor attitude' were also stressed. These included being 'more interested in research than teaching'. There is a certain amount of pressure to separate out the various aspects of the job and get different people to perform them. One view put forward was that there should be 'categorization of "lecturers" into pure lecturers, pure researchers and departmental administrators, but regular seminars from the latter two'. It is often suggested that there should be a purely administrative head of department: as one student argued, 'after all, it is not economical to pay professors to do administrative work'.

Though satisfaction with teaching at the University is generally high, additional sources of unease in the relationship between staff and students are centred here. What students require of a lecturer and what he provides, are systematically different. Many students see study as a means to getting a degree. A degree gives them access to a preferred occupation. They do not necessarily value knowledge of an academic subject for its own sake, nor do they place emphasis on ideas which are theoretically important. Most staff do both these things. Hence the complaint that lectures are 'too theoretical and remote from real life'. Differences in values underlie felt problems in the teaching sphere.

In addition, there are conflicts of substantive interest between staff and students. Students require more individual contact and more informal contact with staff. Lecturers need to have time for research. Promotion for university teachers is linked more to research and publication than it is to teaching. In addition,

members of staff need to have time, both for their other professional duties and their domestic duties. The conflict of interests is
as irreconcilable as any in industry. One thing is certain – it will
not disappear through an increase in the knowledge which
students have about what lecturers do. This is not a problem
merely of communication.

When differences of values and conflicts of interests are involved, university teachers will resist the demands of students. In
resisting the demands, they are defining in a different way the
role of the university lecturer.

The Wall of Darkness: Subjective Operationality and the Promotion System among Clerical Workers
D. T. H. Weir

This extract has been specially prepared for this volume and has
not previously been published in this form.

Many studies have shown that white-collar workers put a high
emphasis on 'security and a steady income' in assessing the factors which they consider to be important about a job. This
emphasis is quite compatible with the conventional view of the
clerk as a sober, steady and rather unimaginative kind of person.
It is a justifiable view too, for, historically, the greater safety of
the white-collar job compared to that of the manual worker
has been an important point in its favour, and has made it
relatively more attractive despite the fact that the manual worker
might enjoy higher earnings in the short-term in some jobs.

In discussing the findings of the Luton Study, Goldthorpe
considered the affluent manual workers '. . . not primarily as
members of a given industrial organization but rather . . . as
men who, in some more or less conscious way have "projects"
for themselves and their families which they seek to realize
through work in one form or another'. He used the term 'project'
to refer to 'some *chosen course of action* through which the
individual seeks to create for himself a new life situation'.

Is the comparable 'project' for the white-collar workers merely tied up with the search for security, then, or are his horizons more extensive? We need to examine the significance of expectations for upward mobility, for a 'career', and for promotion, to supervisory positions in the first instance and thus to 'management' levels, in order to make sense of the typical 'projects' of typical clerks. Such a progression involves greater rewards in terms not merely of pay and conditions of employment, but also in terms of the enhanced prestige which derives from occupying a position of authority and responsibility. Moreover, such a position of authority and responsibility may in itself be very attractive to the white-collar worker because it provides a source of satisfaction *intrinsic* to work itself. As well as these advantages, the man promoted to a management position tends to occupy a more privileged position in the community as a whole, and his general social status is thus higher.

All of this is obvious and, to a certain extent, trivial, but it appears both obvious and trivial because it forms part of a general typification of white-collar attitudes, of a general 'myth' of clerical behaviour. If we take him to be the modal lower-middle-class man, the white-collar worker, *par excellence*, should be the most enamoured of career goals, and the most likely to affiliate to the values which justify and support these goals, which are in general distinctively 'middle-class'. Central to this typification is the notion of the career progression of the individual through individualized stages.

Many commentators on the work situation of lower-middle-class white-collar workers have emphasized the crucial importance of 'promotion', both as subjectively perceived and as objectively experienced by individuals. Lockwood, for example, quotes Hilferding as arguing that 'the possibility of advancement [is] the basic factor making for the individualistic outlook of the blackcoated worker'. Lockwood's own analysis attaches much importance to the 'chances of rising to managerial, quasi-managerial, and supervisory positions'. This feature also distinguishes the *male* black-coated workers not only from wage-workers, but also from female clerks who tend to be employed in positions where the work is routine, and the possibility of promotion is slight. This is so, not merely because they are women, but also because *as women*, they have rather little chance of developing the skills and experience which would enable them to *qualify* as 'promotable'. They are never allowed therefore to emerge as potential promotees.

Sykes has argued that opportunities for promotion constitute a fundamental reason for what he calls the 'different industrial ethos' of clerks, as compared with manual workers. A similar point is made by the Luton team when they say of their sample of affluent manual workers, 'promotion is not automatically accepted as desirable, as with white-collar workers for whom a career is a moral expectation'. March and Simon, summarizing and reformulating the results of over 500 empirical studies of organizations, conclude that 'for a majority of blue-collar workers in most organizations promotional rewards are almost non-existent'.

Promotion, and the prospects of obtaining promotion, are thus important in three ways to the analysis of the work situation of clerks:

1. As aspects and reflections of social values which are in fact rather generally available in Western society, but are held to be most strongly internalized by white-collar workers because of their position in the middle of the class structure.

2. As aspects of the *market* situation of white-collar workers, and thus as a basis for a profound distinction between the market situation of the *clerk* and that of the industrial manual worker.

3. As aspects of the *normative* dimension of the work situation: they set bounds to expectations, channelling them, and preventing them becoming 'boundless', by institutionalizing precise and predictable criteria of 'success' and 'failure'. There is a more generalized effect as well in that it is the fact that, for the clerk, there exists a chance that he may be promoted to management level which influences his relationships, based on the extent and nature of his interaction with management as individuals. This could be put more briefly by saying that it is the possibility of entry to management, conceived of as a cadre, which is held to account for the development of mechanisms of anticipatory socialization to management as a class.

Thus 'promotion' is a concept which does not merely *describe* a certain sort of behaviour and certain specific events at the workplace; it is a concept which illuminates the unique position of the clerk in the class structure.

The analysis which follows is based on a study of white-collar workers undertaken in the Hull area between 1963 and 1968. In all, over 1,400 white-collar workers were interviewed, but the analysis of this paper is based on a group of 154 male clerks, aged between 22 and 49, all of whom were married. 98 of them were employed in private firms and 56 in organizations in the public sector.

One important factor is the state of the local labour market, both for manual and for white-collar jobs. Over the post-war period, during which our respondents had spent most of their working life, the employment situation in the Hull area was very different from that in Luton, the locale of the 'Affluent Worker' study. Unemployment, never as high as in the North-East or Scotland, was none the less above the national average and it could be argued that, for the average manual worker at least, this must have represented a constraint on his freedom to change jobs that warranted serious consideration. However, rather few of the white-collar workers in the sample did in fact experience unemployment during this period, and this is consistent with the low proportion of white-collar workers among the unemployed locally, according to figures provided by the Department of Employment.

These respondents are not 'wage-workers' in the commonly accepted sense either: they are not in Goldthorpe's terms 'men who have achieved their present affluent condition primarily through selling their labour power to the highest bidder'. Although in strict Marxist terms it may be possible to characterize the white-collar employees in Hull as 'wage-workers', the label seems to be a somewhat misleading one. All the workers in our sample were on a salaried rather than an hourly or weekly wage basis. All, moreover, enjoyed 'staff status'. (Wedderburn has shown how ubiquitous the phenomenon of staff status is, and how it provides a basis for discrimination between different categories of worker.) *All* of our respondents had protection from arbitrary and precipitate dismissal or changes in their work situation, and the construction of the sample ensured that those who were interviewed were drawn from a group who occupied an intermediate position in the structure of authority of the organization. The 'objective' basis for a threat to the job security of these white-collar workers did not therefore exist in the case of most *manual* workers as a matter of course, as an ever-present and real threat to their chances of retaining their jobs for as long as they want to hold them.

We asked respondents to narrow down their perspectives on security of employment in general, and to consider the situation in their own firm, by asking 'Would you say that your job was dead safe, fairly safe, rather insecure, or very insecure?'

Table 1. Perceptions of job security

% replying to the question 'Would you say your job was very safe . . . ?'

	Clerks in	
	Private industry	Public sector
Dead safe	34	84
Fairly safe	58	16
Rather insecure, very insecure, others, don't know etc.	8	0
	100	100

Clearly the clerks in private industry were rather less confident about their future than were those in the public service. This is to be expected of course, because, objectively, jobs in local government and the civil service, once attained, do have a high degree of security. Moreover, this was a question which might be expected to produce an unambiguous set of responses, in that job security was important and significant enough for respondents to have reasonably clear-cut views which could be fairly readily reported on. But when asked further why they considered their own job to be 'safe' or 'unsafe' the answers of respondents in these two categories illustrated rather different perspectives on the organization as a whole. For the clerks in private industry referred either to aspects of the market situation for the products manufactured and distributed by their firms or to the market situation more specifically in terms of their estimate of the probable demand for the skills they possessed, or the experience they had amassed. Respondents in the first category would say 'That depends on conditions in the industry', or 'That is outside the control of the firm, I'm sorry to say', 'This is a very unstable industry', 'The firm is not likely to go bankrupt, touch wood', or 'We have plenty of work: we are well established'. The second type of answer was in such terms as 'I have my qualifications, so I can go anywhere within reason', 'I have the seniority, so I wouldn't be the first to go', 'I feel I'm giving satisfaction, and as long as I do, I am all right'.

The public employees, however, did not tend to refer to the *market situation* from either an organizational or an individual perspective but instead related their discussion of job security to aspects of the structure of the organization or of public policy which were *predictable* and *understandable* to them, and to some extent *controllable* by them. Thus they tended to say 'If you keep to the rules, no one can touch you', 'With my seniority, I'm absolutely safe', 'I have passed my exams and have done as much or more as I could be expected to do'. The clerk in private industry, however, perceives that there is an uncertainty built into the structure of the situation which makes his future and his economic security not susceptible to rational prediction. Table 2 illustrates this. When he looks forward towards his organizational future he perceives only a 'wall of darkness'.

Table 2. Reasons for perceiving one's job as 'safe' or 'unsafe'

	Clerks in			
	Private industry		Public sector	
% of all those who rated their own job as 'safe' or as 'dead safe'				
Reasons related to:				
The structure of the organization	17		27	
The controllable behaviour of the individual	16		29	
All 'predictable'		(33)		(56)
The market situation faced by the individual	17		19	
The market situation faced by the organization	50		25	
All 'unpredictable'		(67)		(44)
	100	(100)	100	(100)

Neither of these types of response is akin to the simple 'fatalism' which Goldthorpe argues was the lot of the average industrial worker in the past, and which might be expected in an area without much experience of consistent prosperity. Nor are they clearly related to the market situation which obtains in the community *in general* or for white-collar workers in general. Rather they refer to particular aspects of the position and role occupied by specific types of clerical worker in a specific and limited market situation.

Overall, too, there were clear differences between the clerks in private firms and those employed in the public bureaucracies in terms of their attitudes to promotion. These are summarized in Table 3. Having noted these differences, we suggest that they are not of random nature, but are systematically related to the systems of promotion which obtain in these two types of organization.

The private clerks were more likely to feel that they would lose friends if they accepted a significant promotion, and less likely to feel that such a loss could be mediated by the operation of personality factors. It is possible also that the level of identification with the work-group and the satisfaction derived from work-group membership were higher among this group than among the public employees.

A significant difference between the two groups was demonstrated by the proportion of each who were undertaking training with a view to obtaining further qualifications, the public employees being more involved in these activities than the private. We agreed earlier that in the public bureaucracy training and qualifications were more important in their own right and as a means of establishing a claim on the organization for the individual to be recognized as worthy of promotion. *No such clearly visible connection between means and ends existed in the private firms and the motivation to undertake training was accordingly low.*

There was not such a strong difference between public and private clerks in their view of the promotion system as 'fair' or 'unfair', though the proportion considering it fair was slightly higher among the former. But the public clerks were markedly more optimistic about their expectations of upward mobility through the promotion system. Not merely did they expect to get further up the ladder but they were able to predict with more specificity precisely which position they expected to attain.

Although a majority of both groups felt that the holders of top positions in their organization had obtained them by means that were legitimate in terms of the core values of the organization, the minority that did not attribute legitimacy to this process was twice as large among the private as among the public clerks. Despite this, there was not as great a distinction between the two groups in their perception of the entitlement of the top people to hold their posts.

The public clerks were more likely to report that they felt 'part of management' than the private. But the largest difference between the two groups was in potential job security – 84 per cent of the public employees saying that their jobs were 'very safe' as against only 34 per cent of the private clerks. When elaborating on the reasons for this confidence in the security of their employment, the public clerks were more likely to refer to aspects of organization process which were accessible to them and over which they could, at least in principle, exercise some control, than they were to refer to the market situation facing the organization, or other 'uncontrollable' factors.

Another way of putting this distinction is suggested by March and Simon's analysis of the decisions about promotion systems that are made by an organization and that condition the employee's motivation to be involved in that organization. They argue that, if promotion depends on the attainment of some performance criterion, the weights assigned to the several factors which combine to constitute the performance criteria must include how the factors are to be measured. If the 'subjective operationality' of the performance measures is low, it will be difficult for the participant to obtain guidance as to the consequences attached to specific behaviour and to relate this behaviour to some perceived outcome. Thus they hypothesize that 'the greater the subjective operationality of criteria used in promotion decisions, the greater the effect of the promotion system on the perceived consequences of action'. This hypothesis is supported by the results of psychological studies of individual motivation and learning behaviour: thus 'most participants in an organization probably want to evaluate the success of their actions, and standards of success undoubtedly further both learning and satisfaction'.

In more straightforward terminology, no matter how strongly an organization pressurizes individuals towards promotion, they themselves will not necessarily feel highly motivated to do as the organization wants them to, unless they can see very clearly and precisely what is expected of them. They need not merely to want to be saved, but to know what to do in order to achieve salvation.

We would argue, then, that the subjective operationality of performance criteria and of promotion norms may be higher in the public bureaucracy than it is in the private enterprise firms. Thus, although the *desire* for promotion may be equally strongly held by participants in both kinds of organization, its translation into motives for action is conditioned by their perception of the performance and promotion criteria, and thus of the feasibility of their incorporation into strategies of effective action for the individual employee.

Table 3. Attitudes towards promotion of clerks in private industry and public sector

%	Clerks in Private industry	Public sector
Saying they would lose old friends by accepting promotion	39	22
Undertaking training	12	36
Saying promotion system fair	60	73
Expecting to get to top	26	57
Unable to specify how far they expected to get	29	16
Saying top people got there by illegitimate means	32	15
Saying top people entitled to their position	67	78
Identifying with management	29	46
Saying job very safe	34	84
Referring to predictable aspects of organization in explaining why job safe	33	56

It is probable that this is related to the greater predictability of events and the greater meaningfulness of action in what we conventionally regard as bureaucracies. But much sociological work has argued the opposite. For instance, Seeman discusses five aspects of alienation. These are 'meaninglessness, powerlessness, normlessness, isolation, and self-estrangement'. Blauner developed one of these themes arguing that 'bureaucratic structures seem to encourage feelings of meaninglessness. As division of labour increases in complexity in large-scale organizations, individual roles may seem to lack organic connection with the whole structure of roles, and the result is that the employee may lack understanding of the co-ordinated activity and a sense of purpose in his work'.

Mannheim distinguished between 'functional rationalization' and 'substantial rationality'. The former 'refers to the idea that in a modern organization everything is geared to the highest efficiency . . . the rationale of the technical and social organization is comprehended fully only by a few top managers, if indeed by anyone at all. . . . But along with the greater efficiency and rationality of the whole, the substantial rationality of the individuals who make up the system declines. The man who has a highly subdivided job in a complex factory and the clerk working in a huge government bureau need only know very limited tasks. They need not know anyone else's job and may not even know what happens in the departments of the organization next to them. They need not know how their own small task fits into the entire operation.'

The result of this process as far as the individual employee is concerned is, according to the Mannheim-Blauner analysis, a decline in the 'capacity to act intelligently in a given situation on the basis of one's own insight into the inter-relations of events'.

But the data we have presented do not seem to bear out this interpretation, rather the reverse. It is in the *more* bureaucratized organization that the most 'meaning' is apparent in the process of work and this is true of the operation of the promotion system as well. It was in the private organizations that the motivation to attend courses, undertake training and acquire qualifications was weakest, because there did not appear to be any predictable and regular connection between doing so, and the attainment of promotion.

Gouldner discusses a similar situation in the context of factory work. He points out that regarding factory workers' promotional opportunities and conditions of dismissal there is relatively little that is predictable. Gardner made a similar point when he concluded that 'channels of advancement are not clear, the how and the when of getting ahead are not defined. When they ask their boss how they can get ahead, he can only say that if they work hard, do a good job, behave themselves and learn about the work, eventually they will be given a chance at better jobs. He cannot say if they do this and this and this, they will be promoted at the end of so many months.'

We are arguing then that the clerk in private industry faces this sort of dilemma. He wishes to know 'the how and the when of getting ahead' and he needs a schedule of activities to perform ('. . . this and this and this . . .') and he needs a fairly definite expectation of 'how many months . . .' the process is expected to take. *Indeed his whole training and the requirements of his occupational role lead him to the belief that this is the correct and proper way for promotions to be organized.*

Crozier sees the search for security as being of pre-eminent significance in understanding the white-collar worker's involvement in the promotion system. The security may be obtained by means of either collective or individual action. The former is normally undertaken as a defensive tactic, such as, for instance, becoming a member of a trade union. The latter is a positive search for congruence within the individual's organizational identity, and is achieved by attempting to align one's organizational status with one's ambitions. The existence of incongruence between various aspects of an individual's organizational status is used by the individual as a lever for demanding congruence at a higher level; thus the individual tends to align himself with behaviour patterns he considers to be superior. But final congruence is unattainable, because aspirations enlarge as the individual becomes involved in interaction with representatives of not merely higher, but more disparate status levels. Thus the incongruence becomes a 'permanent stimulus for advancement and more active participation'. Successful playing of the promotion game generates a demand for more involvement in it.

We have argued that the white-collar worker perceives the promotion system in which he is involved as constituting not so much a set of external constraints upon his behaviour, but rather as providing the parameters within which he can consciously evolve a strategy for action, conceived in terms of some notions, not necessarily very long-term, of a career with an anchorage point at some place in the future. To this extent Crozier's analysis is compatible with the findings we have presented. But we would give more weight to the perceived aspects of organizational structure and in particular to its *comprehensibility* and *predictability* for the individual. It is these, we argue which are more clearly demonstrated by the organizations in the public sector and which are lacking in the private firms. Paradoxically, it is the ideology of individual achievement which is associated with organization structures which deny the individual the precise and operationizable knowledge about how he can achieve, and of what is to count as achievement. In March and Simon's terms, the *subjective operationality* is lower in the private firms. It is this which underlies the greater reluctance to engage in activities which to the outside observer would appear to offer some guarantee to the individual of emerging as 'promotable', such as undertaking training with a view to obtaining qualifications. There is a conflict, then, between the objective rationality and the subjective rationality of the clerk.

Subjective operationality is particularly associated with the much greater job security felt by the clerks in public organizations. They are secure in two ways. Firstly because the organization offers them security and a guaranteed safety of revenue. But they are secure too because they know, in precise and quantifiable terms, what course of action will give them the security of attaining a higher position. Their successful playing of the organizational promotion game, by obtaining qualifications, giving themselves a *claim* on the job they presently hold, and a springboard for advance to a higher one, reinforces this felt security.

They feel the loss of friends in the work-group less keenly than the private clerks, because their identification with the work-group is lower. This is because their felt job security is higher, so they need the work groups rather less as a means of social and psychic support and because they are more confident and more precise about their personal mobility prospects. This denial of the work group is associated with a tendency to identify with management.

The greater perceived meaningfulness of the organization structure leads to a tendency to perceive the organization as a legitimate structure of authority, and successful experience of following organizational prescriptions and meeting organizational demands tends to reinforce this perception of legitimacy. The incumbents of top positions in the organization are perceived as 'entitled' to their position, and this in turn strengthens the clerks' tendency to identify with management.

This analysis differs somewhat from those conventionally offered, in particular in its interpretation of the significance of the clerks' tendency to identify with management. We have treated this as a dependent, rather than an independent variable with respect to the clerk's perception of and experience within the system of promotion. So far from this factor exercising a crucial and *general* constraining influence on the clerical career, we argue that it is mediated quite significantly by aspects of organization structure, and in particular by the clerk's experience of meaningfulness and the subjective operationality of injunctions for individual action implied by the promotion system. Thus it is the clerks in the public sector organizations who tend to identify with management more; they perceive more clearly what they have to do to obtain promotion, and they are more confident of attaining top positions.

Dual-career Families

M. P. Fogarty, R. Rapoport and R. P. Rapoport

Reprinted with permission from *Sex, Career and the Family*,
P.E.P., 1971, pp. 336–9, 340–5, 378–80.

The pattern which has been traditional in our society since the
Industrial Revolution and earlier is neither universal nor inevitable. While men have tended everywhere and always to be
concerned with warfare and women with infant nurturance, this
is not absolutely inevitable. The legendary Amazons aside, one
finds among some of the 'developing' countries such phenomena
as women paratroopers and, in the most highly civilized societies,
men child welfare officers. In some societies women have held the
chief responsibility for finance in the family, as in the markets of
some African and South American countries. In some societies
it is the women who do the arduous physical labour, for example
the farming among the Alorese; indeed, where the couvade is
practised, women are found returning to their work in the fields
immediately following childbirth while the men take to their
hammocks to protect the newborn infant from evil spirits.

The degree to which the separation of work and family life
has been emphasized in our own society owes something to the
Protestant Ethic and the capitalist form of organization of
industry, though there are deep roots in the whole Judaeo-
Christian-Islamic tradition that emphasize the women's place
in the shelter of the home. The Industrial Revolution and the rise
of capitalism brought about a 'rationalization' of the workplace
through the separation of the fiscal affairs of the enterprise from
those of the family – allowing entrepreneurs to employ the most
competent help independently of familial obligations so as to be
better able to compete on the open market. Secondarily, humane
tendencies were operating to protect women from the odious
conditions of work that sometimes prevailed in the earlier industrial situations. As a consequence of this, a sharp division has
resulted between the domestic side of life, which is under the
guardianship of women, and the workplace, which is under the
control of men who funnel the economic benefits of productive
industry into the household. As the household shed its productive

functions and became a unit of consumption, the economic dependence of the women on their men became increasingly marked. Women's participation in work at these earlier stages reflected deficiencies in the male role in the family – as with widows, spinsters, divorcees, etc. More recently there are new trends at work associated with increased education and universal education for both sexes.

While the world as a whole has been moving towards a conception of family life which, in most cases, tends to produce something like the Western nuclear family, the situation in the Western countries is one of differentiation. As the nature of work changes and as men and women are exposed more equally to educational influences – with their value and skill components – a range of patterns emerges within the basic framework of the nuclear family. Women are beginning to articulate with the world of work as effectively as men – with the differences increasingly being due to differences in individual competence rather than to sex-linked stereo-typed conceptions of work capacity. With women's jobs ranging as variously as men's, an enormous spectrum of possible combinations is coming into being. Husband and wife may work together or separately; they may work at similar or different kinds of jobs; they may be commensurate or incommensurate in their earnings or fame or power; they may be similar or different in relation to the importance of work to them as individuals. Similarly, family considerations and participation may vary greatly for different men and women.

The place of the dual-career family

The dual-career family is a statistically minor variant. A recent survey of all English working women shows that even among the most highly qualified women there is a strong tendency to drop out of work at the time of having the first baby and not to return until many years later. Where the return is successfully negotiated, this becomes the 'in-out-in' pattern· referred to above. The length of the 'out' period varies greatly according to the size of the family and the environmental circumstances of the individual woman – as well as her personal level of ambition and her husband's attitudes, etc. The analyses presented above indicate how some of these variables operate in a sample of university graduates. Our reason for concentrating in this chapter on the small minority of 'dual-career' families, in which the woman maintains the involvement fairly continuously, is that it is disproportionately from within this group that the women with senior accomplishments and responsibilities are found. To the extent that this becomes a more important pattern in future, the small group now demonstrating this pattern may be thought of as 'pioneers', or as a 'creative minority'. These are not pioneers in the sense used earlier in describing women and their careers – of breaking new ground in professions previously closed to women. That battle has been nearly successfully concluded – or at least its end is in sight. Today's pioneers are the men and women who work out new patterns of relationships between work and family that will facilitate the wife's pursuit of an effective career if she wants this.

The life career of a highly qualified woman may be defined in critical path terms with various options available at different points. The life career as a whole is punctuated by critical transitions. Traversing them in a given way constitutes a career pathway. Regarding specifically the work-family aspects of the pathway, the following diagram presents a simplified version of some major options.

Underlying each choice of option is a motivational syndrome. One marries or does not marry according to one's motivation

FIGURE 1

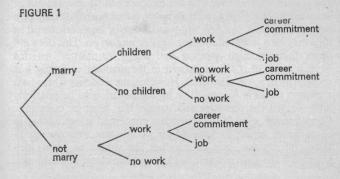

and circumstances. Our data provide much suggestive material about the single people (both men and women) that indicates the nature of some of these motivational syndromes. The same is true of the decision to have children. The culturally normal and statistically normal situation is to marry and have children, but important variant patterns exist. Similarly, the culturally normative pattern is for the man only to work, particularly in the period of early child-rearing. But here, as in the other variant patterns, important variations are seen and are becoming more prevalent. Indeed, it is one of our basic observations that in periods of social change, it is from among the variant patterns that the most creative innovations may be found. In relation to women's careers, the dual-career family pattern is in this category.

Aside from the motivational syndromes influencing the acceptance of some options and not others, consideration must be given to the consequences of having embarked on a given pathway, in terms of the satisfactions experienced by the person in the pattern. Thus, the person who decides to marry, have children and not work may either be a satisfied conventional housewife, or a dissatisfied 'captive housewife'. Similarly, not all the workers are happy in this situation. Two major orientations to work are contrasted – the 'career orientation', where work is highly important to the person and an organized developmental job sequence is sought, and the 'job-orientation' where work is engaged in for other reasons and without an organized sequence. The person who married and has children but who works out of economic necessity (e.g. with an improvident husband) may be a reluctant worker, the one who works out of boredom to fill in time may be a low commitment worker, and so on. This does not mean that the high aspiring and highly committed married women careerist – classic partner in the dual-career family – is necessarily happy and satisfied. However, the tendency where such a pattern exists is for the drive in this direction to be relatively high – given the obstacles and stresses that must be overcome. Consequently, even if the individual concerned is not willing to characterize herself as 'satisfied', it would seem from our qualitative information safe to say that she would be highly dissatisfied if she were not able to carry out her career commitment.

The dual-career families in the study

Intensive studies were made of the life careers, family backgrounds, marital relationships and patterns of working of 13 fully functioning dual-career families from a range of occupations. In addition, three families were studied in which the women, though highly qualified and formerly on the way to success in their professions, had decided to stop working for an indefinite period.

*   *   *

An overall picture of these couples can be obtained from the following general description of their family backgrounds and current attitudes:

These are families in which both husbands and wives value the possibility of the women continuing in their careers. They feel that various arrangements should be made, or at least the options provided, to facilitate this. The reasons for this kind of view tend to be multiple. Some men profess strong egalitarian values. Others, who are away from home frequently, prefer to know that their wives are feeling happy and fulfilled by working rather than being pent-up and lonely at home. Others like to share the financial burden and the higher level of income that this makes available to the family. Still others like to work with their wives, or at least to interact with them over work issues. They enjoy sharing the elements both of their domestic lives and of their intellectual or professional lives. The motivational syndromes underlying these attitudes are discussed in greater detail below.

The husband-wife relationship in the fully functioning dual-career families tends to be egalitarian, with a good deal of mutual accommodation. While there is wide variation in styles of relating, degree of closeness, volatility, tension and so on, the common factor to all the couples is that neither of the partners considers the relationship in a hierarchical framework – husband as the 'lord and master', and wife as chattel, to caricature the conventional attitude. This is a general trend in contemporary society and the dual-career families are not much distinguished from others in this respect.

The support provided for one another by the dual-career couple should not be idealized. There are many stresses and strains involved, ambivalence and undercutting, conflicts and so on. These are described in the next section. However, it should be stated at the outset that the balance in the families studied was positive; the benefits were perceived as outweighing the costs. Dual-career families that had broken up were not studied. Only families with an intact marriage as well as two careers were selected. No information is available about the relative incidence of broken homes among dual-career families and other kinds of families.

The overwhelming tendency – though not the universal feature – in these families is that both husband and wife value family life and children as well as involvement in careers. On the whole these people are very busy. They have to cut down, for the most part, on their formal leisure and community participation activities. These have to take place at weekends, and tend to be organized around household and children though, to different extents, friends and relatives play a part.

One of the striking features about child-rearing practices in the families studied is the degree to which the children are brought into their parents' lives and participate in many of the interests and concerns of the parents, becoming part of the egalitarian ethos of the families.

Analysis of important dimensions in the lives of the dual-career family

In analysing the ways in which the dual-career family 'works', i.e. how the couples have managed to accomplish what is for them a pattern of life consistent with their egalitarian ideals, various approaches could be used. The three approaches taken here reflect the concerns of the couples studied; they are also important in the analysis of trends of social change that are central to this study. The three dimensions discussed are:

a dilemmas confronted by the couples: the strains imposed by these dilemmas and how the couples manage them.

b motivational syndromes: the types of motives that seem to underlie a woman's desire to work and the likelihood of her husband making it possible or allowing it in the context of a continuing marital relationship.

c viability factors: the elements in the situation other than personal motives which make it possible for a woman to have a career and at the same time to reconcile it with family life – such factors as possibilities for organizing time schedules, making job demands flexible, and finding helpers or facilitators to enable the woman to involve herself in her career in spite of her handicaps (seen in terms both of stereotyped prejudices and of competing family demands).

DILEMMAS CONFRONTED BY THE COUPLES

There are many dilemmas that might be abstracted from the data. Indeed, it is obvious that in the lives of complex people living in complex metropolitan society, life is continually punctuated with dilemmas. However, five areas of dilemma are selected which seem to represent foci around which many of the important sources of strain cohere. These are not exhaustive but they cover a good deal of the ground, at least as experienced by the couples studied. The five foci are:

i. Dilemmas arising from sheer 'overload'.
ii. Dilemmas arising from experiencing in one's important environment strongly conflicting ideas and directions about what is considered right and proper in a given area of behaviour.
iii. Dilemmas arising from conflicts within oneself about whether one is being a good person (good human being, good wife and mother, good woman) in leading a certain type of existence.
iv. Dilemmas arising from conflicts in obligations, attachments, desires, and so on relative to one's network of relatives, friends and associates.
v. Dilemmas arising from the conflicts between roles that may be variable in their demands at different times – e.g. the marital role demands in relation to the work demands of each partner at different points in the life cycle.

Overload dilemmas

'It always seems to me as far as our own situation is concerned, that it is tremendously dependent on good health; this husband and wife team, and the survival of the pair with individual work potential, is almost entirely an energy thing. It may be that a lot of the fall-out (i.e. women dropping out) is actually physical . . . you do run out of steam. We know two couples – one of the children's teachers, both husband and wife teach and the children are about the same age as ours. It's extraordinary the energy pull of that family. I'm always amazed how they survive until the holidays. You can actually see them physically diminishing as the term runs on because it is so physically taxing.'

The old folk expression 'behind every successful man there is a woman' stands not only for a social psychological situation where the wife gives emotional support and advice, but also for a whole culture complex of activities and relationships within which the wife is a helpmeet – attending to the shopping, child rearing, housekeeping and general social tasks necessary to provide a smoothly operating base to which the male can retreat after the rigours of a day's work and from which he can sally forth refreshed and emotionally supported. One of the couples studied began the interview by reversing the expression, stating that 'behind every successful woman there is a man'. What they meant by this, however, was that the man encouraged his wife to face and cope with problems arising in her work, provided consultation on financial matters and co-operated in various ways. They did *not* mean to indicate that the husband gave the same sort of backing – through shopping, mending, cooking, child minding and so on that would be the obverse of the traditional picture. When only the man is following a career, it is usual for his wife to provide the domestic 'back up', but in a dual-career family there is not usually a total reversal of the traditional roles (though role reversals do exist). The most usual situation among the study couples where both husband and wife pursue careers is a rearrangement of the domestic side of their lives. Some of the household tasks are delegated to others and the remainder is reapportioned between husband, wife and children. In effect, each member of the couple both pursues a career and performs some household and child rearing activities. Among the couples studied, the overload experienced seems to have been a function of at least four factors.

a The degree to which having children and a family (as distinct from simply being married) *is salient*. With the exception of one of the couples studied, family life in general and rearing children in particular was highly salient. The couples were very concerned with the possible effects on their children of their both pursuing careers. This implied a limitation in the degree to which the couples were willing to delegate child care, even assuming the availability of satisfactory resources. Aside from the sheer number of things to be done by the conjugal pair who are both working and who, at the same time, value and enjoy interaction with their families, there is an element of psychic strain involved in allowing two major areas of life, so different in their demands and characteristics, to be highly important. The overload involved here, then, is not a simply arithmetical increase in the number of tasks to be accomplished, but is related to the duality of emotional commitment and concern, and is thus far more difficult to assess.

b The degree to which the couple aspire to a high standard of domestic living. Most of the couples aspired to a high standard of living, including a pleasant home and garden and high standards of decor, cleanliness, cooking and so on. This made the problem of managing the domestic side of their lives more complex, albeit by choice, than if they had kept to a lower standard. The notion of a lower maternal standard, though, is almost a contradiction in terms of the notion of career success, since a certain standard of life is implied in occupational achievement. The process in fact tends to become circular in that once a taste for high standards has been acquired, the impetus to continue working and career development is increased.

c The degree to which satisfactory arrangements for the re-apportionment of tasks is possible. Here we found various combinations of conjugal role reorganizations and delegations of parts of the domestic work to children and helpers of various kinds.

d The degree to which the sheer physical overload of tasks and their apportionment is adumbrated by a social-psychological overload which comes from struggling with the conflicts that are described in the issues that follow: normative conflict, sex role identity maintenance, network management and role-cycling. Couples vary enormously in the degree to which these other sources of tensions feed into the family system and the degree to which they can manage them once they are present.

For all the couples the overload issue was salient; they all emphasized the importance of physical health and energy as a prerequisite for making the dual career family a possibility. They regarded it as important for their children to be healthy too. Generally speaking there was little room for illness in the systems that were evolved. For example, Mr Y says: 'I don't think that we're particularly fit or anything, but we're never ill in any serious sense, and I think that we attach more importance to that one fact for our survival capacity than anything else.' To help them to deal with the overload issues, all of the dual-career families studied spent much thought and effort on arranging a system of domestic help. This problem can be seen as having two sides: the availability of different kinds of domestic helpers on the one hand and the preferences of the couples as to which elements of the domestic roles they wish to delegate.

*   *   *

VIABILITY FACTORS

What makes the dual-career family viable?

At the heart of the factors that make a dual-career family viable lie the motivational syndromes of both husband and wife, which we refer to as dual-salience. Work and family are important spheres of involvement, and for both husband and wife there is a will to find a pattern that will make it possible for each of them to enjoy involvement in these spheres. True, this is a matter of degree; there are families even in the dual-career situation where the husband tolerates rather than assists his wife in her drive towards combining both sets of activities, and there are other families in which a very actively helping, even pushing, husband presses the wife over a line of hesitancy in working out this pattern. These variations, however, fall within a more limited range than prevails in the population as a whole, where the man is expected to maximize his involvement in career and the woman in family – whatever residues of time and interest each may have in the sphere that is primarily salient for the other.

There are also some pre-conditions which must be present to make the pattern work – both in the personal motivational syndromes of the participants and in their external environment. The individuals concerned must have a relatively high energy level because so much of what is involved at the present time is contrary to custom and requires extra energy, and in addition there are too few supportive external institutions to help take up the slack. This means that if the pattern is to work, a great deal depends upon the individuals' sheer drive and persistence.

The issue of flexibility in the work and family situations was one which is much discussed by the study couples and various viewpoints were presented. One thing is clear as a *sine qua non*, and that is that there must be *some flexibility* in both the work and the family situation – ideally in co-ordination with one another. That is, when there are domestic crises, the work situation must be such as to allow the employed person a means of dealing with them. This is true for men as well as women, only more so for women at the present time because the assumption is that domestic crises are largely her responsibility. It is felt to be illusory however to assert that complete flexibility is the answer. Women, for example, who are artists, writers or architects and who work at home may find that their creativity and productiveness are inhibited because they are subject to continuous interruptions and do not have the supports of an external work situation. On the other hand, complete rigidity of the work environment is not conducive to the dual-career family situation – either for the man or the women – because in many of these instances the man covers whatever rigidities there may be in the woman's situation by coping himself with specific domestic crises. Many of the women in the study would like to see both an element of structure and an element of flexibility. When the work situation is structured, for example, one knows that the work is finished at 6 pm, and that there will not be a great deal of carry over into evenings and weekends. On the other hand some employers, recognizing that flexibility is of great assistance to women, have allowed the women to do the job in their own time according to their own hours, making it possible for them, for example, to be with their children in the afternoons. In such situations the danger is that the women will be loaded with impossible expectations because only a limited amount of energy, time, and so on is available for everything. The work may, under such circumstances, go uncompleted, and the employer may draw the erroneous conclusion that flexibility is a wrong idea. The point is, of course, that flexibility is not enough. There is an optimum combination of flexibility and structure – different for different occupations and for different family constellations – which makes the pattern viable.

Added to these factors there are a whole series of *coping mechanisms*, which individuals and couples develop apart from their personalities *per se* and their external situations which allow them to deal with the situations in which they find themselves. These are learned patterns of behaviour which make it possible for the couples so to organize their time, energy, finances and other resources that the kind of life they have chosen can be seen as feasible. In this sense the family-work situation may be viewed in a management framework. Some of the couples are better than others at, for instance, managing their resources, delegating housework (and office work), gathering necessary information and making decisions, and delineating issues and drawing boundaries about what is legitimate and possible by way of involvements.

Further Reading: Community and Role Conflict

E. BOTT, *Family and Social Network*, London, Tavistock, 1957.

M. P. FOGARTY, A. J. ALLEN, ISOBEL ALLEN and PATRICIA WALTERS, *Women in Top Jobs*, P.E.P., 1971.

*H. GAVRON, *The Captive Wife*, London, Penguin, 1968.

*E. GOFFMAN, *The Presentation of Self in Everyday Life*, New York, Doubleday, 1959.

P. HAMMOND, *Sociologists at Work*, New York, Basic Books, 1964 (especially article by Lipset).

S. M. LIPSET, M. A. TROW and J. S. COLEMAN, *Union Democracy*, Glencoe, Illinois, The Free Press, 1956.

*P. TOWNSEND, *The Family Life of Old People*, London, Penguin, 1963.

S. YUDKIN and A. HOLME, *Working Mothers and their Children*, London, Michael Joseph, 1963.

* Available in paperback

Chapter Six

The Process of Work 3: Ideology and Attitudes

Surely there never was such fragile chinaware as that of which the millers of Coketown were made . . . they were ruined when inspectors considered it doubtful whether they were quite justified in chopping people up with their machinery.

Charles Dickens, Hard Times

An individual may bring many expectations to his work role, and however these expectations may turn out to be falsified by the subsequent events of his occupational and organizational experience there comes, for most individuals, a point at which we may justly say of them and they may equally accept that they have 'become' in some way the person that their occupational and organizational roles define them to be. Most doctors *do* behave in most of the relevant respects like medically trained, qualified practitioners *and* most garage mechanics do wear overalls and pour lubricants into the recesses of motor car engines. And to each occupational role some characteristic pattern of belief pertains.

Since the initial work of Goldthorpe in 1966 and the subsequent attempt at a formalization of 'action theory' by Silverman, the concept of workers' orientation to the situation has become widely used in studies of industrial and other workers. The study by Beynon and Blackburn, referred to in Further Reading, considers groups of workers who '. . . worked in the same environment, subject to the same management, and with the same conditions of service, including systems of payment and fringe benefits, social facilities and so on'. Also there was only one union to represent them and a system of joint consultation which applied to the whole factory. But individual workers understood their work situations differently and likewise their own position in it.

Objectively, the main differences between groups of workers

were between men and women, day-shift and night-shift and full-time and part-time workers. Not all of the possible combinations of these distinctions occurred because night-shift work was reserved for men over 21 and part-time work was for women. But these objective, structural features of the work situation were important bases for the differentiation of workers' attitudes as well as behaviour. The groups also tended to differ in the social characteristics which they brought in to work, and in particular according to their position in the family.

Nichols studied the views of sixty-five directors and senior managers in fifteen large companies in a northern city. He asked those respondents to tell him whether they agreed or disagreed with a series of statements about business and the role of the businessman with particular reference to four key areas of business activity. These were redundancy, the purpose and goals of industrial companies, giving information to employees, and the role of the businessman in public life. These statements were not taken at random but were drawn from three broad conceptions about the role of business and of businessmen to which it was expected the respondents would subscribe.

These key areas were 'laisser-faire', 'long-term company interest' and 'social responsibility'. However, although these distinctions were analytically possible, they appeared somewhat less clear cut in practice. Certainly few businessmen favoured the laisser-faire ideology. But what was more interesting was that many respondents did not see a consistent distinction between the ideals of social responsibility and those of long-term company interest. As Nichols concludes 'socially responsible' policies were in keeping with the pursuit of the company's long-term interests and the pursuit of the company's long-term interests was in keeping with implementing management's 'social responsibilities'. The conflict which exists logically, on paper, between these philosophies, and existed in the way in which the researcher structured his questions did not seem to exist in the minds of the businessmen of 'Northern City'.

The navvies who are the subject of Sykes' paper were characteristically hostile to their employer, although, unusually among lower-paid manual workers, their sentiments were not expressed in terms of collective action. They sought to *evade* rather than to *oppose* the employer. A high value was set on individual independence and on the evasion of obligations to others. This set of attitudes also enables one to see why workers who had stayed with one employer for a long period of time tended to be rather looked down on, and in some cases discriminated against in the allocation of jobs. The prevailing ethos among the navvies was that such men had been 'bought' and become 'bosses' men'. Sometimes men in a stable work situation would deliberately leave – create an instability in their own lives – in order to avoid such an accusation.

Although discrimination is based on more than the mere tendency to be prejudiced towards a member of another group, or towards one who does not conform to one's own values, in some cases there *is* a clear connection.

There have been many studies of the assimilation of coloured workers, immigrants and native British, in the community, while many researchers have concentrated on integration in terms of housing and education, but there have been rather fewer studies of coloured workers in British industry. Wright's account is both illuminating and rather salutory. He points out that many British workers initially structure the coloured worker as a 'stranger', as one who is in but not one of the host community. He is therefore a prime target of suspicion, because even his attempts to conform to what he believes or perceives to be the local norm only serve to persuade the in-group of native British workers that he is 'trying to be something he isn't' and *is for that reason also* untrustworthy. Schutz and Simmel both analyse the peculiar role of the stranger in works listed under Further Reading at the end of this chapter.

Wright's study also illustrates the generally low level of information about coloured people, for instance the belief that English is 'not really the West Indian's native language'. Again there is a tendency to believe that coloured workers are *intrinsically* inferior in their capacity to do a job, or even '. . . a bit like little kids'. It may be encouraging or it may be pathetic to see Wright's comment that '. . . the interviews with West Indian workers suggest that relations with white workers were much closer and more friendly than appeared to be the case with British respondents, both managers and workers'. But Wright's conclusion is a damning one: 'the evidence of the present research . . . suggests that if the coloured immigrant does not have a status in the British hierarchy, it is because he is unwilling to accept the one available for him, that of a coloured man who "knows" he is coloured and is willing to accept a lower status role'.

Seear's analysis of the position of women in industry which we referred to in the introduction to the last chapter may be compared not too disingenuously with that of the coloured worker. For, like him, there is a status available for her . . . if she wants to take it. But now women are no longer prepared to accept a male-dominated society's low evaluation of their contribution to the economy, no longer able to stomach the statistical function that the work of a housewife, because 'unpaid' is not really 'work' at all. Seear concludes that 'a change in public opinion is an essential condition if any real advance is to be made'.

Others would argue that major structural reversals must precede such changes of opinion, however widespread.

Business Ideology in Northern City

W. A. T. Nichols

Reprinted with permission from *Ownership, Control and Ideology*,
George Allen and Unwin, 1969, pp. 166–70, 179–82.

Three hypothetical ideologies

The data collected in Northern City refers to the views of sixty-
five directors and senior managers in fifteen of its largest companies. In order to gain some knowledge of the value structure
and frames of reference of these directors we took a series of
statements about business and the role of the businessman which
had particular reference to four topics. The topics presented were
concerned with,.

(a) redundancy (Group A)
(b) the purpose and goals of industrial companies (Group B)
(c) giving information to employees (Group C); and
(d) the role of the businessman in public life (Group D)

Each of the three statements within each group was designed
to fit in with one of three broad conceptions about the role of
business and the businessman. We termed these '*laisser-faire*',
'long-term-company-interest' and 'social responsibility'. For
heuristic purposes it was hypothesized that any one businessman
would make all four of his choices in line with one, and only
one, of these 'ideological sets'. For example, it was predicted that
if he chose the *laisser-faire* item in Group A, then he would
proceed to choose similar items in the other three groups.

The salient differences between these three ideological sets
may be put as follows. The *laisser-faire* set is conformable
to what Sutton *et al.* and other writers have referred to as the
'classical' ideology. It expressed the view that businessmen are
primarily concerned with economic matters and that consideration
of ethical issues and social consequences should be outside the
ambit of policy making. Both the Long-Term-Company-Interest
and the Social Responsibility sets differ from the Laisser-Faire
items in this respect. They both emphasize that the businessman
must be directly concerned with the social consequences of his
actions.

The difference between the LTCI and SR views is mainly one

of motive. Thus, the distinction between them does not rest upon whether apparently socially responsible behaviour is favoured but upon the motives which lead to its acceptance. The SR set embodies a specifically moral element in the sense that the businessman is depicted as choosing between alternative policies on the basis of *ethical* rather than *practical* (i.e. predominately economic) considerations. The LTCI set, on the other hand, puts the view that policy formulation should take account of social and other aspects of the problem because this is the *practical* thing to do.

At this point, perhaps, it would be prudent to enter a disclaimer. It is quite clear that any social scientist who concerns himself with the ethics of others is likely to find himself on shifting sand. But unless one takes the view that morality is the manifestation of divine intervention or guidance there seems no good reason why we should not investigate its relation to alleged or actual changes in the structure of industry and society. This is all that we intend to do in our attempt to distinguish between the LTCI and SR ideologies. Thus, even though we have couched the SR statements in 'moral' terms we do not wish to imply that they are any more, or less, 'moral' than other statements. Nor do we wish to imply that the choices with which we confronted businessmen are the only possible ones.

Quite the contrary to this, it is our intention to attempt to assess whether, in fact, Northern City directors will accept the choices we offer them, which ones they will opt for and with which degree of consistency. If there is no clear pattern of choice, or if choices are made inconsistently (i.e. if they are split between the three ideological sets), this will tell us something about the ideology of contemporary directors. In particular, we hope that it will tell us something about what social responsibility means to businessmen and whether in fact their views are conformable with the expectations of some of the writers whose work we reviewed in Part I [not reprinted here]. The imputation of moral choice is implicit in some of their work (e.g. Berle) and one of our objectives is to enquire into the businessman's perception of this choice.

Before we proceed to consider the results of this study there is one further and related preliminary point which we must make. This is that there are certain values implicit in some of the items – e.g. some of them even contain the word 'moral'. As a consequence of this some care had to be taken to avoid the inference, in other items, that those who agreed with them might, so to speak, be 'beating their employees'. This was a major problem with the LF items which we have attempted to 'soften' by including certain escape clauses. Thus we have included phrases about 'the country's economic position', suggested that redundancy is 'simply a risk which all those in industry have to bear', that employees 'do not want' information, and that 'a manager has work enough to do'. Similar clauses have been incorporated into the LTCI items. However, we think it doubtful that they invalidate the items used. It is the essence of an ideology that it is made up of just such statements.

The general orientation which we attempted to build into each ideological set is presented below:

Laisser-faire. Managers should not concern themselves with social and moral consequences: if they did, the result would be economic disaster for us all. The manager's place is with his firm, and he's enough work to do there without becoming a leading figure in the community. Business exists for one purpose only, to satisfy a need at a profit. Unemployment is a risk we all live with but it's no part of management's responsibility to make provision to safeguard their employees. Nor is it desirable to provide employees with company information; they don't want it and its circulation might injure the company.

Long-term-company-interest. It's true that profit is the one absolute in business and it's a good thing for the nation that this is so. But in its own interest every firm must gain the sympathetic understanding and co-operation of all concerned. This means that the public must accept us as thinking people. We should try to bring this about by taking every opportunity to put our views across. It also means that we should convince the worker that we are concerned for his welfare and make him feel secure so that he will work better. This can be done by some form of redundancy provision, and also by providing him with information. Giving information to employees can make them feel an important part of the team and make their co-operation more likely.

Social responsibility. A business conducted solely for the profit of shareholders is unethical. The firm is a social institution and its management is an arbiter with responsibilities to serve the social and economic needs of employees, customers, shareholders and the local and national communities. In the case of the community, both the firm and its senior executives have a duty to make what contribution they can to public life. Similarly, management has a moral responsibility to safeguard workers from redundancy and to provide them with full information about their own and their company's position.

The predominant types of choice

The results gained from the forced choice questionnaire demonstrate one fact quite clearly. This is that, at least in Northern City, very few businessmen favoured the LF or 'classical' ideology. Only 27, or 10 per cent of the possible total of 260 choices (65 subjects with four choices each), were made in favour

Table 1. The distribution of choices between the three ideological sets

Ideological set	% of choices	No. of choices
LF	10·4	27
LTCI	57·3	149
SR	32·3	84
	100	260

of the LF items. Furthermore, as can be seen in Table 1 , there is little evidence to indicate that this was because a majority of businessmen chose the SR items. In fact only 32 per cent of choices were made in this way and the majority, 57 per cent, were made for the LTCI items. .

*　　　*　　　*

Given these results there is some evidence to indicate that the general value orientation of these directors was much closer to that presented by the items in the LTCI set than in either the SR or LF.

*　　　*　　　*

This question of the extent to which the LTCI or SR sets of items were each regarded by directors as mutually exclusive alternatives is of some significance for any assessment of managerial theory. As we saw in Part I there is a division within managerialism as a whole between those we termed sectional and nonsectional managerialists. And if the latter are to be regarded as the representative of a reasonably distinct variant of managerial theory it must be admitted that one of their distinctive characteristics is that they impute an ethical choice to the businessman.

They imply that he does recognize a choice between acting in terms of the values presented in the LTCI and SR sets of items and that he formulates his policies in accordance with the criteria associated with the latter. Quite clearly we cannot 'prove' or 'disprove' such assumptions in a study of this kind.

*   *   *

It was quite common for the interviewer to be greeted with some such phrase as 'you know this is all very interesting, I've never thought about things like this before' and far from being mere pleasantries, such remarks were often substantiated by the ensuing conversation. Directors often had difficulty in seeing any difference between the LTCI and SR statements and some of their reasons for opting for SR items were more closely related to the 'letter' than the 'spirit' of the statements concerned.

Table 2. Distribution of choices by subject group

| Ideological set | Subject group | | | |
	A (Redundancy)	B (Purpose)	C (Information)	D (Public life)
LF	10	0	4	13
LTCI	30	52	53	14
SR	25	13	8	38
Total no. of choices	65	65	65	65

Thus, we find that those subject groups in which SR items were most likely to be chosen were A and D. *Prima facie*, this might be taken to indicate that businessmen believed that managements had a 'moral responsibility' to make provision for redundant workers – as opposed to believing that such provision was desirable on the 'practical' grounds that 'the secure contented employee . . . will work better' – and that they believed it was 'the duty' of senior executives to fulfil their business's social responsibilities by contributing their skills and knowledge to community life – as opposed to believing that it was desirable to be publicly active on the 'practical' grounds that this would improve the public image of their business. However, a closer look at the items concerned suggests that such an interpretation is not the only possible one. Neither of the SR items concerned

(A3 and D2) constitute simple statements which the respondent could accept or reject: both of them are 'double-barrelled'.

The most obvious case of this is D2 which posits (*a*) that 'every business has a social responsibility to the community' and (*b*) that 'it is the duty of senior executives to fulfil this by contributing their skills and knowledge to public life'. We were aware of the nature of this item at the pilot stage: we retained it because it seemed an admirable tool by which to assess how far the individual businessman felt obligated to the corporation in his non-work activities and social life. However, the double-barrelled nature of item A3 was not apparent to us at the pilot stage. Yet this item did appear to consist of two discrete propositions in the eyes of many businessmen.

Thus although all 25 of those who opted for this item quite clearly believed that 'management has a moral responsibility *to guard against redundancy*', 17 of them said they had chosen this item because – unlike A1 – it did not necessarily imply 'some form of redundancy *payment*'. To complicate matters still further it should be noted that of the 30 who opted for A1 none came from companies which had any established form of redundancy payment system for (manual) workers. The view generally expressed about redundancy provision for workers was that 'it will come' and except for Zed's directors, and one other, we met no strong feeling that the interviewee's own company should have taken the initiative and already introduced such a scheme.

It would seem, then, that the differences we built into the three ideological sets were not always readily perceived by businessmen and that the reasons underlying the choice of SR items in the two groups from which they were chosen most often (A and D), were, to say the least, not always the expected ones.

As we have already pointed out, the perceived 'distance' between the LF and the LTCI or SR sets was much greater than that between the LTCI and SR ones. Businessmen generally had no problems at all about recognizing that the LF statements were radically different. Some made the comment that a particular LF item was 'pure laisser-faire', or 'real nineteenth-century stuff'. When it came to justifying the choices made between the LTCI and SR items, however, no such clear distinction was evident. This perhaps is best illustrated by a brief reference to the case of U-Products.

U-Products is the regional branch of one of the largest British companies. Furthermore, it is one of those companies which has sometimes been cited as an example of the 'managerial revolution' – and indeed of the emergence of a social responsibility ethic. Only one of the six businessmen we interviewed in this firm was a main board director but all of them had worked in the company's other offices and factories and in some cases had done so overseas. In this sense, then, they could well be described as 'managerial spiralists'.

We found that the directors of U-Products were second only to those of Zed Ltd in their choice of SR items. There can be no doubt that the actual phrase 'social responsibility' was part of their vocabulary before we met them. Nor can there be any doubt that they were sincere in their belief that U-Products was a socially responsible company. It is thus worthy of our attention that with the exception of one man (perhaps significantly an ex-trade union official) their conception of social responsibility differed radically from that held at Zed.

As far as we could judge they had generally chosen the social responsibility items because they believed themselves and their company to be socially responsible but – and this would seem to be of the utmost importance – they did not think in terms of a distinction between (*a*) policies designed to serve the long-term interests of the company and (*b*) policies which are formulated on the basis of an ethical framework. As far as they were concerned SR was in no way an *ethical* alternative to LTCI policies. For them, *'socially responsible' policies were in keeping with the pursuit of the company's long-term interests and the pursuit of the company's long-term interests was in keeping with implementing management's social responsibilities.*

Work Attitudes of Navvies
A. J. M. Sykes

Reprinted with permission from *Sociology*, Vol. 3, 1969, pp. 21–34.

This paper describes a participant-observer study carried out in 1953 on a hydroelectric construction site in the north of Scotland. The purpose was to study patterns of group behaviour among the navvies in order to compare them with those found in printing and other industries previously studied. It was found that the patterns of group behaviour among the navvies were unusually weak and ill-defined. In the other industries studied the workers showed attitudes of hostility to their employers whom they opposed by means of collective action. Cohesive work groups were formed and *group* rather than *individual* responses to the work situation was cultivated. The navvies showed similar attitudes of hostility but they sought to *evade* rather than to *oppose* the employer. A high value was set on individual independence and on the evasion of obligations to others. This led very weak work groups and to an emphasis upon an individual rather than a group response to aspects of the work situation.

The author lived for five weeks in a camp in Northern Scotland at a site for the construction of a hydro-electric generating station. The period of observation was brought to an end by an accident which led to a week's hospitalization in Inverness – also among navvies. As navvies are intensely suspicious of outsiders, participant observation seemed the only way by which an effective study could be made. To check on the representativeness of the author's observations in the one camp, he made frequent visits during the study to the bars in two adjacent camps belonging to other firms. Later a series of interviews, both formal and informal, were held with navvies, trade union officials and engineers with experience in the civil engineering industry: these were held in Glasgow and Edinburgh, the navvies being mostly men in transit through Glasgow. Finally, the results of study were checked against published accounts of the industry. These other sources of information suggest that the attitudes and ethos found in the camp studied were widely held throughout the industry.

The camp had a labour force of 208 men, excluding foremen and office staff, at the commencement of the research; during the next five weeks, 44 men left and 69 others were taken on. The management regarded this turnover rate over this period as normal. Most of the men in the camp had worked at several other sites during the previous twelve months, some boasted that they had worked on as many as twenty sites in the period. This high labour turnover indicates that the men in the camp did not form an isolated group that could have developed attitudes and an ethos peculiar to itself. As so many of the men were constantly changing their place of employment the ethos and attitudes they displayed could not have been learned in any one camp but must have been acquired within the industry at large.

The camp was composed of wooden army type huts and included an office building and accommodation for office workers and camp staff; these were separated by a cook house and canteen from the part in which the men lived. Here there were huts for the navvies, a sick-bay, a store and post office, and a bar. The bar sold only beer for in such camps the sale of spirits is believed to lead to too much fighting and disorder. The men were accommodated in large huts, each holding twenty-two beds; some huts were divided into cubicles for two men: these forms of accommodation cost 10s and 15s respectively. Only a few of the charge-hands and tradesmen used the cubicles; the men expressed a preference for the social life of the undivided huts. The canteen provided three meals a day for a total sum of £2 10s per week. The standard of food and accommodation could be summed up as 'rough'. Apart from the bar and the sleeping huts there was nowhere a man could go after work. There were two similar camps within three miles but the nearest village was ten miles away and was visited only at weekends. This meant that the social life of the camp centred on the huts and constant visiting went on between them.

Of the 208 men employed on the site 87 were Scots, 108 Irish, 12 Poles, and there was one Spaniard. Included in the total were 34 tradesmen; 23 Scots, and 11 Irish. Of the non-tradesmen, the Irish worked mainly in the various navvy gangs which were overwhelmingly Irish in composition. The Scots provided a large majority of the skilled men such as joiners, electricians, and fitters; and workers in the semi-skilled jobs such as steel-benders and fixers, lorry drivers and storemen; and also provided the cooks, sick-bay orderly, and keepers of the camp shop and bar. The camp office staff was entirely Scots. The Scots who came from distant parts of the country were mostly joiners, steel-benders and fixers; they were distinct from the local Scots who provided some of the joiners and lorry drivers and a few labourers.

The Irish came almost entirely from Donegal. There is a long tradition of Donegal men working in Scotland. With the exception of the eleven who were tradesmen (all joiners) they could all be described as peasants. Most of them were the sons of small farmers and several had farms of their own which were not able to support them without other work. The local Scotsmen were of rather similar background, being mainly crofters or labourers; men who before the advent of the hydro-electric scheme had mixed labouring on farms in summer with fishing with the trawling fleet or labouring on public works in winter. In addition there were a few labourers of Irish descent from Glasgow. The Scots tradesmen were of two kinds, country joiners from the locality and from other parts of the Highlands and North-East coast, and joiners and other tradesmen from the Glasgow and Edinburgh area.

The work was hard and frequently dangerous. It consisted of concreting a tunnel from a dam about a mile above the camp, building an inlet to the tunnel, and concreting another tunnel on the other side of the valley. Working conditions were very rough indeed and not at all comparable with those to be found in manufacturing industry or even on building sites. The hours of work were twelve a day in weekdays, nine on Saturdays and Sundays. The only opportunities for relaxation occurred after work at the weekends. The men preferred the long hours because they meant more pay and, as they put it, 'What the hell is there to do here except work?'

Attitudes to employers

The navvies in the camp displayed attitudes of hostility towards the employers in the industry generally. In comparing them (and they frequently did) the men made certain differentiations: all were regarded as bad employers but some ran better, or worse, camps than others in respect of the quality of food and living accommodation. The employer in this particular camp was regarded as average, neither particularly good nor particularly bad. All the employers in the industry were regarded as being entirely ruthless, holding their workers in contempt and having not the slightest interest in their welfare. The interviews that were held with management, staff, and trade union officials confirmed that these attitudes are general within the industry. The management and staff interviewed, both in this camp and elsewhere, made no attempt to hide their contempt; in more than one interview they referred to the men as 'animals' and the kindest estimates of them placed them as people outside society. Neither side expected any consideration from the other, or gave it. The navvies in discussing the industry constantly used such phrases as: 'it's every man for himself'; 'you've got to be able to look after yourself'; 'you get no quarter in this game'. At the same time the men made it clear that this was the way they preferred it; although they grumbled about conditions they showed no interest at all in the possibilities of improving them or of establishing better relations with the employer. Both sides took a pride in the toughness and brutality of the industry, as one manager summed it up: 'this is a hard life and we are tough'. Among the men there was a pride in the fact that they were under no obligation to the employer and as a result they were free and independent or, as they put it, 'we owe him nothing'.

The relationship between the men and their employers can be illustrated by describing the situation regarding industrial accidents. The work in itself was dangerous and was made more so by the disregard of safety precautions by both management and men. The men complained that in all sites the management were careless about safety and would sack any man who wasted time by following even rudimentary safety procedures. But the men on the site (and, according to the trade union officials, the men on most sites) were themselves extremely careless about safety. The men claimed accidents were due to the negligence of the employer, who would accuse the person injured of negligence, refuse to pay compensation, and immediately sack all witnesses of the accident. The men often discussed such accidents and described cases to each other at length. It was accepted that the management would take no interest in safety but would cheat a man, or his widow, out of compensation if possible: 'they'll spend a hundred pounds on lawyers before they'll give you a penny of compensation'. The navvies regarded accidents as a lottery, a form of gambling. Minor accidents occurred daily and were ignored, but a serious accident set off a contest between the injured individual and the employer. If the employer won, the man got little or nothing; if the man won, by exaggerating his injuries and the employer's negligence, he secured excessive compensation. The men would discuss with glee how particular individuals had 'done the firm'. For example, they told how a man recently killed had been drunk at the time but they had kept this information from the employer who had compensated the widow. The men told various stories about men who had simulated crippling injuries and in consequence received vast sums in compensation – sums far greater than any Scottish court would have paid for such injuries.

When the writer was injured he was warmly congratulated on his luck, and advised on how to 'play it up'. Men who had never spoken to him before came up and said: 'you've a good one there; don't let them beat you down, get a good lawyer'; 'watch them, don't take a thing until they settle'; 'be careful, don't do a stroke of work until it's all settled'. Discussion as to what the accident would be worth and what was the best way to handle it was general for some time. In hospital injured navvies discussed at length what had happened to them and what they intended to claim, detailing how they intended to exaggerate their injuries. The general attitude to an accident was summed up perfectly by one who said; 'It's like drawing a horse in the Irish Sweep, now you have to try and get him placed'. The situation undoubtedly appealed to the men: while they disliked the employer and resented the way in which they were treated they enjoyed pitting their wits against him, or seeing other men do so. A man who won gained great credit for being 'fly' or 'long-headed'; if he lost he was written off as stupid or 'soft'. The credit of having beaten the employer seemed to be as important as the money to be gained. The men showed equal hostility and distrust towards the management and staff within the camp. Although there was little direct contact the men were completely convinced that the management and the office staff, both separately and in collusion, were out to cheat them. The men claimed that the hydro-board paid a subsistence allowance which was being embezzled by the office staff who were also cheating them over their pay allowances and food. The general situation was summed up as, 'They are all bloody rogues.'

In most industries hostility towards the employer is expressed through collective action. Navvies are an exception. Each navvy tries to be as independent as possible and to avoid being obliged to any one employer. This attitude was continually expressed in their everyday behaviour, most notably in respect of their willingness to leave any particular job. Thus the navvies stated that it was contemptible for a man to 'belong' to any one employer. To call a man by an employer's name, 'A Wimpey's man', 'A Costain's man', 'A Carmichael's man', etc., was regarded as an insult. Men who had been in the camp for more than a few weeks were liable to be 'kidded' mercilessly for *belonging* to the employer. The father and son in the writer's hut had been in the camp for nearly two years, and the other men were constantly joking about this. For example, a man at one end of the hut would shout to someone at the other end: 'did you ever hear tell of the man who stayed with X for two years', to this the other would pretend incredulity and shout back, 'you're codding, no one ever stayed six months with X, it's a bloody impossibility'. Variations on this theme were played out almost every evening. Another man in the hut who was similarly teased one evening for having been in the camp nearly a year became very upset and left the next day. In conversation, the navvies referred to men who had been in the camp any length of time as 'men who have to buy their jobs'. It was assumed that only bad workers who had to 'buy a job' and who could not get a job on their merits would stay with one employer. To stay constantly with the one employer was contemptible, something that only a cripple or a poor worker would do, no 'decent' man would do it. Men who were attached to a particular firm were also referred to as 'boss's men'. This is a term common enough in other industries for people who are on the boss's 'side' as opposed to the men's 'side', but the navvies used it of any man who, by staying with one particular employer, acknowledged him as his 'boss'. The other navvies were quick to point out that they acknowledged no boss; they came and went as they liked and never stayed long enough with any one employer for him to become their boss. Zweig, discussing labour in building and civil engineering, makes a similar point: 'The casual labour is really employed by the industry as such, not by an individual employer. They stand in no personal relationship to a particular employer and have no loyalty to him, more often following the foreman.'

The navvies emphasized their independence of the employer by constantly *jacking* or threatening to *jack*. To *jack* means to put in one's notice and leave: it has been used in this sense in the industry for at least sixty years. The term implies more immediate action than is conveyed by the normal industrial expressions of 'putting in your notice', or 'asking for your cards'. The conditions of employment in the industry require two hours notice of termination on either side, so when a navvy talks of jacking he implies a sudden decision translated into immediate action. Zweig says of this two hours notice: 'When I questioned a Trade Union official about this state of affairs, the answer was that the men in Civil Engineering prefer that sort of termination because it gives them a greater sense of freedom.' This 'greater sense of freedom' is the reason for the stress men put upon jacking. His ability to leave any time, suddenly and on the merest whim, gives a man a feeling of freedom and independence. The navvies were constantly talking of jacking, and boasting of how they jacked from previous jobs. If a man did not like the way the work was going, or the way the foreman spoke to him, or his food, or even if the weather was depressing, he would threaten to jack. Men not only talked of leaving but implemented their

threats at any hour of the day. There was little doubt, judging by
the men's boasting, that the less the reason for jacking and the
more sudden the decision to jack, the more effective it was as a
demonstration of independence. Some of them said: 'If the mood
comes over me I just up and go'; 'If I don't like something I
don't mess about, just up and off, that's me'; and, 'If I suddenly
fancy a change, it's down the road, couldn't stay another minute,
get my pay and off, nothing could hold me'. It is possible that
some of the jacking observed in the camp was premeditated, but
all departures were made with dramatic suddenness and at odd
hours of the day as though completely spontaneous – for example,
a man got up at the end of the morning tea break, said 'I'm off
boys', and walked away.

Jacking suddenly and for little or no reason was regarded as a
demonstration of freedom and independence of the employer.
Men who did not jack and who could not boast of having jacked
from other camps were held in contempt. That navvies were
constantly trying to impress each other in this way there was no
doubt; apart from the constant boasting when the men did jack,
they did so as dramatically as possible. In no case did a man
disappear quietly without announcing that he was going. Although
the men occasionally tried to gain prestige for themselves by
jacking they also seemed to get a genuine feeling of freedom
from such behaviour. In conversation they often referred to the
need to feel free, of hating to be tied down or of 'belonging', and
of 'the feeling they own you' that comes after staying a spell with
one employer. Such statements were made openly to other men
during general conversations and were accepted as commonplace
sentiments which any navvy would share. When men were asked
why they moved so much, why they didn't stay on a good job,
or in a good camp when they found one, the answer that was
given time after time was that they had to be free, that they
couldn't bear to be tied down, that they had to keep their
independence. Thus it would seem that the basic attitudes of the
men to their employers were of hostility to employers generally
and of independence of any particular employer.

Attitudes to trade unions

The only substantial group of trade unionists were the joiners
(carpenters). They were all members of the Amalgamated Society
of Woodworkers or its Irish equivalent, and they were careful
to check that every new joiner who came to the camp had a

union card. It was in their interest to ensure: (a) that they were paid the official tradesman's rate as joiners; (b) that no one was employed as a joiner unless he could prove he had served an apprenticeship to the trade and was a member of the union; (c) that non-tradesmen did not do skilled work. The first two of these objectives was easily achieved as the company employed only union men and paid union rates. The third was more difficult and it meant that the individual joiners had to maintain a constant check on the labourers to ensure that they did not 'handle tools'. Trade union meetings were not held; now and again one of the joiners would complain that it was time they held a meeting but nothing ever came of it. It appeared that they had held one meeting to check union cards some months earlier but, despite the turnover of labour, had held no meetings since. According to the joiners, meetings were equally rare in other camps. As far as they were concerned the chief importance of the union was that it guaranteed their status as joiners; for this purpose alone membership of the union was vital to them.

The labourers in the camp were not members of any union. Many of them claimed to have been members of the Transport and General Workers Union in other camps and admitted that it had done much good in these camps in improving conditions. Nevertheless, they showed little interest in trade unionism. They would join a union if membership was a condition of employment on a particular job but they would drop out of it as soon as they could. Although the men talked incessantly about the work, about the various jobs and camps, they were never heard to mention trade unionism. When they were questioned directly on the subject three points emerged. The first was that they distrusted trade unions just as they distrusted the management and the employers. The situation as they saw it could be summed up in the view that everyone looks after his own interests, and that anyone who is in a position to do so seeks 'to do the puir oul navvy'. Trade union officials were thought to be 'doing well out of it'; to be playing some elaborate game with the employer, and to be uninterested in the welfare of the men. The idea that union officials might be genuinely concerned with their members' interests rather than their own, was regarded as naive. The members might get something out of membership but this could only be an accidental by-product. The second point was closely connected to the first. The navvies stated that every man ought to be able to look after himself and his interests without help from anyone.

In consequence none of them was willing to admit that he needed help from a trade union or any other body or person. Several of the navvies asserted this angrily. Belonging to a trade union temporarily on one particular job they thought harmless. Belonging to a trade union *permanently* was much the same as belonging to an employer: both are states of dependence which no real man could accept. The third point was that when there is a trade union in a camp 'they are always trying to make you do things'. A trade union, like the employers, tries to impose a degree of discipline upon the navvies and this is bitterly resented. Several of the navvies told stories of how unions had tried to enforce various rules and working practices on them; this was regarded as an unwarranted interference with their freedom. In short, the navvies regarded trade unions not as *their own* organizations but as external bodies membership of which was incompatible with their independence as individuals.

Attitudes to work

The navvies worked hard even when unsupervised, and there was no question of restricting output. One never heard complaints about men working too hard. To be known as a hard worker was something to be proud of. Men who worked hard were praised, while poor workers were regarded with contempt. Workers in other industries which the writer has studied – e.g. steel, engineering, printing, and car manufacture – also showed approval of good workers, condemnation of bad ones, but less strongly than the navvies. Workers in the other industries tended to qualify their approval of the good workers by stressing that men should not work too hard lest rates be cut or men be paid off. Among the navvies every man was free to work as hard as he liked and to earn as much as he could. There was little pride in skill, but considerable pride in the ability to work long and hard in bad conditions. The navvies boasted among themselves of the feats of hard work they had achieved or seen others achieve. The younger ones frequently tried to show off by emulating such feats and by competing against each other at work. For example, one young navvy after much boasting worked three successive twelve hour shifts – a straight thirty-six hours without a break. Financially he gained nothing as he spent the next two days in bed, but the feat aroused much interest in the camp and added greatly to his reputation as a worker. On another occasion a squad of four men did a job of moving equipment that was supposed to require ten men and then boasted loudly about it for the rest of the week. The older men sometimes grumbled that such feats were dangerous and upset the whole pattern of work; nevertheless, they would praise any young man who did achieve some feat and would circulate the story round the camp. It was noticeable too, that dodging work was strongly disapproved of; men who tried to avoid work were 'latchicoes', layabouts, and were told so quite brutally.

Such feats were performed for fame and brought no extra payment. But even where extra earnings were involved the same degree of individual freedom applied. Thus men commonly asked for extra shifts and worked them to make more money; this elicited no comment from the other workers. A typical example occurred when the joiners found that on a particular job two out of three joiners had left; the remaining joiner, with the help of a labourer, had taken over the work of all three and was being paid a bonus by the company. The joiners held a meeting and instructed their card steward to check that the labourer was not 'using tools', that is working as a joiner. When they were reassured that the labourer was restricted to unskilled work and did not handle any of the craftsman's tools the joiners made no further objection. Among themselves they commented that the joiner would 'kill himself' and speculated as to how long he would last. There was speculation about the size of the bonus he was paid and discussion by individuals about how much they would want to do the job, yet no one suggested that this behaviour was wrong, 'greedy', or was depriving other men of work.

The navvies' high valuation of individual work ability precluded any collective action to limit production or impose uniformity of earnings. Ability was also valued because it gives a man independence. For, as they put it, 'a good man can get a job anywhere', 'a good worker doesn't need to give a damn for anybody', 'a good worker can go anywhere'. A man can jack freely only if he knows that he will readily get another job, and the ease with which he can get another job depends in turn upon his ability as a worker.

Attitudes to supervision

The attitudes the men showed towards supervision and through this to any externally imposed discipline, were somewhat contradictory. On the one hand they behaved as though they were terrified of the various foremen and would rush about in a panic when one came near them. They did not take a great deal of notice of the leading hands or junior foremen who worked with them but the advent of any of the staff foremen would create a great panic. This was hardly surprising since the behaviour of the foremen was highly dramatic. On every occasion on which a senior foreman appeared – which might be several times in the day – he would attempt to arrive unexpectedly by elaborately stalking from behind the available cover. As the men kept a careful lookout and went to considerable trouble to warn all other squads in the vicinity, these attempts were often unsuccessful. When a foreman came, his invariable practice was to stand quietly for two or three minutes looking at what was going on, and then to explode into action, shouting and cursing that the men were doing nothing, that what they were doing was wrong, that they should stop everything they were doing at once and do something else, or do the same thing in a different way. The chargehand and anyone in the immediate vicinity would get the worst of this. The men would rush about with the chargehand in the lead doing what the foreman wanted, but the moment he had gone and it was signalled he was out of the area they would pause, curse the foreman, and go back to what they were doing before. The foremen's performance was stylized, was taken for granted by the men and had no apparent effect on their work. According to the men it was the normal behaviour to be expected of any foreman on any site; it was what foremen were employed for. One evening in the bar a navvy was heard giving an imitation of a foreman: 'Do you know why a foreman always wears a cap? Wait now till I tell you. What does he do when he comes to a job? He looks at it, then he takes his cap off, throws it on the ground, jumps on it with both feet and shouts "Jesus bloody Christ! That's not what I told yees to do!" I tell you he couldn't do the job without a bloody cap. A foreman without a cap would be like a bull without balls.'

Allowing for some slight exaggeration, this was the foreman's function as the navvies saw it, and it fitted the observations made on the site admirably. In the main the men accepted the aimless bullying without protest as being part of the job, although several of the Scottish workers who had experience in other industries – coal-mining, building and engineering – claimed that they were shocked by the foremen's behaviour and that they had never seen anything like it in other industries. They also claimed that workers in other industries they had experienced would not

tolerate such behaviour. All the author's own industrial experience would go to confirm this. However, this was only one
side of the picture. The other side was that at any time a man
harassed by a foreman might turn on him and abuse him back.
This never led to the dismissal of the man concerned – on only
one such occasion was a man even threatened with dismissal.
Usually, the foreman would just walk away, or laugh and try
to make a joke of the incident, or even try to placate the man
concerned. On some occasions a navvy would become sulky
and say he was going to jack, that he could go anywhere and
wasn't going to stay there and have his work questioned. Where
the navvy concerned was a good worker the foreman would try
to talk him round. The relationship was paradoxical; the behaviour of the foremen was apparently traditional but tempered
by the men's unconcern about getting the sack and the foremen's
desire not to lose good workers.

The navvies' response to supervision was individualistic. They
would warn each other of the movements of the individual foremen and 'covered up' for each other as much as possible, but this
was the limit of collective action. The men grumbled but never
made any collective protest against a foreman or against anything he said or did. On one occasion an old – sixty years old –
navvy was sacked apparently just because he was old. This aroused
a great deal of indignation among the men generally but no
protest was made; some men who claimed to be 'sickened' by the
affair threatened to leave but no one mentioned the possibility
of a collective protest. Apparently none of the navvies in the
camp had been involved in or had even heard of any collective
protest against an unpopular foreman or against any aspect of
discipline that they found objectionable.

The work depended very much on the skill and self-discipline
of the individual navvy. The amount of real direction and supervision that came from the management and foremen was minimal.
The men had a rough idea of what was needed and got on with
it. If totally unsupervised they would sneak the odd five minute
break, but by and large they worked steadily and if an individual
tried to slack he was abused by the others until he did his share.
Work was not precisely allocated; each individual member of a
squad made his own decision as to what was needed. The charge-
hands or foremen rarely tried to allocate jobs; if asked for a job
they were usually nonplussed, and would tell the enquirer to look
around and see what needed doing and 'not waste his bloody time

asking daft questions'. The foreman of one squad was constantly giving orders and advice but no one paid any attention to him nor, apparently, did he expect them to. The navvies clearly accepted the general discipline enforced by the work; they were willing to work hard but they expected to be left alone. Occasional abuse from a foreman was expected but close supervision was strongly disliked; when exchanging notes about other sites, the men would condemn those where the work was highly organized and closely supervised.

Attitudes to pay

The navvies constantly discussed pay and compared the various construction sites in terms of pay. As the rates paid were standardized, comparisons were made in terms of hours per week or in terms of bonus schemes. In the camp studied the hours paid were 91½ per week, made up of twelve hours per day for five days at standard rate, nine hours on Saturday at time and a half, and nine hours on Sunday at double time. For these hours a labourer earned £14 14s a week, a joiner £17 (the study was carried out in 1953 when the weekly earnings of an adult male in manufacturing industry averaged only £9 11s 11d). New men joining the camp gave information on the circumstances at other sites and rumours were constantly sweeping through the camp that employers on other construction sites were offering 96, 100 or, in one case, 108 hours per week, while rumours about the bonus paid at various camps put it as high as £10 per week. Such rumours were everyday gossip in the camps; some men would believe them and talk of moving on to these sites, others would dismiss them as nonsense but all were distinctly interested in the prospects of higher earnings. It was accepted by both men and management that if the number of hours paid fell appreciably – below eighty hours a week was the figure usually quoted – then most of the men would leave and new men would not be attracted to the site. When a camp was opened very long hours were offered to attract men, and when the job neared completion the staff was run down by reducing the number of hours per week. Apart from a few of the older men, the navvies in the camp studied were constantly complaining that the hours were too short; they did all they could to get extra overtime and 'ghosters' (twenty-four-hour shifts occasionally put on for some special purpose). Men frequently grumbled about the working and living conditions but always justified their staying in the industry in terms of the high wages.

They showed a very accurate knowledge of what could be earned in various unskilled jobs in different parts of Britain.

The navvies' interest in high earnings was pursued individually. They did not concern themselves with the way in which the rates for the industry were arrived at, or with the part played by the trade unions in increasing them. They showed no interest at all in collective action to increase rates generally or to secure better rates on a particular job. On the site studied, navvies grumbled that some men were paid a subsistence allowance while others were not, that some men got 'concrete money' and others did not. If a man felt he wasn't getting what he was entitled to, he left. This individualistic outlook dominated all questions of pay. If men wanted more money then they sought it by going to the sites that offered longer hours or bonus earnings. In some cases they sought it by getting better paid jobs on the same site. Some of the men had worked in camps where the trade unions had organized the men and had improved pay and conditions. When questioned, they would mention this but the idea of collective action still did not interest them.

The question arises: why were the men so keen on high earnings? There appeared to be two different reasons: high saving and high consumption. As many of the navvies pointed out, there was no other occupation in which an unskilled man could earn and save so much money; several of the low-spenders were known to be saving and many more claimed to be about to give up heavy drinking in order to save. Among the Scotsmen three were saving in order to get married and gave this as their reason for being in the camp. Two other men claimed to be saving in order to go into business for themselves. Among the Irishmen several were known to be saving to buy or extend a farm, or to buy equipment for it; one man had recently bought a tractor out of his earnings. Information was easy enough to come by as the navvies were intensely curious, had an accurate idea of how much other men were spending or saving, and, in the case of the Irishmen, usually had information on each other's home background and circumstances. It was clear that the men who were genuinely saving were but a tiny minority of those in the camp. Attitudes to these men varied: some were admired, others despised as being miserly, but in all cases they were regarded as being unusual, as only temporarily in the industry, and therefore not accepted as *real* navvies.

The other reason for seeking high wages was the customary

pattern of expenditure. The men always spoke of themselves as being very poor, and, in spite of the high earnings in the industry, navvies traditionally have regarded themselves as among the very poor. At the same time, the navvies boasted a great deal about how heavily they spent money, in particular on drink. Many claimed that they had to work in civil engineering as the earnings in other industries were too low and, so they claimed, they couldn't live on 'the pay they would get'. Three of the Scots joiners said that they could get 'good money' on building sites in the city, but that the opportunities for drinking were so frequent that they never had any money. Several of the labourers also said that they did not like to work where the facilities for drinking were too convenient. One evening there was a long discussion on the subject of earnings occasioned by a young Irishman, new to the industry, who announced that he couldn't stand the work any longer and was going off to Glasgow for a job. A group of half a dozen men formed round his bed and, helped by most of the men in the hut, they all tried to persuade him not to leave the industry. The one argument they all used was that he would not be able to live in Glasgow: 'All you can make is £10 to £12 a week, you just couldn't live on it.' There was little doubt that the men genuinely believed that one could not live properly on wages of under £12 a week.

A rough estimate of what the men spent was made on the basis of the cost of food and lodgings in the camp, £3 per week, and the weekly sales of beer and tobacco in the camp bar and shop, which averaged £3 per man per week. To this has to be added the substantial but incalculable amounts spent on extra food (for nearly all the men bought extra food), the heavy drinking outside the camp at weekends, the cost of clothing, and the amounts spent on gambling of all kinds from cards to football pools. No real figures for overall expenditure could be built up but it was clear that after taxation and sending something home to the wife or parents, there was nothing to spare. The men openly admitted that they were grossly self-indulgent and constantly talked of 'reforming'. Such confessions were but part of the boasting which was a favourite pastime. Men were frequently heard protesting that 'they couldn't stay off the drink', or of losing some large sum (a hundred pounds was often mentioned) in a single night's gambling. The research took place shortly after the summer holiday and men were still boasting to each other that they had been drunk for a fortnight, that they had gone home with large sums of pay, bonus, holiday money, etc., and that they were 'broke' before the end of the holiday. The Irishmen told each other stories of navvies they knew who had stayed in the local pub for days on end buying drink for everyone until the money ran out. Although the men could be very sceptical about each other on occasion, such stories were accepted at face value and never questioned even in the teller's absence. The navvies liked to think of themselves as 'wild men', completely reckless about money, complaining 'no matter how much I earn I never have a penny; I can't keep money, it just slips through my fingers'. A minority of the men had to get 'subs' from their wages every week to pay for their day to day expenditure and several were known to be in debt.

Conclusions

The navvies show attitudes of hostility to the employer. This is common enough, but other industrial workers who display such attitudes usually *oppose* the employer and do so by *collective* action. The navvies do not oppose but try, individually, to evade a relationship with the employer and to preserve their independence of him. The reasons for this appear to lie in the conditions of the industry – both historically and at the present day. Civil Engineering employers retain – and have always retained – only very small permanent staffs, recruiting men when needed and paying them off when a job is completed. In consequence the navvies' lot has always been one of casual employment. This makes organized opposition – or any other relationship – to the employer very difficult, particularly since there has usually been a plentiful supply of unskilled labour on which the employer could draw. On the other hand conditions make it possible for navvies to evade a permanent relationship with any one employer and to maintain individual independence of him: being unskilled, navvies have no status to lose by moving to other work and being mobile they can travel anywhere there is work available. Hence they respond to the employer by individual evasion rather than by collective opposition. This individual response, and the like interest and social value arising from it, dominates the navvies' attitudes and behaviour towards the other major aspects of life in the industry. Thus they reject trade unionism because of its essentially collective approach; stress individual ability as a worker and reject any collective restriction of effort; accept the need for severe self-discipline at work, resent supervision, and react to excessive supervision by leaving individually rather than by collective protest; they are very interested in maximizing their earnings but do so entirely by individual means and do not combine for collective action to increase earnings.

The Coloured Worker in British Industry
P. L. Wright

Reprinted with permission from *The Coloured Worker in British Industry*, The Institute of Race Relations, Oxford University Press, 1968, pp. 188–99.

More important than beliefs concerning particular values seems to have been the image of the coloured man as a stranger – someone unacquainted with British norms and values in general. This seems to have been at the root of much of the initial resistance to coloured workers reported in several firms.

'We had quite a lot of difficulty getting coloured workers accepted at first. At that time it was something new. . . . It was just the fact that they were a different nationality.' (Shop steward, Major Castings Ltd)

'In the early days, there was a certain amount of natural resentment at the chargehand level. This was probably just because they were different. Over time, particularly when they got to know them as individuals, this began to break down.' (Personnel Officer, Leigham Cannery)

'When the blacks first came, they [the white workers] were afraid of them. There wasn't any trouble between them, but they were afraid of them – some of them were hot-heads.' (White worker, Steel Bars Ltd)

'Actually, when they first came, I didn't fancy the idea, but it's turned out all right. It was just that strangeness you know.' (White worker, Pentland Alloys Ltd)

As we have already noted, and as the above examples indicate, this initial resistance to coloured workers tended to diminish in time. The white workers became accustomed to the coloured immigrants, sufficiently at least to accept them as workers, and in some cases friendships developed. The last respondent above, for example, in spite of his initial misgivings over the employment of coloured workers, said of his West Indian mate during the interview: 'He's one of the nicest personalities I've ever met. He takes everything in his stride. You can't help but like him.' More often, however, the white workers' image of the coloured immigrant as a stranger seems to have inhibited the growth of close social relationships.

This was particularly so in the case of Asian workers, where the desire to maintain social distance was often attributed directly to cultural differences in cultural background.

'It's not a matter of colour – it's their way of life.' (White worker, Omega Metals Ltd, with respect to Pakistanis)

'Myself, I can tolerate them, but I can't be friendly towards them. If you're friendly they take advantage of the fact. If they would change their ways and habits, there would be no difference.' (Chargehand, Edge Tools Ltd, with respect to Indians and Pakistanis)

'They're different. They had different habits, different religion, different hygiene.' (Shop steward, Major Castings Ltd with respect to Pakistanis)

West Indians, on the other hand, tended to be regarded as being less different from British people and therefore easier to get on with and easier to understand, both in terms of language and motivation. This seems to have been the main reason for the somewhat higher level of social acceptance of West Indians noted above.

'I would rather have the Jamaican. He has the same way of life. He eats the same way as you do. He speaks the same language. When in Rome do as the Romans do – if you want to get on with him.' (White worker, Omega Metals Ltd)

'They're too sly and oily for me. You can see it when they look at you, in their eyes. It isn't the Jamaicans I'm against – there are some decent chaps amongst the Jamaicans – it's these Indians.' (White worker, Edge Tools Ltd)

'West Indians are all right – they do know our language. I would prefer them to Arabs or Pakistanis. The West Indians, they understand. The Arabs and Pakistanis, maybe they understand – when they want to. They're not out in the open like the West Indians.' (White worker, Leigham Cannery)

'The Jamaicans seem to be the easiest going. Some Pakistanis seem a bit moody.' (White worker, Leigham Cannery)

Nevertheless, there was still a tendency for West Indians to be regarded as being, to some extent at least, strangers. A supervisor in Omega Metals Ltd, for example, stated that he preferred West Indians because their way of life was more similar to his own *up to a point*. In Pentland Alloys Ltd a white worker spoke of some West Indians appearing to have come 'straight from the jungle'. He stated:

'They come over here with remarkable ideas. One of them was a voodoo worshipper – he went off the rails eventually. . . . One thing I get on to them about is the way that they jabber when they get excited. I have to tell them to slow down so that I can understand what they're talking about.'

Another white worker, in Leigham Cannery, was under the impression that English was not the West Indians' native language. He thought that they were taught it in the schools. Similarly two West Indians in Hamilton Engineering Co. commented, somewhat ruefully, that some English people were surprised that they could speak English so well.

Apart from the fact that white workers tended to regard coloured immigrants as being strangers, however, there is also evidence to suggest that they regarded them as being of lower status. One indication is the greater reluctance to accept coloured workers in the higher status jobs and particularly as supervisors. Another is the reluctance, noted in Drop Forgings Ltd, to work for a firm which has acquired the reputation of being a coloured works. A third is to be found in a report of one of the questionnaire firms that 'The white workers expect higher earnings than the coloured man despite the fact that they may be doing the same job.'

Furthermore, there was a tendency among white workers to regard themselves as being better workmen than the coloured immigrants. Among the twenty-five white workers interviewed, twelve thought that coloured workers were slower to learn than British workers, eighteen that they showed little initiative, ten that they were less intelligent than British workers, and sixteen that they required more supervision. After the first eleven interviews, a further question was asked regarding the skill level of coloured workers. Ten respondents stated that they were less skilled than British workers, three that they were 'about the same' and one gave a non-committal answer.

This is not to say that these respondents had a uniformly low opinion of coloured immigrants as workmen. There was a considerable range of opinion and some of the answers were quite favourable. Nevertheless, all but two of the twenty-five respondents stated that coloured workers were inferior to white workers in at least one of the factors we have considered – skill, speed of learning, initiative, intelligence, and supervisory requirements – and none said that they were superior.

Some further comments made during the interviews also suggested that the white workers felt that they had superior status.

'These blokes here, cheap labour that's all it is. They have a low standard of living in their own country. . . . The boss would like to bring us down to their level if he could.' (Omega Metals Ltd)

'Some of the coloured workers on night duty work very hard. Mind you, when you've finished, they're only doing woman's work. Women do their jobs in the day time.' (Leigham Cannery)

'I don't think a white man would come and do the kind of jobs they get. . . . There isn't so many white labourers now; they are mainly black men.' (Hamilton Engineering Co.)

'Some of the Arabs are pretty docile – a bit like little kids.' (Steel Bars Ltd)

'You've got to use your patience to teach them because coming to work over here must be a terrible jolt to these kids.' (Pentland Alloys Ltd)

However, it is not sufficient merely to show that the white workers believed that coloured immigrants were of a lower social status, we must also demonstrate that these beliefs affected the level of social acceptance. The evidence here is mainly of an indirect nature. Banton suggested that British people were not sure of the correct norms of conduct concerning coloured immigrants, mainly because the latter refused to enter into relationships in the role of a social inferior. There were several indications in the present research that the white workers experienced some difficulty in achieving a pattern of behaviour in relation to coloured immigrants which was acceptable to both parties.

In Major Castings Ltd a shop steward stated: 'I've always found it best to lean over backwards to be fair. They've had preferential treatment. We have always been very careful not to give them the chance to claim they they were not getting fair treatment because of their colour.'

Similarly, in Torrington Cutlers, the Works Director said of the white workers: 'They will sometimes be particularly nice to the coloured workers. More so than they would be to their own colleagues under the same circumstances. . . . This would appear to be a special attempt not to be condescending to the coloured people.'

In the same firm a white worker stated: 'We always have the difficulty that when we try to tell them anything, they think we are trying to impose on them. . . . The chap in our department has come with a chip on his shoulder. His attitude is that, when we are trying to teach him anything, we are trying to take advantage of him.'

Nevertheless, the respondent stated that, in a way, he got on very well with the coloured worker concerned. 'He resents being pushed around, but looks upon me as a father confessor in a way. Anything he doesn't understand, he'll come and ask me.'

This suggests that as long as the coloured worker was prepared to accept the role of a social inferior, asking for advice, he was accepted, but resentment arose when he refused to accept this kind of relationship. Further evidence to this effect was found in other firms. In Precision Engineers Ltd, it was stated that West Indians were very popular because they could be kidded, for instance, on how many wives or children they had, the coloured workers accepting such kidding with good humour. However, the fact that West Indians were sometimes able to buy a car (a symbol of status) by clubbing together, caused resentment among the white workers who could not afford one. In one of the questionnaire firms, where Indian workers were not socially accepted, it was said that resentment arose because they 'aped superiority' over the white workers. On the other hand, in Steel Bars Ltd, where the Arab workers were accepted socially, a white worker stated: 'I'll say this for them; if you do them an act of kindness of any kind, they do appreciate it.'

Finally, there were two cases in which white respondents were very favourably disposed towards particular coloured workers because they accepted the role of a coloured man. In Pentland Alloys Ltd a white worker stated:

'We have had incidents – one in particular is very touchy – if you snap at them, they say it's because they're coloured. My mate knows he's coloured. We had seen something on television about coloured Americans, and he said, "Well, I'm a coloured Englishman", and I said "Of course you are." . . . He's a great kid, my mate, but we've had some funny ones. He doesn't interfere. I like him.'

And in Sovereign Steel Works a foreman stated with respect to a Somali: 'You couldn't hope to meet a nicer bloke. We know 80 per cent of them's no good, but he's a real good bloke. One thing about him, he *knows* he's coloured. You can say to him: "Why don't you come in early one morning and we'll take a scrubbing brush and see if it will come off," and he sees the joke and laughs with you.'

Thus far, we have been concerned mainly with the attitudes of the white workers. As the above examples indicate, however, the attitudes of the coloured workers are also of vital importance in determining the pattern of inter-group relations at work. In the questionnaire survey respondents were asked whether the coloured workers showed willingness to mix socially with white workers or seemed to prefer to keep to themselves. The answers obtained are presented in Table 1.

Table 1. Coloured workers' orientations towards social relationships with white workers

	No. of firms replying for each group	No. stating prefer to keep to themselves	%
West Indians	36	24	67
Indians	13	10	77
Africans	11	9	82
Arabs	12	11	92
Pakistanis	31	29	94

In one firm, employing West Indians, Arabs, and Pakistanis, the following additional comment was made: 'Socially, the coloured workers tend to keep to themselves. This is in no way as a result of a "cold shoulder" by the whites, and is more a voluntary situation. In other words, segregation is as much the choice of the coloureds as the whites. We have a social club, membership of which is open to all employees, coloured and white, but the coloured population are not interested.'

It will be noted, however, that in general the tendency to remain in separate social groups was more marked in the case of Asian workers, particularly Pakistanis. The main reason for this would seem to be radical cultural differences between Asian and British workers. Of primary importance, of course, is the language barrier; the Asian workers do not speak English as their native language and relatively few have learned it. Nevertheless, this does not provide the whole explanation. Unlike the West Indians, Asian workers have their own distinct culture with customs, habits, and religious beliefs which differ markedly from those of the British workers. In the firms studied during the present research, Asian workers were in general willing to make only those adjustments to the British way of life which were necessary in order to achieve a minimum degree of integration into the work organization. Apart from this, they retained as many of their own cultural traits as possible and therefore tended to remain in their own social groups where little or no adaptation to British ways would be required. In two firms, for example, the Asian workers' eating habits led to voluntary segregation at meal times. The situation in Bradfield Foundry has already been described in the introduction to the present chapter. [not reprinted here] Similarly, in Omega Metals Ltd, the British workers and the one West Indian employed by the firm ate in the works canteen whereas the Pakistanis remained on the shop-floor and 'ate curry out of pans with chapatis'.

In the latter firm, there were also indications that the Pakistanis kept apart from the white workers as a means of avoiding friction. When asked how the British and the Pakistani workers got on together, the Pakistani chargehand stated that they were, '. . . not friendly, but not unfriendly. They [the Pakistanis] can't speak English so nobody quarrels. They don't argue, they just keep working.'

The greater willingness of the West Indians to mix socially may be attributed to the fact that, not only is their cultural background more similar to that of the white workers, but also, due to the 'mother country' image of Britain in the West Indies, they are much more willing to seek full acceptance into British society. Nevertheless, the fact remains that in a high proportion of firms, they tended to remain in their own social groups. Part of the explanation may be that, although there were no radical cultural differences, as in the case of Asian workers, there still existed differences in interests and topics of conversation sufficient to make the West Indians feel more at ease in the company of their fellow countrymen. One white worker stated that West Indians remained in their own social groups because they had 'their own things to talk about' and another stated: 'It's just the ordinary talk of everyday things they can't get into.' It is quite possible, of course, that the white workers merely assumed that the West Indians had different interests and therefore made no effort to associate with them. However, a similar point was made by a West Indian in Torrington Cutler who stated: 'I've got on all right with white workers because I like sports – football, racing, cricket – so we talk about it. But if I didn't have this, I wouldn't get on so well.'

On the other hand, it would seem that the West Indians' tendency to remain with their own social groups resulted, to some extent at least, from the lack of social acceptance on the part of the white workers. When asked why the coloured workers tended to keep to themselves, a white worker in Quality Steel Co. stated: 'It's not language – Jamaicans speak good English. There's some of them think and others know that they are not wanted here.' Similarly, in Sovereign Steel Works, the Personnel Manager stated:

'You tend to see them sitting having a meal in a corner rather than mixing in a group. They tend to have a chip on their shoulder. . . . There is a tendency to carry a constant concern about their relations with white people and it will be many years before they lose this. They carry their own colour bar about with them and tend to view our approaches a little suspiciously. They tend to meet people who do not treat them well – the odd one or two – so you can't blame them.'

In its extreme form, this attitude was rarely encountered among the West Indians interviewed during the present research. In only two cases was any marked resentment of white workers expressed. In Torrington Cutlers a West Indian worker stated:

'I'll tell you one thing I don't like. The reason why some of us have a chip on our shoulder is because people say: "Why you come here?" They think that we come here to steal their jobs. But the world owes everyone a living. If they came to Jamaica we would welcome them. We would not ask why they come.'

And in Omega Metals Ltd a West Indian was extremely bitter about his relations with white workers. He stated: 'Well I'll be frank with you . . . you get some of them – they're educated, but they're ignorant – they've got a chip on their shoulder. In the canteen the other day, one of them said: "If there was another war, I bet you would go back to Jamaica." I said, yes I would. If you live in a country, you ought to fight for it, but what's the point if you are just a "wog" or a "black" after the fighting has finished. The way things are going, if you were in the trenches, one of them would kill you instead of the enemy.'

However, twenty-six of the twenty-seven West Indians interviewed, including the first respondent above, stated that they got on all right with the British workers. Sixteen respondents stated that they had found white workers friendly, and in two cases highly favourable attitudes towards white workers were encountered.

'Well I'll tell you, I'm finding it all right. People have treated me very well. You couldn't have expected them to be any better. While I have been in this country there has been no one who hasn't been good. We are all living just the same and working just the same.' (West Indian, Hamilton Engineering Co.)

'I get on very well with the white workers. They are very friendly. It's better than with my own people.' (West Indian, Pentland Alloys Ltd)

In six cases it was said that while the majority of white workers were friendly, there were some who were not. However, little resentment was expressed and the general attitude seemed to be that it was best to ignore any unpleasantness which occurred.

'I get on all right. You will find a few who are awkward, but if you don't take any notice, it don't go far.' (West Indian, Annerley Iron Foundry)

'I get along all right with them and they get along all right with me. There's a few of course that's nasty, but there's good and bad in every nation. . . . You haven't got to take any notice. You might hear people say bad things, but the best thing to do is to take no notice.' (West Indian, Edge Tools Ltd)

In only one case, however, was there any evidence that the West Indians kept apart from white workers as a result of the white workers' behaviour. A respondent in Torrington Cutlers stated: 'I don't put it in their way to make any fuss. If you're working here and you don't talk to me, I just don't talk.'

Thus in general, the interviews with West Indian workers suggest that relations with white workers were much closer and more friendly than appeared to be the case in the interviews with British respondents, both managers and workers. This inconsistency, the writer would suggest, results from a tendency on the part of the West Indians to present a more favourable account of inter-group relations at work than was actually justified. This may be attributed to two factors. Firstly, the West Indians were hurt and disappointed by the fact that the level of social acceptance was lower than they had expected and therefore tended to ignore as much as possible the incidence of unfriendliness or antagonism on the part of white workers. In Edge Tools Ltd, for example, a West Indian worker stated: 'I would like to say that they are friendly because they haven't treated me bad. Until they do, I would like to say that they are friendly.' And in the same firm, another West Indian said: 'I would have to say that they have treated me well. I haven't had any fuss – I just get along. If somebody else have difference, that's not my business.' Thus in both cases, the respondents stated that the white workers had treated them well or had been friendly simply because they had not been actively unfriendly. Under these circumstances it seems likely that the West Indians would remain within their own groups as a means of avoiding overt social rejection on the part of the white workers.

Secondly, the writer gained the impression during the interviews with coloured workers that the fact that the interviews were carried out within the works environment with the approval of management tended to make respondents reluctant to be critical either of working conditions or of their relations with white workers. An attempt was therefore made to arrange interviews outside work, but with little success. Ironically enough, at a meeting of a West Indian society visited for this purpose, one of the workers interviewed in Hamilton Engineering Co. approached the writer and said that he had not given an accurate account of the situation at his firm because it was impossible to do so at work. However, he refused to provide any further information, and none of the other West Indians present were willing to be interviewed.

We may now summarize our data and conclusions with regard to social relations between white and coloured workers. The relatively low level of social as opposed to work integration may be attributed both to a lower level of social acceptance on the part of the white workers and to a tendency for the coloured workers to remain with their own social groups. In the case of the white workers, avoidance of coloured immigrants in social situations seems to result from two main factors. Firstly, coloured immigrants tend to be regarded as strangers – people unused to British ways. This is most marked in the case of Asian workers, where fundamental differences in cultural background exist. However, West Indians are also regarded as strangers to some extent; they are thought to have different interests and in some cases erroneous beliefs concerning their cultural background were encountered. Secondly, coloured immigrants were regarded as being of lower social status. There was little evidence to suggest that this was a direct cause of avoidance of immigrants in social situations, although this may well be the case in view of the fact that the question of status seems to be an important factor in the avoidance of coloured immigrants in certain work relationships. However, there was evidence that ambiguities in the status of coloured immigrants did affect the pattern of inter-group relations. Richmond suggests avoidance of coloured people arises not because they have low status, but because they do not fit into the British system of social stratification at all. The evidence of the present research, on the other hand, suggests that if the coloured immigrant does not have a status in the British hierarchy, it is because he is unwilling to accept the one available to him, that of a coloured man who 'knows' he is coloured and is willing to accept a lower status role.

The Position of Women in Industry

Nancy Seear

Reprinted with permission from *Research Paper 11: The Position of Women in Industry*, Royal Commission on Trade Unions and Employers Associations, London, HMSO, 1968, pp. 14–26.

If better use is to be made of today's womenpower and if the more serious situation foreseeable in the future is to be avoided, then first and foremost a change is needed in the climate of opinion regarding women's work. In addition women must be offered new opportunities and must be given positive encouragement to accept them.

The effect of the climate of opinion on women's attitudes to work has not been measured and it would be difficult if not impossible to measure with any precision. Yet it is not unreasonable to suggest that this is the single biggest factor influencing the use made of womenpower. In subtle and not so subtle ways an atmosphere is created and sustained which still makes it appear peculiar or comical for women to be both feminine and using their capacities to the full. This attitude thrives while a book reviewer in even a serious journal thinks it relevant to refer to an authoress as 'handsome', while BBC commentators make facetious asides about women in scientific and managerial jobs, while the public and Press chatter nervously about the way to address a woman judge, while a schoolgirl in a mixed comprehensive school can be told that 'technical drawing is only for boys'. All these instances in themselves are trivial – too trivial to record it may be thought – but they could be multiplied a hundredfold and are both symptoms of present opinion and a way in which such opinion is reinforced. Changes of attitude are notoriously difficult to achieve but without a change of attitude the present situation will go on with a small advance here and there and the continued occasional emergence of a woman whose achievements and success are too outstanding to be denied, but who is explained away as the exception which proves the rule. Real changes of attitude cannot take place unless the reasons for the attitudes are understood by those who hold them, the fears on which they are based are met, and the persons concerned are directly involved in the process of change. Public opinion is based on the opinions of individual men and women, of men in all levels of work and of women both at work and at home. At one level men's objections to opening up new opportunities for women are entirely rational. Organized skilled occupations and learned professions have always contained an element of exclusiveness, based partly on a genuine desire to maintain high levels of performance, partly on a sensible understanding of the advantages to be gained by restricting supply. To open the door to women either in the skilled trades or in the ranks of management would make the competition tougher for men and would weaken their bargaining position in the labour market. In companies or trades which are failing to grow or are positively contracting such additional strains would prove intolerable and such changes should probably not be attempted. Where, however, as in the case of the new science-based industries in general and of such scarce occupations as draughtsmen, there are chronic and serious shortages, the threat is greatly reduced. If a deliberate attempt were made in such areas to attract, train, and where necessary re-train, women this would do more than any other single thing to influence the climate of opinion among men and to reduce the apprehension with which women's advent is viewed.

Men's opposition to women in responsible posts is not however solely based on rational considerations of the labour market. The position of women in the family and the extent to which they are able to maintain themselves without dependence on the family have changed very rapidly in the last generation. This is not the place to discuss the difficult psychological and sociological adjustments which such changes demand. Even the most mature and well-adjusted men often find it a conscious effort to accept such alterations. The wife who works frequently brings many assets to home and family, but there may well be a price to be paid in terms of the man's comfort and convenience. Many men have adapted remarkably to a regular quota of shared chores and baby-minding but it must often have been a considerable wrench to sacrifice their traditional domestic leisure.

Nor should it be suggested that men's resistance to these changes is purely selfish. Much of the talk of families neglected by working mothers has been exaggerated, emotional and unsubstantiated, but such neglect has, on occasion, occurred and it is not sufficient, though true, to point out that mothers who do not work are also sometimes negligent. Careful studies such as that undertaken by Professor Yudkin and Anthea Holme have shown the conditions under which mothers working can strengthen rather than weaken the family, but there are real threats and it is surely right that society should voice its legitimate anxiety in so vital a matter.

These fears have not so far been fully answered and until they are, public opinion will continue to view working mothers with some suspicion, and the mothers themselves are likely to approach jobs with some degree of conflict of mind, a situation in which they may well make the worst of both worlds. To solve these problems more research is needed into the effect of wives that work on their families at various stages of the family's development, and determined efforts must be made to see that services exist to enable women to meet the dual obligations of home and work. Where possible, these facilities should be run on an economic basis since in the long run it is no help to the position of women if their work is subsidized by a reluctant taxpayer.

Men's dislike and fear of women in responsible positions are not based solely however on rational objections which, given the will, can be met without too great difficulty. It is probably true that an emotionally insecure or an immature man sees a woman in authority as a psychological threat. The problems of relations of men and women at work cannot be separated from the more general problems of the relations of men and women, and any attempt to deal with the work situation will fail unless this fact is appreciated. Much more research into and open discussion of these problems is needed and until this happens public opinion, insofar as it is male opinion, is unlikely to shift to the extent needed if more than marginal changes are to take place.

Public opinion is not of course solely masculine. Most working women would agree that women are by no means always helped by the attitudes of other women. For the more successful career woman there is a certain satisfaction in being one of the few women moving in a masculine world. Such a position can provide powerful compensation to sexually unsuccessful women who find it attractive and flattering to be regarded by male colleagues as different from other women. This type of satisfaction depends on scarcity value, and such women may well subconsciously be unwilling to alter this personally satisfying state of affairs. So far from promoting opportunities for other women they may in fact positively block them.

If career women do not always go out of their way to help other women to scale the ladder, it is not surprising that little support is forthcoming from the housewife living at home. Yet the housewives' attitudes may in the long run be the most important of all in shaping public opinion, since the standards and expectations of the mother are likely to have considerable influence on the attitudes of both her daughters and her sons. Many a man who is unwilling to see women emerge from women's traditional limited work roles may well be reflecting standards and prejudices absorbed from a mother who viewed independent and successful career women with a mixture of envy and disapproval.

We do not know enough about these attitudes or the feelings underlying them to understand how change could be brought about. It may however be connected with the feeling, common it seems among a number of women who do not go out to work, that housewives are not held in high regard – 'I am only a housewife.' Since it would be a very uncomfortable world if there were no women left with a little time to spare, and a lost world if there were no mothers devoting most of their time and thought to their husbands and children, this attitude needs to be firmly resisted. Housewives made more confident of their own role would be able to be more generous towards women at work outside the home. It is only as such changes come about in public opinion that action will in fact be taken to create new opportunities for women at work.

Since training is the key to opportunity, education and training must be the first line of attack. The science and mathematics teaching in girls schools is often woefully deficient through the schools' sheer inability to attract qualified staff. Everything possible must be done as a matter of urgency to help schools to find solutions to their staffing problems. Quotas for teaching staff, based on a desire to secure fair shares for all schools, should not lead, as it sometimes does, to a refusal to engage qualified married women on a part-time basis, women whose presence as an addition to the school's staff would give to some girls opportunities which would otherwise be denied them. Girls and parents need also to be convinced that prolonged education is a very good investment for the future. The need to learn and re-learn in middle age is constantly stressed, but it is not so forcibly emphasized that learning is a habit hard to acquire and easy to lose. Broadly speaking, the longer a person goes on learning the longer he can – the sooner learning stops, the more difficult it is to re-acquire the knack. Girls who leave school at the earliest possible moment are likely to be severely handicapped when re-training is needed twenty years later.

After leaving school, whether at the statutory leaving age or later, the choice of job has to be faced and the possibilities of vocational training considered. Of recent years careers advice has been improving, as the report of the Albemarle Committee made clear. Very many people would agree, however, that such advice is too often not given soon enough to help a girl to select her optional subjects at school with her ultimate career require-ments in mind. Since it is improbable that youngsters will make a firm career decision at the age of 13 or 14, or even earlier, it needs to be stressed to both parents and girls that to abandon such subjects as mathematics at an early age almost certainly means abandoning career possibilities which subsequently might appear highly attractive. There is also no doubt that many girls remain totally ignorant of the diverse and developing work going on in industry. Writing in 1964 of interviews held with 290 sixth form girls, Mrs V. Roberts commented: 'Engineering particularly was unpopular as a career. Dislike of it was based on a bias against industry, on a belief that there were a great deal of prejudices against girls, and of considerable ignorance of the range of work covered by the term. There was some difficulty experienced even by girls who were interested, in finding out about science careers. They maintained that careers advice in sufficient detail was not always available to them, and that ad-visers were not always well informed.' Girls' individual comments included such remarks as 'I shall take a mathematics degree. I would be interested in engineering on the electrical, scientific instrument, or heating and ventilating sides, but it is too hard to get a training', and 'I would like engineering but I don't think I have the training because I have not done technical drawing', 'Girls don't have training for engineering', 'I would like to know about jobs using mathematics and science openings. I might like engineering. My father is an electrical engineer, but girls don't know anything about openings in engineering for them.'

The need to arouse the interest of girls and their parents in technical careers and the opportunities for technical training has been recognized in other countries. In October 1967, the French Minister for National Education sent a circular to all headmasters pointing out that technical and professional training opportunities should be available to both boys and girls without any discrimination on the grounds of sex. Such an emphatic lead from Government, employers and trade unions, and in particular from the industrial training boards, might bring about substantial changes in this country.

The problem of training is not only a problem for school leavers. Because nearly all women leave employment on the birth of their first child their re-entry to employment is as important, if not more important, than their first job on leaving school or college. Since in the future the vast majority of all women at work will be older married women, the utilization of these women is of great economic importance. The better education and training they have had before giving up employment, the more easily will they be re-absorbed. But even the highly educated and professionally trained will be far more effective if they are helped to keep in the closest possible touch with their profession while not actually employed, and if refresher courses are tailor-made to meet the needs of the older women with some considerable continuing domestic responsibilities. Cash through tax adjustments, domestic assistance and favourable public opinion are the most necessary requirements. The trained women returning to work in their own field of employment are probably the easiest group with which to deal. Many women of good education, but whose original training has been inappropriate for the work available will need a full training scheme, not a refresher course. These women at present easily slip into work which is much below their potential level. Much better vocational guidance should be given to such women, and training carefully planned with their special requirements in mind. It ought not, for example, to be impossible to commence training while the mother is still tied to the home for most of the week. A good deal of progress in some fields could be made with private study assignments guided through small tutorial groups held once or twice a week at times convenient to the students. Such women would also greatly benefit from programmes organized through the University of the Air.

Opportunities for training are the first essential steps but they are only a beginning and much training must in any case take place in industry both in formal apprenticeship and learnership schemes and through the essential learning that can only come through experience on the job. It is here, in particular, that a part must be played by trade unions and professional associations. It is alleged that women have done little to help themselves through active membership of trade unions. As has been shown, this failure has been somewhat exaggerated and the position has undoubtedly improved in the post-war period. But the blame for women's slow progress in union activity does not lie with women alone. There is not much evidence that men trade unionists as a whole, with many outstanding personal exceptions, have been greatly concerned with the position of women workers except in circumstances in which the exploitation of women has been seen as a threat to the position of men. Although in the nineteenth century such unions as the Amalgamated Cotton Spinners Association and the National Union of Boot and Shoe Operatives accepted women members, many others regarded women as interlopers. Even in 1890 one trade union still had a rule stating: 'No female allowed in the capacity of either piecemaker, turner or bottomer. Any member working where a female does either process shall be forfeit £1, and, should he continue to do so, shall be excluded.' Though this was no doubt an extreme view, male unionists were on the whole content to see women fight their battles alone, even though too often the battles were lost. Even since the Second World War there has been little evidence of active assistance for women in the union movement as a whole. As long ago as 1957, Lord (then Mr) Carron of the AEU pointed out that girls were eligible for engineering apprenticeship. It is difficult to believe that if his union had really wanted to see an improvement in training opportunities for girls the figures a decade later would be as low. If the unions were concerned to improve the status of women, steps would be taken to bring women into positions of influence within the union movement itself. There have of course been very distinguished women trade unionists, and a woman chairman of the TUC, but they must be regarded as completely atypical. In 1966, for instance, in the Transport and General Workers' Union with 195,577 women comprising 13 per cent of total union membership there were only two women national officers, no women officers at all at regional or district level, one woman on a trade group executive, and one woman member of the TUC General Council. The same union runs one week training courses for members which provide excellent opportunities to help women to be more effective as trade unionists. Yet of all those attending only 3·9 per cent were women in 1964, 4·7 per cent in 1965, and 5·7 per cent in 1966. Neither in relation to employers nor in internal trade union affairs does it appear that the trade union movement as a whole has regarded the position of women as a matter calling for vigorous action.

If women need opportunities for training and job experience, they also need positive encouragement if they are to make the effort necessary to stay the course in training and employment to the point at which they make the contribution of which they are capable. It is a main theme of this paper that, with many exceptions, women are not at present greatly concerned about their employment situation. This implies that the country as a whole, which stands to gain from an improvement in the effective use of women, needs to take positive action to change this state of affairs. Women rightly expect to marry, and married women can usually rely on support from husbands, even if the standard of living provided is lower.

The case for equal pay has long been accepted in principle by the trade union movement and in other quarters. It is a principle supported by the ILO in the Equal Remuneration Convention and Recommendation adopted in 1951, but not ratified by this country. The Treaty of Rome (Article 119) also accepts the obligation to introduce equal pay. Article 119 makes it clear that equal remuneration means that: 'Remuneration for the same work at piece rates shall be calculated on the basis of the same unit of measurement and that remuneration of work at time rates shall be the same for the same job.' In 1961 a conference of Member States of the European Economic Community passed a Resolution on Equal Pay and dealt with the interpretation of the policy by explicitly prohibiting (1) the application of a legal minimum rate to men only, or by fixing different minimum levels for men and women (a point of interest in view of renewed discussion in some quarters in this country regarding the establishment of a national minimum wage); (2) collective agreements which fix pay at different levels according to sex (the normal practice in this country); (3) different bases for time rates and piece rates for men and women; (4) the use of job methods systematically to down-grade women and the use of comparison factors having no connection with the objective conditions in which the work is carried out.

Progress in implementing the Equal Pay policy in the Community has in fact been slow, and it is admitted that the countries have not kept to the timetable laid down. The 1961 Resolution does however spell out an interpretation of equal pay which could have very important consequences for women in employment.

Discussions on equal pay in the United Kingdom have been taking place in 1967 between the TUC and the CBI. It has not however been possible for them to agree on a definition of the term. If, as in the past, the issue of equal pay is said to arise only when a man and a woman do the same job agreement might not be difficult, but the improvement from the women's point of view would be slight since in only a relatively small number of cases in manufacturing industry can it be said that men and women are in fact doing the same work. The distinction between a customary man's job and a customary woman's job has been maintained too rigorously to allow this situation to occur frequently. It is only if equal pay is interpreted, as the TUC argued it should be, to imply equal pay for work of the same value that sufficiently substantial changes would take place to give a new significance to women's employment. Even if this interpretation were finally agreed, pitfalls would still remain. The concept of equal pay for work of the same value would if applied lead to the establishment of a single base rate, the same for men and women alike. With this rate as the foundation appropriate wage structures would then be worked out. If, however, women were consistently found to occupy the great majority of jobs at or only slightly above the minimum level, and few if any of the jobs on the higher rungs of the ladder, then the achievement of equal pay would have been a hollow victory.

If an attempt is to be made to make more effective use of womanpower the question of equal pay cannot be indefinitely deferred. If it is not possible to implement it in a single step, then a planned programme such as was used in the Civil Service could be worked out. When fully applied an equal pay policy would tend to eliminate women who give little consideration to the demands of the job, but who are tolerated because they are cheap, and would greatly encourage the women who are able and anxious to tackle demanding work.

While better pay and prospects are the forms of encouragement most likely to achieve results, there are other important ways in which women could be helped to make a more effective contribution at work. The burden of the dual job is heavy. It can be relieved either by help on the domestic front or by reducing the demands at work.

A married woman who goes out to work can ease the weight of

her domestic tasks either by employing someone to help her in her home or by using public services, or by both these means. If a woman is carrying a responsible full-time job, which often entails out-of-hours activities, she is in a position to pay an economic rate to attract someone to work for her at home. It can, however, be argued that the payment made by a wife who goes out to work to someone who replaces her in the home is a cost of working, and should be allowed to attract tax relief.

Assistance on the domestic front can also take the form of the widespread establishment of day nurseries and nursery schools. Such provision has been advocated by the ILO, but development in this country has been slow. So far as day nurseries are concerned, this is partly because in some quarters it is strongly argued that it is highly desirable for children under the age of two to be looked after by their own mothers in their own homes, and partly because the establishment and running of satisfactory day nurseries is very expensive and is not always justified economically in terms of the value of the work produced by the mothers released for employment. There is no doubt, however, that there is a demand for day nursery places which is not being met. A strong argument in their favour is the widespread growth of private child-minding arrangements. Some such schemes are very satisfactory, and the law requires registration and supervision, but there is no doubt that in a number of cases registration is evaded and supervision difficult to exercise. There have been horrifying cases of child neglect which have come to light only as the result of tragic accidents, and which have strengthened the case for day nursery provision. Legislation is currently being prepared to make the child-minding regulations more stringent, but it is hard to see how evasion can be stopped. Once again, if women's earnings were raised it would be possible for a charge for day nurseries to be made which would at any rate reduce, if not eliminate, the high cost of running them.

Whether or not the case is accepted for day nurseries to assist mothers with pre-school age children, the biggest problem encountered by the working mother of schoolchildren is adequate provision during school holidays. In other European countries a great deal more is done than in the United Kingdom to provide formal holiday centres and camps. Such facilities, if developed here, would do much to cut down the unavoidable absenteeism of the working mother who feels obliged to supervise her children when they are not at school. Such absence from work involves, of course, loss of production and loss of earnings.

A further change which would greatly assist women at work involves not the provision of a new service but the breakdown of a long-established traditional practice. Regulations governing the hours at which shops may be opened were drawn up in order to protect shop workers, but legislation passed by an earlier generation to assist the workers at that time bears heavily on the women workers of today. It seems absurd that the time at which most women leave work is also the time at which shops shut. Women working full-time must in consequence either sacrifice their lunch-hour or do all their shopping at the weekend. With shift working an increasingly common practice in industry it is impossible to believe that measures cannot be devised to give adequate protection to shop workers while at the same time enabling working women to shop at leisure and with some pleasure when their own day's work is over. This is surely a matter on which unions representing shop workers and unions seeking the support of women working in factories and offices might well get together to devise an appropriate scheme.

For many women it is not possible to reduce domestic tasks to the point at which a full-time job is a practical proposition. For such women the most valuable form of assistance is the opportunity to work part-time. Many employers are reluctant to adjust working hours to suit married women and have normally done so only where the shortage of labour has given them no alternative. In teaching, nursing and retail distribution, where the lack of staff has created acute problems, many very ingenious arrangements have been worked out. In manufacturing industry, however, many employers have been unwilling to introduce part-time working, partly because of the high cost of idle plant and factory space. The percentage of women working thirty hours a week or less in manufacturing industry has risen slowly and in 1966 it reached only $17\frac{1}{2}$ per cent of the total female working force. The difficulty in obtaining part-time work has no doubt been increased by the obligation laid on employers to pay full national insurance contributions for part-time employees, an additional tax which they have, not unnaturally, been unwilling to shoulder.

This brief account of the low level of rewards for women's work, of their restricted opportunities for training and promotion, of the inadequate social provision to assist the working wife, shows clearly that those who possess power in this country – in Government, among employers and in the trade unions – have never seriously considered the whole problem of women's employment. They have not examined it, either from the point of view of the national economy or from the angle of the needs and desires of the individual women concerned.

Trade unions have always seen the protection and assistance of workers as their primary responsibility, and particularly the protection and assistance of those least able to help themselves. The story of women's employment suggests that in this sphere unions have either tried and failed or they have simply never really tried. Today, trade unions are increasingly concerned not only with the interests of their own members but with the national wealth. Economic growth, productivity and modernization are seen to be matters in which unions are directly involved. Half the population and one third of the country's labour force are women. It is this group above all others which has been denied opportunity and where the greatest potential for rapid advance can now be found.

From the facts available it is clear that the majority of women are being employed in both non-manual and manual work in industry on semi-skilled and unskilled jobs. This can be frustrating for individuals and is certainly wasteful in terms of national manpower resources.

The work on which women are employed is to a large extent in the jobs most likely to be modified or eliminated by technical change. It is necessary to prepare for the time when there will be far fewer routine jobs and when far more people will be needed in technical and skilled grades.

The customary arguments used to justify the refusal to train and promote women can all be supported to some extent, but in no case can they be accepted without qualification. In particular, a woman's working life can no longer be considered solely in terms of the years before her first child is born since an increasing number of women now plan to return to work and are returning after their last child goes to school. This second period is in fact the longer and more important from industry's point of view.

The argument that women care too little about their working life to organize effectively in trade unions must also be modified in view of the growth of unionization among women since the Second World War. There is, on the other hand, little evidence of sustained support from trade unions in the attempt to improve women's conditions and prospects.

If women are to be used more effectively in the future opportunities at present denied to them must be made available. Conventional ideas of women's work in such occupations as draughtsmanship and in the engineering and electrical industries in particular must be reviewed and training facilities must be made available. The minute proportion of girls in any form of apprenticeship makes clear the need for change by both employers and trade unions if the necessary fundamental alterations in the use of womanpower are to take place. It is possible for the Training Boards set up under the Industrial Training Act to make a decisive advance in the training of women, but so far there is little evidence that this is taking place. Training opportunities for married women returning for their second phase of employment are as important, if not more important, than the training of school leavers.

Women need not only opportunity but also encouragement. The present level of women's average earnings in manual work is approximately half of men's average earnings. In future the great majority of women in employment will be married, and the rewards of working are not high enough to encourage married women to overcome the domestic problems that frequently interfere with sustained performance at work. With the support given at any rate in theory to the principle of equal pay in the Treaty of Rome, it will not be possible to continue to avoid facing this issue in this country. But even if it is finally accepted that equal pay implies 'equal pay for work of equal value' this will not really meet the needs of women if women continue to be employed almost exclusively in jobs of least value. Encouragement implies not only equal pay, but also access to better paid jobs.

Adjustments in social policy are also needed. For many women paid employment must be restricted to part-time work. There are too few part-time openings for women seeking them, and this position is made worse by the existing social insurance requirements. Policy with regard to day nurseries, nursery schools and holiday centres and camps for children needs to be reviewed, as do the requirements governing the closing time of shops.

The available information on the problems of women and work is very slight. In particular we need more detailed studies of the use being made of the vast army of women, often with good school records, in clerical and office work, and of the part played by women in trade unions.

The progress of women is undoubtedly hampered by public

opinion. This involves social and psychological factors of considerable importance and more research and education in this field is needed. A change in public opinion is an essential condition if any real advance is to be made, but if such a change could be brought about the improvement in the range and quality of women's work might well be dramatic.

Further Reading: Ideology and Attitudes

*H. BEYNON and R. M. BLACKBURN, *Perceptions of Work: Variations within a Factory*, Cambridge, Cambridge University Press, 1972.

E. A. FRIEDMANN and R. HAVIGHURST, *The Meaning of Work and Retirement*, Chicago, University of Chicago Press, 1954.

*J. H. GOLDTHORPE, D. LOCKWOOD, F. BECHOFER and J. PLATT, *Industrial Attitudes and Behaviour*, Cambridge, Cambridge University Press, 1968.

J. KLEIN, *Sample from English Cultures*, London, Routledge and Kegan Paul, 1965.

*A. OAKLEY, *Sex, Gender and Society*, London, Maurice Temple Smith, 1972.

B. OLLMAN, *Alienation*, Cambridge, Cambridge University Press, 1971.

A. SCHUTZ, *Collected Papers:* Vols. 1, 2, 3, The Hague, M. Nijhoff, 1962, 1964, 1966.

*D. SILVERMAN, *The Theory of Organizations*, London, Heinemann, 1970.

H. WAGNER (ed.), *Alfred Schutz on Phenomenology and Social Relations*, Chicago, University of Chicago Press, 1971.

K. WOLFF, *The Sociology of Georg Simmel*, Glencoe, Illinois, The Free Press, 1950.

* Available in paperback

Chapter Seven

The Texture of Work 1:
Slaves to the Machine

I am a disappointed craftsman,
And Colby is a disappointed composer.

. . . .

We have both chosen . . . obedience to the facts.

T. S. Eliot, The Confidential Clerk

Weber's analysis of bureaucracy and Marx's of the system of
factory production share many characteristics in common.
They illustrate the ultimate tyranny of forms of social
organization based on 'rational' principles. Analyses of
organizations in the field of management studies also make
certain assumptions about human nature. As March and Simon
put it, '. . . traditional organization theory views the human
organization as a simple machine. In this model, leaders are
limited in their achievement of organization goals only by the
constraints imposed by the capacities, speeds, durabilities and
costs of these simple machines.' The organization must
therefore assume that individual occupants of organizational
roles will tend to behave only in certain rather predictable ways.
But individuals bring with them into the organization a wider
range of expectations and therefore a more varied pattern of
response to the requirements of the organization than the latter
can permit. This variety must be at least curbed, possibly even
extinguished, or it is likely to prove to be subversive of the
organizational goals. To this extent individuals become
enslaved. The extracts in this chapter all deal with ways in
which the role and status requirements of specific
organizational contexts tend to limit the role-performance of
individuals to certain specific and predictable routines.

The obvious and usual way of doing this would be to turn
to that most characteristic cliche of the field of organizational
and occupational sociology – 'the man on the assembly line'

or some other example drawn from the area of manual work. But to do this would be banal and might even serve to obscure the *general* nature of the processes we are attempting to illustrate. For those who wish to utilize this sort of example and to refer to studies of factory work, the further reading should, we hope, be helpful.

The Morrises' study of Pentonville offers an opportunity to examine the operation of one of the most successful 'machines' of its type and time – the Victorian prison system. Constructed after widespread capital punishment had become unacceptable, as an alternative to transportation and as the means by which the system of penal servitude was implemented, the 'Pentonville' system enjoyed several decades of outstanding 'success' in realizing the organizational goals of containment and fairly minimal rehabilitation. The growth in size of the prison population has tended to exacerbate the affects of what the Morrises call the 'mass situation' in which treating representations of the 'other' group in a *stereotyped* way is facilitated. In smaller groups the situation may be more flexible and open-ended, but in some circumstances, even more dangerous. (This extract relates closely to Robert's account of 'The Custodians' which is reprinted in *Social Problems of Modern Britain*.)

At first sight it may appear to be rather wilfully obscure and perverse to treat journalists as 'slaves to the machine'. After all, in Tunstall's own terms 'news itself is a vague entity . . . and journalism [is] an indeterminate occupation'. But while journalism is in one sense 'non-routine work' with a high value placed on innovation and creativity, none the less a clear and relatively stable organization structure does tend to emerge. The key element in the emergence of stability is the 'desk': it is the rigorous 'deadlining' imposed by the desk which timetables and shapes all the non-routine work activities of the news journalist.

Within the highly programmed, severely timetabled situation role conflicts are, of course, likely to occur. It is not always possible, even in the custodial institution, like the long-term prison or mental hospital, to specify exactly what the single job, or the most important goal in a hierarchy of goals should be. Moreover, there may be conflicts about the relation of organizational goals to the activities of organizational participants. Lane's study of publishing house managers illuminates these problems quite clearly. The different definitions of culture which are offered by the organization and accepted by the managers coalesce with a differentiated authority structure in such a way as to produce a structural conflict between the managers and the directors. Such conflicts are likely to take particular forms when the goals of the organization are 'cultural'.

The 'cloistered elite' of Wakeford's title are the inmates of a different kind of institution, the public school. He shows how the staff who fail, or who choose not to meet the requirements of the school in occupying a certain kind of position, playing certain characteristic roles, and living a certain kind of life, tend to become marginal to the system. But their marginality is an important asset to the system for it provides the lower participants – in this case the boys – with a plug-in point which may be a means of releasing tensions and de-escalating threats to the school's authority-structure.

Another kind of enslavement is represented by the situation of the agricultural worker. Only recently has he become more than a 'hired man', an objectified type of labour. But his isolation from other workers and the high degree of personal contact and interaction with his employer combine to produce both a low level of unionization and a deferential image of society.

Possibly the greatest tyranny of all forms of actual dominance is that of the institutionalized exploitation of belief. Perhaps it is most clearly met within the form of the triumph of positivism in the late Victorian educational system. Thus, in Mr Gradgrind's school in Dickens' Coketown the tyranny of fact extinguished the breath of fancy for '. . . facts alone are wanted in life. Plant nothing else, and root out everything else. You can only form the minds of reasoning animals upon facts: nothing else will ever be of any service to them . . . in this life we want nothing but facts, sir – nothing but facts.'

Moorhouse's book is entitled *Against All Reason* and there is much point in the title. The expectations of Western society, the purpose and meaning of living, are very largely bound up with work. Self-conceptions derived from the successful performance of the tasks assigned to an individual by his work role are vital in defining our place in society. Ours is a society in which we are, to a large degree, what our work role is. Moorhouse's penetrating and careful account of the monastic life is worth reading in full in order to pick up the subtle resonance of a way of life in which work retains some of the timbre of the 'world we have lost'. The purpose of this enslavement may be, for some, the enlargement of another kind of personal freedom. One monk says 'There is no more virtue in working in freedom from the worry of making ends meet and coping with the income tax than there is in trying unsuccessfully to cope with these things and paralysing the rest of one's work. There is no more virtue in accommodating one's idiosyncrasies, talents, opinions and inabilities to the mind and milieu of the community than to that of the office or family.' In terms of the structure and organization of work in contemporary society, this is a revolutionary and subversive notion.

The Prison Officer
T. and P. Morris

Reprinted with permission from *Pentonville*,
Routledge and Kegan Paul, 1963, pp. 267–73.

The discipline officer can in reality make a prisoner's life difficult, and it is undoubtedly true that favouritism and victimization occur. The average discipline officer, however, is in close contact with a comparatively small number of prisoners so that the subtleties of such discrimination are limited; this does not stop some paranoid individuals from making claims that they are victimized. The prison sees such complaints as 'false and malicious allegations' and punishes them if need be; it does not see them primarily as manifestations of character disorders. Thus one prisoner claimed that on one occasion he reported 'special sick' but instead of being taken to the hospital he was 'placed on report for disobeying an order'. He must have known that the research staff knew that this story was untrue, for 'special sick' requests are always dealt with, and although the prisoner may get into trouble it always comes afterwards. On the other hand, the maxim that 'if a screw wants to get you, he will get you' has some basis in reality. Furthermore, the possibility of an officer 'planting' unauthorized objects in a man's cell is not out of the question, for the honesty of *all* officers is not unimpeachable, and (during the research) no fewer than three officers on the staff of Pentonville were subsequently indicted on serious criminal charges, two of them receiving prison sentences.

Probably the most important determining factor in the character of relationships between custodian and captive is the scale of the group situation in which they confront each other. When both are remote – in the large workshops, the great exercise yards, or the long galleries of the cell houses – prisoners and staff tend to see each other in mass terms. Because the mass situation permits little differentiation the relationship is dominated by the persistent stereotypes which divide the prison community into evil criminals and contemptible screws. As the size of the group increases so stereotypy hampers effective communication and the mutual pursuit of the common task. Where prisoners and officers spend time together in small groups they are compelled to regard each other as individuals. The factor of mutual selection enters in here, for the small groups are invariably work groups which depend for their effectiveness upon mutual tolerance. Thus the officer tends to select certain prisoners towards whom he is well disposed either on grounds of personality or work competence and to reject, or get transferred, those who are unacceptable to him. Similarly prisoners seek to leave such groups if the officer is unacceptable, or if the advantages stemming from the job do not outweigh such disadvantages.

The nature of Pentonville's social organization, however, creates other face-to-face situations which are not small group situations in the same sense, in that the group is not involved in a collective activity. These situations exist on the landings, between the officers allocated to them, and the prisoners located on them. The routine of locking and unlocking, the prisoner's need to frequent the Wing Office, and to make routine enquiries of his landing officer, involve relationships which are often closer than those in the large workshop or in the yards. But the ratio of prisoners to landing officers is high, and staff tend to be frequently moved from one landing to another, or to other duties. In such situations officers and prisoners are brought into face-to-face contact, but without the mutual knowledge and understanding which is the normal by-product of prolonged contact in the small work group situation. It is not without significance that some of the most explosive and violent staff–prisoner conflict occurs in such situations where the group is too small to permit complete depersonalization, small enough to allow emotional involvement, and yet insufficiently permanent for relationships to develop in depth. The development of the 'Norwich' system, which seeks to link the individual officer more or less permanently with a group of a dozen prisoners or less, is clearly one solution to this problem. But H Wing in Pentonville exemplifies two limitations of the system: (1) that when the group becomes too large the benefits tend to be lost, and (2) that without specialized staff training, explicit objectives and the use of socio-therapeutic techniques such as group counselling, officers and prisoners sink into a dangerous tolerance of each other's shortcomings.

While there are some officers who seek to avoid conflict with their captives by simple appeasement, there are others who recognize that the rewards for industry and good behaviour in Pentonville (outside H Wing) are conspicuously lacking. Accordingly, they strive to reward prisoners in a variety of subtle ways for work well done, and at the same time achieve compliance not by the crude devices of coercion but by the subtle manipulation of incentives. Further, there are some officers who go out of their way to assist prisoners constructively.

For example, two officers in a fixed post, both men of long service, by the nature of their job were brought into continuous contact with prisoners' domestic problems. Unofficially, men managed to come from all over the prison to discuss problems with them to get a sympathetic, though often firm, hearing. On one occasion a man who kept fainting intended to report sick the next day. Instead he was taken into the office and given the opportunity to talk over his domestic affairs about which he was extremely worried, and then taken to the hospital, given a sedative, and another for the night. Although such handling was outside the strict confines of the officer's role, it produced a significant lessening of tension. It was no coincidence that a few days earlier one of these officers had presented to him a tinned metal beaker, which he placed on his desk. It was inscribed: 'J . . . – the best screw in the nick.'

On an individual basis other officers are able to handle even difficult men. Once the Governor and Deputy Governor were discussing the case of a mentally sick man who, in the Governor's view, ought to have been not in prison but in hospital. The Deputy Governor said he was refusing to grant the man's continual applications to leave a particular shop because: '. . . it's the only place where he can do nothing and not get into trouble – [the instructor] understands him and doesn't put him on report.'

The extent to which prisoners and officers can joke together is another measure of the relative stability of their relationships. Providing that the prisoner does not 'go over the mark' he can indulge in a joking relationship which assists in the maintenance of cordial relations. Moreover, the officer can do the same, providing he does not provoke the prisoner too far. Obscenity may, as in some primitive societies, be present. For example, a man in a workshop asks to go to the lavatory and the instructor replies, 'But you went last week!'

The closest relationships between staff and prisoners are those in the smaller work groups – in the élites of the large workshops, in the small groups who work alongside trade assistants doing engineering maintenance and constructional tasks, and in strategic office jobs, such as Reception and the Pay Office. When men are

concerned with really useful and constructive work the relationships which emerge are akin to those of workman and foreman.
Discussions about the job are serious and to the point, and
indicate a commitment to the task. All over the prison there are
small groups of staff and prisoners in which jokes are made, tea
is drunk and cigarettes smoked, which are of their very nature
paradoxical in the total setting of the prison.

There are, nevertheless, situations in which role reversal tends
to occur. The red-band in the Library drafts the weekly report on
educational classes, an orderly in Reception fills out much of
the information on newly received prisoners' files and handles
committal warrants, and in the mess the orderly exercises most of
the functions of a head waiter. In the officers' mess the complaint,
'It's the prisoners that run the prison', could scarcely be more
opposite. One of the main activities of the senior waiter was,
however, concerned not with food, but with football pools. Each
week he would work on a permutation for a syndicate of officers,
and managed to win them steady, if unspectacular, sums.

It is the essence of the Sykes hypothesis that the prison cannot
exert total power by reason of the inherent defects of coercion.
The informal rewards and compromises that the prison officer
must make in order to secure compliance result in the corruption
of his authority. Thus, '. . . the theoretical dominance of the
guard is undermined in actuality by the innocuous encroachment
of the prisoner on the guard's duties. Inmates in this position . . .
may wield power and influence far beyond the nominal definition
of their role . . . the guard may find that much of the power he
is supposed to exercise has slipped from his grasp.' Once in this
position it is difficult to regain his authority.

In Pentonville, there are situations which bear remarkable
similarity, not so much because of the 'laziness, indifference, or
naïveté' which is allegedly characteristic of the Trenton guards,
but largely through understaffing. Thus one officer in charge of a
fixed office post could say: 'I know for certain that it is quite
impossible for me to do the whole job on my own, therefore I
have to rely on prisoners doing my job for me. In many ways I am
completely in their power. If they want to fiddle things I either
have to condone it or report it. If I reported it the work simply
wouldn't get done and I also stand the risk of being assaulted.'

But although such feelings are widespread (and some officers
think that if their colleagues spent less time in the mess drinking

tea, it would not be necessary for prisoners to do so much of their work), there are important flaws in the Sykes hypothesis.

It assumes a heterogeneity on the part of the custodial staff which does not exist. It is only those officers who have specialized work tasks to perform that find reward and incentive essential to obtain compliance. Indeed, allocation to a special work task is itself a reward, and there is often a queue of potential successors eager to succeed any incumbent who fails to work well. It is only where the prisoner's skills have a significant scarcity value that the staff are at a real disadvantage. In many situations crude coercion and physical force are remarkably effective in obtaining at least temporary compliance. Nor are all those officers who seek to provide their captives with incentives 'corrupted' for they may well withhold them, or even remove them altogether, without major difficulty. Prisoners individually may, in fact, of their own volition seek to please the staff in the hope of obtaining favours, or in the case of some personalities, out of a sense of passive obedience to authority deriving from long years of conditioning in residential institutions of custodial character.

Nor does it reckon with the officer who, by virtue of his personality, accepts every challenge in the contest of wills between himself and rebellious prisoners, nor with the whole range of subtle devices whereby he can make the prisoner's life intolerable. Even the threat of physical violence to him is minimized by the fact that in the process of taking a violent prisoner to the cells 'legitimate force' will almost invariably be used. If the physical reprisals which occur informally and the official punishments which follow do not protect him by their deterrent implications, he may at least savour the notion that revenge is sweet. If the bureaucratic devices of social control are ineffective by reason of their complex inefficiency the informal system of rewards and punishments is not.

The Sykes argument does not take into account the fact that in certain circumstances the officer actually cares little about the prisoner's compliance. Cynicism and apathy, at least in Pentonville, are sufficiently widespread to make it a matter of little importance to some officers whether prisoners are clean or dirty, whether their cells are neat or squalid, or whether they work industriously or idle their work time away. For the staff who merely watch the clock anything beyond the performance of the minimal tasks of their role is too much bother and they neither attempt to coerce prisoners nor enter into bargains to secure compliance. Nor is it always true that breaches of the rules are *invariably* regarded as invidious reflections upon the staff, for it is constantly reaffirmed among the uniformed ranks that the staff are grossly overworked, the prison is overcrowded, and the delinquent and deceitful character of prisoners is such that it is hardly surprising that they are always up to some mischief.

Finally, it provides no adequate explanation for the behaviour of the truly corrupted official, namely, the 'bent screw'. The bent screw who trafficks in tobacco or who offers to assist in an escape by letting a prisoner copy his keys, plays an alienative role *vis-à-vis* his peers and his superiors which is not dissimilar from that of the Robber Baron. He is a man who seeks to manipulate situations for personal gain at the expense of the group of which he is a member and towards whom his loyalties ought logically to be directed. Just as the Robber Baron tends to negate the collective efforts of his fellow prisoners to achieve an equitable distribution of the means whereby his imprisonment may be made less painful, the bent screw negates the collective efforts of his fellow custodians to achieve containment and control.

Journalists at Work

J. Tunstall

Reprinted with permission from *Journalists at Work*, London, Constable, 1971, pp. 10–36.

An indeterminate and segmented occupation

When an occupation deals with a fairly specific line of activity it becomes possible to lay down specific training and other regulations and hence to make the occupation more determinate still. Such determinate occupations include ones like 'medical doctor' or 'plumber'. 'Indeterminate' occupations include jobs like 'sales representative', which cover a very wide range of activities and lack prescribed arrangements for entry or training. In journalism, also, 'the range of expected tasks' is wide and is likely to change 'from one workplace to another'.

In journalism there is no single clear 'core activity' (in Everett Hughes' terminology). News itself is a vague entity and on a national daily about half the journalists are not gathering news at all – but processing it, or acting as executives and deskmen. Although individual journalists may show some interest in the overall occupation of journalism, they are usually oriented mainly towards a more specific segment of journalism, or of the world outside, or both.

Indeterminate occupations also often contain elements which become interested in narrowing down the range of work tasks, specifying training, restricting entry and raising status. The main body attempting this in Britain is the National Union of Journalists; but a trade union is presented by an indeterminate occupation with some acute and perhaps insoluble problems. Efforts to make the occupation more determinate involve efforts to limit the power of employing organizations. But news organizations seem likely to retain much power over journalists – at least in Britain – and for many journalists their work situation drives them into some degree of identification with the organization. Newsgatherers tend to become more, but not entirely, oriented towards the fields where they gather news. And the national newspaper Football specialist may feel he has little in common with the Knitting columnist on a women's magazine, or, for that matter, with the Editor of a rural weekly newspaper.

Journalists tend to rate journalists in other sub-fields in terms of the prevalent level of criticism. *National* journalism aimed at general audiences is generally believed to be the best and the most critical. Journalism which is either local or aimed at specialized audiences is believed in most cases to be less critical and of lower quality. '*House journals*' are believed to be highly uncritical and are scarcely regarded as being journalism at all. Another separate segment of journalism is the world of *consumer magazines*, which are believed by many other journalists to be an extension of the advertising world rather than of journalism. The *trade and technical magazines* are a separate world again, with each one oriented primarily to the interest or industry which provides not only its readers and its advertising but also its news sources. Many journalists on these publications have previously worked in the industry about which they now write. *Provincial daily* newspapers are more highly regarded by national jounalists – although primarily as a training ground for London journalism.

Even within a national newspaper there is a high level of segmentation. The editorial is largely cut off from the commercial departments. Among the journalists there is a basic distinction between *gatherers* and *processors*. Newsgathering journalists are also divided by time, place and the kinds of stories they cover. An Aviation correspondent may not know a Football correspondent who has a desk twenty yards away. The Financial specialists spend all their time at a separate office in the City of London; the Political men are always down at Westminster; the Foreign correspondents are at their foreign postings. The open floor office system which is designed to speed face-to-face communication appears to do so only between people in closely related work roles.

In broadcast journalism segmentation is no less marked than in the press. Firstly, broadcast journalism is physically separate from the press in Fleet Street. Secondly, the two broadcast news services are separate from each other. And, thirdly, the BBC in particular is internally segmented.

*   *   *

Non-routine news organization

Journalism is *non-routine* work. Firstly, 'exceptional cases encountered in the work' are numerous – news values stress the exceptional. Secondly, 'search' is not logical ,systematic or analytical; on the contrary 'search procedures' in journalism stress talking to people on a non-systematic 'personal' basis; 'experience' and 'intuition' (or 'news sense') are highly valued.

In non-routine work (personal services, symbol processing, innovating, or 'one-off' production) the hierarchy may be unclear – in sharp contrast to the pyramidal Weberian bureaucratic model. Non-routine work favours an unclear authority structure, shallow hierarchy, and broad lateral span. The emphasis on innovation and creativity requires quick communication with the top – and hence non-routine work follows a shapeless, or apparently 'chaotic', arrangement.

Journalism has such working arrangements. There is no steep hierarchy, but a large bulge in the middle. This can be seen in terms of pay. 78·5 per cent of all London newspaper journalists were earning around (one-third more or less than) £45 a week. Moving away from this bulge at the middle (or lower middle) one notices smaller numbers higher up the pay scales, but an interesting category of 7·4 per cent in the top pay grade. Apart from a few star specialists and others, these highly paid journalists are primarily editorial 'executives'. It is only over-simplifying a little

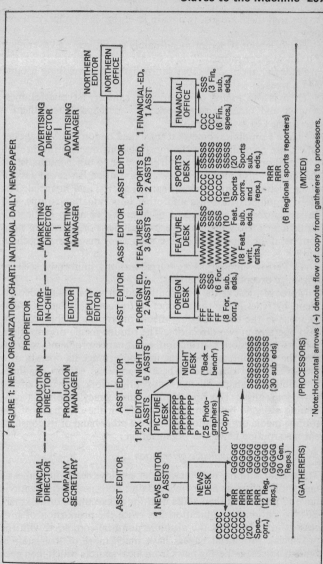

FIGURE 1: NEWS ORGANIZATION CHART: NATIONAL DAILY NEWSPAPER

Note: Horizontal arrows (→) denote flow of copy from gatherers to processors.

M.W.M.B.

I

to say that there are just two main levels inside a typical national news organization.

Firstly, about 20 senior men (mainly executives) and averaging £100 a week or more.

Secondly, about 280 other journalists – all averaging around £45 a week.

There is also a *third*, non-journalist, category (secretaries, messengers and other clerical workers) – perhaps 200 of them – averaging £20 a week or so.

Figure 1 simplifies somewhat since the London and Manchester offices are combined. But the most obvious mechanism through which 20 or so executives 'control' 280 or so other journalists is the 'desk'. This (imaginary) news organization has seven desks – news, picture, night, foreign, feature, sports, and financial. The 'desk', equipped with files and other impersonal apparatus, will be recognized by any student of Max Weber as an element of bureaucracy. How then can we still call news organizations non-routine, if the impersonal desk is such a key managerial mechanism?

As Perrow himself says: 'Organizations uniformly seek to minimize exceptional situations.'

Moreover, just as the non-routine editorial (or design) department, by redesigning the product so frequently, influences what happens in the encompassing media organization, this relationship operates in two directions. The routine media organization, with its production, distribution, and finance problems, requires that the non-routine news organization arrange its operation to meet very rigid deadlines. These remorseless edition deadlines timetable and shape all the non-routine work activities of the news journalists. The non-routine bureaucracy involves a continuing struggle between the demands on the one hand of the routine media organization and on the other hand of its constituent non-routine news and organization.

News processing: audience orientation

The typical national daily newspaper employs nearly five times as many journalists as a provincial daily; both news organizations have 17 per cent of their staffs working as executives or deskmen. But the national organization has twice the proportion of processors (and 10 times the absolute number) compared with the provincial. Provincial papers have much more of their staff in branch offices, gathering news from local sources which then goes into fixed slots in the paper; provincials also use more agency copy. Nationals, on the other hand, use more freelance material, which is re-written by sub-editors. Most nationals have more complicated edition changes and the popular nationals generally use more aggressive sub-editing.

The divide between sub-editors and all other journalists, which is the major internal functional boundary within the occupation, depends partly on different work functions and partly upon differences in previous career and future expectations. One fundamental difference is the orientation towards different outside groups and different organizational goals. The gatherers are oriented towards their news sources, the processors towards the ultimate audience. The processors regard gatherers as over-involved in their particular subjects; the gatherers see the processors as playing *down* to the audience. This conflict, partly concerned with the overall goal of the organization, cannot easily be resolved since most news organizations lack clearly defined goals.

Sub-editors and other processors on newspapers prepare copy for the printers. They work later hours, inside the office, under the direction of a night editor and his assistants – the 'backbench'. Here is one senior processor describing the characteristics of an ideal sub-editor:

'1. A capacity to check and check and check. . . .
2. An organized mind. . . .
3. A sense of time. A good sub must always watch the clock. . . .
4. An understanding of type. . . .
5. An ability to assess length. . . .
6. An ability to count headlines. . . .
7. An ability to write clearly in a well-ordered way. . . .
8. An ability to write bright headlines. . . .
9. The knack of getting to the heart of the story. . . .
10. A clear understanding of when re-writing is necessary and when it's not. . . .
11. A continuing sense of excitement about change. . . .
12. A capacity to cope with dull stories and get the best out of them. . . .'

The gatherers accuse the processors of cutting stories needlessly, lacking judgment, and being envious of gatherers. The sub-editor's basic pay is slightly higher than the reporter's and a daily man can increase it by working on Saturday as a 'casual' for a Sunday paper. But the gatherers' incomes vary more – partly according to their inclination to do extra work.

Over half the national newspaper sub-editors have been in their present job for less than four years – whereas specialist gatherers are much less mobile. More than gatherers, sub-editors conform to the 'provincial tradition'. A sub-editor would seldom be hired on to a national without previous daily experience. He is also much less likely to have been educated beyond 17 than a gatherer. Among sub-editors university graduates are rare. Some newsgatherers claim that most sub-editors lead mole lives in the outer suburbs of South-East London, which they leave only during the hours of darkness, and where they share a socially and sexually frustrated existence with a wife whom they met years ago when working on a small provincial newspaper. Sub-editors are accused by gatherers of thinking that the reader always wants to see a few more square inches of female flesh.

In 1965 a *Financial Times* journalist got six times as many column inches into his paper as did a *Daily Express* journalist, five times as much as a *Daily Mirror* or *Sun* man and twice as much as a *Guardian* or *Times* journalist. There were strong inverse correlations of column inches per staff member with both total numbers of journalists and size of circulation. On a paper like the *Daily Express*, where each member of editorial staff produced only 3·2 column inches per working day, the processing of news was much more aggressive than on the *Financial Times* where each man got over six times as much – 19·8 inches – into the paper.

The usual physical arrangement of the night-desk is a 'back-bench' – such senior processors as the Night editor, deputy night editor and chief sub-editor – facing two or more long tables of sub-editors. Much of the work must be done in about three hours. During this intensive period no one man can read all the words which will constitute the first edition of a daily newspaper. Large quantities of material will be rejected – or 'spiked' – so total reading is even more impossible. Further, the processors do not merely read but also cut, re-write, update stories with new matter, check spellings and write headlines. There is some division of labour: *Firstly*, by pages – front, sports, features, etc.; *secondly*, processors specialize according to the stage in the flow. Some processors gatekeep for others farther on in the flow. After the copy has left the news-desk it will be 'copy-tasted'; if not rejected, it then goes to an executive (e.g. deputy night editor) who will give it a 'catchline' (preliminary title) and a rough indication of the number of words required; a sub-editor then does the detailed processing. The processed story is next returned to the backbench where, if accepted and of suitable size, it will be allotted perhaps half a column on page 3 by an executive – say, the chief sub-editor – who is 'laying out' this page. Later still, yet another gatekeeper, a 'stone sub-editor', with proof in hand and the story set in the composing room, may make another cut. So, after leaving the news-desk the piece of copy passes perhaps five or six gatekeepers before reaching print.

Such specialization of gatekeepers at different stages in the flow (and at different hierarchical levels) contrasts with news-gathering, where specialization is primarily by subject-matter. A senior gatherer will deal with just one subject, but a senior processor may deal with all the 'inside' news pages – for which he will select 'page leads' from political, crime, human interest, aviation, beauty queen, animal, and other stories. Processors must also consider appearance. Within a very few minutes a chief processor will (in consultation with his picture editor) select a picture of a photogenic kitten, while throwing a pile of glossy dog, panda and pony pictures on the floor; next he selects one girl who provides the best combination of leg quality and photographic quality, while other assorted starlets and débutantes join the ponies and pandas on the floor; then he interrogates the office lawyer about possible libel in a crime story; next on to a late arriving United Nations story.

Pages are made up around advertisements, with pictures and headlines especially affected. Using blue pencil, scissors and paste, processors must rapidly butcher copy upon which other men and women have spent their whole day. There is some specialization by subjects (e.g. sport), but much less than in gathering; newspapers like the *Daily Express* and *Daily Mirror* which had substantial staffs of Foreign correspondents nevertheless process their foreign and domestic news together. The 'splash' sub-editor processes the front-page lead story regardless of its subject. A story is assigned to a sub-editor primarily according to its importance and to his seniority 'up the table' (that is physically closer to the backbench).

The gatekeeping role of copy-tasters includes regulating the total flow to the processing executive – according to space available at the time and date (which depends on the amount of advertising, the number of pages for that day's paper and whether it is a busy or slack day for news). Further on in the processing flow is the 'revise' sub-editor or 'prodnose', who reads proofs, and checks for matters of house style, policy or inconsistencies between stories.

As each edition time approaches, the processing team works at great speed and pressure. If a reporter hands his copy in at the news-desk, but does not see it in the paper next morning, all he will know is that it disappeared somewhere in the processing process.

Newsgathering: source orientation

Processors have a distinct hierarchy and a basic orientation towards audience and revenue. Gatherers, however, are primarily oriented towards performers in entertainment, politics, or some other field of performance.

Among newsgatherers the *feature writers* claim to deal with background, perspective and the like. A feature writer – who may do a political story this week, and an aviation story next week – tends to see himself as more independent of news sources than is a *specialist* newsgatherer who will need the source again to-morrow. Feature writers see specialists as often uncritical and superficially factual, while the specialists see feature writers as piratical and usually ignorant intruders.

The *columnist* may specialize in politics, finance, sport or show business. Although unlikely to achieve the status of the national American columnist – whose strength is based on syndication in many local publications – the Fleet Street columnist is encouraged to be 'independent', outspoken and personal. His seniority, his 'name', his licence to pontificate and his fixed space leave him free of much processing; his prominence and previous career will have established favourable contacts with sources; being defined as general but 'prestige', his column need not appeal to any narrowly defined audience group. His major orientation is likely to be to the broad world on which he comments.

Diary writers or 'gossip columnists' usually work in an anonymous team. Diaries, like features, tend to be 'locked up' early and to conflict with other gatherers in the same news organization; juicy gossip items may be 'poached' or dull items may be 'dumped' on the diary. Many diary items are based on following up previously reported events for an additional personal angle. Gossip journalists may have family connections in gossip-source areas – such as literature or diplomacy. The orientation of diary journalism to its source area is also noticeable in the stage vocabulary of some gossip writers.

General reporters (10 per cent of national daily newspaper journalists) mostly do not wish to remain permanently as ordinary general reporters. Some are aiming for the job of their current boss – the News editor; and there is a hierarchy leading up through the news-desk assistant posts. Other career ambitions include becoming a specialist newsgatherer, or a feature writer, or perhaps a star reporter – doing some foreign 'fireman' trips plus unusual reporting assignments within Britain.

General reporters come to the news-desk for assignments each day, and return their completed copy to the news-desk; when out of the office, on a story, reporters are expected to telephone in at regular intervals. A general reporter may on the first day of the week be assigned to cover an unofficial strike meeting, the next day a beauty show for dogs or girls, the third day a mystery explosion, the fourth day a story about petty criminals in the East End, the fifth day a 'colour' story about the demolition of an ancient factory. However, even general reporters tend to specialize a little. Some deputize on the Aviation, Crime or Labour correspondent's day off. Especially good shorthand, or being female, or having a particular social background may seem (to the news-desk) relevant to some categories of story. Most general reporter's assignments are those which specialists do not think adequately interesting. But there is always the chance – even for a junior reporter – that his story will turn into the front-page splash. One ambition predominates among young general reporters – to become a Foreign correspondent. There is much competition to get these few jobs which cost the news organization more than can be justified in revenue terms. This reflects the prestige of the Foreign correspondent's job, as well as the marked lack of revenue-orientation among most young general reporters.

The *News editor* is a senior executive in newsgathering, although an 'assistant editor (news)' may come in the hierarchy between him and the Editor. The news-desk may have a normal staff of the News editor, plus his deputy, plus three assistants. But, since the news-desk on a national daily paper is manned day and night six days a week, the total regular news-desk staff will be nearer to ten. An important object on the news-desk is the list of local correspondents (some are freelance agencies, others news editors or branch-office men on local papers). Another prop is the 'Enter Ups' – a filing system of forth-coming events, appropriate invitations, and notes to check back on fresh developments. Across the news-desk there flow even larger quantities of paper than across the night-desk. A major news-desk activity is the 'copy-tasting' of material from agencies, stories phoned in by stringers (and typed out by 'copytakers'), and various kinds of public relations material. During one day at a news-desk an estimated 75 to 90 per cent of this material was rejected without even reaching the News editor. If material does reach the News editor it then has a fair chance of being assigned to a reporter.

There is a tendency for News editors on 'popular' media to have come up through the more junior jobs on the news-desk, and for prestige paper News editors to have been senior specialist newsgatherers. To the source orientation which a newsgathering background normally entails, the News editor must add an ability to match the personality of an available reporter to a news source's anticipated type of personality. His work role thus forces the News editor (and his staff) to remain primarily source-oriented.

Publishing Managers, Publishing House Organization and Role Conflict
M. Lane

Reprinted with permission from *Sociology*, Vol. 4, 1970, pp. 367–83.

The sample

A number of occupational roles outside custodial total institutions might be expected to be subject to problems arising out of the difficulties of specifying a single or clear goal. Members of some of the traditional professions strive, presumably, to achieve both high incomes and other officially defined ends. However, in just those situations where this might be problematic, such professionals – barristers and doctors, for example – work independently of formal organizations. Hence their situation is not analogous to that described earlier. On the other hand, though works of art–painting, sculpture, poetry, plays, novels–are created by individuals, generally they can only reach the audiences for which they are designed by way of organizations of one kind or another. This is particularly the case where literature is concerned: books are both individual creations and manufactured objects which have certain characteristic, normative properties which most objects of production do not possess. In any society with an extended tradition of literacy they act as one of the most important repositories of the society's culture, both in the limited sense of recording its repertory of technical skills, and in the broader sense of embodying its accumulated wisdom and values. This being the case, those organizations which produce books – i.e. publishing houses – are highly likely to suffer some degree of goal ambiguity. Insofar as these attributes of books alluded to above affect them, publishers have a cultural goal; insofar as publishers are in business and must remain at least minimally financially viable, they also pursue economic goals. Not all publishers, of course, produce books having the characteristics I have touched upon. Those that do – literary publishing houses – have certain structural resemblances (at least in respect to goals) to the total institutions referred to earlier. We might, then, expect to find in them roles subject to conflicting expectations analogous to those in prisons and mental hospitals, affecting high as well as low status staff.

To investigate this hypothesis a sample was drawn from the managerial staff of London publishing houses. One part of the sample, on which this paper focuses, consisted of all the managerial staff of a single firm with a distinct literary character which will be referred to as 'Critical Books'. In order to guard against the possibility that the conflict phenomena described are a product of book publishing in general, rather than specific to literary publishers with mixed goals, a second, control group, was sampled from nine other publishing houses. Data were collected by means of structured interviews, and in the case of Critical Books, by extended periods of non-participant observation. The organization of Critical Books, though possibly an extreme case in certain respects, is by no means unique in publishing. A medium size company in terms of output, it produces on average one hundred and fifty new titles a year. Unlike many publishers of its size and type it has remained completely independent through a period when the trade as a whole has seen a great many mergers and take-overs. There are six directors, all save one of whom are full-time working members of the firm. The exception works half-time with Critical Books and devotes the remainder of the time to another publishing company of which he is also a director.

Though all the directors have alternative sources of income, Critical Books provides the *major* source of income in three of the five cases, if we ignore the half-time director. All voting shares – and hence the control of policy – are held by the active directors, though some non-voting shares are held by members of the board who have since retired.

All aspects of the publishing, marketing, and distributing operation are concentrated in a single building, since Critical Books does not use any of the ware-housing and distributive facilities set up to service the whole book trade. Altogether some sixty employees work in the building. Of these two-thirds are semi-skilled manual workers employed in the packing room and warehouse, or routine non-manual workers occupied with accounts, filing, and the other low-grade clerical tasks. The remaining third correspond to middle and upper level grades of management in other industrial and commercial organizations. Of these five are members of the editorial staff – two general list editors, two educational books editors, and a children's books editor. Next, there are five members of the sales and marketing department, consisting of a sales manager, a publicity manager, and three sales/publicity assistants. There are five members of the production department, consisting of a production manager, an assistant production manager, a designer and assistant designer, and the head of the rights department. Finally, there are a total of five that I have designated administrators. These consist of four directors' secretaries and an editorial secretary who is treated from now on as a member of the editorial department. I have called these secretaries 'administrators' because the tasks they perform are essentially managerial and are elsewhere the province of those officially designated as such. Of these twenty, I interviewed sixteen.

The control sample consists of ten editorial staff, ten production staff, ten sales staff, and ten administrators. The most notable difference between the two samples *in toto* lies in the nature of the administrative sector. It is becoming increasingly common to find in publishing middle level managers attached to one of the three main departments (editorial, production, sales), but whose work is of a purely internally administrative or 'progress-chasing' nature. They correspond to what in the USA are called variously, 'Managing Editors', or 'Production Editors'. Their rise seems to be attributable to three main causes. They have come into being first, by reason of the sheer inefficiency of three parallel and virtually hermetically sealed departments, in which communications exist only at the top and are bad because none understands the others' specialisms; second, because the volume of publishing has increased so enormously in the last ten years the total number of employees at this level in each firm has increased to some two or three times its original size; finally, by virtue of the decay of the private company in which the directors were expert, active and retained a high degree of the decision-making power, and could hence resolve day-to-day administrative problems. We should not discount the external pressures towards higher efficiency exerted by printers, authors, and their agents, booksellers and other publishers (particularly abroad), on whom increasing dependence is laid. Finally we must recognize the cross-fertilization of ideas from other industrial and commercial concerns who now own and finance many publishing companies.

The firms from whom the control were drawn represent the full spectrum of publishing activity. At one extreme lies a paperback firm, which is part of an international group whose avowed intent is in the maximization of profits; and whose policy it is not to consider a book for publication unless it has already achieved marked commercial success in hard covers; their minimum print order is for over 100,000 copies. At the opposite extreme lies a University Press which regularly publishes books whose print order is less than 1,000.

Goals, roles, and conflict

What objective evidence is there for my earlier assertion that publishers are confronted with a potential conflict between cultural and economic goals? I have, elsewhere, discussed the basis of this conflict and possible organizational responses to it in more detail. Here my attention must be restricted to a particular case. Critical Books has a fifty-year-old tradition of literary and literary-critical publishing. In that time it has been in the forefront of most of the important movements in that field. A large proportion of the novelists and poets that emerged in the inter-war years, and several since, originally appeared under its imprint and many now major figures continue to do so. Out of the annual total of approximately 150 new titles some 6–10 on average are volumes of poetry, and a further 10–15 are first novels. Thus $13\frac{1}{2}$ per cent of the output is devoted to works which are considered to be, on the available evidence, sure losers of money. In addition, it publishes a further 10–15 novels a year which have, at the very best, an extremely slender chance of being profitable. Outside this area the emphasis is on 'highbrow' critical works with a leavening of books on history and current affairs that are primarily written for or by academics. All in all, it is a list that common sense belief among publishers would confirm as being, at best, only marginally profitable. Though precise figures were not available, the evidence suggested that the company achieved a return on capital of less than 5 per cent. In fact, this is not a level at which commercial survival is possible, nor indeed does it represent the actual figures of profits from year to year. These are only assured by the existence of a backlist of titles in steady demand which show high margins because the costs of production were fully covered several printings since. If we accept that any new title is a risk (even publishers whose explicit single goal is to make money make mistakes from time to time), directors intent on the maximization of profits still have available to them the option, exercised a few years ago by a company then in a very

Table 1. Respondents' perception of primary goal for own firm

	Critical Books	Control
Economic goal	3	16
Cultural goal	10	14
Doubtful	3	10
	16	40

similar situation to Critical Books now, of ceasing publication of new titles and concentrating exclusively on the provenly profitable areas of the backlist. We may say in conclusion, then, that since survival depends on making at least a minimum amount of money, but that since much more could be made if sought, Critical Books has by definition, mixed cultural and economic goals on *objective* criteria.

In order to obtain a subjective measure of organizational goals the respondents were asked to say, ignoring their own values, what was the primary aim of the company for which they worked. On the basis of their answers (Table 1), firms appear to be divisible into three categories: those whose employees consider them to have a cultural orientation; those whose employees consider them to have an economic orientation, and those whose employees are doubtful. Of the ten respondents in the 'doubtful' class in the control sample some were very junior employees who were generally uncertain and reticent in their responses, while others worked for a medical publisher. One of these said that though he was sure his directors regarded themselves as 'philanthropists helping sick mankind' they must none the less have realized that the books they produced were guaranteed a market in quantities, and at prices that gave a sound return on capital and certain prospects of growth. Of the three Critical Books 'doubtfuls' one was a newcomer, while the other two felt the definition of 'Culture' to which directors subscribed to be so alien to them that they were unable to see any goal orientated action on the part of the firm.

This contrast between Critical Books managers and those in the control sample is brought out even more sharply in Table 2. Whereas rather less than two-thirds of the former perceive their company's goal as specifically cultural, three-quarters of them go

Table 2. Respondents reporting firm would publish book for purely economic reasons

	Critical Books	Control
Would publish	1	20
Would not publish	12	16
Don't know	3	4
	16	40

as far as to say that they do not believe that their firm would publish a book for purely economic reasons. They were insistent that the directors would reject a manuscript which did not in some way stand for, support, or represent the values to which they subscribe, even if they could be sure in advance that it would make a great deal of money.

It is perfectly clear from the interview schedules that though Critical Books must objectively have always both economic and cultural goals in view, the managers employed there are aware only of the latter and experience no sense of conflict between the two. Yet the same schedules make it equally clear that the respondents perceive themselves as subject to shifting, uncertain, and contradictory expectations about the roles they perform within the organization. Since there is apparent consensus on organizational goals two specific, closely related questions must be asked. First, precisely what are these expectations? Second, from whom do they emanate?

It is a commonplace of organization theorists that where economic goals are sought there may be conflict over the means to achieve them, but there will be a high degree of unanimity over both the definition of the end and the operationalization of that definition. Agreement will be both nominal and substantive. In contrast, acute cognitive disagreements arise over both ends and means if the sought goals are cultural. This is pre-eminently the publishing situation.

Fifty-six per cent gave as their reason for having gone to work at Critical Books the fact that they admired or respected a publisher with the authors on its list that Critical Books has. All of these had, none the less, become disillusioned since starting work at Critical Books. They defined the specific content of culture as a goal constantly changing. What they wanted to do was to publish books that they perceived as the present-day equivalents of the works on Critical Books' backlist they admired: instead what they saw was the directors of the firm intent upon publishing books whose style and content was unchanged, pastiches or historic relics of a culture that had passed. They see themselves compelled to work upon what are, to them, 'old-fashioned, pale imitations' of the books they admire. Worse still, the directors evaluate these in terms which put the new and the old on equal levels. At the same time they feel unable to be as critical as they would wish because this is, after all, the firm that in its own time did what they want it to do now.

In effect, the first source of role conflict is this. On the one hand the directors expect their managers to work on texts which represent or contribute to the directors' definition of a cultural goal whose content has been shaped by and fixed at a specific period. On the other hand, the managers themselves infer from the backlist and reputation of the firm expectations that they will work towards a cultural goal whose content is in constant flux. To this is added a further dimension. The managers define the firm as having, by its past record, established a relationship to the literary world and its public which imposes obligations that Critical Books is not fulfilling. Editors especially see their role as being expert representatives of this literary and public world, a position which they have achieved through academic success and job experience. As such, they feel themselves subject to expectations that they will support and implement the cultural values of their group. In their role as paid employees they are subject to the expectation that they will implement a policy that the directors decide upon. When the perceived content of the abstract ideals of the group and the directors' policy is more or less synonymous, the situation is unproblematic; once the two diverge to any noticeable degree the managers are subjected to conflicting and incompatible demands.

One final factor needs to be considered here. Given the location of the publisher midway between the author – 'maker' – and the public – 'consumer' – it is relevant to ask towards which of these two the manager sees himself as primarily orientated.

Table 3. Respondents' perception of responsibility to author/ public, by sample

	Critical Books	Control
Author	8	12
Public	5	18
Both equally	2	6
Don't know	1	4
	16	40

As Table 3 shows, neither orientation commands an overall majority. It is, nevertheless, suggestive in that the Critical Books managers show some tendency to see their role as orientated towards an author while those employed by other publishers tend to see their role as oriented to the public. Altogether less than a quarter of the respondents did not commit themselves, and fewer than one in ten had no opinion on the subject. The interviews suggested that it was an issue that had been considerably thought about, and opinions were firmly held with, on occasion, a positive moral fervour. No matter which group the managers feel themselves oriented towards it is seen as a source of legitimate role expectations. If it is authors, editors perceive an obligation not to publish work which they value much below that of the idealized author, for fear the latter be, in a manner of speaking, contaminated or devalued by propinquity. In the case of the reading public, editors feel an obligation not to publish work of low standard – as they define it – which the public will be deceived into buying and reading by a halo effect from the firm's established reputation.

The analysis of the situation may be summarized. The available evidence does not support the hypothesis that the role conflicts are the product of contrary expectations arising out of the pursuit of both cultural and economic goals. Instead, they would seem to be the result of disagreements about what is properly to be understood as literary culture. On the one hand, managers' roles are defined by the directors' understanding of culture. These expectations are legitimated by the directors' hierarchical position, and buttressed by the cultural tradition of the firm which the directors themselves created. On the other hand, the managers perceive themselves as subject to expectations that in their work roles they will realize an entirely different culture. It is more difficult to specify the source of these contradictory expectations, not least because the respondents themselves are unable to give clear-cut answers about them. In effect, we can distinguish two, very closely related points from which these expectations emanate, both of them 'symbolic' in the sense in which Sarbin and Allen use the term. First, managers come to and occupy their roles in the organization as highly educated, highly skilled representatives of the intellectual-cultural elite. They see their responsibility as primarily to, and sanctioned by the ideas of this elite, and only secondarily to the firm with whom they are working. Parallel to, and partly a product of this they see themselves subject to the expectations of the firm's distinguished authors and the imprint's loyal public that they will continue to sustain high cultural and literary standards.

*   *   *

Conclusion

When idealistic policies provide the motive for joining and work-ing in an organization there is nearly always a conflict between the ideal and the reality. In publishing, for instance, this conflict at first sight appeared to be between publishing worthwhile books as an ideal, and the practical problem of staying in business to be able to publish worthwhile books as the reality. It may be that the conflict in this form still exists, underlying the alternative basis of conflict that I have described, where the disagreements and the consequent incompatible expectations are not so much between economic and cultural goals, as between two conflicting definitions of culture. After all, the version of culture to which the directors adhere does, in the form of the backlist, make consider-able profits.

Nevertheless, such pervasive and inherent conflict is a general and recurrent feature of all idealistic organizations and need not generate intense role conflict as long as there are systematic, agreed methods of resolving inconsistencies or reducing the tensions that arise from them. The directors of Critical Books depend upon their managers' commitment to an ideal as a motive for adequate role performance. Yet the directors, rather than the managers, define the ideal that will be pursued in a way that conflicts with that of the subordinates, and with that of certain symbolic groups to whose values the subordinates are committed. This role conflict, created by the requirement that the manager be idealistically committed to ideals other than his own, tends to produce distinctive sources of dissatisfaction with work. The institutionalization of rules of interaction which emphasize diffuse cultural commitment, though perhaps designed by the directors to resolve conflicts, serve only to sharpen them, not least by eliminating the possibility of employing certain commonly found techniques for reducing role strain.

The Public School Master
J. Wakeford

Reprinted with permission from *The Cloistered Elite*, Macmillan, 1969, pp. 161–7, 168–9.

The public boarding school when recruiting its teaching staff takes into account the multiple tasks and roles that they will be expected to undertake. Although, on average, a full-time staff member teaches 27 to 29 periods each week, that is, 18 to 19 hours per week, with reduced teaching loads in some schools for housemasters, about 45 per cent of the masters at public boarding schools, according to the data Kalton presents, are involved in formal duties directly related to boarding. Apart from the preparation and marking of school work the master, but not the housemaster, is formally free after school hours, but most staff are either appointed on the understanding that they will take on further responsibilities at a later stage in their career at the school, or are encouraged to do so when they arrive. In the research school ten of the sixty teaching staff had received commissions from the War Office and ran the school CCF; three or four organized the two scout troops; others ran the societies, were responsible for the magazine, library, the school printing press, and assisted in the refereeing of games, in judging competitions and in training boys in school and house games teams. The school, in effect, makes extensive demands beyond those of the classroom on the time and energies of all members of the teaching staff. They are expected to attend a variety of school functions, especially the chapel services, school prayers, and the official public ceremonies, and are thus involved in school affairs for a major part of their time during term. Their holidays, however, usually in the region of 16 weeks a year, are about four weeks longer than those customary in the state sector.

The staff are indirectly rewarded by their social environment both during and outside term. The research school, for instance, is situated, like the majority of such schools, in a small-town community where the staff member shares the prestige of the school, and usually receives privileged treatment in the locality, treatment which is not generally experienced by others in the same occupation in the state sector. Within the school the staff have authority over a large number of boys and in most of their interactions are treated with deference and referred to respectfully by the boys. They wear distinctive dress both in and outside the school buildings for a significant proportion of the time – consisting of a black academic gown, to which is added on certain occasions (such as school chapel services) a lined hood appropriate to their university degree. They drive cars around a town where the majority of boys must walk. They occupy positions of precedence at formal ceremonies, and they and their families are accorded the right to use certain school facilities for their enjoyment. The research school, for instance, owns the only chlorinated swimming pool in the town, and its use, during the school holidays, is limited to staff and their families (and to certain residents who can, by their close association with the school, receive permission from the headmaster to use it). In the term time special times are reserved for 'staff families' to use the pool. Similarly, staff members and their families have the best seats at school film shows reserved for them. In particular, the wives of the staff share aspects of their husband's status: '. . . . the head-masters' wife will organize flag days and deputy assistant masters' wives to carry the flags, visit the boarding house matrons and invite them out to supper or to the theatre; and similarly the wives of housemasters have a status slightly superior to other wives.'

Perhaps more significant than the nature of the task and the conspicuous returns for the job is the fact that many individuals taking employment on the teaching staff of a public boarding school will be returning to a familiar social environment, and in a role that they, presumably, have earlier come to esteem. Their experiences and socialization within the residential environment of a public school, especially if followed by a collegiate life at university, and by service in the forces, often appears to lead to a preference for a continuation of a similar way of life. John Wilson states categorically that, from his experiences of the public school system, staff do choose this career 'to clothe themselves (or reclothe themselves) in the public school aura which they knew as boys; to be able to feel part of a community, at once respected and respectable, earning a reasonable salary and being honoured both within the community and outside it. Though they have not as much money as the Jaguar-owning parents who crowd the chapel on Sundays, and proudly watch the young men whom they pay to educate their young process in gowns and hoods down the aisle, they can meet them on equal terms. Their position in the chain of command and precedence, their exact status in the school, is clearly defined and secure. They like calling the headmaster "sir", and being called "sir" by the boys.'

Certainly, nearly three-quarters of the public boarding school masters in Kalton's survey had attended a public school themselves, and approximately one in eight had attended the school at which they were now teaching.

At the research school 10 to 15 per cent of the staff over the last 15 years have been past pupils of the school. Kalton also reports from his data that over half of the staff in the schools surveyed had taught at no other type of school, including the 40 per cent who have taught *at no other school*, that 31 per cent had taught at their present school for over 15 years, and that 93 per cent of the teaching staff with 20 or more years teaching experience had spent ten or more of these years at their present school. 25 of the 60 teaching staff in the research school in 1963 had been teaching there in 1950; none of these 25 had moved to other posts by 1967.

The teaching staff of public boarding schools are predominantly male, aged between 25 and 60, more than half being under 40. About three-quarters of the masters are married, whereas, in the girls' public schools, two-thirds of the mistresses are single. On the whole they have good academic qualifications – 60 per cent of the masters holding degrees with first- or second-class honours.

But there are a small, but significant, number – about 12 per cent according to Kalton – without a degree. Of those with degrees, two-thirds had read arts subjects and one-third science. At the time of the research 12 of the research school staff had taken a first in one or both parts of their degree examinations, and six, including some of these, held higher degrees. 83 per cent of the graduate staff in Kalton's survey had received Oxford or Cambridge degrees. It is worth noting however, without assessing the causal factor behind his finding, that Szreter maintains that the overall trend between 1939 and 1964 indicated a decline in Oxford and Cambridge graduates on the staff of public schools. The Public Schools' Commission's figures appear to give weight to this finding.

About two-thirds of the staff had no formal qualification in teaching. All McConnell considers necessary for new staff at Eton is an introductory course on how Eton works.

'The supposition here [Eton] is that a man either can or cannot teach and no amount of theory can alter the fact. New masters are given their classes and they must either sink or swim. . . . At Eton . . . one must develop a technique which can be discovered nowhere else. Eton has no 'method'. The curriculum is there, the syllabus is there. How a master gets through it is his own affair, so long as he does it.'

It is not usual for a teacher's performance in the public boarding school to be rated on a universalistic basis among his colleagues in the common-room; the latter in general do not distinguish between the objective assessment of a master's teaching (and counselling) methods and his adherence to the staff code – especially that aspect which concerns the maintenance of the social distance between the staff and the boys. Masters who do attempt to maintain a close and informal contact with boys usually have to do this covertly, and to be discreet about it during their conversations with other members of staff. In the majority of instances a master is assessed not so much by the effect he has had in an academic sense on individual boys but rather by his ability to maintain order in his classes, his house or in any group for which he has been allocated responsibility.

On appointment a new master is usually in his early twenties. If, after three or four years, his performance in the tasks and roles to which he has been allocated is considered satisfactory, he may be appointed a house tutor or allocated some specific organizational responsibility. He will be considered by the headmaster for a housemastership within a further 5 to 10 years, a post which he will be allowed to hold for 15 years. By then, his duties in the school organization will have become more numerous, his responsibilities will have widened, and typically his private life increasingly embraces the life of the school. During his term of office as housemaster he will probably identify with his house to an extent which is unusual among the boys in it, interpreting all kinds of individual performance in terms of house performance and prestige. He may become more excited than the boys in his house over successes in inter-house competitions. A research school boy perceived the situation in his house in the following terms:

'——loves to have his head of house head of school. . . . This gives him a good feeling. He gets as many school prefects in the house as possible. Because it meant that his house was obviously top house. There's a lot of this petty pushing between housemasters. . . . It's ridiculous. It's like a lot of racehorses. Each housemaster has to feel that his house is doing well. If somebody gets expelled from your house, it means that you would be rather afraid of showing your face in the Common Room, because some idiot like——would start making cutting comments, "It's a disgrace to the house, etcetera." ' (Recorded interview, sixth former)

Housemasters and other senior staff often constitute a conservative core within the school with which the headmaster has to contend. This was illustrated in the research school when the bursar decided to combine the arrangements for providing house meals into a more centralized system. The first move was to build a new refectory block for three adjacent houses, comprising a kitchen, run by a caterer/supervisor, and dining facilities for the boys. But the refusal of the three housemasters involved to compromise over the exact times, over the seating layout and over the arrangements of the accommodation meant that the school had to provide instead three separate dining halls in the same block with separate entrances, each with its own timetable and design.

*   *   *

Most schools contain a small number of staff who, as a consequence of their position in the school can, if they choose, adopt a different mode of adaptation to their staff role and can have a significant influence in the school system partly because they gain access to the subculture or 'underlife' of the boys. Such staff frequently lack some or all of the accepted credentials of staff membership. They may have had a grammar school rather than a public school education, have no degree or one from a provincial, or foreign, university, and/or hold a part-time post with no further duties outside their immediate specialism. They may in some cases have a role involving duties defined by the other staff as, at most, only marginally academic – being responsible for art, individual music lessons, the CCF, sporting activities or even the library. In different schools different roles carry the stigma of marginality among staff members as a whole. The implications of marginality also vary between the schools. Such staff may not be automatically accepted as full members of staff, may consistently be given lower priority in school functions, or not allocated the privileges, particularly the use of certain school facilities, accorded to other staff, nor perhaps may they wield the same authority. In the research school those teaching non-examined subjects such as art and music, those with staff status but without any recognized academic role, such as matrons, gardeners and domestic staff, could be said to fall into this category. But the relevant point as far as this research is concerned is that in most of the schools these staff contained among their number one or two who provided facilities for certain boys to retreat, for short periods, into a valued environment where the direct influence and control of the school appeared minimal.

In the research school, a number of marginal staff members – in some houses the house matron, in others the boilerman or gardener – provided this facility. During the research period one of the music masters allowed his house to become the best-known and the most significant retreat for a number of discontented senior boys. His role was in no way public and many of the staff neither knew, nor probably would have wanted to know, about his role, but in an informal way he risked the disapproval of the senior staff by using his house as the meeting place for a small number of retreatist and intransigent boys, and one or two of the rebels.

The Farm Worker

H. Newby

Reprinted with permission from *Sociological Review*,
Vol. 20, No. 3, August 1972, pp. 413–27.

Market situation

The agricultural worker is the archetypal 'hired man'. In former
years his weak market situation was symbolized by the hiring
fairs in the north and west of the country and by casualization and
laying-off on wet days in the south and east. The Second World
War and state intervention removed these and other abuses, but
the agricultural worker continues to be subject to the vagaries
of a situation in which, as a group of economists concluded after
an analysis of wages, 'agriculture approximates most closely to a
perfectly competitive labour market'. In such a situation the most
sensitive indicator of trends is probably income, but other aspects
of the market situation are also relevant.

(a) Job security

The most important feature of the size of the agricultural labour
force it that it is in marked decline. From a post-war peak of
438,300 in 1949, the number of adult, regular, whole-time males
employed in agriculture in England and Wales declined by more
than half to 200,400 in 1969. From 1948 to 1968 the average yearly
decrease was 18,700 or 3·6 per cent. Even allowing for the understatement in the Agricultural Returns of the growing number of
workers employed by agricultural contractors, agriculture continues to be an industry with a rapidly shrinking labour force.
This is clearly a potential threat to the job security of the agricultural worker, but the impact of this decline can only be fully
assessed by taking other factors into account.

The decline in the labour force has been spread evenly over
most sizes of farms and across all types of labour. The only
exception to this has been where increasing specialization has
occurred. Specialized farms have lost less labour, or have even
gained labour, at the expense of the others. There is a growing
demand for highly skilled specialists, particularly in stockbreed-
ing, but these workers still form a small percentage of the total

labour force (less than 15 per cent). Though the decline has thus been fairly uniform as far as the employment structure of the industry is concerned, a more skewed distribution emerges when one considers the age-range of the labour force: one-third of all agricultural workers being within twenty years of retirement. The under-representation of workers under the age of forty-five is not due to a lack of school-leavers entering agriculture – though there has been a fall in recruits since 1964, it is still not on a scale sufficient to cause a decline in the labour force on its own. The loss of labour in agriculture is primarily accounted for by the outward mobility of workers in the twenty-one to forty-five age group. The extent to which this occupational mobility is caused by the disappearance of employment opportunities in agriculture as opposed to a choice taken by the worker to leave agriculture for employment elsewhere enables an assessment of job insecurity to be made.

Econometric analysis has shown that the best predictor of the volume of labour outflow from agriculture is the employment situation in other industries, so that the loss of workers shows a distinct pattern that correlates closely with the business cycle. Underlying these year-to-year fluctuations, however, there is an 'underlying, strong, basic trend towards a reduction in the total labour force'. Even in years of high unemployment in industry there is a decline in employment opportunities in agriculture owing to continuing mechanization and adoption of other labour-saving techniques; although the extent to which this exerts an influence on the total labour ouflow is also a function of regional and sub-regional factors. Though the rates of decline have varied between different counties, the overall pattern is such that the *volume* of decline has been greatest where the largest number of workers are concentrated, but the rate of loss has been greatest in the counties lying in the main industrial belt of the country. The differences are even greater at a more localized level, where trends may cut across the overall regional pattern. At this level the importance of disappearing employment opportunities as a causal factor of the total labour outflow varies not only with the state of employment in industry, but also with access to this employment. Other things being equal, job insecurity will be more prevalent in relatively isolated rural areas than in areas near towns.

These extreme variations in labour outflow suggest, then, that the areas which are meaningful as labour markets to agricultural workers are small, so that 'differences within almost individual parishes are very significant. One of the most important points that can be made about the agricultural worker's market situation is, therefore, the extent to which the market in which he sells his labour is a *local* one, with all the constraints on choice that this implies. These constraints are reinforced by the fact that, almost by definition, the range of occupational choice in rural areas is small, and that the demand for labour has fallen due to mechanization. Although the range of skills possessed by agricultural workers has, also as a result of mechanization, become increasingly transferable to other industries and although rural areas have become less isolated from the flow of information concerning urban earnings and conditions, the increasing cost and declining availability of transport in rural areas have worked against these trends to keep the labour force captive. In many rural areas it is now very definitely a buyer's market for labour – with agriculture in a near-monopoly position – to the extent that the continuing high recruitment of school-leavers can seriously be attributed to the gap between the school-leaving age and the age at which a driving licence becomes obtainable.

(b) *Earnings and conditions*

As noted above, income is probably the most sensitive indicator of the agricultural worker's market situation. At the end of 1971 the statutory minimum wage in agriculture was £14·80 for a 42 hour week. Earnings in the year ending September 1970 averaged £18·30 for a working week of 49·1 hours, compared with average industrial earnings of £28·05 for 45·7 hours. Earnings in agriculture are lower than in any other industry covered by the Department of Employment and Productivity's six-monthly earnings surveys. Other conditions tend to be merely a reflection of the low level of earnings. Employers may ask their workers to stand by at weekends to await improvement in the weather (usually for sowing or harvesting) without payment. There is no compulsory sickness pay scheme in agriculture. More than half the labour force receive no contracts of employment letter, and the absence of timesheets and itemized wage packets is not uncommon.

The minimum standards of wages and conditions in agriculture are laid down by an industrial council, the Agricultural Wages Board. On the whole the AWB has been rather conservative with its awards and the percentage of workers earning no more than the minimum wage has declined from 33·7 per cent in 1950 to

12·1 per cent in 1965, which suggests that a growing proportion of agricultural workers achieve more in their own negotiations with their employer at a face-to-face level than do their national representatives. Thus the AWB has been more of a restraining than an inflationary influence on wages. However, it does perform a 'safety-net' function for the approximately 10 per cent of workers – chiefly in the south-west, Wales and East Anglia – who remain on the minimum wage. It also possesses an important enforcement function – its decisions are legally binding – which continues to win it the support of the agricultural trade unions.

The very existence of the AWB is a symbol of the poor market situation of the agricultural worker. Trade unionism in agriculture is weak. The principal union is the National Union of Agricultural and Allied Workers (NUAAW) with approximately 115,000 members (not all of them agricultural workers), but the agricultural section of the Transport and General Workers Union also contains about 13,000 agricultural workers. Estimates of the level of unionization vary between 17·63 per cent and 37 per cent; about one-third seems to be a widely accepted figure. There are wide regional variations, however, and trade unionism is particularly strong in eastern England, but even in the areas of union strength the level of unionization is insufficient to influence the level of wages. East Anglia, despite being a union stronghold, remains the area where weekly earnings are the lowest in the country. Like other manual workers, the power of agricultural workers to improve their earnings and conditions rests to a great extent on their ability to achieve a partial or complete withdrawal of labour. The last strike in agriculture was in 1923, in what amounted to a test case against wage reductions. In the union's strongest area in the whole country – west and north Norfolk – a limited success was achieved; but out of 20,000 strike notices sent out, the largest number of members who stopped work was only 5,000 and the strike nearly bankrupted the union. This strike was the last of a series of sporadic outbreaks of labour unrest in agriculture in the years shortly before and after the Great War, when the NUAAW was in its infancy. These strikes enable a pattern of response on both sides to be discerned which subsequent developments in agriculture are unlikely to have altered a great deal.

The low level of unionization in agriculture, together with the sheer organizational difficulties of policing a strike among a membership scattered in very small groups over the whole of the country, has meant that agricultural trade unions have never contemplated national strike action, but have chosen selected areas, and even selected farms within these areas, as test cases. The high number of family farms means that a withdrawal of hired labour is unable to bring about a total curtailment of output in any case, so that not all farms can be equally affected. This inability to affect the production of all farms seriously weakens the power of trade union action, for it only needs some form of organizational unity among farmers, and a pledge from those who are not affected to those who are, to decisively shift the balance of power. The National Farmers' Union, for instance, founded in Lincolnshire in 1908, was a direct response to the growth of trade unionism and the threat of strike action in eastern England. The characteristic employers' response to collective action on the part of their employees has therefore been a collective response of their own – the lock-out. It has been used extremely effectively, for reasons which were outlined in the discussion of the agricultural workers' market situation. The lock-out is a powerful weapon in an industry with a falling demand for labour, which typically is carried out in areas where there are few alternative employment opportunities and where the possibilities of finding alternative accommodation are poor if farmers decide to evict strikers from their tied cottages. In arable areas, where trade unions have traditionally chosen their ground because of their greater degree of unionization, these problems are overlaid by the lengthy nature of the production cycle. At only two periods of the year – sowing and harvesting – is the withdrawal of hired labour a serious embarrassment to the farmer. By choosing the time of year for their counter-offensive, employers have therefore been able to undertake an extended war of attrition in which they are likely to have the resources to withstand far better than their employees. Hence agricultural trade unionism is denied the ultimate sanction in wage negotiations. The union leadership now seems reconciled to the virtual impossibility of strike action, but is must be added that rank-and-file opinion has also not favoured a withdrawal of labour.

The AWB is therefore the institutional alternative to a trial of strength which farmworkers would inevitably lose. And although a diminishing proportion of agricultural workers earn only the statutory minimum wage, the decisions of the AWB continue to wield a good deal of influence over average earnings due to the narrow range of 'premium' payments. Two investigations by the

Prices and Incomes Board have concluded that, in the words of the first report, 'the concentration of low paid workers is higher than elsewhere . . . Few industries, if any, provide for all payments above the minimum (other than overtime) within such a narrow span.'

*　　*　　*

Apologists for the low level of earnings among agricultural workers often point to the extent of payments in kind. Their significance is, however, grossly over-exaggerated: total payments in kind as a percentage of the contract wage for all hired men have declined from 4·7 per cent in 1950 to 2·1 per cent in 1969. One form of payment in kind consists of cheap farm produce, chiefly milk and potatoes, but their provision on many farms is being eliminated by increased specialization. The other form of payment concerns subsidized housing which affects two groups of workers. First there are those who pay board and/or lodging for 'living in' on the farm. The proportion doing so has declined slightly from 5·4 per cent in 1956 to 4·7 per cent in 1969. The other form of subsidized housing is the tied cottage: the proportion of workers living in them has *increased* from 34·3 per cent in 1948 51·9 per cent in 1969.

The significance of the tied cottage to the agricultural worker extends beyond its cash value – to many agricultural workers and outsiders alike it continues to be a symbol of his dependent social status. The lingering sense of insecurity which the tied cottage system generates can pervade all other aspects of the farm worker's class position and it is probably the cause of more bitterness in the relationships between worker and employer than any other single issue. In 1970 the NUAAW handled 417 cases of threatened eviction in the county courts compared with 210 in 1964. As far as the workers' market situation is concerned, however, the tied cottage can literally tie agricultural workers to working on the land. While it may facilitate labour mobility within agriculture, it adds to the financial barriers of anyone wishing to find other forms of employment. Added to the constraints of the labour market are the constraints of the rural housing market which increase as the growing urbanization of rural areas inflates house prices. On the other hand, the maximum rent of 30p per week which AWB orders stipulate, makes the tied cottage an attractive proposition in view of the low level of agricultural earnings. But this means that the agricultural worker is frequently faced by the dilemma that he cannot afford *not* to take on the tenancy of a tied cottage; but, once in one, he cannot afford to seek higher earnings elsewhere. Today the tied cottage is no longer the instrument of anti-trade union oppression it used to be – rather it is the carrot which may make a worker accept his low wage.

Parity of earnings with workers in other industries is a long-cherished ambition of agricultural trade unions. Data on how far this has been achieved are conflicting and frequently fail to take account of the longer hours worked by agricultural workers. Hourly earnings in agriculture are gradually falling behind those in industry. The growth in the general level of earnings increased the absolute size of the gap from just under £2 in 1949 to just under £10 in 1970.

(c) *Training and promotion*

The generally poorer facilities in rural schools compared with those in towns mean that rural school-leavers enter agriculture with in-built disadvantages in securing the kind of universalistic qualifications which are aids to labour mobility. In addition, attempts to introduce a formal training scheme in agriculture are notoriously ineffectual due to the refusal of farmers to accept 'paper' qualifications and an insistence that only they know how to train their own workers. Training therefore tends to be particularistic and not conducive to labour mobility. There is also resistance among workers on instrumental grounds since the large number of small employers in agriculture allows no 'promotion ladder' that might provide the incentive for formal training to be undertaken. The wages structure, although it will increase the relevance of training, will not alter this structural disincentive – generally speaking, promotion will continue to be gained only by moving to a larger farm. The prospects of farm ownership – the agricultural ladder – remain principally a myth of rural revivalists, the first rung of the ladder being well beyond the means of most agricultural workers. Nalson, for instance, in an upland area of North Staffordshire, where farms are small and comparatively cheap, found only four farmers out of a total of 172 who were the sons of farm workers. He concluded that, 'such a ladder is not characteristic of this area. Indeed it is doubtful whether this notion of mobility within the farming industry has any basis in reality anywhere.'

The alternatives to outright purchase, the smallholdings let by either county councils or the Ministry of Agriculture through the

Land Settlement Association, give preference to agricultural workers, but a recent Committee of Inquiry reported that, 'On the whole statutory smallholdings have not provided the tenants with incomes high enough to enable them to build up sufficient capital to move to larger farms.'

Under the local authority scheme only 55 out of 15,000 tenants had succeeded in this.

The constraints of the agricultural worker's market situation are therefore such that his 'life chances' are severely curtailed. Nor is there any evidence to suggest that these constraints are substantially weakening. On the contrary, his level of earnings continues to fall further behind that of his industrial counterparts, a greater proportion of agricultural workers are living in tied cottages and there is a continuing diminution of employment opportunities which threatens job security. As far as his market situation is concerned, the agricultural worker appears to be receiving fewer and fewer tangible benefits from his 'exchange of deference for paternalism'.

Work situation

If the work situation is defined, following Lockwood, as 'the set of social relationships in which the individual is involved at work by virtue of his position in the division of labour', then it has an almost zero value when applied to agricultural workers, for their social relationships with other individuals while at work are few. This individuality (and even autonomy) is a function of both the enterprise structure and changes in work that have been induced by technological developments.

Though the trend is towards larger units, both in terms of production and acreage, British agriculture still consists predominantly of small farms. The average British holding in 1968 consisted of only eighty-five acres and nearly 57 per cent of holdings were smaller than fifty acres. Though small acreage is not always accompanied by small-scale production, this skewed distribution towards small units is reflected in the size distribution of output – 50 per cent of holdings produce only 6 per cent of output, while the largest 12 per cent produce 54 per cent. Similarly the labour force is very unevenly distributed. In 1968, 67 per cent of the holdings in England and Wales employed no whole-time, regular male workers at all and a further 17 per cent employed only one. Only 6 per cent of holdings employed four or more workers. These holdings, however, are the larger farms that account for a disproportionate amount of production.

Nevertheless, though agricultural workers are concentrated on large *farms*, they remain concentrated among small *employing units*. The decline in the labour force is sufficiently outpacing the amalgamation of holdings to reduce the average size of the farm labour force – from 2·1 hired workers per holding in 1965 to 1·8 in 1968. In 1968 only 39 per cent of the labour force worked on farms employing five or more men.

One result of the characteristically small size of each farm's labour force is that it allows the frequent face-to-face interaction of employer and employee. A number of studies have shown how the more wide-spread level of interaction in small organizations may produce an interaction network with a high degree of 'connectedness' which not only fosters a high level of organizational identification but may create a normative system which governs instrumental activities. In such small organizations the nature of employer-employee relationships are particularistic rather than universalistic and diffuse rather than specific (instrumental). The prevalence of such 'gaffer-to-man' relationships in agriculture implies that the modes of control operated by the farmer over his hired employees is at the informal, personal level rather than by reference to impersonal mechanisms of control operated through a set of formalized procedural rules. Indeed the relationship between farmer and worker often includes consultation on day-to-day farm management and frequently extends outside working hours and (due largely to the tied cottage which is usually located on the farm rather than in the village) into the domestic sphere. While such a relationship contains its own peculiar problems, it also tends to increase the agricultural worker's identification with his farm. Hence 'a worker tends to enjoy easy (which is not to say equal) relations with the farmer'. In the context of this close *personal* contact between employer and employee, deprivations which might warrant industrial action in large organizations, such as the lack of timesheets, itemized wage packets and so forth, might seem irrelevant trivia. Moreover the falling number of workers per farm indicates a trend towards *greater* personal contact between farmer and agricultural worker.

Clearly this personal relationship is not likely to engender formal industrial action – a work-to-rule, for instance, is difficult to apply to agriculture, even allowing for the rudimentary division of labour, simply because this relationship is so diffuse. Neither is it conducive to unionization, since trade unions are frequently anxious for recruiting purposes to stress the potential conflict between employer and employee and to erect and maintain a series of rules and procedures that will mediate in this conflict. There is, however, no place for shop stewards in agriculture. In addition the apparent irrelevance of trade unionism is increased by the growing proportion of workers who obtain better pay and conditions from their employers than those negotiated at the national level. To the individual worker it may well seem that the way to improve his earnings is not to join a trade union or undertake some form of industrial action but to foster, by increased efficiency, even better relations with his employer. The precise role of trade unionism within the framework of deferential industrial relations must, however, await the outcome of further research.

Even on the very large bureaucratically run farms, other factors in the work situation militate against the growth of a normative system among agricultural workers that may foster a more 'proletarian' form of class consciousness. These factors are largely related to advances in the technology of agricultural production. Mechanization has not only drastically reduced the number of workers per farm but has removed the need for gangs of labour for most jobs in agriculture. Thus while 'vertical' interaction with the farmer has increased, 'horizontal' interaction between employees has been reduced. The agricultural worker now works predominantly on his own. Ostracism as a means of exerting normative pressure thus could have little effect on most farm workers. In addition, except perhaps where 'factory-farming' methods have been introduced into intensive livestock production, advances in agricultural technology have not increased the division of labour in agriculture. Rather mechanization has removed much of the routine drudgery from agricultural work and has allowed an increasing amount of job rotation, so that one worker may now perform a number of tasks – mechanic, driver, stockman, general labourer – each of which was formerly undertaken by one man.

For how long the decline in the labour force will continue to out-pace farm amalgamation and specialization – and therefore demand this degree of versatility – is a matter for speculation. However, the length and rhythm of the production cycle in agriculture will always introduce a wide degree of variety into agricultural work compared with most manual employment in industry, and it is doubtful whether the division of labour will ever be as extreme as in many factories. Compared with most other manual work, agriculture offers far greater non-economic rewards in terms of job interest, judgment, discretion, challenge, responsibility and control and is likely to continue to do so. For those who seek such non-economic rewards job satisfaction is thus likely to be high. Data on labour turnover, absenteeism and job satisfaction in agriculture, are rather meagre, although absenteeism is universally believed to be virtually non-existent and job satisfaction very high. In a small scale (N=55) survey in North Norfolk in 1969, 96 per cent of the agricultural workers interviewed found their jobs 'interesting nearly all the time' or 'mostly interesting'. This compares with the levels of job satisfaction reported by Blauner of 66 per cent among automobile workers, 82 per cent among textile workers, 90 per cent among chemical workers and 95 per cent among printing workers. In the light of Blauner's work, however, it is interesting to note that the absence of division of labour and the diffuseness of the work situation makes this operationalization of the concept of alienation very difficult to apply to agricultural workers.

The work situation of agricultural workers therefore conforms closely to the characteristic work situation of deferential workers outlined by Lockwood and Parkin. Moreover the trend is towards an increasing level of interaction with the employer and decreasing interaction with other workers. Other things being equal, this would tend to reinforce the agricultural worker's 'deferential' image of society.

The Monastic Life

G. Moorhouse

Reprinted with permission from *Against all Reason*, Weidenfeld and Nicolson, 1969, pp. 223–6, 235–40.

It is almost commonplace to find in a religious community people who have been there for half a century and more. And there is maybe nothing more astonishing to a secular world, which is permanently and continuously in a state of vivid flux, which is forever packed with incident, where high contrast in every form shapes the pattern of days, than the fact that there are many people who have lived for so long a life of comparative monotony

and immobility and who can say at the end of it that never for one
moment have they doubted that this was indeed their vocation.
But there are. More frequently they will say, like this monk of
three decades, that they have not *always* felt absolutely sure of
their vocation but that 'on the whole, by and large, I have grown
more sure. I have, indeed, been through experiences of very
considerable abandonment by God but this, I think, is very usual
in the religious life.' A nun who has just celebrated her jubilee
says that she has never seriously doubted the rightness of her
option for the religious life: 'Occasionally I have wanted or tried
to do so in moments, hardly even hours, of stress, but have never
succeeded.'

Stress usually derives from some personal friction or else from
some collision with the vow of obedience, in which case it can
take the oddest forms. A septuagenarian nun recalls that

'It was not until 1945, when I had been professed fifteen years,
that I had a terrible shake over the question of obedience. We had
been told that, although we were enclosed, the Bishop had given
us permission to go out to vote for Sir Winston Churchill in the
general election. Greatly as I admired Sir Winston as a war leader
I could not vote for that Conservative programme. So I stated
my difficulty and was of course allowed not to vote (the Labour
candidate was divorced and in favour of easier divorce). No one
was unkind to me, but it gave me a queer sort of shock. It was
only a priest who said to me, "Remember – 'Ye have not chosen
me, but I have chosen you' " that brought me back to the certainty and wonder of vocation.'

A wavering vocation is more likely to be felt by the young,
rather than the old in religion. A thirty-one-year-old Benedictine
monk says that 'Of course, one still has moments of doubt and
dissatisfaction with oneself. But reflection and prayer usually
seem to restore the balance. My doubts and misgivings are about
my own inadequacy, not about the certainty of my vocation.' An
Anglican monk of thirty-eight does not think that his vocation has
ever seriously faltered 'though there was a time not long ago
when I did have a depressing stretch. I am sure that this was owing
to the kind of work and the place where I was. As the tensions
were not just something that I felt myself, but were common to
the other brethren in that particular house I did not take seriously
any temptation to throw in the sponge.' A forty-five-year-old

contemplative nun who has been professed with her order only two years can say:

'that almost from the beginning of my life in the community I have had a deep, underlying conviction that this was God's call for me. But at all stages I have had times of rebellion and been tempted to give up and return to an easier life in the world, because I was unwilling to bear the cost of the necessary purgation of my inherent selfishness. Thus, as a postulant or novice and since profession, at times an inner voice has said, "Why carry on what seems a stupid waste of my life when I could have a good job, be successful in the world, comfortably off financially? Why not return home to my mother and so prove my love for her? Why not use my medical training and experience in the world and have the satisfaction of knowing I was helping people?" And at times there has been the whisper, "Is there a God at all?" I am sure that those times will go on, as faith will only grow and mature as it is tested; but knowing that the testing will never be beyond what God knows each one can endure.'

A forty-two-year-old sister, professed with her community for ten years, says briskly: 'Since becoming a religious the conscious certainty of my vocation has been almost entirely absent. This is neither unusual or important. It was a functional thing which served its purpose in enabling me to know God's will for my life – it was not intended to be a permanent prop of reassurance.'

And the purpose of it all? There are some religious who see it almost entirely in personal terms, like this monk.

'There is no particular virtue in living the Christian life in community as opposed to the world of the parish, the factory, the commercial undertaking, the Services or the home. Neither is there any particular virtue in l iving it in those worlds rather than in the cloister. There is no more virtue in working in freedom from the worry of making ends meet and coping with the income tax than there is in trying unsuccessfully to cope with these things and paralysing the rest of one's work. There is no more virtue in accommodating one's idiosyncrasies, talents, opinions and inabilities to the mind and milieu of the community than to that of the office or family. The commitment for life certainly plunges a brother into the joys, distresses, responsibilty and creative activity of a family; into the work of a corporation or cooperative society; into a freedom in which he is relieved of many difficulties which he is by nature incapable of solving; into a brotherhood in which he is supported by corporate prayer and intention. The immediate worship and service of God (which is the first requisite of all Christian work) is not the monopoly of the monastic, but is practised among all the faithful, priests and laity. For me personally, the religious life has made this practice possible again. I might also add that it has given an untidy mind a framework in which to pray, think and live.'

Others see their life as a signal to the rest of the world. A monk says:

'Although we reckon to have certain aims in the order I would say that we are here to demonstrate the truth of learning obedience by the things we suffer. We appear to give up all sorts of things, but if this is where we should be, then we are happy with the things that are provided for us here, we are the praying heart of the Church, and therefore the worship of God is first in our lives. Everything that people see, and by which they mostly judge our lives and our usefulness, is the outcome of this life of worship and prayer. Our founder said that we were a lot of men trying to be good. I think that this still holds – because it is what we are that is more important than what we do.'

A contemplative nun compares the convent to 'an experimental laboratory into which some are called to work out in a particular way the problem of how man can give himself to God and to his neighbour, and if this is the basic spiritual need of human life, then it is worth doing. This experiment involves every part of one's being – physical, mental, emotional and spiritual. If any part is left outside the experiment goes wrong, the gift of oneself to God is incomplete, and we have nothing authentic to give to others. People come to us either in person or by letter, expecting to receive the results of our experiences in Christian living and community, that they may work out the principles in their own particular vocations. This is part of the overspill from our prayers which they have a right to expect from us.'

Another nun appears, in the more conventional language of piety, to collect all these ideas and wrap them into one generalized diagnosis of the religious life. The object, she says, is 'that all the members of the community should become mature persons, unified in themselves and in ever-deepening relationships with God and so with each other; and so be a family of love, and by doing so to fulfil the purpose for which they were created, and so to give glory to God. By their increasing growth in sanctification and union with God to be channels of this love to the world, participants in this thirst that all men and all creatures should be drawn to unity, to respond to his love for their healing. Thus called to share in God's reconciliation, to stand in the centre of the world's forces of evil in the victory of Love's triumph on the Cross.'

So far, we have had religious talking piecemeal about a number of sides to their vocation; the quotations have been deliberately extracted from often lengthy answers to a questionnaire in order to form a coherent pattern of experience and belief in a highly complex subject. By contrast, here is an unedited statement of vocation and what it means to one man.

*   *   *

The monk's story

(A Benedictine monk, aged thirty-two. He took simple vows eight years ago and solemn vows five years ago.)

About the age of thirteen I was conscious of a desire to do something large and generous with my life. I had no notion what this could be, and the desire itself was completely formless except that, having had from my Irish mother a 'good Catholic upbringing', I felt the Church to be the biggest thing around, in fact the only true thing. Therefore my life must in some way be involved in it. I didn't equate this with being a priest, but because my then Jesuit form-master at the local Catholic grammar school was the most loving and lovable person I had so far met I wondered whether his life was the thing for me. The 'religious' and priestly ideal meant nothing, or at least was completely remote; but this man somehow broke the conventional Jesuit behaviour pattern by showing an unconditional and disinterested concern for us, for our growth. I remember in particular that he took what I said with complete and unaffected seriousness in a way no one else quite did, which may explain why my one-year contact with him left a deep impression which still remains. Without moralizing he communicated a sense that life, our life, was intensely worthwhile, wholesome, and could be terrific fun. I don't think there was much, if any, romanticism or fantasy in my view of him; I wasn't shattered, though naturally puzzled and dismayed, to hear of his very severe mental breakdown soon after leaving us. He remained for me a vital person.

Through later school years and two years' National Service, I had no deep desire to do anything in particular with my life. My non-Christian father, remote in childhood owing to physical separation during the war years, was a solicitor and joining him seemed a sensible thing to do, especially as his business was self-made and the idea of a son inheriting it meant much to him. So it was with this fairly formed intention that I went from National Service to university, yet with a sense that this career, and indeed any career acceptable to most people I knew, was not quite real for me, somehow not adequate to my deepest desire and need. My father had very generously made it clear that any desire to be a priest would have his support, but this was not then appealing.

At university my only intimate friends were Old Boys of the school run by my present monastery. Through them and some of the younger monks also at university I came here first, largely out of curiosity to see the place which had produced my friends. The sophistication of their minds and the depth of their thinking about religion were a revelation after the prosaic and second-hand quality of religious instruction at the grammar school. Coming to the monastery for a few days was a deeply moving experience; a glimpse of a new, strange and curiously attractive world of which I wanted to be a part. I had no intellectual notion of what the monastic life was about – I wanted to be whatever these men were. Very simple so far.

At school I always moved happily in a like-minded group of friends, free of any emotional intensity. This pattern more or less repeated itself on National Service, except that the RC bit gave me a certain sense of apartness in this new irreligious atmosphere. My faith now demanded at least some degree of nonconformity to the group ethos, at least in terms of Sunday Mass and saying night prayers by my billet bed, scrutinized by at least one hostile witness. But I was on easy terms with almost everybody, and very dependent on a group of new but firm friends. It was at university (age twenty-one) that I first consciously and intensely loved anyone in particular. My narrowly formed RC conscience turned this experience into a morbid, guilt-ridden infatuation. This temporarily fixated relationship clogged the vocational issue because the person I loved (A) intended to join this monastery after university. This was at once a draw to the monastery and a repulsion from it; while desperately wanting to be always with A I felt guilty about this desire, which seemed a radical disqualification for the monastic life. Another friend, whom I now realize I loved more deeply (B), joined the monastery a year before I left university. I missed B very much in my last year and the thought of him in the monastery was a terrific pull, unclouded by the increasingly paralysing guilt associated with my immediate contemporary. My desire to be with my friends won out, although I seriously considered joining another monastery.

It seems clear to me now that it was quite simply human love which brought me here, although the attraction and inspiration of the place as a whole suggested a larger worth-whileness in living the life my friends proposed to lead. In letting my love lead me in this way I wondered very much whether I was really escaping, doing the nearest and most immediately appealing thing instead of something less congenial and more mundane, like my father's job. I couldn't exercise this doubt, and entered the monastery hoping rather desperately that all this would be resolved positively or negatively in the noviciate. It wasn't!

Things were further complicated by the noviciate-induced feeling that the search for and service of God were paramount, with love of other people as a kind of by-product of the God-and-prayer business. This made my emotional involvements a worry, a distracting irrelevance; yet I could never feel in my bones that they were no more than that. The fact that other people were absolutely important for me suggested that I was really in bad faith and should leave, or at least make the kind of psychological break with my friends which others seemed to find workable but which I felt to be beyond me. The recognized guides (books and older monks) had things to say about 'the problem of particular friendships', but they weren't adequate; they treated this as a *problem on its own*, never suggesting how such a relationship could be creative.

Sex was a closed book, so that the fact that my love included sexual attraction and desire made me think, at least with a part of myself, that it was outrageous, sinful, lustful, sacrilegious even. Words like 'sublimation', heard occasionally in the monastery, suggested there was an answer to be found, although the word itself was never enlightened in any practical way by the speaker. But I could never feel in my bones that loving another monk in this way was simply taboo, although often thinking that I ought to leave because of the intensity of the emotional-sexual pressure in the rather hothouse enclosed noviciate atmosphere. A further complication was the sense of not-quite-really about so much of the God-and-prayer business; this, I felt, was something I had to be able to take on and make my own, yet it never really connected with the rest of my life in any satisfactory way.

The first glimpse of anything I could honestly call 'certainty' about my vocation came in my fourth year here, when I began to be deeply influenced by an older monk. This was the year in which I had to try to reach a final decision about solemn vows, due that September. The terms in which superiors posed the problem – 'Do you really want to serve God in the monastic life?' – were artificial, presenting me with what I felt to be an unreal and therefore artificial question, although part of me felt this *ought* to be the real, decisive question. So it was a flash of light when this older monk (C), who had recently taken a more genuinely personal interest in me than any other older monk, suddenly said: 'The real vocational question is "Do you want to share the problems of this community?"' This struck home because it pin-pointed the sort of bond I already felt with the monastery in a way which seemed to unify all my hitherto fragmented concerns. The tension involved in my love for B was by no means resolved, but here at last was a conviction which made sense; a desire to help and serve this community in any way I could. In particular I thought of the commitment as helping the monks to resolve a spiritual crisis which their communal and personal history had clearly left radically unresolved at the time. I don't know what I thought I could do, but I wanted to be in on anything that happened. C communicated a strong sense that out of so much darkness and confusion some tremendous good would surely come. A deeply intuitive person, this conviction possessed him. Then, in the pre-solemn vows retreat, an old monk with the reputation of a highly intelligent eccentric, suddenly said, 'The eyes of the heart should be on all the brethren all the time.' I wondered why I had had to wait four years to hear this from a monastic preacher: I took solemn vows.

Subsequently I became ever more involved in C's struggle to articulate his new-found conviction about the Christian life and the monk's life ('You either marry or go it alone – if you take the second option it turns out to be going it with everybody.') His preaching was the service of the community as the key to what it meant to be a Christian and a monk. Deeply influenced by Teil-hard de Chardin, he discerned a unity in the whole of creation and in personal experience, which was for me a liberation. I could never understand how I was such a help to him, since I seemed little more than a sounding-board for his ideas. He was so con-scious of the mawkish sterility of even the most positive elements in the received teaching on particular friendship that he seemed to deny the relevance of emotional intensity between people, despite a message of love. So while giving me a firm conviction that we were working towards a re-birth of our own community in an unimaginable oneness of mind and heart, he couldn't fully resolve my personal uncertainty. I thought he would have been dismayed and outraged had I told him of my real feelings towards my contemporaries. There was very great emotional intensity in his talking and teaching, but a very deep inhibition prevented any clear articulation of this.

Recently we have been given a new insight into the equation of the communal and the personal which simplifies the whole busi-ness and leaves me with a new and deeper certainty that the love of one another is the only worthwhile thing, that it is this and only this which creates community, that only growth in this love will equip us for service in the wider world beyond the monastery to which we must increasingly look. This is no longer a largely notional conviction, still less a maudlin sentimentality, but an increasing intuitive awareness of the reality of others and of how we can in fact help to create each others' lives. The obverse of this is an increasing realism about the impossibility of really loving, the recognition that whatever real further change we can initiate in one another will be, like what has happened to us so far, a gift to us all.

This, then, is my present vocational certainty: a clear-headed involvement in the creation of a community to serve the world in a way which will hasten its end. I see this as the unification of my hitherto fragmented experience in the ability at last to begin to love others straightforwardly and wholeheartedly without fear or scruple. One consequence is that the options are now open in a new way: I am no longer worried as to whether or not I am a 'queer', but neither am I worried about what would happen if I were to fall in love with a woman. Ultimately I doubt whether full spiritual freedom can be reached without an intense man–woman relationship, but I don't see the sexual consummation as essential. Indeed, it seems that relationships which by-pass the immediate consummation have a special function in building up the whole human community and precipitating its final fulfilment in God – this is what I mean by the end of the world.

I should add that what has brought me to my present certainty is a sense of *being loved* unequivocally. The sense of being wholesomely and unconditionally loved has begun to release in me the power to love, so that more and more people are now clear to me as growing vessels of the Spirit, in whose growth is my salvation. This may sound a piece of abstract or pietistic wishful thinking, but I am writing out of an experience which has rapidly stripped me of many illusions and self-defences, out of a newly discovered sense of my own real self and others' real selves which is deeply unromantic and open-ended (but emphatically not *unfelt*). An older confrère not at present resident in the monastery has called this the recovery of sanity; if it reads like the belated discovery by a deeply neurotic person of a basic human truth familiar in childhood to more normal people then my language has failed me.

This is a love which *is* for ever; I am certain of my brethren, whatever they may do, say or think, now or in the future. This certainty works outwards into other relationships, producing for instance a new and exciting freedom in family relationships and leading to an increasingly direct and genuine contact with a wider range of people.

As hinted above, I think the purpose of our life together is to bring the world to an end by the practice of an all-embracing, open-ended love. Few monks would accept this without cavil – many would find it incomprehensible or shocking. And this conviction would be an absurd, delusive fantasy if it didn't illuminate Christian and monastic tradition. But all the classical monastic doctrines now take on a new fullness of meaning: the search for God, loving obedience, communal prayer (effective sign of our love's present achievement and future fulfilment), so-called private or personal prayer (to facilitate some depth of reflective awareness of reality, of all that is and how it moves), the flight from the world (i.e., the darkness, whatever requires exorcism in Harvey Cox's sense, of *The Secular City*). The world is intensely present in the monastery; this stripped-down way of living together heightens consciousness of what is truly dark and unresolved in all our lives.

The monk least of all can avoid the burden of consciousness of the whole human spectrum and the insistent challenge to new ways of spiritual action which that consciousness provokes.

Perhaps we can define the monastery's function as exorcism. True, that is the Church's function – but the monks are explicitly and consciously committed to this task. If a monastic community can be exorcised, what task is beyond it? I have known sufficient exorcism to believe total exorcism possible.

Further Reading: Slaves to the Machine

J. G. ABEGGLEN, *The Japanese Factory*, Glencoe, Illinois, The Free Press, 1958.

*R. BLAUNER, *Alienation and Freedom*, Chicago, University of Chicago Press, 1964.

*T. BURNS, *Industrial Man*, London, Penguin, 1969.

*N. DENNIS, F. HENRIQUES and C. SLAUGHTER, *Coal is our Life*, London, Eyre and Spottiswoode, 1956.

*A. ETZIONI, *A Comparative Analysis of Complex Organizations*, New York, The Free Press, 1961.

P. R. LAWRENCE and J. W. LORSCH, *Organization and Environment*, Boston, Harvard University, 1967.

LIVERPOOL UNIVERSITY DEPT. SOCIAL SCIENCE, *The Dock Worker*, Liverpool University Press, 1954.

*D. LOCKWOOD, *The Blackcoated Worker*, London, Allen and Unwin, 1958.

J. G. MARCH and H. A. SIMON, *Organizations*, New York, Wiley, 1958.

*S. MARCSON, *Automation, Alienation and Anomie*, London, Harper and Row, 1970.

V. H. VROOM, *Work and Motivation*, New York, Wiley, 1964.

C. R. WALKER and R. H. GUEST, *The Man on the Assembly Line*, New Haven, Yale University Press, 1957.

W. F. WHYTE, *Men at Work*, Homewood, Illinois, Irwin-Dorsey, 1961.

* Available in paperback.

Chapter Eight

The Texture of Work 2:
The Pursuit of Autonomy

... When I was a boy
I loved to shape things. I loved form and colour
And I loved the material that the potter handles,
. . . .
For me, they are life itself. To be among such things
If it is an escape, is escape into living,
Escape from a sordid world to a pure one

T. S. Eliot, The Confidential Clerk

An hour alone spells freedom to the slave

Pete Atkin

Most sociologists would agree that the immediate deprivations
and discomforts of working life are not the most important
components of alienation. More fundamental reasons for the
feelings of powerlessness, normlessness, meaninglessness and the
lack of capacity to control one's own destiny are related to
men's self-conception of themselves as workers. Innumerable
studies have documented the tendency for workers to attempt
to control their own level of output in relation to some notion
of 'acceptable' standards of reward and remuneration. Others
have shown how individuals may try to extend their range of
satisfactions from inherently unrewarding work by 'messing
about' and horseplay. The extracts reprinted in this chapter do
not all fall directly into this tradition, but rather illustrate a
few of the organizational situations which can permit
individuals to pursue an autonomy in *their* work which may be
denied to others.

Thus the systems analysts and programmers interviewed by
Mumford regard their work as satisfying because it provides
them with interest and variety. As one said 'What more could
one ask for? It is intellectually satisfying and interesting. One

is in the midst of innovation. One meets people who are controlling the situation everywhere.' But there were other satisfactions, too, to be derived from 'working with people' and human relations skills were also stressed.

Hollowell's lorry drivers pursue autonomy in a fairly similar way to the navvies studied by Sykes in Chapter 6. Like them there are strong distinctions of status between types of drivers. Like them, too, there is a good deal of geographical mobility. But the drivers' individualism meshes in well with the situation of 'mock-bureaucracy' because of the collusion of management and workers to evade nationally imposed regulations. Lack of adequate maintenance of vehicles and the practice of 'flogging his log' (less exciting than it sounds) combine to keep the lorry-driver, even the respectable hard-working 'trucker' at the top of the status hierarchy, in a rather marginal position in relation to the authorities.

Ronald Blythe's *Akenfield* perhaps comes closest of all contemporary work to recapturing the clarity of social relations within 'the world we have lost'. Terry Lloyd, pig farmer, is confident, and to the head-start of four acres and an old barn he has added the formal symbols of qualification through the day-release agriculture centre. Although the natural rhythm of the seasons does not determine the whole of his life as it might have done that of his forefathers he has never had a holiday since he left school. When he says 'It's a long day and I don't mind', the reason lies in his autonomy: as he points out 'I am lucky, I work for myself'.

The 'new craftsmen' studied by Williams are supported by a bureaucracy, the Rural Industries Bureau. They are clearly different from the traditional craftsmen, not merely in terms of the nature of their craft, but because of their social origins and their expectations that a certain pattern of life will consequently follow on this adoption of a certain type of work. Their pursuit of autonomy has taken them out of the industrial urban system, but their existence in the rural economy may be tenuous for 'they are not members of a community except in the most formal sense, and economically they are linked most closely to the towns'. Possibly these, more than Terry Lloyd, the pig farmer, will be more representative of rural workers during the next few years.

Pamela Bradney shows the importance of joking in relieving the burdens of working in a large department store. It may be

useful for students to compare this analysis with that of
W. F. Whyte in his study of restaurant employees in the USA.
Joking, as Bradney describes it, is not perhaps accurately
enough identified as another way of pursuing autonomy – but
it indicates some ways in which the analysis of apparently
casual or idiosyncratic forms of behaviour may help us to
understand the system of social relations in which 'work' of a
particular type is embedded. Joking, too, may be seen as a
response to deprivation: in Chapter 9 we look further into
some of the more formalized ways in which workers have
historically tried to defend their position.

Computer Programmers and Systems Analysts

E. Mumford

Reprinted with permission from *Job Satisfaction: a Study of Computer Specialists*, Longman, 1972, pp. 160–1, 164–70.

Work content and job satisfaction in our firms

When examining the nature of the task contract in our firms –
that is the extent to which the kind of work provided by employers met the needs of their employees for variety, interest,
challenge, etc., – one thing stands out immediately. This is the
apparent success of employers in providing their data processing
staff with the kind of work they enjoyed. The answers to two
questions show this clearly. These questions were, 'Have you ever
regretted your decision to become a programmer (analyst)?', 'If
yes or no why is this?'

Table 1. Degree of satisfaction with work choice (percentages)

Have you ever regretted your decision to become a programmer
(analyst)?

	Yes	No	No answer
Users	13	87	—
Manufacturers	4	91	5
Consultants	3	93	4

If you have no regrets why is this?

	Likes the work	Other answers (Career prospects/ potential of computers)
Users	65	35
Manufacturers	50	50
Consultants	73	27

People who said they liked the work expressed great satisfaction with its interest and variety:

'The work is interesting and varied and I am my own boss.'

'I am never bored or idle, all the jobs are different.'

'What more could one ask for? It is intellectually satisfying and interesting. One is in the midst of innovation. One meets people who are controlling the situation everywhere.'

'My only regret is that I did not move into the work earlier.'

There must be very few jobs in industry which evoke this unbounded enthusiasm. It seems that data processing provides a continuously challenging work state for those people involved in it and many experts believe that this is the most satisfying factor in work. Leavitt suggests that people tend to programme their activities so that these become routine, and then to complain that their work is uninteresting. They ask for the certainty of highly detailed job specifications and then complain about 'deskilling'. He believes that where tasks can be made challenging, they should be, and that this process provides greater satisfaction than the much recommended 'participation' in taking decisions and defining objectives.

Let us now look in more detail at the jobs of programmers and systems analysts using whenever appropriate Cooper's categories of physical variety, goal structure, control over work and task identity.

*　　　*　　　*

Table 2. Job content (percentages)

	Technical only	Technical and administrative or technical and human relations	Technical administrative and human relations	Total
		Job described as		
All programmers	44	36	20	100
All systems analysts	12	46	42	100

Many programmers saw their skills being used only in technical areas, while systems analysts saw their skills as having a technical, administrative and human relations orientation. In all three groups – users, manufacturers and consultants – those who saw their jobs as primarily technical tended to be under twenty-one while those who described activities which were technical, administrative and involved dealing with people were likely to be over twenty-six years of age. The fact of working for a user, manufacturer or consultant appeared to exert little influence on the distribution of work activities within the three categories. Consultants, however, had no systems analysts who saw their work as solely technical.

This breakdown gives some indication of the content of programmers' and systems analysts' jobs, but a better estimate of the number and different kinds of skills required in programming and systems analysis can be derived from examining the activities that people referred to when describing the technical, administrative and human relations aspects of their work. Let us consider programmers first.

Programmers

If we begin by looking at *technical* job content a measure of skill variety can be obtained by distinguishing conventional programming activity from other activities which programmers may perform and which require different kinds of skill and knowledge. Conventional programming is defined here as covering the functions described by Papetti. These are:

Detailed planning of programs.

Study of diagrams and flow charts and their documentation.

Drawing up the sequence of instructions making up programs.

Testing the programs on the computer, correcting them and making adjustments.

Documentation of the programs.

Maintenance of the programs and software.

Revision of the programs as a result of changes in processing requirements.

Operational responsibilities associated with the provision of a data processing service.

In addition to these functions some programmers had responsibility for certain aspects of systems analysis and systems design; others were required to have a wide knowledge of computer hardware, software and applications; others again undertook customer liaison in order to familiarize themselves with customer programming requirements. These programmers can be categorized as having specialized areas of skill and knowledge. A further small group were engaged in research and had responsibility for the development of new programming applications.

If we now analyse the activities of programmers in our firms the pattern emerges as shown in Table 3.

Table 3. Activities of programmers (percentages)

		Conventional programming	Specialized areas of skill, knowledge and responsibility	Research and innovation
Users		94	6	—
Manufacturers	A	26	68	6
	B	75	25	—
Consultants	A	22	—	78
	B	34	66	—
	C	64	28	8

These very different percentages require some explanation. In our user firms we interviewed the commercial programming groups who were generally engaged in routine programming activities. Both Industrial Products and the government department also had specialized programmers who did not come within the scope of our survey. In computer Manufacturer A programmers were concerned with sales-customer liaison and many were required to have extensive knowledge of the Company's hardware and software and to be able to advise customers on the nature of their data processing problems. These responsibilities required the majority of programmers to have a range of skill and knowledge wider than that found in the user group. In computer Manufacturer B, in the section where interviewing was carried out there was less direct contact with the customer and programming activities were more comparable with those found in the user group. The three consultants differed from each other in the kinds of skills they required of their programming staff. Consultant A was a research-based organization and programmers there were working on highly innovative aspects of data processing. For example, the design of information retrieval systems, including on-line retrieval, on-line patient monitoring for hospitals, computer-aided systems analysis, etc. Consultant B's programmers had considerable customer contact and many of them had to have a wide knowledge of equipment and computer applications. Consultant C's programmers also had this kind of knowledge although it appeared to be located in a numerically smaller group. Once again it must be stressed that consultant programmers and systems analysts were hard to distinguish from each other.

If the interfirm differences are ignored it can be seen that there is a progression in programmer skill variety from user group to consultant.

Table 4. Progression in programmer skill

	Conventional programming knowledge	Specialized areas of skill and knowledge	Research
Users	94	6	—
Manufacturers	50	47	3
Consultants	40	31	29

It is dangerous to generalize from these results that consultancy work always offers more skill variety than that of manufacturers and users. It would be strongly argued by both our computer manufacturers and at least one of our user firms that some of the more specialized staff working in their research and development sections would have just as much skill variety in their jobs as those of consultants. Nevertheless the trend is probably correct and it is reasonable to expect to find more people with a large amount of technical skill variety in their jobs working for consultants than working for users. It must be emphasized that these differences in skill variety were in no sense a source of job dissatisfaction. In the user, manufacturer and consultant groups the vast majority of programmers had never regretted their decision to make data processing their career and were enthusiastic about their work. The fit between the amount of skill variety [not reprinted here] that programmers were looking for and the amount provided by the firm seemed everywhere to be a good one.

In our original discussion of skill variety we pointed out that Cooper saw it covering three things: *object variety* – the number and complexity of problem areas in the task; *responsibility*, and *required interaction* with others which contained an element of uncertainty. Responsibility is impossible to define in the present context as we have no way of knowing how employers weighted the different tasks they required their programming staff to undertake. Interaction with different groups as a factor in skill variety is quite easy to evaluate. Here we found that in the user group required interaction was usually within the programming group or with the systems analysts group. In the manufacturers, in addition to interaction with internal groups, there was also interaction with clients – particularly in Manufacturer A. In the consultant group many programmers had considerable contact with clients. Interaction with others as one aspect of skill variety therefore increased as one moved from user to consultant.

It can be seen that there are considerable variations in the number and kind of technical skills found in the programming group with consultant staff generally using the greater variety of skills. Let us now see whether a variety of skills were required in the programmers' *administrative* activities. An examination of programmers' descriptions of the administrative content of their jobs shows that, in fact, administration is not an important aspect of programming. In the user group the most common form of administration was related to responsibility for a small group of subordinates. There were also a few references, but not very many, to the necessity for documenting programmes and to other aspects of the planning and organization of programming work. In the manufacturer group programme documentation *was* administration for the majority of programmers. In the consultant group the programmers of Consultants A and B said that they had little or no administrative responsibilities and the programmers of Consultant C referred again to documentation. The stress laid on programme documentation by the computer manufacturer's programmers suggests that it was in this group that most emphasis was given to this activity. In general, administration was not an area which provided much opportunity for the exercise of a number of different skills.

Programmers were asked to indicate how much and what kind of human relations skill they required in their work. It can be argued that those EDP staff who have to interact with non-data processing departments in their firms or with customers in other firms will operate in a more uncertain environment and require a broader range of human relations skills than those who merely relate with data processing colleagues. With the manufacturers and consultants, success in customer relationships is a major factor in success in business. In all three groups the successful implementation of EDP projects depended on effective human relationships with user areas. Set out in Table 5 are the groups where programmers told us their human relations responsibilities were primarily located.

Table 5. Programmers, human relations responsibilities (percentages)

		Own department only	User departments in own firm	EDP departments and user departments in clients' firms
User firms		90	10	
Computer	A	—	—	100
manufacturers	B	67	—	33
Consultants		57	—	43

Programmers working for computer manufacturers and consultants have to liaise with the customer and therefore require human relations skills. This was especially true of computer Manufacturer A's programmers who all claimed to have some customer contact. They said: 'This is a difficult area for us. The programmer is the link man between the systems analyst and the client and the machine. He has to explain machine faults in a way that both the systems analyst and the client can understand. Therefore he must use a great deal of tact.'

Systems analysts

The job of the systems analyst is tremendously varied and provides opportunity for the use of many complex skills. Papetti defines it as covering the following activities:

1. Ascertaining existing manual or mechanized procedures and their documentation.
2. Analysis of the requirements and automation possibilities of the procedures ascertained.
3. Definition of the new organization procedures and their documentation.

4. Design of the processes for automatic data processing and their documentation.

5. Definition of the programming systems for the implementation of processes designed.

6. Training of personnel in the organizational units concerned in the new automated procedures.

7. Starting up and implementation of the new automated procedures.

The systems analyst has therefore to use his observational and analytical skills to understand the workings of the manual system. He has to weigh up the deficiencies of the manual system and decide how it can be improved, using the potential of the computer to assist this improvement. Once he has formulated a solution to the problem he must design the new processes and procedures which form part of this solution and, on occasion, define the programming requirements of his new system. He must ensure that staff in the user department are trained to operate the new system and he must see that the new system is successfully implemented.

Because these steps are so comprehensive and complex it was difficult to spot differences in the technical skill variety of systems analysts working for users, manufacturers and consultants. Descriptions of the technical content of their jobs given by user systems analysts fitted well into Papetti's definition: 'I am looking at the present organization of work in user departments and trying to find better, more advantageous ways of running these departments. I then implement these new systems.'

Systems analysts working for computer manufacturers also described the technical content of their jobs in these terms but, like their programmer colleagues, they spoke a great deal about their need for considerable hardware and software knowledge, and about their advisory role. 'I must have a fairly high level of understanding of equipment and its limitations. I need a good knowledge of those computer applications which are relevant to industry's requirements.'

Once again the consultant group came out as having a wide variety of technical skills. There were references to the need for management science and operational research expertise; for management ability and for the knowledge and experience to deal with many different kinds of applications. The Consultant A systems analysts described in detail the highly innovative local government, hospital and other projects on which they were working.

'The technical content of my job varies from project to project. I must determine a client's requirements, design computer systems to meet these requirements and get hardware specifications from the computer manufacturers. I must evaluate the computer manufacturer's proposals. I must also control and direct the work of the systems analysts; produce time tables and progress the work; manage a team of people, and do public relations work with the clients.'

Whereas programmers had laid claims to few administrative skills, many systems analysts saw these as a major part of their activities. One told us: 'I am an administrator. I implement new ideas and call on my experience of previous situations.'

In user firms, systems analysts saw their administrative responsibilities as covering four principal areas. The first was the organization of their own work; the second, the management of the work of a team of systems analysts; the third, project administration covering every aspect of the implementation of a new computer system, and the fourth, documentation such as the production of proposals, reports, contracts and information for the customer.

Although major differences in the technical skills required by systems analysts have proved difficult to identify, administrative differences were much clearer, as Table 6 below shows.

Table 6. Administrative skills required by systems analysts (percentages)

	Own work only	Managing EDP team	Project administration	Report writing etc.
User firms	37	30	15	18
Manufacturers	24	19	22	65
Consultants	21	28	39	12

Few user systems analysts had a great deal of administration, other than organizing their own activities and looking after a small team of analysts. Manufacturers' staff described the greater part of their administrative responsibilities as preparing documents of one kind or another for their customers. Consultants, in contrast, said that their administration was primarily concerned with project management and control. This was particularly the case in Consultant B, whose staff were encouraged to assume a DP management role when working with clients.

All systems analysts gave the same degree of emphasis to their human relations skill area. This involved encouraging users to look at their work from new angles, maintaining good relationships, 'selling ideas' and generally communicating what they were trying to do in a meaningful manner. Many systems analysts saw 'human relations' as the most uncertain, difficult and important part of their work.

'This [human relations content of job] is very important. It involves introducing new methods to traditional people and selling my ideas.'

'It is a most important area. We work with top management and have to be able to communicate and to assist in the formulation of objectives and rational methods of managing. We have both a line and staff role when we are in a client company.'

This analysis of the variety of skills required by programmers and systems analysts shows clearly that both specialisms require a multitude of skills and the use of these appears to be an important factor in job satisfaction. Indeed when asked 'What aspects of your work do you find most rewarding?' both groups tended to answer in terms of the totality of work operations.

'When one is able to create successfully by one's own efforts. One has a sense of achievement, an ability to influence events [a programmer].'

'It is succeeding with a project, selling it and having it go like a bomb. Pleasing people and saving time and effort.'

Programmers tended to stress the technical aspect of their work and as one moved from user firm to consultant there appeared to be an increase in technical complexity. This was not true of systems analysts and the greatest difference between those working for users and those employed by consultants was the amount and kind of administrative responsibility they were required to assume. All systems analysts placed great stress on their need for human relations skills.

The Lorry Driver
P. G. Hollowell

Reprinted with permission from *The Lorry Driver*,
London, Routledge and Kegan Paul, 1968, pp. 27–70.

Types of lorry driving job

One cannot look at a lorry driver as he passes by and predict precisely what his job entails. Many lorry drivers do not work in the road transport industry, a factor which alters their conditions of work greatly. For those who do work in the road transport industry there is a great deal of variation. Many sorts of loads are carried in many different makes of vehicle and to meet the needs of manufacturing industry arrangements have to be made for specialized working. The customers of the road haulage industry are probably the cause of task specialization within lorry driving itself. Within the road haulage industry the lorry driver may take one of three specialized jobs. The jobs are those of the Shunter, the Trunker, and the Tramper.

(a) *Shunting*

A 'shunter' can be almost any kind of local delivery driver. He may just be called a local or general delivery driver if his lorry is below a certain weight, perhaps three or even five tons. Usually in the road transport industry a shunter is a driver of a vehicle of around fifteen to eighteen tons capacity. He drives a big vehicle, but usually only within a certain radius of the depot. More often than not, every shunter on a firm has a trunker whose lorry he takes over and delivers the load that the trunker has brought down overnight. The shunter is a driver who spends perhaps more than half his time in loading and unloading his vehicle. He begins his day by offloading vehicles at factories, warehouses and docks. Once the shunter has delivered his load, which may include several 'drops' (deliveries), he then calls at the places where he can obtain another load for his vehicle. He loads his vehicle and then takes it back to the depot and, if it is at the end of his shift, he checks the oil and petrol and lights to make sure that the vehicle is ready for the night trunker. He may load several vehicles in a day according to the cargo and return them to the depot for the trunkers.

(b) *Trunking*

A 'trunker' is a lorry driver who drives a lorry from point A to point B or perhaps, if he is on a 'changeover trunk', he drives the vehicle (usually an articulated vehicle consisting of a unit and trailer) from point A to a point halfway to point B where he changes trailers, according to a pre-arrangement, with a driver from point B. The changeover point may be at a café and is usually so but not always. Consignment notes are usually exchanged at these points. A changeover trunker returns to home base by the morning, and thus although he is a long distance driver he always sleeps in his own bed every day. However, some trunkers may go from point A to point B, stay the day at point B in transport accommodation, and then bring their reloaded vehicle from point B to point A the following night. The archetype of trunk driver just drives; he does not load or unload his vehicle, nor does he deliver loads to customers, or pick up items for transportation. At the depot he picks up his loaded vehicle, which the shunter has left for him, and delivers a loaded vehicle for his shunter in the morning.

(c) *Tramping*

A tramper (otherwise called a 'rover' or 'roamer') is a driver who, unlike the trunker, has no set route. He starts out from the depot perhaps on a Sunday or Monday morning. He collects a load and loads his vehicle himself. As soon as he collects the load the tramper knows the first destination in his week's work. He may deliver the first load in one 'drop' or there may be several 'drops' in one load. If there is a whole load for point B, then the tramper may pick up another load at point B, which may take him to point C. At point C he may load for point D, and so on, until at the end of the week he gets a load for point A, his home base again. The journey described above is only one possible journey of a tramper, the important point to note is that the tramper has no fixed route normally. He is a lorry driver who really does not know where his week's work will take him. A tramper loads and unloads his lorry and delivers goods to customers. His job is probably more physically arduous, because of the loading and unloading that he does, than the trunker's job. A tramper's job is characterized by more variety and less regularity than is a trunker's job. Another characteristic of tramping is that the tramper may himself be left to his own devices to find and organize a return load, or a load to some other place than by his depot. This is why he has no set programme since, until he gets a load from a clearing house or some other place such as the docks, he will not know where he is to go.

All the three jobs in driving have a great deal in common but they have a good deal that is distinct between them. The local driver or shunter is still within his own community when he works by day. In fact as he is travelling about in his community he probably knows it much better than people in less mobile occupations. The long distance drivers, the trunkers and trampers, spend most of their working time away from their community. The trunker goes away at night and even when he is on a 'changeover' he spends most of his time at home asleep. In fact a six-night-per-week trunker may mean that the trunker has very little community life of any kind, either in his own community or another. The tramper spends perhaps as much as a week (more in some cases) away from home and after his day's work he eats and sleeps in transport accommodation. Thus, although all three categories of drivers may be seen by the casual observer to be doing the same job, in fact both working and leisure time conditions are very different between the three.

*   *   *

The lorry driver is a skilled workman with a responsible job and one which can be dangerous. The type of skill required, together with expansion of the road haulage industry, tends to skew the age distribution of the lorry-driving population towards youth. On the other hand, some of the most desirable characteristics a good lorry driver should possess are considerable experience and emotional stability, a maturity and reliability that usually only come with age. The interplay of these two factors, physical ability and maturity, turn out to be important determinants of the lorry driver's career pattern.

For all his skill and responsibility, the lorry driver is not all that well paid. His basic rate of pay varies according to age up to 21 years and then by carrying capacity of the vehicle. Average hourly earnings are well below those in 'All industry' (exclusive of agriculture), although average weekly earnings approach the average for all industry since the lorry driver works long hours. An eleven-hour-shift is prevalent among private haulage drivers and BRS drivers have a ten-hour-shift. Working conditions in the road haulage industry vary a great deal from firm to firm. It would seem that the drivers of goods vehicles with 'C' licences have better conditions than drivers in the road haulage industry. Conditions in British Road Services are laid down with the agreement of the union and are clearly defined. The trade union is an accepted part of the industrial relations system at BRS but this is not always the case in the private firms. This fact and the regional location and employment position make for variation in working conditions in private firms. There is less variation in wage rates than in a free market as firms can be prosecuted for paying below the minimum required by the Road Haulage Wages Council Orders. However, many private firms pay over the rate or give excellent bonuses which make some lorry drivers' earnings very high.

From this summary, the lorry driver emerges as something of an 'individualist'. His job, the driving itself, is done in semi-isolation where communication is by signals because of the boundary of the cab. The managements interviewed generally believed that lorry drivers like to have a large area of discretion in their job. This area of discretion arises from the separation of the driver from his depot and management for most of his working hours. The amount of discretion varies according to the type of driving job the driver has, whether it is shunting, tramping or trunking. Paradoxical to this substantive discretion is the fact that the work situation is a complex of rules which emanate from various agencies. The driver's individualism may make him much more conscious of the rules in the total work situation. This consciousness will also vary between firms, the discretion of the driver will be less in the nationalized BRS with its formalized set of rules, than in the smaller private haulage firms. The private firms can have a less formal system and allow greater discretion since the managements can have a personal knowledge of the drivers they employ.

It is possibly the way the industry has evolved which has created the individualism among lorry drivers. The chaotic conditions of the 1920s have subsided with the regulations imposed by the 1933 Road and Rail Traffic Act. In spite of this Act, the rapid growth of the industry since the war, coupled with the freeing of road haulage in 1953 has produced conditions in which the many rules and regulations are evaded. The evidence is that, in Gouldner's terms, the rules of the Ministry of Transport have to be seen as 'mock bureaucracy'. Either the lorry drivers do not obey them, or the firms do not, or there is collusion between the two parties to evade them. This collusion takes place in the private enterprise road haulage firms, whereas BRS are on the whole extremely observant of the rules.

The trade unions are only weakly equipped to deal with the abuses that go on. The lorry driver is difficult to organize, particularly by a general union as big and diversified as the TGWU. The emergence of more specialized associations, known generally as 'Drivers' clubs' are representative, at least to some extent, of competition for the trade unions. The clubs attempt to help the lorry driver without attempting to restrict him formally, although informally, attempts are made to induce him to behave in a way which is agreeable to the community as a whole.

There is an objective situation in the work environment which makes for the inability of the lorry driver to achieve and maintain a status ranking in the eyes of the general public. The existence of 'mock bureaucracy' through collusion of the managements of smaller private firms and their drivers in order to compete in what is a very competitive industry has produced scandals. The lorry driver may well be driving an ill-maintained vehicle and is very likely to be 'flogging his log' by working hours which are over the legal maximum. If managements see the lorry driver as an 'individualist', and attempt to conform with such expectations, then the lorry driver will inevitably see a deficit in terms of the social reputation of his group.

*   *   *

Driving experience and career progression

An examination of the experience of the drivers in the sample in the various driving jobs supports the supposition that drivers progress by age from local driving to shunting, to tramping, trunking and finally back to shunting. This progression is shown in diagrammatic form as Figure 1. If the supposition about the age progression is correct, it is to be expected that trunkers will, for the most part, have held both shunting and tramping jobs, and that trampers will have held jobs in shunting but not in trunking. Shunters have already been presented as being divided into two categories, the younger age group has had little experience other than shunting, and the older age group of shunters have very likely had experience in either trunking or tramping or both.

With all three types of driver interviewed, the mention of entry

into the various types of driving followed the supposed pattern.
For all three types of driver the age on entry into shunting or
local driving is lower than the age on entry into tramping. Both
these entry ages were lower than the entry into trunking. The
order of age progression is that trunkers progressed through all
the categories at an earlier age than trampers, who progressed
through at an earlier age than the shunters. Trunkers have, for the
most part, had some experience in the other types of driving.
Over three-quarters of the trunkers have been trampers or
shunters at ages lower than their entry into trunking. Trampers on
the other hand have much less experience of trunking (only
18 per cent of trampers have been trunkers) than shunting (82 per
cent of trampers have been shunters). For shunters the percentage
who have been trunkers is 34 per cent compared with 58 per cent
who have had experience as trampers. The lower percentage of
shunters who have been trunkers may be explainable in terms of
the job content in relation to age; it may be that a trunker gets set
in his ways and out of practice at lifting heavy weights which the
job of shunting demands. It may be that a trunker is physically
incapable of doing a shunting job after being a trunker for so
long. Many trunkers probably retire from lorry driving altogether
after they are no longer able to go trunking. The attitude to
shunting, as a job, will be the key to discovering why more
trunkers do not return to shunting.

Aspiration to the various types of driving job

How far do lorry drivers have a 'perception of the whole occupational system and their places in it?' To what degree is any
particular driving job recognized as the 'top' driving job? The
vertical axis in Figure 1 is essentially an indication of prestige.
Trunking is shown as the job with the highest prestige, while
tramping holds second place, and shunting has the lowest
prestige, as it is either the first or the last job held.

There seems to be some kind of recognition of the prestige of
driving jobs and the career progression by the lorry drivers
themselves, though this is not entirely unambiguous. This perspective is the basis of the indicator used for the prestige axis. However the recognition is not completely in pure career terms but
rather in terms of the relative advantages and disadvantages of the
different kinds of driving. For instance, there are domestic and
social advantages of having a trunking or shunting job as opposed
to being a tramper.

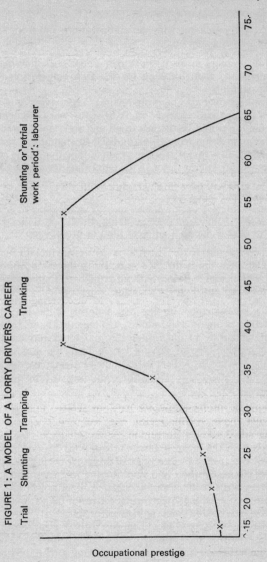

FIGURE 1: A MODEL OF A LORRY DRIVER'S CAREER

Trial Shunting Tramping Trunking Shunting or 'retrial work period': labourer

Occupational prestige

'The trunk work is for the convenience of my wife – there was difficulty at home, my wife had an operation; and from "shunt" to "trunk" is a step up.'

Money enters in also: 'Fortnight about (i.e. shunting for a fortnight and then trunking for the following fortnight) is a better paid job.'

Trunking may also be more secure: 'Years ago if you were a trunk driver they kept their trunk drivers – when the depression was on you would be the last to go and service would count.'

The progression from trunking back to shunting is also mentioned. In this case a trunker predicts that this is the way his career will go, but for this man the family factor was also relevant.

'The girls will have finished school and I'll apply for a lighter job when I'm about 55.'

Another trunker who was talking about the status of lorry drivers gave a clue to a different kind of progression.

'The wife tends to think that lorry drivers are fucking bums and what disturbs me is that she must think the same of me. The progression used to be local, tramp, trunk, and that's as far as you could go, but not today – shunting is the top job.'

This last statement implies that shunting is the job which is aspired to as opposed to trunking. On the other hand, the following statement by a trunker indicates that some trunkers at least, perceive their type of driving job to have the most skill and prestige. 'Trunking – there's less traffic at night. You can keep to your time, and you're with your own class of people – you all know one another.'

Certainly, the figures used to illustrate career continuity show a similarity between trunkers and shunters, which tends to put in doubt a hypothesis that trunking is the driving job for the lorry drivers with the greatest career orientation. The aspirations of lorry drivers to the various types of driving job will show whether in fact the recognition of a 'top' driving job exists and to what extent it exists. If the aspiration pattern does not fit in with the progression, then the drivers' perspectives of the various types of driving job should reveal the reason for this.

There is a strong identification with present occupation: 67 per cent of trunkers think the best job is trunking; 52 per cent of trampers think tramping the best driving job; and 58 per cent

Table 1. Determinants in the lorry driver's career pattern

Age	15–20 years	21–25 years	26–35 years	36–55 years	56–65 years
	Trial work period	Shunting (1)	Tramping	Trunking	Shunting (2) or retrial work period
Situation	Incumbence in a non-driving mobile occupation or an occupation from which driving is a 'visible' occupation.	More a local delivery driving job than a real shunting job, where trunkers are serviced. If the driver is between 17 and 21 the vehicle driven will be under 3 tons.	Driving heavy goods vehicles to all parts of the country on a schedule determined by where the work is to be found. Loading and unloading as well as driving.	Set journeys: night work with the possibility of staying one day in two away from home compared with 4 days to the week in tramping.	Shunting on local work, 'servicing' trunkers vehicles; often loaded and unloaded by cranes.
Factors in movement into an occupation.	General but the 'trial work period' is enforced by legal restrictions on the ages of drivers.	Gaining experience before insurance restrictions are lifted. Socialization.	Socialization; learning to load various types of goods, to sheet and rope a load and unloading. Also where to pick up loads.	Trunking: a job for experienced drivers.	Needs a lighter local job such as shunting where loads handled by crane. May move into labouring of one kind or another since transport firms may not have any jobs other than for drivers.
Factors in movement out of an occupation.	The 'visibility' of driving making it a natural next move. Also possibly alienation from other occupations.	Long distance work is more adventurous and less monotonous than local work. The driver has by now family responsibilities which can be financed by long-distance work. Long-distance driving is a natural progression from short distance work.	The age-strength threshold is reached. The driver can no longer load or unload easily. Family and community pressure. The comforts of home and companionship of friends in home community, the loneliness of wives and the desire for family life.	Psycho-physiological changes – vision – the homeostatic mechanism. Night work. Domestic problems: wife needs company. More community life needed by the driver himself.	Retirement.

of shunters think shunting the best job. Overall, however, trunking is the preferred job, with 40 per cent of the sample mentioning it. Shunting is next with 35 per cent and tramping least favoured with 25 per cent of drivers in the sample preferring it. In the private haulage firm tramping is definitely the least favoured job and trunking definitely the most favoured. At BRS shunting is the most favoured job and tramping and trunking are favoured equally. Within the occupational categories the most noticeable thing is the lack of preference for tramping. No shunters say they prefer tramping, while only 4 (11 per cent) of trunkers opt for tramping. On the other hand, 16 (32 per cent) of trampers prefer, and 16 (42 per cent) of shunters prefer trunking.

Indication of the progression being aspired to is apparent from the table but rather tenuously so. More trunkers prefer shunting than prefer tramping. More trampers prefer trunking than shunting, and shunters prefer shunting and trunking but not tramping. This information, coupled with a knowledge of the relative present ages of the types of driver, shows an aspiration pattern along the lines of the suggested progression from shunting and local, to tramp, trunk and back to shunting.

Terry Lloyd . . . Pig Farmer
R. Blythe

Reprinted with permission from *Akenfield: Portrait of an English Village*, Allen Lane, Penguin Press, 1969, pp. 212–22.

In spite of the sweet reasonableness or dire warnings offered by the advocates of bigger units, Britain remains remarkably full of farmers going it alone, or who would go it alone given half a chance. The young men aren't showing lack of greed but realism when they say 'ten acres will do'. Whether it is some far cry back to the old pre-Enclosure days or the same uncooperating spirit which confronts the French agricultural economists with the blunt fact of *two million* or so small farms, the truth is that the almost sensuous contentment of doing what you like on your own bit of land persists as strongly now as ever it did. The Akenfield small-holders will tell you that they have to work all the hours that God ever made, that they never have a holiday and that they have to watch every penny. Yet even William, the young shepherd, with his new estate house, bigger than most wages, responsible work and generally superior prospects, dreams of 'getting out and having a little place of our own. My wife wouldn't mind; she'd do anything to help me. It is all she wants too.'

Terry Lloyd achieved this enviable state the week he left school at fifteen, when his father gave him four acres and an old barn. At twenty-one he shows some of the conventional signs of the freelance, a precariousness accepted as an ordinary condition of being alive, enough fear not to do anything silly and quite a bit of unegotistical self-assurance. He is a small, quiet, thoughtful young man, mature in his outlook but without that essential limitation or simplicity which makes things comfortable. He is a thinker. His mind is restless in the way that the Suffolk rivers are restless. The water hardly seems to move at all, yet it reaches the sea. He is a natural maverick, a masterless one. There is a searching quality in his manner, as though he is looking for somebody who will instruct him in the basic grammar of an as yet faintly grasped language, some key which will lead to 'all the rest'. Books? The question brings the inevitable embarrassment. The village people of all ages seem frightened at the mere mention of books. Why isn't this book-fear dispersed at an early time? Why should it exist at all? A seventeen-year-old wrought-iron worker from the village, a good craftsman and an apparently lively youngster, said, 'Yes, I have read books. I read Enid Blyton when I was at school.' The normality of reading scarcely exists. To nearly every person interviewed, it was a strange thing to have read a book. The book is a kind of frontier across which few seem to have the nerve to pass, even when, as in Terry's case, it is the only way out.

The county day-release agriculture centres are producing interesting side-effects. In the purely social sense, they have contributed more to the destruction of the derelict vision of the farmworker as a kind of sub-standard human being than any previous plan to improve his status. But something else is also taking place. The mere process of class attendance and an intelligent interest in his affairs by equal-seeming adults has set the learning process in motion for the first time for many youngsters who left school at fifteen. This is what has happened to Terry, now in his last year at the Centre. One master in particular has helped him, and others like him. What has emerged from this still fairly new – about ten years old – governmental further education programme is that one part of a student's intelligence cannot be trained to the degree necessary for him to learn the new sophisticated farming methods without his whole intellectual nature being awakened. Terry is grateful for the extraordinary amount of tangential information Mr Austin has been able to throw off upon such subjects as natural history, politics, current affairs – even art. To an outsider, many of the students appear famished, starving for something more than the curriculum provides, and there seems to be a unique opportunity to accomplish on the young adult scale something comparable to what Sybil Marshall achieved in her condemned Cambridgeshire playground and described in *An Experiment in Education.*

The truth is that there is a void where the old village culture existed. Ideas, beliefs and civilizing factors belonging to their grandfathers are not just being abandoned by the young countrymen, they are scarcely known. A motor-bike or universal pop might appear to be a reasonable exchange – but not after you have begun to think.

I went to day-release about five years ago. It starts off pretty basically – machinery, crop husbandry, stock husbandry – and then, in the second year, it goes on to the farm institute level. I am taking the management course at the moment. It is made up of two parts, records and accounts and general management. I feel myself that the day-release scheme really offers more than the full institute course. It has certainly made all the difference in the world to my life. There are five masters at the Centre. I get on very well with Mr Austin – we all do. He'll discuss anything with us – insurance, history, morals, religion, sex – anything. It is tremendous. Something completely different. Other industries have had their training schemes for years and, as usual, the poor old farmworker gets his last! Anyway, we've got it now. It isn't philanthropy. There was suddenly a need to train the village boys to use machinery and understand the new scientific methods. There is such a massive amount of machinery used in farming now. The men are going down, down, down on the farms and the machines up, up. What men are left have got to be real good – different to what they used to be.

I always wanted to work on a farm – but I was born in Leeds! I can't remember Leeds because I was so little when we left, nor can I ever imagine myself as being there. Me in Leeds – impossible! But I was. Then we went to Scotland, where I went to school in a little town in the mountains. Everything was beautiful there. But if you want to know how I came to Suffolk, you will have to hear about my grandfather Merriam Lloyd, who farmed the Dove. And if you haven't heard of him, then you're a newcomer yourself. He wasn't really a farmer, in fact he was a bicycle-shop owner by trade. He came to Suffolk in 1910 and bought the Dove for about £500. He was a bachelor who walked about with a gun – you know the sort. He was very independent and nobody could tell him anything. He knew it all. His farm wasn't much when he bought it, by all accounts, but it was a sight worse when the Second World War broke out. He hadn't done a thing except walk round it. Of course the War Ag. told him to plough up his meadows – told him! Of course, he wasn't having that. He took no notice. So they pushed him out. Some men came and literally pushed him out of his own front door. Then they brought some bits of furniture out and stood it round him on the lawn. They wanted the house, you see, for administration. Well, he went to live in a shepherd's hut in the orchard, where he stayed all through the war and doing absolutely nothing, of course, and the Dove was given to Jolly Beeston to farm. Jolly was nothing then but he's very big now. The war made him. He paid a florin a year on each acre for the Dove, just to make it legal. He ploughed it all up, ploughed all his own margins and wastes up, got subsidies – he was quids in. He was made. He's never looked back. The war put him on his feet and, do you know, although he didn't do one single stroke of work, it made my grandfather quite well off too. He was so lazy that he didn't fill in his compensation claim forms until after 1951 – and he was still living in the shepherd's hut – but eventually they sent him £350 damages for putting Nissen huts in the Dove garden. So he had a good war. I don't blame the farmers for the war fortunes; I'm glad it happened. But, all the same, when I see their big cars and little swimming pools, and think how, before 1939, some of them were riding around on bikes and having to sell a calf on Tuesday to pay the men on Friday, well it is amazing. Some of them really suffered. They won't, they *can't* talk about the old days. Not because they are ashamed of them but because they were so badly hurt. Some of them can't rid themselves of little economical habits which can't possibly matter any more. Like Mr Clary, who must be worth a couple of hundred thousand, but who still sweeps the last drop of barley from the barn floor himself.

The war and the price of the land going up has made them all.

And good; the land shouldn't rot. But it has also made it quite impossible for someone like myself to go into arable farming. The net profit on an acre of barley is about £10 and wheat about £17. Put this against land worth £300 an acre with ingoing valuation – it's about three per cent! Well you can't do it. Everybody is trying to manage bigger acres with bigger machines and less labour. Put it like this, to manage 200 acres you need two tractors, but with two tractors you could also manage 250–80 acres. You see, you have to try and spread the machine cost over as many acres as you can.

Then you have another problem – labour. Although labour is being cut and fewer and fewer men are needed to work the farms, it is still hard to find them. They are all going away from the land. An intelligent young married chap simply can't afford to be a farm-worker. Those who stay, the bright ones, I mean, stay because they really love the land. A young man like this can be found working all hours of the sun. This love-the-work business is all very well but sooner or later these clever, hard-working countrymen will have to be seen as experts, and paid accordingly. Otherwise they will simply have to drift off into the service industries like the Milk Marketing Board and the seed and fertilizer merchants.

I am lucky, I work for myself. When I left school at fifteen, my father let me have four acres of his ground rent free. So I got a job on a farm at £4 7s a week. I gave mother £2 for my keep, put £2 in the bank and spent the seven bob. I never spent notes, only silver. I saved for about six months and then I had enough to buy three little pigs. I fattened them, sold them, and bought five. One of these was a gilt. £45 it cost me. I've still got this same gilt today. She's had ten litters and I'm very fond of her. I kept on selling off the litters because this makes a quick turnover. You buy a gilt in pig and take the pigs off her when they are eight weeks old and sell them as stores, and the money turns over nice and quick. You've got to pay for the gilt's keep from the minute you've bought her. You must turn her out on the meadow, put her in pig, care for her. Anyway, eventually I've built up until I now have thirty sows, which are as many as I can manage. I daren't do any more to it, not yet, anyway.

I've got a boar. I haven't been too choosey about him because I'm not fattening. A good boar is very expensive – about £90. Mine was cheap – he cost me £37. He's a pretty good buy.

I like the work so much. I have to do it all. So I wouldn't step the sows up any more. I feel that the more you get the less well you can do the work. So many people say, 'Ah, we've done very well, we've made so many pounds profit, so look what would happen if we got 100 pigs! We would be home and dry.' But it doesn't work out like this, because you either have to pay wages or not be able to give so many pigs the same attention which you can give a few.

I breed Essex pigs, which are very good mothers. They produce a blue pig which sells pretty well and is very hardy. I do all the buying and selling myself, and have this sense of freedom. It is wonderful. Freedom, if you would like to know about it, is getting up at 6.30 every morning, having a wash and breakfast and being outside by seven to start feeding. I feed all the pregnant sows on the meadow by throwing sow-cake down on the grass. I'm very lucky, I've got this little stream running through my land, so I water from it. After feeding and watering, I start cleaning out. I do it twice a day. The old traditional method was to clean out once a week but it is much simpler to do a bit each day and work right through. Then I water everybody and go home to eat a proper breakfast. After breakfast, I might go to market at Campsey Ash with the pigs which are fit to sell. I like to watch them being sold. If they don't make the right price, back they come! I used to have a man cart for me but now I take them in a little pick-up which I managed to buy. I'm not very fond of people who live by carting animals around, they tend to knock them about and pigs especially look very bad when they are bruised.

The market is full of dealers forming a ring. They're whispering at the tops of their voices, as you might say. It's 'bid for this' and 'don't bid for them'. But if there happens to be a scarcity they will bid for anything. They go mad for pigs. I like to introduce a smart pig right off the teat at eight weeks. You can actually take a pig off at three weeks, but I'm not very fond of this practice. You get five litters in two years with three-week weanings – two and a half litters against two of the eight-week method. But it is a very expensive system because you have to buy a special milk substitute feed for them which works out at £70 a ton. The best way I know is the outdoor weaning system, with your pigs out on grass in little bale shelters. You build up disease if you keep pigs in the same building year in, year out.

I have dinner at twelve, do all kinds of jobs until half-past four, then it's feeding again. I have tea at six and at eleven, just before

I tuck in myself, I have a walk round to see if everybody is cosy. Pigs are funny animals and like a sense of being cared for.

It's a long day but I don't mind. I've never had a holiday since I left school. I have been out of the county now and then but I always get back the same day in time to feed. I honestly don't mind. I think that once you've started this animal business, you've started a way of life within yourself. I couldn't live without a pig, which might seem a funny statement to you. I work every Sunday. It seems worse when you're talking about it than when you're doing it. East Anglia is now *the* pig area and the chief thing about myself is that I tend not to join in the huge Suffolk pig world. I may see it all differently later on. Maybe.

It is a very precarious business. Pigs are a difficult stock to control. They don't stay steady, they waver from surplus to shortage. What happens is that, in February, the Government assesses what the nation's pig requirements will be for the next year and guarantee what they call the 'middle band'. The middle band consists of between six and eight million pigs. It has a guaranteed price. This year it was 45s 5d a score. If production falls under this band, the Government steps up the guarantee to encourage production; anything over, and the price just drops off. This is how it is supposed to work, but it doesn't unfortunately. There will be pig surpluses at the end of 1968 – even if foot-and-mouth really hits us. At the moment about one pig in 200 is being slaughtered. It is nothing! One gilt will produce twenty pigs a year. You could, if you wished to, keep the ten or so gilts out of this twenty and breed them – and so on. I don't belong to any of the groups like Porcofram. I work alone and sell on the open market. I have to do this, it is the way I am. I am all right now but when the surplus time comes I shall get hit. The price on the open market will sink; I will know all too well that it would have paid me to be in the group.

Walls have really spoilt the pig market round here. When they first introduced their pig scheme they said, 'Right! produce a pig for us as fat as it is long!' They weren't interested in grading. They wanted a big pig of between 250–300 pounds – a heavy hog, a cutting pig. The legs of this pig went into hams, the rest into sausages and pies, and the fat into ice-cream. Well, eventually they got so much of this pig fat stored away into the hangers and Nissen huts of an aerodrome that they said, 'Right! We've got enough.' And so they packed their big pig scheme up – and a lot of pig-farmers came unstuck.

I am a member of the Young Farmers' Club. It is not a thriving club. A lot of these YFCs lack something, I don't know what exactly. They're made up of sixty per cent farmers' sons, thirty per cent young men from the service industries and a sprinkling of farm-workers' children. The service industry people are reps or officials. The reps join because it's the policy of the feeding stuffs and fertilizer firms to establish friendships between their young representatives and the boys who are soon going to own or manage farms. I joined to get to know people. No, this isn't exactly true; I joined to get an education. That was the real reason. We go on farm walks and that sort of thing. But the fact is that these clubs offer the working man's son very little. They cater for boys with £1,000 a year and a sports car. The clubs are rather snobbish and even if you don't care about snobbery you can't help seeing it. It is the bugbear of the clubs, spoiling everything. To tell you the truth, I feel completely out of it. Some of the members simply don't want to associate with you. You are not in their class, they think. They have been to Framlingham or Woodbridge School. Or even to Felstead. They either won't or can't conceal that they are 'different'. I tolerate all this simply because of the educational side of it but I have learnt that if you don't have certain kinds of clothes, a car like theirs and spare money, then you don't just belong – even if you're a member! All the clubs have this atmosphere. I keep away from the strictly social activities and only attend the walks and talks. Very few girls come to the clubs – at this particular branch, anyway. I often wish that I had joined the Ipswich branch. The atmosphere could be better there. It is so hard to get accepted. I never understood anything about this until I joined the club. I don't want to 'get in', as they say; I just want to go and be ordinary. I am the only member of this club who isn't a farmer's son – my father is a farm-worker – or a rep. The gentlemen-farmers' sons are quite different. For instance, they arrive in sloppy jumpers and jeans when everybody else wears Simpson's hacking jackets. These boys haven't a clue what it is all about and obviously can't tell me from the rest. But Suffolk isn't really a snobbish place. I wouldn't like you to think that.

The Agricultural Training Centre is a far better meeting place than any YFC. I belong to the Stockman's Club there – what a difference in the atmosphere! It is a wonderful club, really useful. It costs 5s a year to join – and 25s a year to belong to the YFC.

Working on my own tends to cut me off from people. I am involved in the little circle around me but, so far, I have never managed to make a successful move out of this circle. Even with a car.

I do quite a bit of reading. I have read a novel sometimes but most of my reading is connected with pigs. It would do me good to broaden my outlook, I suppose. The trouble with my life is that, except for Mr Austin, nobody has ever talked to me about anything except farming. I watch television but if you look back on television – it is the saddest thing. I like the News. And documentary programmes, like that old film about the Russian Revolution.

We often have discussions at the YFC but the members, although they are not much more than boys, have already learned to shut their eyes to what is going on in the world. They have firm opinions about everything. They can't debate, they make statements such as 'The Americans are doing a good job in Vietnam, stopping Communism'. Full stop. What is the point of arguing? they seem to say. When I told my father he said, 'Funf has spoken' – it is an old wartime joke. I told the YFC that the Vietnamese were really just farmers in revolution, but nobody spoke – except to say that the Americans are doing a good job, etc. I am astonished that they are able to hold such strong, solid opinions about things which they can't possibly know a thing about. A lot of them are the sons and grandsons of self-made men who worked very hard until the war made them rich.

I am a member of NUAW. I think it is a very bad thing when young men don't join the Agricultural Union. Everybody connected with modern farming should be united in this way. The pity is that the young men are affected by the 'beaten' men. But the beaten men are all so old now – over fifty, so why worry what they say? You take George Annerley, he has the fear on him still. Farmer-fear – it went all through Suffolk. George thinks that he is betraying his farmer if he joins the Union, and I know plenty like him, men who would sooner admit to anything than that they were socialists. Catch them putting an election poster in their cottage window! The young men are absolutely different. They speak their minds. The boys who go to the Training Centre aren't fools; they know that they are able to do specialist work on the farms and that a good worker isn't going to be sacked because of his politics. A good worker can get a farming job in a day. A lot of us think outside all the newspaper talk and believe in the Labour Party – not just the Prime Minister, but in the socialist movement. But I haven't very strong political feelings myself and I am not an outright socialist. I just want to go forward and to stop this everlasting looking back.

I am recruiting for the Union. I got six members in one week! All from one farm, and not one of them had thought about joining before. One of the older chaps said that he couldn't see what good the Union did because it wasn't getting us the money up. But how I look at it is this, unless there is a complete and intelligent new support for the Union, how can you expect it to work? Too many of the members do nothing but look back into the past. The past is finished. Over. Whatever happens, it will never be like that again. These old farm men make you feel so damned miserable. Be what you are, say what you have to say. Stop staring over your shoulder. Laugh at old Sammy Eden. Do you know what happened on his farm during the election before last? All his men stuck red rosettes on the tractors and things and drove around all day before he spotted them. That night he sacked the whole bunch – and then three days later he had to re-employ them all again because he knew he'd got the best men in the whole neighbourhood.

I don't feel all that personally attached to Suffolk. I often fancy Scotland. I dream of Scotland. I think it would suit me. It was the Scottish farmers who came down here before the war and worked harder than the Suffolk men, and began to put new life into the place. A lot of these men farmed on the rock. Think of farming on the rock and then drawing a plough through this rich earth! How surprised they must have been. But I don't think a lot about the future. I find life quite enjoyable. What I would like would be to farm like the Barber brothers. There are four of them and they've got about sixty acres each. They aren't mechanized but they are wonderful farmers. They follow the Norfolk four-course plan of wheat, barley, beans and roots. Mind you, they live virtually hand-to-mouth, as you might say, yet comfortable. Their fields are beautifully clean. Everything is traditional, but without the struggle and misery. I would love a little traditional farm, plenty of muck, plenty of grass. I would go right in and say, 'For the first two or three years I shall rob this land and get a return'. When I talk of 'robbing', I mean that where there's plenty of grass and muck there will also be plenty of phosphate and potash in the soil. My fertilizers would be cut right down. I could rob and get away with a good start, and probably take off three crops of wheat before I had to start spending real money.

East Anglian country people work very hard. The young men

will do anything to make a start. The working-class village boy gets on because he won't mind what he does or how long he does it to get a start. A lot of boys start with a partnership. When he has proved that he can make a bit of money, another young man will go in with him and the pair of them won't marry or spend a penny for several years. They live very carefully. They will sell beansticks to the gardens on the Ipswich estates. They don't have such a strong sense of missing things as the town boys have. Not many country boys round here have record-players, so pop music doesn't 'take' in the same way as it does in London. The boys will listen to the music on the radio but they won't buy records. And most of them won't buy the fashions because one of the things about a village is that you never give anyone anything to talk about if you can help it. That is why I admire Hughie. Do you know Hughie? Hair like a girl and trousers so tight you wonder he can breathe. What a nerve he's got! The old women clack about him and the men whistle. But he takes no notice at all. But why shouldn't he do as he likes?

I haven't got a girl-friend. Plenty of time. And I'm not promiscuous either – what a word! Sometimes I go to the dances in Ipswich but it is very, very hard to get a partner. The girls come with their boy-friends and won't dance with anybody else. The boys are mostly mods. Not many boys from the village go to these dances. I have also been to the Saturday-night dances at Framlingham but it seems virtually impossible to meet a girl in this way. The village girls like to get married very young but the boys don't. Many of the boys don't want to marry until they are about thirty, although plenty of them have to long before then. I have a friend whose girl made all the running before they were wed, now he has to beg for it. I sometimes get lonely for girls.

I have been to London three times but have always returned the same day. I have never slept there. It means getting up very early in the morning, getting all the work done in advance, having a bath, getting there – real drudgery! But it is only once a year. I go to the Smithfield Show. But I think I will try and take a proper holiday this year. You might say that I have had an awful warning! It was like this. A chap I know down the lane, a very hard-working chap who started up like me, only twenty or more years ago, has just had to sell half his farm. It seems that he was so busy working, saving, making sacrifices, that he forgot how to bargain. So here he was, buying his clothes from the second-hand shop in Ipswich, getting streaky bacon ends from Sainsbury's at twopence a pound, never having a day off and working like a black. This was how he got on when he started but now that he's getting old – forty-five or more – he has become lackadaisical in the strangest way. You would think that he was working for somebody else instead of himself. You could say, 'This hay is £20 a ton' – and although it might be the biggest rubbish, he'd buy it! Everybody was having him on. Things began to fall down on his 120-acre farm. Then there was a creditors' meeting. It was a wonderful thing for him. He saw the light. He said to me after last harvest, 'Fenner the contractor tried to charge me 7d a bale for this baling hay. A bit dear, ain't it? I said. I cut him down and got it for 5d.' Now the deed of agreement has been drawn up, this small farmer has become a saved man. He's paying cash for everything. He's a saved man. Redeemed by the auditors! So perhaps I shall get to Scotland for a week this summer – let my brother look after the pigs. I mustn't get like old Charlie. I am getting on. I shall be twenty-two on Valentine's Day.

But I am forgetting, I do quite a lot of things. I shoot. Commotion – and not just for the birds. I've got these four acres and if I see a pheasant on them, I might shoot him. But no sooner than the gun is heard there is somebody rushing round, wanting to know this, wanting to know that. It is nothing to do with them. They are my fields, it is my gun. I have a licence for it. The pheasant is the god, you see. People like me aren't supposed to pot at the god. But I do – I have just done so. With any luck I am just picking him up when this face appears over the hedge. 'I thought I heard a shot,' says this man. He looks as if he could burst or faint or something. He wants to shout, 'Sacrilege! sacrilege!'

There is something else I do – silversmithing. I learnt it at evening classes. I have made a beer-mug and a chalice.

The Joking Relationship in Industry
P. Bradney

Reprinted with permission from *Human Relations*, 1957, pp. 179–87.

It became clear in the course of some research in a London department store that it may be possible to apply usefully in industry certain concepts that have emerged in the study of primitive societies. Although in industrial research an attempt is often made to apply concepts and methods of social anthropology, the result of this is never recognizably anthropological. It is generally just a case of using big, meaningless terms like 'culture' in a way that adds nothing to the understanding or the analysis. In this study of a store, however, two specific forms of relationship, widely investigated by anthropologists, have been found helpful in understanding the work group situation: first, the joking relationship; second, the relationship between members of a family. It is with joking in the store that I wish to deal here.

*   *   *

The store is one of the largest of the department stores, selling a wide variety of merchandise from haberdashery to all types of household equipment. With the exception of such sections as Men's Wear, Sports Equipment, and Furniture, it is staffed mainly by women. The immediate group under study is that of the individual sales department, selling a particular type of commodity and occupying a limited floor area within the store building. At the head of each such group is a 'buyer' who runs the department and is ultimately responsible both for the success of its merchandise and the efficiency of its members. An 'underbuyer' assists the buyer and is responsible for the day-to-day running of the department and the direct control of the selling staff. The number of sales assistants varies according to the size of the department; the average is about seven or eight. Each has her own section of the counter or floor space on which to sell (allocated by the under-buyer), and a commission of $\frac{1}{2}$ per cent is paid on all sales in addition to a basic weekly wage. There are also usually one or two 'juniors' attached to the department, who are training to be sales assistants and act as messengers and light porters for the buyer and underbuyer.

For the sales assistant there are three main groups of external factors controlling her activities. These are the internal plan of the department and its relation to the store as an architectural unit; the various store procedures, primarily that of selling; and the staff hierarchy. In making a transaction with a customer an assistant has to know where to go in the particular departmental arrangement for the variety of goods she needs and the necessary wrapping materials, etc.; she has to sell the goods in accordance with the correct method of sale appropriate to the customer's wishes; and finally, she has to perform this operation while continually open to orders from the buyer and underbuyer controlling the department and interruptions from co-workers who are her rivals.

* * *

The third and most important of the controlling circumstances that affect the assistant are the contacts made with her by other members of the work group. These contacts are of two kinds: first, those made with her by either the buyer or underbuyer; second, those made by her co-workers. The buyer may at any time ask to see an assistant or get her to do a special job, and the underbuyer, in carrying out her daily organization of staff, arranging meal breaks, etc., and dealing with queries from both staff and customers as they arise, frequently has to interrupt an assistant to tell her, for example, that a special order has arrived and may be dispatched or to ask her how a particular 'line' is selling. More frequent interruptions, however, come from the second type of contact – that with co-workers. There is so much to learn and know about where things are situated in both the department and the store as a whole, so much to know about the sales procedure, etc., that working side by side as the assistants do, it is inevitable that they refer to each other from time to time about these matters, often interrupting a sale in doing so. Interruptions also come from members of other departments.

The three types of difficulty described are, of course, simple and natural enough. They are only to be expected in an organization like a store and most likely may be seen to exist in nearly all human activity. However, the sales assistant's activity is one that requires a special effort of concentration and for her the time factor is of considerable importance. This is because she is working on a commission basis, which means the quicker she can apply herself to finding out a customer's requirements, producing the goods from the department, and convincing the customer that these are just what she is looking for, the quicker the sale is completed, the commission on it assured, and the assistant ready for another sale. Time is money in this business and by making the most of it an assistant not only satisfies a personal goal – to maximize her earnings – but also consolidates her position in the eyes of the buyer and underbuyer and achieves considerable prestige in the eyes of other assistants.

Seen in this light it is clear that in each case the difficulties described are a direct hindrance to the rapid completion of a sale.

In each case the first two types of difficulty are inevitable: whatever the sale, it has to be made in the particular geographical setting of the department and it has to be made in accordance with one of the prescribed procedures. The third type of difficulty, that of interruption by other members of the staff is not, however, inevitable, and in fact sales do occur without such interruptions. It is usually when the department becomes busy and all the assistants are serving that demands and questions become most frequent and coming as they do, particularly at times like this, they are a sort of 'straw to break the camel's back' for the assistant.

It is at this point, then, when an interruption comes from another member of staff to hinder a sale and waste valuable selling time that one would expect to find friction in the department. One would expect to find the relationship between the assistants on such occasions tense and offhand, with a tendency to quick temper and harsh language. But what *do* we find? We find a 'joking relationship'.

To take an example: a window-dresser, on approaching an assistant during a busy period to ask her to get out some stock for the windows, said, in a cheeky joking manner, 'I've come to bother my favourite blonde again!' and she replied, jokingly and with only a pretence of grievance, 'Why do you have to pick on me? What've I done?' In any other context the sentences spoken might have been regarded as impertinent or angry, but because of the tone of voice used and the understanding between the members concerned, it was a joke. They both smiled and the assistant was soon attending to the window-dresser's requirements.

Before considering in greater detail the function in store life of this joking relationship, and whether in fact it may be regarded as a joking relationship in any way akin to that usually connoted by the terms, let us consider Radcliffe-Brown's definition of joking relationships and the part he considered them to play in primitive societies.

Radcliffe-Brown defined the 'joking relationship' as 'a relation between two persons in which one is by custom permitted and in some instances required, to tease or make fun of the other, who, in turn, is required to take no offence'. He wrote: 'The joking relationship is a peculiar combination of friendliness and antagonism. The behaviour is such that in any other social context it would express and arouse hostility, but it is not meant seriously and must not be taken seriously. There is a pretence of hostility and a real friendliness. To put it another way, – the relation is one of permitted disrespect.' Radcliffe-Brown also distinguished between 'symmetrical' and 'asymmetrical' relationships: in the first, 'each of two persons teases or makes fun of the other'; and in the second 'A jokes at the expense of B and B accepts the teasing good-humouredly but without retaliating; or A teases B as much as he pleases and B in return teases A only a little'. Radcliffe-Brown stated that in some instances the joking or teasing is only verbal, while in others it includes horse-play; in some the joking includes elements of obscenity, in others not.

The main function which the joking relation seems to have in primitive societies is to maintain a satisfactory relationship between persons and parties who as a result of their particular social ties might be inclined to feel some hostility towards each other but between whom it is important, from the society's point of view, that the relationship should not become strained. For instance, as Radcliffe-Brown put it, 'in the relation between a man and his wife's family there is both social disjunction and social conjunction – the man is an outsider to his wife's family, and vice versa, yet after marriage there is a continuance of a wife's relations with her family which has a continued interest in her and her children'. 'Social disjunction implies divergence of interests and therefore the possibility of conflict and hostility, while conjunction requires the avoidance of strife.' 'Any serious hostility is prevented by the playful antagonism of teasing and this in its regular repetition is a constant expression or reminder of that social disjunction which is one of the essential components of the relationship, while the social conjunction is maintained by the friendliness that takes no offence at insult.'

The joking relationship in the store does seem to be similar to that defined by Radcliffe-Brown, in regard to its function: there is clearly a divergence of interests among sales assistants, i.e. 'social disjunction', as a result of their formal relationship. Each wants to increase her own sales – to earn both a better living and the approval of her employer – and is in competition with the others to do this. There is also every likelihood of hostility and conflict between them when they interrupt and hinder each other just at a time when this interferes most with selling. Yet it is essential, for a number of reasons, that the relationship between assistants should not become strained. If this did happen, in the first place they might cease to help each other with their queries and work problems. They might even purposely get in each other's way or refuse to cooperate; customers would witness this hostile behaviour and the generally unpleasant atmosphere resulting might increase labour turnover. All this would undoubtedly mean a loss of sales which would be bad both for the organization as a whole and for the individual employee. The 'social conjunction' between the assistants – because they are working for the same organization, on the success of which their livelihood ultimately depends – makes essential the avoidance of strife in the department, and it is at the point where conflict is most likely to arise that the joking occurs.

The type and method of joking in the store are also similar to that found in primitive societies, although there is both a slightly wider variety of method and a very much wider variety of subject-matter than that mentioned by Radcliffe-Brown. Store joking is altogether less formalized than that of primitive societies. In the store, joking occurs not only between two persons, but also between one person and a group and sometimes even between two groups. It occurs both in contacts necessitated by the system and in personal contacts and may consist of either one of the following or a combination of these – a jovial manner of passing the time of day or commenting on the weather or some other matter of topical interest; mutual teasing about personal habits, appearance, love experience, morality, and, in particular, work and method of work; telling funny stories about members of the store and telling other funny stories in some way relevant to the subject of conversation. Unlike joking in primitive societies, this joking is not confined to teasing and being teased.

These different types of joking extend from the lower to the higher ranks of the organization in roughly the order in which they are listed above, i.e. there is a tendency for lower ranks to adopt a jovial or teasing manner in their contacts and for higher ranks to tell funny stories. This may be due to the fact that members of higher rank spend more time in social contact with each other in the course of their work, whereas sales assistants do not have the opportunity to tell long stories while they are serving. All the subjects listed are used in carrying out the day-to-day work of the store, i.e. in the course of the social contacts this necessitates.

To take a few more examples: on a particularly busy afternoon when a porter went into a selling department to empty the waste bin, inevitably hindering for a moment or two the movements of the assistants inside the counter, he said in a jovial way, 'Gets more like Christmas every day, don't it?'

When a new girl appeared to be working overhard and taking her work too seriously, one of the old hands (to whom the new-comer had put yet another query to help her with a sale) said, 'You want to sell up the shop today, don't you?' – in a friendly joking manner even though it did conceal a reprimand.

Buyers and underbuyers are continually telling anecdotes in the course of their work, e.g. one story that frequently cropped up, particularly at underbuyer level, concerned the piano department, which had the reputation in the store studied of being moved around more frequently than any other department. The story was that when a customer asked (as customers always do) where she could find that department the assistant replied, 'If you'd be good enough to wait here, madam, it's sure to be passing by.'

From these examples it may be seen that the joke can be made either by the one likely to offend, by the one likely to be offended, or by any employee about an objective occurrence or situation generally recognized as likely to create considerable difficulties for those involved in it. The joking of assistants is mainly related to their own particular work problems, whereas the joking of buyers and others is concerned with their problems and covers a much wider field – taking in the whole store.

Horse-play in store joking is very rare. If it occurs at all it is only between juniors or young male assistants. However, both the symmetrical and asymmetrical type of joking relationship is to be found in the store, as in primitive societies, and seems in this case to bear a definite relation to status. In general, joking is established more quickly and easily between members of the same status either in the same or in different departments when they happen to come in contact, i.e. between juniors, between sales assistants, between one underbuyer and another, and so on. The assistant says to the liftman (who is of assistant status), 'How's my best boy-friend today?'

'I shall be all right now I've seen you!' he replies.

This exemplifies a typical symmetrical relationship. However, joking also occurs between members of *different* status. The joke may be made by a member of higher status in an attempt to disarm a subordinate member of any antagonism and maintain a good relationship. Joking may also be used in order to give a reprimand without offending – though these methods are not consciously understood by those using them. For example, one of the buyers, on seeing a junior carrying out her duties in a slow and lazy manner, said to her, 'Miss —— [i.e. the junior herself] looks as if her heart's in her boots today! Don't you like work today, dear?' There is no reply made to a remark of this kind. On the other hand, members of low status may sometimes purposely joke with members of higher status partly because it gives them a sense of bravado and partly because by means of it they are able to assume at least temporarily an equality of status with those whom they are addressing, e.g. juniors often attempt to joke with the sales assistants but the latter seldom joke back as it would be lowering to their dignity. A symmetrical relationship between members of different levels is established quite frequently where the relation is one of constant instruction and training or continuous giving and taking of orders, and a relationship established in this way is often maintained even after the parties concerned no longer have any direct contact in the business, i.e. it is exhibited in chance meetings. A relationship of this kind is very often found between underbuyers and juniors. It is the underbuyers who are responsible for training juniors and for organizing their work. In the course of this the juniors usually tease and joke with the underbuyer endlessly, and she for her part finds that a better relationship is maintained if she takes the joking in a good-humoured way and is ready to have a joke back at them. In general, the *symmetrical* type of joking relationship occurs most frequently, and such *asymmetrical* joking as does take place is usually aimed by superiors at subordinates.

Joking is usually learned by a newcomer after she has been in the store about three weeks and it takes about the same length of time for her to be accepted as a 'joker' by the rest of the department. It is a very uncomfortable period for her, and this may largely account for the fact that the biggest labour turnover in the store occurs during the first few weeks of employment. Definite sanctions exist and operate both to establish and to maintain the required joking, and brief mention will now be made of these in order to give some indication of what a newcomer suffers before she has learned the 'art'. This will also help to give some understanding of the actual function of the joking in store routine.

The store sanctions of the joking relationship and other aspects of the informal tradition operate quickly and effectively because the salesgirl knows that she has joined a group in which it is essential for her to conform if she is to earn her living. She is therefore sensitive to all types of sanction and seldom thinks of trying to distinguish between formal and informal sanctions. In the old days conformity with the demands of the formal side of the system would in fact have been enough, but nowadays the personnel officer always wants to know whether a newcomer is 'fitting in' with the rest of the department – although personnel staff are, of course, unaware that this 'fitting in' means conforming with a permanent informal tradition of the work group, one aspect of which is the joking relationship.

There are three main types of sanction that should be distinguished: first, 'formal' sanctions – by these are meant not only management rules but all actions and expressions of individuals and groups that are generally recognized as following a prescribed method and are used again and again. Second, 'informal' sanctions – these cover all those actions and expressions of individuals and groups that are not generally recognized as following a prescribed method and are often spontaneous although not necessarily so. Third – for want of a better term – 'automatic' sanctions. These, unlike the first two types of sanction, do not involve expressions and actions indicating approval or disapproval, they merely serve to enforce the required behaviour by proving it successful, and vice versa. Examples of these will now be given.

As neither management nor staff are aware of the part played by the joking relationship it is not surprising to find little or no formal sanction of it. However, a sort of formal sanction of the relationship, in which joking is also the method of sanction, does tend to develop in the individual department, e.g. one of the assistants said that in her department whenever someone was sent to help or to work there who was rather 'snobbish' and would not talk to them, they all made a point of joking at her continuously in a good-humoured way and she soon 'came off it'. The activity which this department adopted in making a newcomer take a hail-fellow-well-met attitude had thus become to some extent formalized.

Informal sanctioning of the joking relationship, both of a positive and of a negative type, occurs much more frequently. Employees often say the reason they like working in the store is that they have such fun in carrying out their routine jobs. They say they would not care to work in a particular department because its members 'take life much too seriously'. A member will often say how much she likes another member because the latter is 'always ready for a joke' and 'full of fun'. Those who joke readily are obviously very much more popular than those who do not. They are approached more often by other members. They elicit a more favourable reaction than others when they make an approach themselves and they are never seen to sit alone during their meal breaks. This informal sanctioning of the joking tradition is in fact extremely varied and complicated and can be observed not only in the form of verbal expressions and obvious avoidance behaviour but also in tone of voice, method of speech, and manner of approach. It should also be noted that in the course of operating these sanctions employees are not only training new members in the store way of life but are also giving themselves and each other a continuous refresher course in these ways.

Finally, the 'automatic' sanctions: these operate continuously every time a member either behaves in accordance with the tradition or does not behave in accordance with it. Once a member has acquired the knack of joking in the right sort of way she finds that all the approaches necessitated by the system can be made much more smoothly. Simply because a contact made with the correct type of joking attitude achieves the purpose of the contact more quickly and easily, a member tends to repeat this type of joking in further contacts. If her attitude in making the approach was not correct the fact that it elicits a rather less satisfactory reaction discourages her from using it again – although neither positive nor negative use of these sanctions is necessarily conscious.

Nor is this the only form of automatic sanction. Both the mental and physical pleasure which the joking gives is a sanction in itself. It has been shown how in the course of carrying out her duties there are times when the sales assistant's anxiety about selling enough to earn her adequate commission and the approval of her superiors is likely to reach exasperation point as a result of the way in which the three types of controlling circumstances (store layout, selling system, and staff hierarchy) operate as a handicap to her. Occurring as it does at this point, the joking not only acts as a relief to the anxiety and prevents it developing into something worse but also provides positive enjoyment for those participating.

It is clear, therefore, that by means of a tradition of joking behaviour between its members, which is quite unknown to the management, this store is able to avoid considerable tension and disagreement that would be likely to occur as a result of the difficulties inherent in its formal structure. In so doing it also gives the employees a source of positive enjoyment in carrying out their routine activities and incidentally, by means of this, renews their energy to cope even more adequately with their routine problems.

Joking is not a general characteristic of stores – even those of a particular area. In the course of some further research in a different organization – a group of multiple stores – I have found that in a branch only a few yards away from the department store described here, there is no customary joking behaviour at all. However, the multiple store has an extremely simple layout and system, and therefore less need of a supporting tradition. It is not yet clear how a joking relationship is established, but in view of its obvious importance in a particular type of formal structure, further research into its mode of origin would undoubtedly be of value.

Further Reading: The Pursuit of Autonomy

C. ARGYRIS, *Personality and Organization*, New York, Harper and Row, 1957.

E. FROMM, *The Fear of Freedom*, London, Routledge and Kegan Paul, 1942.

G. FRIEDMANN, *Industrial Society*, Glencoe, Illinois, The Free Press, 1964.

G. FRIEDMANN, *The Anatomy of Work*, London, Heinemann, 1961.

A. W. GOULDNER, *Wildcat Strike*, London, Routledge and Kegan Paul, 1955.

F. HERZBERG, B. MAUSNER and B. SNYDERMAN, *The Motivation to Work*, New York, Wiley, 1959.

J. M. HILL and E. L. TRIST, *Industrial Accidents, Sickness and other Absence*, London, Tavistock, 1962.

E. JACQUES, *The Changing Culture of a Factory*, London, Tavistock, 1951.

C. W. MILLS, *White Collar*, New York, Oxford University Press, 1956.

A. R. RADCLIFFE-BROWN, *Structure and Function in Primitive Society*, London, Cohen and West, 1952.

W. H. WHYTE, *The Organization Man*, London, Penguin, 1961.

W. F. WHYTE, *Human Relations in the Restaurant Industry*, New York, McGraw-Hill, 1948.

W. M. WILLIAMS, *The Country Craftsmen*, London, Routledge and Kegan Paul, 1958.

Chapter Nine

The Texture of Work 3: Workers and Trade Unions

An individual helps not; only he
who unites with many at the proper time
Goethe

They can't hurt me, I'm in a union
Woody Guthrie

Don't waste time mourning, organize !
Joe Hill

Throughout the last two chapters we examined the ways in which people's work was influenced by the fact that they were employed in organizations of a certain type and this involved them in differing possibilities of realizing their individual potential. We distinguished crudely and simplistically between those who were 'slaves to the machine' and those whose work allowed them at least the illusion that they could strive towards autonomous goals. But even when individuals are employed in a totally bureaucratized situation they have traditionally attempted to combine in occupational associations in order to protect themselves against any lowering of standards of pay or conditions, or to protect the privileges they have previously acquired.

But, as Fox puts it, '. . . a collectivity is a concentration of power. Once that concentration of power exists, an additional determinant has appeared on the scene. For the collectivity itself will be able to exercise social control over the individual and to create channels of communication which will assist in manipulating his consciousness.' Just as the organization will tend to pressurize him to regard himself as an 'organization man' so the union will wish him to perceive the various activities on his behalf as legitimate and to behave as a 'union man'.

The Industrial Relations Act of 1971 was both a change in the industrial balance of power and an attempt to provide a legal framework for industrial relations in Great Britain which was consistent with a particular view of the national interest. It created a National Industrial Relations Court and thus brought the 'order' which had developed through several decades of experience of collective bargaining within a more conventional framework of 'law'. Moreover, it reversed a trend which had been growing since the early years of this century by embodying in statutory form the legal right *not* to be a trade unionist. It also gave the authorities clearer, but more limited, guidance as to their conduct during a situation of industrial confrontation by permitting the court to designate an 'emergency' and to order a sixty-day 'cooling-off' period. Such procedures had been part of other countries' industrial relations law for some time, notably in the US since the Taft-Hartley Act. But their efficiency was doubted by some, for instance, K. W. Wedderburn, who commented that 'until 1971 the English law was envied by many whose legal systems tried to provide compulsory procedures or prohibitions for industrial conflict that gave rise to an emergency'. Wedderburn argued that the Act could be seen by many workers as a palliative to middle-class opinion and he questioned why '. . . this comprehensive new code to set right industrial ills included no "emergency powers" to deal with mass lay-offs, plant closures or dismissals by which unemployment of a scale amounting to a national emergency has already been created.' The answer is, of course, that to the legislators those aspects of industrial life were not 'problems' in the same way as the activities of trade unions were.

It may be that the report of the Donovan Commission two years earlier can be seen in retrospect as part of a 'softening-up' process, helping to condition the intelligentsia to the view that 'something would have to be done about the unions'. If this seems too harsh a judgment, a close study of the report as a whole would certainly be valuable, but the extract we present here is arguably fairly representative. In it the emergence of the role of the shop steward in industry is related to the tasks he performs. The basis of his power is the work group. Because of this power he is often able to avoid 'joint consultation' procedures which leave the ultimate decision-making power to the management, or transform them into negotiating and decision-taking machinery. He himself may be limited in the exercise of his discretionary power by 'custom and practice'. While he is often misinterpreted, according to the Report, as a 'trouble-maker' it may well be that 'trouble is thrust upon them'. Similar analyses of the activities of unions in their more official aspect and of the attitudes of participants on both management and workers' sides appear to indicate that the role of the shop steward is well regarded and is of positive benefit to the system of industrial relations as a whole. Managers *and* shop stewards retain considerable authority and apparently normally use it reasonably and positively to their mutual benefit. The arrangement is a flexible one and disputes can be resolved on their merits; moreover 'a very high degree of self-government in industry is provided'. But while the Report concedes these to be 'considerable benefits' they are not enough for 'decentralization, degeneration into indecision, anarchy, inefficiency and . . . resistance to change'. The overriding requirements of the need for economic growth in a situation of rapid technical change makes these, in the eyes of the Report, damning criticisms. There is a clear implication that a move in the direction of centralization of decision-taking on the part of trade unions would be in the 'national interest'.

Martin examines the implications of Michels' aphorism that 'who says organization says oligarchy' and the varying extent to which trade unions in Britain conform to either democratic principles or 'bureaucratized oligarchy'. While he claims that his paper represents no more than 'a first skirmish with the complexities of the problem', he does provide an analytic framework which permits the comparison of one union with another in terms of the nature and range of factors which may constrain the behaviour and decision-making of union leaders. Each of these factors relates to the executive's capacity to control the emergence of opposition. It is implicit in this approach that union executives will tend to see internal opposition as inherently negative and destructive and tending to give aid and succour to the economic enemy – the employer. The rest of Martin's paper, which is not reprinted here, examines the impact of these factors by means of a systematic comparison of the AEU and the NUR.

The fact that unions, which play such a key part in the democratic process in industry on the macro-level, as it were, may nonetheless be highly 'suspect' in terms of democratic ideology and practice is one of the key points of concern for writers like Blumberg. In his study of industrial democracy (recommended for further reading) the chief examples drawn on are from outside Britain. But he analyses the reasons for the retreat from workers' control in Britain, not only among trade union bureaucracies but in the world of academic writing on industrial relations. His critique is in part, therefore, a critique of the whole philosophy which implicitly permeates the Donovan Report.

He argues that the generally accepted view of industrial relations in Britain derives in large measure from the work of Clegg and his colleagues and has become a 'conventional wisdom'. For writers like Clegg, 'industrial democracy' can be defined in terms of the existence of an opposition to the established regime; it is not related to the capacity of the members of the 'constituency' which is being represented to make their views felt to their leaders, and thus make the leaders accountable to them. James Burnham had earlier traced the changes in the corporate structure of capitalism which had led to the separation of ownership from control and the emergence of a new class of managers who were free of the need to be accountable to shareholders; they were 'controllers' only, not 'owners' of industrial capital. But the analogy of 'government' and 'opposition' in the industrial relations sphere breaks down because the 'opposition' can only oppose, it can never take over the functions of the government.

Blumberg argues that Clegg and his colleagues cannot have it both ways: either democracy consists in the alternation of governments, each equally capable of governing, or it is a misleading description of the system which actually applies, one of permanently embattled 'government' and 'opposition'. In either case, the ownership of the means of production, distribution and exchange is, for Clegg, merely a sentimental irrelevance, obscuring the *real* need of building up strong trade unions, independent of both state and management, which alone can represent the workers' industrial interests. Blumberg argues that the experience of co-determination in West Germany, and of the Histadrut in Germany, in both of which the trade unions participate directly in management, indicates that the Clegg analysis is at best only partial, at most seriously misleading. He argues that different lessons can be learnt from the Histadrut experience – that trade unions which wish to participate in management and to remain as effective bargainers and negotiators for their members, must develop a more complex organizational structure, possibly consisting of 'the hierarchies, independent from one another, but both responsive and accountable to the rank and file'. Only the successful experience of the Histadrut prevents the immediate response that this sounds like a recipe for organizational failure.

There is a great shortage of well-documented sociological analysis of possible alternatives to the contemporary statements of worker-management confrontation, notwithstanding such recent and dramatic events as the Clyde shipyard work-ins. This is one reason why the following extract, by Scott and others, is from a Report published a generation ago. But some of its findings, while apparently trite, are still worth studying. First among these is their methodological posture which is that 'any formal superstructure such as a system of joint consultation, must be appraised in terms of the totality of relationships in an industrial organization'.

Secondly, there is their judgment that however well-planned and co-ordinated such a system might be and however well-intentioned its members, it will not work if 'the majority of the persons in an organization feel divorced from the process'. Finally, there is the implication that such changes in formal organization depend for their success on changes in the attitudes and expectations of participants and these in their turn depend on the view that these participants take of the environment in which the firm is operating. Thus, where there are pressures from many sources on employers 'the prevalent uncertainty in the minds of many employees as to whether the present conditions of industrial stability are likely to continue makes a reconciliation of these institutional demands difficult for them to achieve'.

Allen is as critical of the status quo in British industrial relations as was the Donovan Report, but from a different perspective. The activities of trade unions in contemporary British society are related to the factors which constrain the behaviour of union officials. These are twofold: firstly, 'the process of socialization whereby the role of union officials has been conditioned to be consistent with the norms and roles of a capitalist society'. The other important constraint derives from the process, described by Michel as inevitable, and analysed earlier in this chapter by Martin, of the bureaucratization of union organizations. While things go well for the economy at large trade unions can develop aims which are 'legitimate' within the system of industrial capitalism, but when the environment changes, inconsistencies develop. Thus, if Allen's analysis is correct to the extent that rapid and largely negative changes are taking place in the position of Britain in the world economy, 'trade unions now are not capable by themselves of achieving satisfactorily even their limited aims'.

Hyman takes this theme further. He argues that while managers may complain bitterly and publicly about the loss of production caused by strikes, or even about the effects on other workers, a stronger reason for their belief that the strike constitutes a 'problem' for them is rather different. By striking or threatening to strike the workers are demonstrating that there are limits to the degree to which managers can control them, s well as providing a 'persistent practical contradiction of the ideology of harmony of interests which assigns legitimacy to managerial power'. But there are also problems for the worker in too liberal a use of the strike weapon. The liberating and educational experience of being involved in a strike, perhaps especially a successful strike, may cause a gradual redirection of his aspirations. Once his 'industrial virginity' is lost, new horizons are opened up, but the reality of the organization of production continually frustrates his subsequent attempts to achieve them. Thus, for the striker, the *real* problems are 'the actions of management which violate his expectation; the features of management which violate his expectation; the features of the employment relationship which degrade and oppress him . . . the social values which deny the legitimacy of his struggle to defend or improve his conditions . . .'.

Trade Unions, Shop Stewards and Work Groups

Donovan Report

Reprinted with permission from *Royal Commission on Trade Unions and Employers Associations*, 1968, HMSO, pp. 25–33.

Shop stewards and work groups

In most factories in which trade unions are strong their members in each workshop choose one of their number to speak for them. If there is more than one union, each usually has its own representative, although in some instances one representative speaks for two or more unions. He or she may go under a number of titles, but the most common is 'shop steward'. In some undertakings works committees or councils are elected by all the workers, regardless of union membership. Where this is so, the shop steward may be elected to the committee, or the committee member may be accepted as the steward, as in the railways' Local Departmental Committees. In some unions in which the branch is based on the factory, branch officers carry out the tasks which shop stewards perform elsewhere.

These tasks include recruiting new members and seeing that existing members do not lapse. The stewards may be helped in this by an understanding that only union members will be employed. About two out of five of Britain's trade unionists are covered by some such understanding. A small minority of these arrangements are formal closed-shop agreements between unions and employers, but the great majority are informally sustained, mainly by the vigilance of shop stewards. In many instances shop stewards are also responsible for collecting union subscriptions. Some unions provide for separate collecting stewards appointed by the branch, but the two offices are frequently held by the same person. In addition shop stewards have a responsibility for communications between unions and members; and with average attendance at branch meetings well below 10 per cent, this is the main link between unions and their members.

These are important services. Without shop stewards, trade unions would lack for members, for money, and for means of keeping in touch with their members. Even so none of them is the most important of the British shop steward's tasks. That is the service which he performs by helping to regulate workers' pay and working conditions and by representing them in dealings with management.

Until a few years ago little was known for certain about this part of the steward's work, but several studies have now appeared and are summarized in our first research paper. Their findings have now been generally confirmed by the enquiry conducted for us by the Social Survey. First of all it must be emphasized that there is no uniformity. A minority of stewards do not negotiate with managers at all, whereas some of them negotiate over a wide range of issues. But over half of them regularly deal with managers over some aspect of pay and about half of them deal regularly with some question relating to hours of work, the most common being the level and distribution of overtime. About a third of them regularly handle disciplinary issues on behalf of their members, and other matters which some of them settle include the distribution of work, the pace of work, the manning of machines, transfers from one job to another, the introduction of new machinery and new jobs, taking on new labour and redundancy. Since there are probably about 175,000 stewards in the country, compared with perhaps 3,000 full-time trade union officers, this suggests that shop stewards must be handling many times the volume of business conducted by their full-time officers.

From where does the shop steward derive his authority to deal with all these items? Where union rule books mention shop stewards, and many of them do not, they generally say something about method of appointment, and the body to whom the steward is nominally responsible. They may mention the duties of recruiting and retaining members, and collecting subscriptions. If the business of representing members is touched on, little is said about it. Most major unions now have *Shop Stewards' Handbooks*, which set out some of these tasks at greater length. But when it comes to telling the steward what issues he is competent to handle and how he should go about raising them, most handbooks refer the steward to the industry-wide agreement in force in his industry. These in their turn are rarely comprehensive. Few say much more than the engineering agreement, which authorizes the steward to take up questions which the worker or workers directly concerned have been unable to settle with the foreman. The engineering steward is to raise them with the 'Shop Manager' and/or Head Shop Foreman and, if need be, to have them considered by a Works Committee.

In dealing with pay or overtime or discipline the steward could be dealing with the application of industry-wide agreements, a responsibility mentioned in most of the handbooks. In fact this rarely happens, for two reasons. In the first place most industry-wide agreements on pay lay down minimum rates or minimum levels of piecework earnings which are very generally exceeded. In dealing with such issues, therefore, the steward must be concerned with obtaining or retaining a concession in excess of the terms in the agreement. In the second place most industry-wide agreements say nothing at all about many of the issues with which the steward deals, such as discipline, the pace of work, the introduction of new machinery and the distribution of overtime.

In dealing with this second class of issue the steward might merely be entering into consultation at the discretion of management on matters outside the industry-wide agreement but nevertheless of interest to the workers. However, case studies show that this is not so. When a decision is reached it is regarded as an agreement even though it may not be recorded. Managers would not normally alter it without further negotiation, and if they did sanctions might be applied. These are not the procedures of joint consultation. Joint consultation, moreover, has never been as popular with shop stewards as with managers. A wealth of evidence supports the conclusions reached by Dr McCarthy that shop stewards regard 'any committee on which they serve which cannot reach decisions . . . as essentially an inferior or inadequate substitute for proper negotiating machinery', and that joint consultative committees in the strict sense 'cannot survive the development of effective shop-floor organization. Either they must change their character and become essentially negotiating committees carrying out functions which are indistinguishable from the processes of shop-floor bargaining, or they are boycotted by shop stewards and, as the influence of the latter grows, fall into disuse.'

In any case there are many shop-floor decisions on these issues in which managers take no part at all. 'Ceilings' on piecework earnings and limits imposed by road haulage drivers on the scheduling of their vehicles are examples of the regulation of work by workers themselves. The distribution of overtime is another matter which may be left to the stewards.

These instances show the basis of the shop steward's power. He could not of his own volition impose a limit on output or a ban on non-unionists. This can only be done by decision of the group of workers which he represents. 'Custom and practice', which settles so much in British industrial relations, consists of the customs and practices observed by work groups. If workers did not keep to them, the customs would cease to exist.

The work group does not derive its power from the union. The printing chapel with its chapel father, the best-organized of all work groups, existed before the printing unions and was subsequently incorporated into their branch structure. Work groups can exert considerable control over their members even where there are no trade unions, or where unions refuse them recognition. Until recently there were no shop stewards in most British docks. Accordingly the 'ganger' or 'hatch-boss' negotiated for the members of the gang in any dispute with management, although he was paid to be the gang's supervisor and all negotiations were supposed to be reserved for full-time officers. In coalmining 'chargemen' performed the same service for facework gangs, although they too were supervisors.

Full employment would in any case have increased the influence of the work group, but British managers have augmented it by their preference for keeping many matters out of agreements, by the inadequacy of their methods of control of systems of payments, by their preference for informality and by their tolerance of custom and practice.

There is no question but that this is largely the choice of management. Previous enquiries have shown that where managers have a choice of dealing with either full-time officers or shop stewards, three-quarters of them choose shop stewards, and our own surveys have confirmed this finding. Their chief reason for this is the 'intimate knowledge of the circumstances of the case' possessed by shop stewards, but this is as much a consequence of their preference as a cause of it. If managers choose to deal with shop stewards on an informal basis, full-time officers cannot be expected to acquire a detailed knowledge of the issues which arise in the factory.

In an earlier survey conducted by Dr McCarthy managers were questioned about their preference for informal and unwritten arrangements. Four reasons were generally put forward. If agreements were formalized they would become established *de jure* rights which could not be withdrawn; even if existing stewards would not abuse formal confirmation the next generation might, and managers like to believe that they can vary privileges according to the response they get; once the process of formalizing began it would extend indefinitely; and, finally, 'some *de facto* concessions could not be written down because management, particularly at board level, would not be prepared to admit publicly that they had been forced to accept such modifications in their managerial prerogatives and formal chains of command'. The more concessions are made the stronger become all these reasons for preferring informality.

It does not follow however that shop stewards and work groups exercise effective control where industry-wide agreements and managers fail to do so. In systems of payment by results with no effective work study, each man may settle his own times with the rate fixer, and this may lead to a wide spread of earnings with an uncontrolled upward drift. In other instances the control of shop stewards over the distribution of overtime may be undermined by workers 'greedy' for overtime earnings. In such circumstances industrial relations can border on anarchy.

Consequently it is often wide of the mark to describe shop stewards as 'trouble-makers'. Trouble is thrust upon them. In circumstances of this kind they may be striving to bring some order into a chaotic situation, and management may rely heavily on their efforts to do so. Both case studies and surveys show that this sort of situation is not uncommon. In addition the shop-floor decisions which generally precede unofficial strikes are often taken against the advice of shop stewards. Thus shop stewards are rarely agitators pushing workers towards unconstitutional action. In some instances they may be the mere mouthpieces of their work groups. But quite commonly they are supporters of order exercising a restraining influence on their members in conditions which promote disorder. To quote our survey of shop stewards and workshop relations: 'For the most part the steward is viewed by others, and views himself, as an accepted, reasonable and even moderating influence; more of a lubricant than an irritant.'

Trade unions

Trade unions have been as guilty as employers' associations and managers of sustaining the facade of industry-wide bargaining with its pretence of dealing with everything of importance for collective agreements. They cannot, however, bear the primary responsibility for the drift of earnings away from wage rates and the growing ineffectiveness of disputes machinery which have weakened industry-wide bargaining. These have been the consequence of the reaction of employers' associations and companies to full employment, a reaction which it was not within the unions' power to control. Moreover there has not been on the unions' side an exact parallel of the decline in authority of employers' associations. Fitfully and haltingly most of the major unions have responded to changing conditions by recognizing shop stewards and making some effort to equip them. Thus it is not so much that the unions have lost power as that there has been a shift of authority within them. Certain features of trade union structure and government have however helped to inflate the power of work groups and shop stewards within the factory.

The first of these is multi-unionism, the existence of two or more unions, sometimes many more, in most British industries and factories. In this respect British trade union structure is extremely complex. Description is hampered by the inadequacy of the types traditionally employed for classifying trade unions – craft, industrial and general. Most major British unions fit none of them. But some outline must be attempted.

In most industries and services it is possible to divide the labour force into groups such as white-collar workers, maintenance workers and process workers. It is common in Britain for each group to have its own union or unions. Further subdivision can separate white-collar employees into clerical workers, supervisors, technicians and administrators; or maintenance workers into members of separate crafts and their mates. It is by no means unusual for each of these sub-groups to have its separate union. It can happen that two or more unions are competing for members in one of these sub-groups. Our surveys suggest that, even if white-collar workers and their unions are left out of account, about four out of every five trade unionists in Britain work in a multi-union establishment, and perhaps one in six of them belongs to a grade of worker in which two or more unions are competing for members.

If this was the whole picture, the British trade union movement would consist of a large number of small unions, and in fact 480 out of Britain's 574 trade unions have less than ten thousand members. At the other extreme, however, nine trade unions, with over a quarter of a million members each, account for more than half the trade unionists in the country. The biggest of them have achieved their position by linking together groups and sub-groups of workers from different industries and services in patterns of astounding complexity which can be given historical explanations, but yield to no logical interpretation.

The Transport and General Workers' Union, for example, organizes the great majority of all grades of worker in one or two industries, such as the bus industry, process workers in most manufacturing industries and labourers in shipbuilding and building. In addition it has a thriving section for clerical and supervisory staff. Its members are to be found in nearly all the country's major industries and services, and in most of them the members of the General and Municipal Workers' Union are to be seen alongside, for its structure is roughly similar. Both began as 'labourers'' unions. Starting from a very different origin two one-time 'craft' societies, the Amalgamated Union of Engineering and Foundry Workers and the Electrical Trades Union, now appear more and more like the general unions in their make-up. Their members also work in nearly every industry and service in the country. In many of them they cover the maintenance crafts-men, and perhaps also their mates, but in engineering and else-where these two unions compete with the general unions in organizing production workers, both men and women. In addi-tion each of them is developing its own white-collar section. The coverage of many other large and middle-sized unions is only somewhat less irrational and complex than the coverage of these four.

This strange structure strengthens the position of work groups, and increases their independence, in three ways. First, many trade union branches consist of small groups of members from a number of different factories or offices. The branch is therefore divorced from the real business of the union at the place of work, but it nevertheless remains the official means of contact between the union and its members. Secondly, full-time union officers cannot easily keep in touch with small groups of members scattered over scores of factories. Thirdly, the several unions within the factory or office have to work together. Our evidence is that more than two-thirds of shop stewards have at their place of work a committee in which they meet with management to discuss and settle problems, and that two-thirds of these com-mittees are multi-union. Where that is so, the committees are not easily made responsible to a trade union authority outside the factory. Perhaps this helps to explain another finding of our surveys, that full-time officers outside the factories seem to find the difficulties arising from multi-unionism more intractable than do shop stewards inside. Only half the stewards who often dealt with multi-union issues thought that it would help if fewer unions were involved, whereas four out of five full-time officers thought it would help.

It is possible, however, to exaggerate the importance of these influences. The overwhelming majority of union members do not attend branch meetings whether the branch is based on the area or the factory. The evidence is that members and stewards follow much the same pattern of behaviour in both types of branch. Equally the fabric of industrial relations seems to be much the same in industries and factories with simple union structures as with complex structures. At one time the contrast between a strike-prone Ford and a strike-free Vauxhall was widely explained by the twenty-odd unions at Ford and the two (subsequently three) at Vauxhall. Since 1962, Ford has radically altered the manner of its industrial relations, reducing the number of its strikes, without a significant change in the number of unions; and in 1967 Vauxhall's record of industrial peace was shattered by a major stoppage.

There is also some truth in the complaint that trade union leadership is 'out of touch'. In the conferences and committees of our major unions there are in fact several obstacles to the effective expression of the members' opinions on industrial issues. Nearly all unions have an annual or biennial conference to make policy and amend the rules. In the largest unions, and in many smaller unions, the delegates to conference come from a number of different industries and services, so that most of them are necessarily uninformed on any specific industrial issue. Some of the unions therefore exclude resolutions on the affairs of a particular industry from conference business. A partial remedy is provided by the thirteen trade groups of the Transport and General Workers' Union, each of which has its own conference, and some other unions employ similar expedients. Even so, most of the trade groups have to deal with the affairs of several kindred industries, and they must in the end be subject to the overriding authority of the union's executive.

The executive committees or councils, responsible for union business between conferences, may also be drawn from a range of different industries, but many of them are now bodies of full-time officers. The members of the executives of the Amalgamated Engineering Union and the Electrical Trades Union are employed full-time as executive members. Half of the ten members of the executive of the General and Municipal Workers' Union are full-time district secretaries. The Mineworkers' executive consists of representatives of its areas, almost all of them leading full-time area officers. These unions have moved a long way from the nineteenth century notion of a trade union executive as a body of men working at their trade, in close touch with the members, and able to see that union business was conducted to the liking of the members.

Multi-unionism adds to the problem. In most major industries and services no single union is in a position to determine what the unions as a whole shall do. This has to be settled at a meeting of them all, where full-time officers generally lead the delegations from each union.

Finally the process of collective bargaining itself is bound to give further power to the officers who conduct the negotiations and make the crucial compromises.

Consequently, it is not surprising if from time to time groups of trade union members protest that industry-wide agreements are not to their liking, and even indulge in mutinous strikes. But such strikes are relatively rare. The great majority of unofficial strikes have nothing to do with industry-wide agreements. It is a mistake therefore to suppose that the shift of power to the work group could have been prevented by a more ready exercise of disciplinary powers by trade union leaders. Even if successful this could do little to halt the transfer of authority from management to the work group. And it is unlikely that it would be successful. Trade union leaders do exercise discipline from time to time, but they cannot be industry's policemen. They are democratic leaders in organizations in which the seat of power has almost always been close to the members. For a brief period between the wars the conjunction of industry-wide bargaining and heavy unemployment gave trade union leaders an unusual ascendancy in their own organizations. Before that, however, power was generally concentrated in the branches and the districts. Since then, workshop organization has taken their place.

Attitudes

It might be expected that arrangements such as have been described would be unpopular with large numbers of those who work under them. Employers' associations might be expected to bemoan their loss of power; managers to decry the power of shop stewards; full-time officers to complain of their exclusion from workshop bargaining. It might also be supposed that shop stewards would be hostile to managers and contemptuous of their full-time officers. It is, however, one of the most consistent findings of the surveys carried out for us that such opinions are to be found among only tiny minorities within each group.

More than four out of five officials of employers' associations said that they had sufficient influence over their members. Only 2 per cent of managers held that shop stewards were unreasonable, 95 per cent taking the view that they were either very reasonable or fairly reasonable. Four managers out of five thought shop stewards were either very efficient or fairly efficient at their job. Nearly a third of them thought that shop stewards were a lot of help to management, and most of the remainder that shop stewards were of some help. Shop stewards reciprocated. Almost all of them thought that management was either 'very reasonable' or 'fairly reasonable' in dealings with them. Although some stewards rarely saw their full-time officer, only 6 per cent complained of difficulty in contacting him when they needed him. More than two-thirds of them thought he played 'a very important part' in local negotiations. The proportion of full-time officers who thought they had sufficient influence over their members was no less than 87 per cent.

Managers were in some ways more critical than the other groups. A quarter of them had complaints about their employers' associations, most commonly on the grounds that they were weak and unable to enforce their decisions. Only 20 per cent of them thought full-time officers were very important in local negotiations. Even among managers, however, the critics are in a minority.

These and other findings suggest that the participants in the current arrangements are, generally speaking, well satisfied with them. How can their attitude be reconciled with the preceding analysis? The only possible answer is that these arrangements have some important advantages which impress themselves upon the participants; and they have.

The first advantage is that they are comfortable arrangements. They do not demand of the officials of employers' associations that they should take on the thankless task of enforcing decisions upon their members who are also their masters. They can devote their time to more manageable tasks. Busy full-time union officers are not called in to deal with trivial details within the factory. They can leave the shop stewards to carry on with the job, expecting the stewards to call them in when an issue cannot be resolved within the factory and has to 'go into procedure'.

Managers have considerable freedom to run their own industrial relations affairs without interference from outside. This also means that shop stewards enjoy considerable authority; but, since stewards are for the most part reasonable people, managers can normally come to an arrangement with them.

Secondly, the arrangements are flexible. They enable managers and stewards to circumvent rules and procedures which might otherwise get in their way; and when employers' associations and full-time trade union officers are called into a dispute, they can usually resolve it 'on its merits', reaching an *ad hoc* settlement without having to worry too much about the consequences elsewhere.

Finally, a very high degree of self-government in industry is provided. Not only do managers and shop stewards have a considerable freedom from outside interference, but above all work groups are given scope to follow their own customs and to take their own decisions.

These are important benefits, enough to explain widespread satisfaction with existing arrangements. They can be condemned only because the benefits are outweighed by the shortcomings: the tendency of extreme decentralization and self-government to degenerate into indecision and anarchy; the propensity to breed inefficiency; and the reluctance to change – all of them characteristics which become more damaging as they develop, as the rate of technical progress increases, and as the need for economic growth becomes more urgent.

Union Democracy, an Explanatory Framework

R. Martin

Reprinted with permission from *Sociology,* Vol. 2, No. 2, 1968, pp. 205–14.

Concern with the impact of bureaucratization upon the prospects for internal democracy in representative institutions, particularly trade unions, has been a prominent strain in sociological analysis since Roberto Michels' *Political Parties* first appeared in English in 1915. His aphorism 'who says organization says oligarchy' has become a sociological commonplace. Yet, despite Michels and his pessimistic followers, democratic ideology and even democratic practice survive. The present paper provides an explanatory framework for the varying degrees to which British trade unions conform to Michels' pattern of bureaucratized oligarchy.

The framework comprises a classification of constraints inhibiting union Executives from destroying internal opposition, together with tentative hypotheses to explain their operation. The hypotheses developed are derived mainly from a detailed comparative study of the Amalgamated Engineering Union (AEU) and the National Union of Railwaymen (NUR), and represent a first skirmish with the complexities of the problem, not its fina conquest. Further empirical investigations will modify, and may refute, some of them. Despite this the 'constraint' approach is presented as the most appropriate approach to the study of union politics, and the most likely to lead eventually to an adequate theory of union democracy.

*　　　*　　　*

What determines the status of union opposition? A step towards understanding the determinants of effective opposition has been taken in J. D. Edelstein's recent paper, *An Organisational Theory of Union Democracy*. His elaborate theory specifies the characteristics of the formal structure of union government likely to create conditions of equality between incumbent and opposition candidates in union elections; the effectiveness of opposition, and thus the degree of union democracy, is measured by the frequency with which incumbent candidates are defeated, and the closeness of the voting. Democracy is most likely when the formal political structure facilitates the emergence of a small number of powerful candidates instead of a large number of weak ones.

Although the model may be appropriate, the measure is inadequate. Overwhelming leadership victories may be due to effectiveness in carrying out the wishes of the majority of union members, not to the lack of union democracy. Close election results and a high turnover in union officials are as likely to indicate incompetence as internal democracy. Indeed, a high turnover in union officials may indicate lack of leadership responsiveness to majority opinion, since removal from office is the ultimate sanction on Executive disregard for membership opinion. Electoral rejection signifies the inadequacy of less drastic sanc-'

tions. Moreover, although Edelstein is right to emphasize formal organization, and particularly the distribution of power between national, district, and local bodies, an organizational theory of union democracy is sociologically inadequate. It may provide a basis for prediction, but not for explanation. Formal organization is a dependent, not an independent variable, reflecting, *inter alia*, the union's history, membership spread (past, present, and future), collective bargaining position and functional needs. An adequate theory of union democracy requires the integration of organizational variables into a wider conceptual framework.

The framework presented here focuses on the constraints upon union leaders to tolerate faction. It assumes that union leaders will not tolerate faction unless constrained to do so, since the existence of any opposition limits the range of alternative choices open. Although this is a logical not an empirical assumption, it is a justifiable one; most union leaders regard opposition as an aid to the economic enemy. The construction of a theory of union democracy therefore involves the classification of these constraints, and if possible their integration into a comprehensive theory.

Although the range of constraints upon union leaders is extremely wide, and their relative importance varies from union to union, and possibly even from official to official, a preliminary attempt at classification is possible. Constraints can be classified into twelve categories: political culture; government attitudes and behaviour; pattern of membership distribution, past, present, and future; industrial setting, including the degree of ownership concentration, and the collective bargaining system; economic environment; technology and rate of technological change; source of union bargaining power; membership characteristics; membership beliefs; opposition expertise and resources; leadership beliefs; and union structure. Each factor affects the chances for union democracy by increasing or reducing the Executive's ability to destroy opposition.

1. *Political culture*

The political culture – the complex of values, beliefs, and emotional attitudes surrounding politica institutions – acts as a constraint upon union leaders directly, and indirectly through its influence upon membership beliefs about the legitimacy of particular political practices. A political culture emphasizing democratic values, including responsiveness to majority opinion, toleration of opposition, and individual freedom, will obviously exert pressure upon union leaders to act accordingly both directly and indirectly by moulding membership expectation of the role behaviour of leaders. The British political culture, with its negative evaluation of expulsion and ballot rigging as political tactics, will influence union leaders to refrain from using them even when they may seem to provide the most effective means of defeating opposition. The furore created by the electoral mal-practices in the Electrical Trades Union between 1955 and 1960 indicates the reality of this constraint. Similarly, an authoritarian political culture, emphasizing obedience, the subordination of the individual to the group, and the duty of private organizations to the state, will exercise a different constraint.

2. Government attitudes and behaviour

Government attitudes and behaviour have had a dual impact upon the democratic potential of trade unions. On the one hand, government pressure for restraint during periods of war or econo-mic crisis can create a division between the leadership and the rank and file, leading to the emergence of 'irresponsible' opposi-tion groups, as in the Engineers and the Miners' Federation during the First World War. In this situation factional conflict, and thus democracy, is likely. On the other hand, the increasing scope of Government influence, particularly its concern to limit wage-inflation and maintain satisfactory working conditions, increases pressure for centralization and bureaucratization, and hence the power of the Executive. Union Executives need authority and expert advice in negotiations with central government; both involve an increase in Executive power.

3. Membership distribution

The distribution of union membership (past, present, and future) conditions the likely pattern of economic interest group conflict between members and thus the likely form of anti-leadership groupings, and largely determines union structure. In general, 'the more homogeneous the interests of the members of the union, the greater chances for democracy', because economic conflict be-tween union members reduces the likelihood of anti-leadership alliances, and thus reduces the threat opposition poses for the leadership. However, the general statement requires elaboration. The basis of cleavage and the pressures making for bureaucratization, and consequently the democratic potential, vary between different types of unions.

In craft unions, like the AEU before the Second World War, occupational homogeneity and industrial heterogeneity provide a basis for both consensus and cleavage. Occupational solidarity, compounded of occupational interests, tradition, and consciousness of difference from industrial workmates, provides a basis for consensus, while industrial differences provide a basis for cleavage. The destructive potential of cleavage is limited by the fact that wage conflict, reflecting knowledge of earnings differentials and wage reference groups, is more likely to be intra-industry than intra-union. Industrial unions, with industrial homogeneity and occupational heterogeneity are less likely to be democratic, for wage rivalry is likely to be intra-union, inhibiting anti-leadership alliances and allowing the Executive to play interest groups off against each other.

The impact of membership spread upon bureaucratization similarly varies between different types of unions. Bureaucratization is most highly developed in general unions with a diverse semi-skilled and unskilled membership, like the National Union of General and Municipal Workers. In unions like the NUGMW the lack of common interest between different groups of members and the unsuitability of settling particular industrial problems at annual representative conferences increases the power of the full-time officials as the only unifying element. The significance of this factor is reduced in craft and industrial unions.

4. Industria environment

The degree of ownership concentration, the level of cooperation between employers, the range of products and product markets, and the collective bargaining system all exert pressure for centralization and bureaucratization, and thus oligarchy. Concentrated ownership, cooperation between employers, and a limited range of products and product markets, all exert pressure for centralized collective bargaining and national regulation, strengthening the position of the Executive and reducing democratic potential. All are features of the railways industry. Similarly, dispersed ownership, rivalry between employers, and a wide range of products and product markets, all characteristics of the engineering industry, minimize the pressures for national regulation and increase democratic potential. The final relevant factor in the industrial environment is the attitude of the employers;

employer hostility places a premium upon internal solidarity, lowering the constraints upon Executive repression of opposition. (Indeed, external hostility as well as historical inevitability contributed to the development of oligarchic tendencies within the German Social Democratic Party analysed in Michels' classic account.)

5. *Economic environment*

The economic situation in the industry or industries covered by the union exercises a dual constraint, on the readiness of the Executive to tolerate opposition, and on the likelihood of the indifferent majority's listening to the proposals of opposition factions. This constrains work in opposite directions. Other things being equal, during prosperity, or in a prosperous industry, the Executive will be able to afford to tolerate opposition, but the impetus to oppose will be weak because discontent will be limited. Factional fights may be frequent, but manageable. During depression, Executive ability to insist upon solidarity will increase, but the appeal of opposition will be greater.

6. *Technology*

Both the content of the industrial technology and the rate of technological change affect the potential for union democracy. Directly, the level of technology conditions the work setting and the work flow, the level of interaction possible between union members on the job, and consequently the opportunities for the evaluation of union personalities and policies. A 'craft' technology (as in printing), with a discontinuous work flow and ample opportunity for face to face contact between union members, provides opportunities for the creation of unofficial solidarity and for political discussion which a 'machine' technology does not. The rate of technological change, independent of its content, increases or diminishes the chances that the Executive will fall out of step with the rank and file. The faster the rate of technological change the greater the likelihood of conflict between the Executive and the membership (or within either group) and the greater the potential for democracy. Under pressure from the employers or the government the Executive may prove too sympathetic to change; or under the domination of old-established power groups the Executive may respond too slowly. Either increases the potential for faction.

7. *Source of bargaining power*

The source of union bargaining power, mass or workshop, affects the potential for opposition directly, by determining the distribution of power between the Executive and substructural groups, and indirectly through the likelihood of unofficial stoppages and the emergence of anti-leadership groups based on unofficial direct action. Mass bargaining power, as in general unions like the NUGMW, is likely to produce a strong Executive, workshop bargaining power, as in the AEU, a weak Executive. In the AEU the constraint exerted by workshop bargaining is increased by the institutional separation between the union structure and the workshop, and the consequent creation of an independent power base for the shop stewards. Moreover, workshop power increases the likelihood of unofficial stoppages, as in the car industry, by rendering Executive support superfluous. The importance of this constraint varies with the level of unemployment; high unemployment reduces workshop power, the feasibility of unofficial action, and thus opposition.

8. *Membership characteristics*

Membership characteristics affect the potential for union democracy directly in so far as they include specific political skills, and indirectly through their impact, upon the level of membership participation. Directly the educational level of the membership determines the level of literacy, the probability of members possessing verbal skills, and thus the differential ability of officials and rank and file to utilize the union political system. The more educated the membership the lower the differential and the greater the constraint on the Executive. Indirectly, membership characteristics influence democratic potential through their effect upon the level of membership participation; although a low level of membership participation does not necessarily indicate the absence of democracy, a high level is likely to provide a firmer basis for opposition than a low level. Membership participation is related to the following membership characteristics: the degree of informal association on or off the job; the degree of isolation from non-members (by work schedule, physical isolation, or status marginality); the number of role relationships between members; the degree of identification with the occupation and the union; and the number of functions performed by the union.

9. *Membership beliefs*

Membership beliefs constrain the Executive directly, where they concern the legitimacy of particular political practices, and indirectly, by limiting Executive interference in particular areas. Membership beliefs about the legitimate degree of Executive interference with branch autonomy reduce Executive ability to root out opposition. In the AEU, for example, Executive attempts to prevent the use of the Branch Local Purposes for affiliation fees to unofficial movements were successfully resisted in 1926 as an infringement of branch prerogatives. Similarly, membership beliefs regarding craft 'custom and practice' circumscribe Executive freedom of action, and provide a 'Sacred Books' basis for resistance to Executive initiatives, as in the National Society Operative Printers and Assistants at the present time.

10. *Opposition expertise and resources*

The level of opposition political expertise is determined by five factors: the number of former union leaders still active within the union; the number of politically experienced lay members; their level of education; their material resources; and their ideological commitment.

Lipset, Trow and Coleman relate the likelihood of former union leaders returning to the rank and file to the status of the occupation and to the chances of maintaining the status of union leader. However, the extremely low turnover in union leaders reduces the importance of this factor. When full time union officials do leave office they either retire completely, enter another branch of the labour movement, or go over to the other side. Moreover, few unionized occupations are likely to attract former union leaders on status or financial grounds; union leaders would return out of solidarity, habit, or not at all. A more important determinant of the level of opposition political expertise is the number of politically experienced rank and file members, trained either within the Labour or Communist parties or within the union itself. The limited transferability of political skills, and the reluctance of Labour of Communist parties to allow able activists to drop out (sometimes counter-balanced by the Communist desire to infiltrate), increases the importance of intra-union training. Hence, the number of responsible posts open to rank and file members is of primary importance. In the AEU, for example, the shop stewards system provides a training ground for opposition members as well as an independent power base, while the Lay District Committees provide a means for lay members to acquire wide experience and to spread their name.

The advantages of a high level of education for union opposition has been discussed above, while the advantages of material resources to pay for meetings, propaganda, and travelling is obvious. More complex is the nature of the relation between ideology and opposition. According to Lipset, Trow, and Coleman, ideological cleavages are more likely to sustain democratic opposition than interest group cleavages. This view requires modification. Within British trade unions ideological cleavages make for permanent, but not for effective, opposition. Ideological, primarily Communist elements form an important part of union opposition, but the majority of union members do not recognize this extra-union ideological commitment as legitimate. Hence, although Communist groups form an ideological nucleus, around which fluctuating economic or policy groups cluster, the price of organizational expertise is compromised legitimacy. Opposition groups which are based upon policy or interest group differences, and which preserve their ideological virginity (or conceal its loss) are more likely to be effective than ideological opposition groups.

11. *Leadership attitudes*

Leadership attitudes can be conceptualized as an independent constraint, determined by individual political beliefs, membership beliefs, rationalization of the functional requirements of leadership roles, and sensitivity to the surrounding political culture. Attitudes emphasizing internal democracy, moderation, and craft custom are more likely to restrict the repression of opposition than attitudes based upon the need to 'trust the leadership'. Commitment to Communism, or extreme anti-Communism, is likely to reduce Executive toleration of opposition by giving a lower priority to democratic procedure than to the need to keep the Communists in (or out).

12. *Union structure*

As the mechanism through which all other pressures operate, union structure is crucially important. The main determinants of the extent to which the formal structure facilitates or hinders the articulation of disagreement are the degree of substructural autonomy and conversely of centralization, the position of full-time *vis-à-vis* lay officials, and the electoral system itself. Union democracy is most likely where substructural autonomy, particularly at regional level, is greatest, and centralization least, where full-time officials are subject to effective lay supervision, and where the electoral system exerts pressure for a small number of powerful rather than a large number of weak candidates. A high degree of national integration and centralization, only formal provisions for lay supervision, and a completely 'open' electoral system reduce the chances for union democracy.

Each constraint discussed circumscribes Executive freedom of action by restricting interference with opposition factions or by increasing the strength of the opposition.

Joint Consultation – an Appraisal
W. H. Scott and others

Reprinted with permission from *Industrial Leadership*,
University Press of Liverpool, 1952, pp. 147–52.

The findings of the present enquiry, insofar as they relate to the organization and techniques of joint consultation, are broadly corroborative of some of the work which has been published previously. The difficulties which arise from the parallel development of Unionization and the internal organization, particularly when employee representation for the two purposes may be divided, are illustrated by the evidence from Firm A. Both the Union and non-Union employee tend to belittle the value of the joint organization, though for different reasons. The Union member, so long as the position of the Union is insecure, regards an increase in its strength and responsibilities as the first requirement, and so long as Union membership is not a condition of candidature for Council and Committee, and the latter are concerned with what he considers to be rather trivial matters, he does not rate them highly; the non-Union employee, since he expects far more of the joint organization that its constitution enables it to do, lacks enthusiasm for this very different reason. In Firm B, on the other hand, the existence of recognized and established Union organizations has tended to weaken the system of formal consultation, although this effect has been aggravated by the conflict between the two bodies of stewards. We also saw in this firm how the experience of pre-war conditions continues to influence the attitudes and behaviour of employee representatives. Insecurity feelings tend to limit the effectiveness of their contribution to joint consultation. The Printing Trade Unions represented in Firm C have been accepted institutions for many years, and although a small minority of employees in this firm were non-members, there was no evidence of feelings of lack of recognition or security on the part of their officials or stewards, and they were neutral in their attitude to the internal machinery. Nevertheless, the apathy of many representatives and a majority of employees, the limited achievements of the Council organization and its preoccupation with 'welfare' matters do not suggest that effective consultative relationships have been achieved. In this connection, in Firm C in particular but also to a marked extent in Firms A and B, the importance of management's role in relation to the Council and Committees was noted. Unless management, as the recognized leadership in the organization, takes the initiative in introducing a range of problems for discussion, meetings are likely to remain concerned almost exclusively with 'welfare' topics. This operational role of management, rather than the mere presence of higher management at meetings, or the attitude of higher management to joint consultation, is an important point which appears to have been neglected in the literature. The paternalistic tradition which is present in all three firms in varying degrees underlies the behaviour of top management, and is responsible for the fact that consultation is not really 'joint', but consists mainly in the submission of problems and requests by employee representatives. It also helps to explain why the latter are preoccupied so exclusively with 'welfare'.

Yet other questions have figured from time to time in the discussions of the Councils and Committees. The 'progress report' in Firm B represented an attempt to keep representatives informed of the commercial position of the Company and new developments that were being planned; and the addresses on the work of particular departments in Firm C were designed to stimulate an interest in departments other than a representative's own and to focus attention on production problems. Yet valuable as such endeavours are, they are mainly informational and rather different from the posing of particular problems for consideration. Furthermore, they do not deal as a rule with the sort of question which arises in an employee's immediate experience on the factory floor. Little attempt was made in any of the three firms to undertake discussion of general problems relating to production, the higher policy of the firm, or its financial structure, and hence there is little empirical evidence from this enquiry on which conclusions about such matters can be based. Yet if such questions are excluded, the prospect of achieving a measure of agreement on the objectives of an organization would appear to be small. As noted earlier, however, most of the employees who were critical of the joint machinery questioned its effectiveness within its existing scope, and few suggested that radical changes should be made. There was much talk of the 'trivialities' which were alleged to dominate proceedings, but few constructive proposals for enlarging the scope of the activities of the joint bodies. Yet when the content of the group discussions is considered as a whole, it is apparent that employees are concerned primarily with the facts of their own immediate experience. The matters which are often considered 'trivial' when handled by the Committees seem to be of some importance to employees when they arise in connection with their own working activities. This apparent paradox suggests, as we shall see below, that the interpretation of these attitudes must be a sociological one. The concern of representatives, on the other hand, with the questions of the scope and power of the joint bodies confirms this view.

The nature of social relationships in industry, and any formal superstructure, such as a system of joint consultation, must be appraised in terms of the totality of relationship in an industrial organization. The validation of this conceptual framework by the evidence of the present enquiry is important not only theoretically, but is also of significance for industrial practice. The purpose underlying the extension of joint consultation has been to achieve more co-operative or more harmonious relationships. Yet it is very doubtful if a committee system can contribute substantially to the achievement of such an objective, however well the committees are organized and administered, however important their functions, or however co-operative the relationships between their members if, for example, the majority of the persons in an organization feel divorced from the process. Changes in relationships are not to be attained simply by agreement between representatives of various groups – even if such agreement could always be achieved – but require prior changes in the attitudes and behaviour of at least a majority of all the persons concerned.

The isolation from the process of consultation of a large proportion of employees in all three firms seems explicable only in terms of two crucial sectors of their relationships. Firstly, in many departments of the firms there was no close and effective relationship between representatives and employees. This was due in part to the operation of shiftwork and the absence of specific facilities for representatives to meet their constituents during working hours. Such a relationship does not develop at other times owing to the residential dispersion of the labour force of the firms. Moreover, representatives were often unaware of any necessity or responsibility to keep in close touch with the rank and file, although few of them were natural leaders of well-knit groups of employees. Secondly, the relationships between employees and their immediate superiors were very different from those which were believed to obtain at the Council and Committee level. In fact the contrast is not as great as it seems to many employees, because, as we have seen, the role of management at joint meetings tends to be passive. Thus the employee does not feel that he has a consultative relationship with either his representative or his supervisor. In some ways this means more than that the establishment of joint consultation has failed to influence the day-to-day relationships of most employees. In many cases the system has increased the insecurity feelings of intermediate and lower management, and, so far as the rank and file are concerned, the institution of joint consultation between higher management and employee representatives has probably increased their dissatisfaction with the authoritarian regime which they experience on the shop floor. Yet there is no widespread desire to compensate for this by seeking election as representatives. Most employees are reluctant to allow their names to go forward. A disinclination to assume responsibility, and some of the other reasons which were given, such as a lack of facility in speaking, particularly in the presence of superiors, provide a partial explanation. The employee's conception of management's attitude towards employee representation is probably equally if not more important, and this will be determined largely by the employee's own experience of managerial staff. There is still a feeling among employees that the representative 'can be branded as an agitator', or that 'victimization can take place'. Moreover, the steward or councillor 'gets the kicks from both sides'; he is not always *persona grata* with management, nor does he find it easy to establish and maintain a satisfying relationship with employees. In this connection, written or verbal assurances from management are of little avail; it is the actual behaviour of managers that determines employee attitudes. Thus the employee still doubts whether management is really convinced of the desirability of developing democratic rights and procedures. In sum, it may be said that the evidence about day-to-day social relationships in these firms demonstrates that the pattern which they follow is in conflict with that which obtains, or is believed to obtain, in Council or Committee. Joint consultation has had little influence on established relationships, whether these exist between persons at different levels in the line organization, between supervisors and workpeople, between representatives and their constituents, or between the members of various groups of employees. Indeed, in some cases it may have led to a deterioration of such relationships, as for example between junior management and their superiors, or between supervisors and representatives, or even perhaps between rank and file employees and their chargehands and foremen. Furthermore it is apparent from what we have said about the role of management in Council and Committee, and about the content of employee submissions to these joint bodies, that the established pattern of relationships has influenced the developing structure of social interaction at the Council level.

In this situation, the employee representative is in the most difficult position of all. In the first place, he is more aware of the conflict between the regime on the factory floor and that which obtains at Council and Committee level, for he has direct experience of both. Top management and his own departmental supervision may differ in the status and treatment which they accord to him. Moreover, he often feels that an inadequate status and degree of recognition is accorded to him by higher management, yet he does not enjoy a secure status as the leader of an integrated group of employees. His insecurity and ambiguous status no doubt contribute to his desire for wider powers for the joint bodies. In one firm known to the writer, in which the background conditions were similar to those obtaining in the firms under review, this factor was manifested in the desire of the convenor and secretary of stewards to gain a position in the supervisory hierarchy for representatives parallel to, yet distinct from, that of foreman. The present position and difficulties of the representatives are a consequence of the conflicting demands of paternalism and Unionism which are at work in these three firms. The representative tends to become involved in a conflict of roles and loyalties. It is not only a question of a combative role on behalf of employees as against a cooperative role in relation to management. This aspect is important, particularly as regards a representative's relationships with his constituents, for when the latter feel that he is co-operating with management in joint proceedings of which they know little, they are likely to conclude that he is neglecting their interests. Yet in these three firms the desire of most representatives, in their Union as well as their Council role, was to *reach agreement* with management, provided a mutually acceptable basis for so doing could be found. The representative's problem is thus to maintain an effective relationship with both management and his constituents; to remain *persona grata* with both management and employees. At the moment his status in the eyes of both groups tends to be insecure, a situation which arises from conflicting institutional pressures. There is a pressure to consolidate the organization of the employee group as such, with a loyalty to a Union which transcends the confines of any particular factory, and there is a contrary emphasis towards integration of the employee group as part of the factory community. This of course is not a new problem, but the demands for co-operation at the factory level and the background of paternalism in these firms have given it a new operational significance. The prevalent uncertainty in the minds of many employees as to whether the present conditions of industrial stability are likely to continue makes a reconciliation of these conflicting institutional demands difficult for them to achieve.

Union Leadership
V. L. Allen

Reprinted with permission from *The Sociology of Industrial Relations*, Longman, 1971, pp. 51–5.

Trade union officials provide leadership at all levels. Because of the inevitable oligarchic control in unions, leadership involves directing the organizations in all of their major activities and is, therefore, a role which must be analysed if the obstacles to the radical character transformation of unions are to be understood.

The role of a union official is set so that the behaviour of any person who becomes an official is almost entirely predictable. The only significant variations which occur are those which exist within the hierarchy of roles in a union. If a person moves from being a local to a national official then different behaviour will be expected of him. The dominance of the role over the individual explains why the union behaviour of communist and anti-communist officials varies so little; why, in other words, there is continuity of activities despite marked changes in personnel. A new union leader might give greater meaning to his role because of his intellectual ability but if this results in a significant difference in the direction of union activities it will be because the environment of the union has also changed.

The behaviour of a union official is confined by various kinds of sanctions which have been created by social and administrative factors. The first set comprise the process of socialization whereby the role of union officials has been conditioned to be consistent with the norms and values of a capitalist society. The second set can be described as the bureaucratization of union organizations.

The process of socialization was an inevitable one, for unions could not perpetually stand out against the system, fail to change it and yet continue to exist without taking on some of the values of the system itself. The consequence has been to make unions work with and to some extent for the system. This is what the non-legalistic integration of trade unions into society is all about. The results of the process can be seen in many ways. A dominant trade union ethic is a belief in solidarity. This was forced on unions by their need for cohesion in a hostile environment, yet their practice of solidarity is disrupted by the way in which each individual union stoutly protects its own vested interests. The trade union movement reflects the competitive nature of British society through the competition of unions with each other over wages policies, members, and, in the case of craft unions, jobs. Trade unions have imbued capitalist values to the extent of becoming involved in the competitive process. The unions have welded themselves to the price mechanism through an uncritical belief in collective bargaining so that it would be difficult for any government, no matter how sympathetic towards trade union aspirations, to interfere with the wage bargaining process without evoking strong union protests and arousing their antipathy. The unions advocate limited forms of planning for other sections of the economy but insist that wage determination, the vital variable in the planning process, should remain free. Unions support the principle of equity and through the introduction of uniform rates for jobs attempt to apply it. Yet in collective bargaining they practise the most iniquitous form of wage determination. Free collective bargaining is an institutionalized way of operating the play of market forces and their interaction with the subsidiary forces which make up the balance of industrial power. Workers, irrespective of their needs, are in a strong or weak bargaining position because of market forces. In the interwar years the coal miners, for instance, suffered privations because the export demand for coal declined; in the immediate post-Second World War period they obtained relatively high wages because the demand for coal increased; now that alternative sources of power are established the demand for coal is again decreasing, with the obvious depressing effect on miners' living standards. The treatment of the miners in the past has been iniquitous, as is that of the railway workers at present compared with motor production workers. The justification for allocating rewards according to market forces is crudely economic; it has no basis in equity.

The acceptance of free collective bargaining has led, too, to what can be called the myth of achievement. This is simply a situation where union officials are so preoccupied with the means of achievement that they create an illusion about the ends. Instead of being directly concerned about the redistribution of income and devising a means to achieve this, they show satisfaction with fractional changes in money wage rates. In doing this they accept the expectations which employers have deemed suitable for them. These expectations are buttressed by disarming notions of compromise and fairmindedness. Any departure from what is equitable can be justified if the result can be construed as being fair, the meaning of which is set by the limits of voluntary concessions from employers. Nothing which is achieved through conflict is considered to be a fair result. The illusion of achievement was doubtless necessary to maintain trade union morale when actual achievements were consistently meagre and for this reason was present to some extent during the whole course of trade union development. But it became enlarged in the decade of trade union seduction from 1868 when employers, politicians and middle-class intellectuals persuaded union leaders that reason discussed over a table could solve questions of industrial conflict to the benefit of trade unionists. Reason, in fact, only prevails when it is consistent with the movement of market forces. Union leaders who accept its validity lose sight of the reality that they are in a conflict situation. But then this, too, is a consequence of socialization. There is an illusion about a harmony of industrial interests which also influences the role of union officials.

The sanctions on union leaders are of a prohibitive, prescriptive or permissive character and can be seen in attitudes to making 'unreasonable' demands, breaking negotiated agreements, refusals to compromise and 'irresponsibility' to society at large. There are also sanctions which are derived from the integration of unions into the political parliamentary democratic system. There have always been occasions when the objectives of unions demanded political action. At first the need was for legislation to protect women and children in industry, then to protect union funds, enforce industrial safety standards and establish minimum wage rates for workers in sweated industries. Now the need arises from the growth of the government as an employer and its frequent and decisive interventions in industry. Unions are forced into an intensive relationship with the government but are confronted by limitations on the political action they can take, which are set by a belief in political democracy in general and party politics in particular. The sanctions from this situation concern acts which challenge the authority of an elected government or usurp the party system. There is, in consequence, a general prohibition on industrial action for political ends; indeed on anything which savours of coercion of the government; and union leaders respect it. When union leaders during the General Strike realized they were challenging the authority of the government they backed down as quickly as they could. The unwillingness of the Trades Union Congress to support the London busmen in the 1958 strike indicated that most union leaders did not want even to appear to challenge the government. These restrictions can be extensive for there can be so many points of conflict between unions and the government and when they are expressed, the government invariably adopts a constitutional position which gives it automatic protection.

Bureaucracy does not belong to any particular economic system but it is authoritarian, and is consistent, therefore, with the private ownership and control of the means of production. It has been associated with achievement and is a dominant feature of contemporary capitalism. It is understandable, though not necessarily justifiable, that unions should copy bureaucratic practices as far as their allegiances to democratic control permit. Whereas the socialization process has set limits to the uses to which the role of union leadership may be put, bureaucratization has prescribed limits to the role itself. It has combined all the roles involved in trade unions in a hierarchical structure with fixed layers of command and lines of communication, and has prescribed their duties. Formally, union officials must act towards each other and committees they serve according to regulations. Their informal relationships may differ from the formal ones but only in so far as this accords either with tradition or greater efficiency. The informal power of a general secretary is generally much greater than that provided for by his union constitution because he commands power as a specialist in addition to his formal authority. This is not usually disputed so long as the specialist power produces greater efficiency. But all the time he has to be guided by the formal limits to his activities.

Bureaucracy inevitably slows down movement, as was mentioned earlier, but it does not necessarily result in faulty movement. Faultiness is the product of an inability to respond to changing circumstances. There are two elements in bureaucratic organizations which make accurate and immediate responses to changes difficult. The first is the constitutional provision for action. Rules and regulations are difficult to change unless the need for change is intense and imperative. Unions, moreover, deliberately make constitution-changing difficult because alterations not associated with variations in circumstances can be a handicap to action. Secondly, it is possible for bureaucratic attitudes to develop which make a ritual of adherence to regulations. If circumstances alter but not the regulations, then people with these attitudes cannot cope with the situation.

Trade unions, then, have acquired aims which are legitimate within the context of a capitalist society. They are limited aims, concerning wages, hours of work and working conditions, which can be achieved without unduly disturbing the fabric of capitalism; without, indeed, unduly disturbing capitalists because it is possible to conceive of them being obtained through labour market pressures. These legitimate aims are pursued through institutionalized practices. So long as the environment of unions remains stable there need be no inconsistency between the aims and the practices; that is, the ordinary members may feel they are getting satisfaction. But if there are sharp environmental changes, equally sharp inconsistencies develop because institutionalized practices are relatively unresponsive to change. This is what has happened in Britain. Trade unions now are not capable by themselves of achieving satisfactorily even their limited aims.

Workers, Management and Strikes
R. Hyman

Reprinted with permission from *Strikes*, Fontana, 1972, pp. 160–72.

Whose strike problem?

It is not enough to accept uncritically the conventional definition of any social phenomenon as a ' problem'. What is assigned problem status by one group in society may not constitute a problem for some other group – or may do so for quite different reasons. This final section considers this aspect of strikes from the contrasting perspectives of managements and workers.

Management's strike problem

Strikes appear as a problem to employers for three main reasons. The least important is that they disrupt the process of production – though this is the reason most frequently cited. What is far more important is the fact that through their actual or potential use of the strike weapon, workers can impose limits to management's control over them. And thirdly, the occurrence of strikes is a persistent practical contradiction of the ideology of harmony of interests which assigns legitimacy to managerial power.

While strikes have always represented a problem for those in control of industrial enterprises, the seriousness of this problem is increasing. But the recent rise in the number and duration of stoppages is only marginally responsible for this. Far more important are contemporary trends in the very nature of industrial organization and production. The development of large-scale multi-national companies; the integration of diverse productive activities; the decreasing life-span of capital equipment which is itself escalating in complexity and cost: all these create a need for long-term centralized planning within modern corporations. And effective planning requires company control over all factors which might otherwise interfere with manufacturing and marketing programmes.

The implications for industrial relations are obvious.

'Planning is not easy, not even for the biggest. One element in particular is intractable – labour. It has a will of its own and more or less independent organizations. It can, and does, take advantage of its own scarcity. Its behaviour, and therefore cost, is fundamentally unpredictable. Yet the big corporation has not given up. It cannot' (Kidron, 1970).

The need for planning has created urgent pressures for new levels of predictability in labour costs and intensity in labour utilization. The passive subjection of workers to managerial control becomes increasingly the key to continued company profitability. Strikes however raise wages, limit managerial autonomy, and represent expressions of working people's self-activity. Not surprisingly, then, they appear increasingly intolerable to managements. Nor is it surprising that companies which have long abandoned the old ideology of *laissez-faire*, and have come to welcome government assistance in all areas of economic life, should turn to the state for aid in combating the strike.

The government's strike problem

The state is widely regarded as a 'neutral' agency, over and above all internal social conflicts. It is scarcely popular to suggest that governments act predominantly in the interests of one particular class within society. The prevalent view of the state tends to match the ideology discussed earlier: governments serve not mere sectional interests but 'the country as a whole' and 'the national interest'.

There are three main reasons why this view is mistaken. First, those who own and control industry are able to exert a crucial influence over the activities of the state. Governments of whatever political label may be expected to give explicit assent to a system of industry geared to producing profits for a wealthy minority. Those who administer government policy – the professional civil servants – also accept this state of affairs as natural and proper. In short, the policies of those with official charge over state power normally derive from an unquestioned assumption that capitalist interests and 'the national interest' are one and the same.

Secondly, even governments which profess some detachment

from business interests are in practice obliged to attend to the expectations of those with economic power. 'The control by business of large and crucially important areas of economic life makes it extremely *difficult* for governments to impose upon it policies to which it is firmly opposed.' The strategy of working within the confines of the existing economic system – which forms part of the consensus of all main political parties – thus entails a critical constraint: the need to maintain the 'confidence of industry', or more accurately of industrialists. Such confidence is necessary since the government's domestic economic policies may otherwise be sabotaged, while speculative pressures may engineer a trade or currency crisis. The experience of the Labour government of 1964–70 bears eloquent witness to the ransom to capital which may be demanded of any would-be reforming administration.

This leads directly to the third point. 'If the social process of investment and accumulation is left to private ownership then the fate of society as a whole is inextricably bound up with the fortunes of the rich. . . . So long as productive resources are in private hands, they must be allowed to produce a sufficient reward to maintain growth.' As long as the capitalist structure of industry is unquestioned, any government is bound to encourage profits. This point has been clearly stated by Michael Shanks, a leading economic commentator and industrialist:

'The need at present is for prices to be allowed to rise, while wages are held back. . . . In other words, what is urgently required in the United Kingdom's economy at the present time is a redistribution of national income away from wages and in favour of profits. It is not perhaps surprising that neither party is very anxious to spell out this awkward but inescapable fact of economic life' (*The Times*, 16 June 1970).

If government policies directed towards the welfare of 'the' economy are in fact directed towards the welfare of a capitalist economy, then any action which benefits the owners of capital – making the rich even richer – must seem perfect economic sense.

Such pressures inevitably shape government attitudes towards strikes. Insofar as strikes are a challenge to managerial interests, they must represent a threat to 'the' economy. The consequences have long been manifest.

'On innumerable occasions, and in all capitalist countries, governments have played a decisive role in defeating strikes, often by the invocation of the coercive power of the state and the use of naked violence; and the fact that they have done so in the name of the national interest, law and order, constitutional government, the protection of "the public", etc., rather than simply to support employers, has not made that intervention any the less useful to these employers' (Miliband, 1969).

Recent dramatic examples of government involvement can be seen in the seamen's strike of 1966, or in subsequent systematic efforts to hold down wages in the public sector. Such confrontations reflect heightened economic pressures on the state as well as on individual companies. Virtual stagnation has meant that improved wages can no longer be financed painlessly out of economic growth; foreign competition limits the extent to which money wage increases can be clawed back through price inflation. The goal of accelerated investment and the pressures of international capital mobility rather necessitate, as Shanks suggests, a redistribution of income away from wages and salaries and towards profits; while concern for increased 'productivity' of labour creates a parallel interest in the consolidation and extension of managerial control at the place of work. Thus governments, like employers, have strong practical reasons for increasing intolerance of strikes. And in addition, striker-baiting is regarded as a fruitful form of party-political capital; strikers also serve as a convenient scapegoat for the abysmal economic records, in international comparative terms, of all recent British governments.

The idea that the state is 'above sectional conflicts' and plays a 'neutral' role in industrial relations is therefore mistaken; but it is of great ideological importance. When the government intervenes in a dispute, on the side of the employer, any attempt by the union concerned to stand firm can be presented as 'undemocratic' and 'a challenge to the constitution'. Where trade unionists themselves regard the state as 'neutral', their resolve is likely to crumble before such an ideological offensive.

The workers' strike problem

Managers and politicians are accustomed to articulating and publicizing their definitions of those areas of social reality which are of concern to them. This is of course not the case for the vast majority of ordinary people, who in any case lack comparable access to the media of communication. For the reasons argued earlier in this chapter, surveys of 'public opinion' are unreliable guides to people's thinking on social questions; they do not indicate, for example, whether people have given such questions serious consideration at all, and thus whether views expressed are likely to be altered by further thought or by practical experience. So statistics which purport to show the attitude to strikes of the general public, or of trade union members, should not be given excessive credence.

It follows however from what was said earlier concerning social values and ideology, that the definitions of industrial conflict constructed by those in positions of social control are likely to exert extensive influence. It follows that workers will tend to use such concepts as 'the country as a whole' or 'the interests of the firm' as part of the frame of reference through which they perceive and evaluate the strikes of other trade unionists. Most workers most of the time may be expected to share in part at least the managerial definition of strikes. This is particularly likely given the defensive and apologetic attitude taken by most trade unions towards strikes, and the open hostility of many of the alleged political representatives of labour.

Strikes are a more immediate problem to those indirectly affected by stoppages. In the car industry, for example, there are signs that workers with experience of lay-offs during strikes unrelated to their own immediate interests have a tendency to react antagonistically towards strikes in general. This is understandable. Since strikes involve initiative by the workers involved, the natural assumption is that they must be the aggressors: natural, that is, unless viewed with a sophistication or class-consciousness which insists that management action may well have precipitated the dispute. Car workers, it has been suggested, may be particularly lacking in 'solidaristic' class-consciousness: when aggrieved at losing money through lay-offs they may regard the strikers as the obvious culprits – particularly since the true causes of the dispute are unlikely to be widely publicized. This in turn may induce some employers to use the 'sympathy lock-out' as a deliberate tactic for putting pressure on strikers to return to work.

Not all trade unionists, however, blame fellow-workers in whose disputes they become indirectly involved. Indeed, the occurrence of sympathy stoppages, collections for strike appeals, and refusals to touch 'black' work indicates that feelings of solidarity remain widespread. The Devlin Report on the docks referred to 'an exaggerated sense of solidarity or loyalty': men accepted without question a policy of 'one out, all out', adopting the 'principle that the man who wants to strike is always right' (1965). Such attitudes, condemned by Devlin as 'irresponsibility', may be viewed in the situation as a perfectly natural extension of trade union ethics. Dockers have learned that strike action is seldom taken frivolously, but reflects an accumulation of grievances; they are therefore willing to support their fellows in dispute without question, knowing that they themselves may some time depend on similar support. The absence of so firm a tradition of solidarity in some other industries may in part indicate a lesser need; under mass-production technology, a sectional group can achieve a similar effect by strike action whether or not other workers in the factory give active support. Nevertheless, an attitude of solidarity towards other workers' strikes can be found even in the car industry: witness the rapid preparations for support at other Ford plants before the Halewood strike was settled. Government attempts to outlaw sympathy strikes and similar action indicate the continuing significance of solidarity.

In any case, however ambivalent – or even downright hostile – some workers may be towards *other* men's stoppages, their views will be quite different when they themselves feel obliged to strike. 'He is an irresponsible wildcat; I am taking legitimate action to defend my rights' – such a viewpoint, probably quite widespread, reflects not so much double standards as the totally different definitions of the situation of the outsider and of those personally involved. Participation in a stoppage can thus transform a worker's viewpoint: the conventional stereotypes and values lose their grip.

'To go on strike is to deny the existing distribution of power and authority. The striker ceases to respond to managerial command; he refuses to do his "work". A new dimension of living can thus be revealed to the striker; an existence in which "ordinary" people are able to control events and command the attention of "them". The experience of this new reality can transform the striker's perceptions of normal life. What was "normal" can no longer be regarded as "natural". Attitudes towards work and authority become critical as opposed to acquiescent' (Lane and Roberts, 1971).

While such a transformation of attitudes normally weakens after a return to work, the effect is unlikely to disappear entirely. Since the inhibiting effect of the dominant social values on potential strikers appears to be weakening; since the statistics suggest that a growing proportion of employees are willing to discard their industrial virginity and turn to strike action as a solution to their grievances; so the effect of such experience on attitudes prevalent among workpeople is likely to extend.

For the striker, clearly, it is not strikes which are the 'problem'. The actions of management which violate his expectations; the features of the employment relationship which degrade and oppress him, generating deprivations and conflicts; the social values which deny the legitimacy of his struggle to defend or improve his conditions; these are the real strike problems for the striker himself. And most of all, attempts to put legal shackles on workers' freedom to withdraw their labour create an intense and urgent 'problem': 'the strike is Labour's expression of free will; surrender that, and the worker becomes the merest wage-slave' (Cole, 1913). For those who are concerned with human freedom, this is today's most burning strike problem.

Alternative solutions

If the nature of the strike problem varies according to the perspective from which it is viewed, so necessarily does the appropriate solution. From the managerial viewpoint analysed above, such a solution is increasingly urgent. And given the convergence of the economic interests of the employers and the state, the same is true of the government also.

The managerial response may take either of two forms. The first is the method of outright coercion. As was seen earlier, the government has on various occasions offered obstinate resistance to unions representing its own employees – often with strong encouragement from industrialists and the press. But the government's writ does not extend to the private sector; and car manufacturers, for example, have felt obliged to adopt a more compromising stance – despite ministerial exhortation to 'stand firm' – when faced by determined action from their own workers. So government policy has extended to a more generally coercive strategy. The deliberate creation of mass unemployment – at the time of writing, roughly a million jobless are officially listed – is one aspect of this approach. This has resulted in 1971 in a substantial reduction in the number of strikes (though their average size and duration has increased). Yet a policy of mass unemployment seems to have failed to reduce union bargaining power to the extent desired, while conflicting with the objective of economic growth.

Hence the use of penal sanctions against strikers has become peculiarly attractive to managerial interests. Such bodies as the Confederation of British Industry and the Engineering Employers' Federation urged this course on the Donovan Commission. While the latter was unpersuaded, both Labour and Conservative governments proved more amenable, and the Industrial Relations Act is the result. Yet as Donovan recognized, the prospects of success for a policy of legal coercion are somewhat doubtful. Sanctions may be directed against trade unions; but since these are so detached from shop-floor industrial relations such sanctions will be largely irrelevant. They may be directed against shop stewards; but since these are rarely the agitators of popular imagination, this may if anything increase conflict. They may be directed against strikers as a whole; but British gaols are already too overcrowded to make such a deterrent credible. Certainly most employers, when confronted by a strike, will be more concerned to negotiate a resumption of production than to compound the conflict by dragging employees before the courts. It is possible that the mere existence of anti-strike legislation may intimidate potential strikers; but given the largely spontaneous origins of most stoppages, this effect will probably be limited. And in any case, while action against strikes is pursued as a means of securing a more compliant labour force, it is more likely to create a body of resentful employees whose resentments are expressed in less overt and less manageable forms of conflict.

The alternative managerial solution is that of manipulation. One example of this strategy goes by the name of 'incomes policy', an increasingly popular device in recent years. Great efforts are devoted to persuading trade unionists to acquiesce in self-emasculation, by agreeing to negotiate pay increases only within rigid limits, or by tying higher wages and salaries to increased 'productivity'. Within the perspective of the ruling ideology, such a policy is manifestly 'fair', since if trade unions hold back 'excessive' pay claims the employers express their readiness to hold back price increases. But any 'incomes policy' of this sort means, at best, that the relative shares of rich and poor – labour and capital – will be frozen; that the privileged position of the wealthy minority will be consolidated; and, if the 'productivity' criterion is rigorously enforced, that workers will have to pay for their own pay improvements through more dehumanizing conditions of labour. Not surprisingly, experience appears to have left many trade unionists unwilling to co-operate in any future exercise of this nature.

There are, however, other possibilities of manipulation. At the level of the individual firm, managerial policy can be adjusted along the lines recommended by human relations theorists or by subsequent breeds of industrial sociologists. At a different level, the type of proposals put forward by Donovan can be adopted: the reform of bargaining procedures, the formalization of industrial relations at factory or company level, the incorporation of shop-floor bargainers within the official institutions of trade unionism. Such a strategy will have genuine pay-offs: undeniably, some strikes are attributable to managerial incompetence, chaotic pay structures, or procedural inadequacies, and such causes are remediable. No doubt the integrating pressures on shop stewards can be stepped up to some effect. Yet as was seen in Chapter Four [not reprinted here], there are limits to the extent to which conflict can be institutionalized and workers' representatives incorporated, without other types of action emerging. Moreover there are increasing signs of resistance from within the trade union movement itself to a policy of 'reforms' designed to intensify managerial control over trade unionists.

It is in any case central to my argument that conflict is generated by the basic structure of industry in our society. If this is so, strikes are unlikely to yield substantially either to manipulation or to legislation. The example of West Germany – often presented as a case of model industrial relations – is illuminating. Free trade unions were smashed by the Nazis and replaced by authoritarian control of labour relations by managements and the state. With the tradition of independent worker organization destroyed, it was possible in the post-war period to establish a system of industrial relations deliberately designed to minimize overt conflict; and until very recently at least, West Germany has had by far the lowest strike figures in any major Western industrial nation. Yet the implications have been clearly stated by an eminent German sociologist: 'the translation of a collective situation into a mass of individual reactions'.

'We find instead of work disputes, individual actions whose connection with social conflicts is barely recognizable at first sight. Sinking work morale, growing fluctuation, indeed even sickness and accident rates may be indicators of such redirections of industrial conflict. In these manifestations, the redirection of conflict . . . approaches repression of its energies. Some of the workers . . . display an attitude of almost hopeless resentment; this may become manifest unannounced and in ways removed from all chance of control' (Dahrendorf, 1968).

In the state capitalist societies of Eastern Europe, where the totalitarian control of a bureaucratic ruling class is used to suppress strikes, there is evidence of a similar redirection of conflict. In Britain today there is little chance that open industrial conflict could be prevented in this way; but if it were, the same result could be predicted: the expression of workers' grievances in less organized and less manageable forms. To this extent management's strike problem, however urgent, can never be satisfactorily resolved.

But equally, the problem as it confronts trade unionists cannot be resolved, so long as their definition of the causes of their grievances and their selection of responses remain at the present level of rationality. The argument of Engels nearly a century ago remains true still: 'The British labour movement is today and for many years has been working in a narrow circle of strikes for higher wages and shorter hours without finding a solution' (letter to Bernstein, 17 June 1879). Grievances are channelled through collective bargaining into demands which accept the legitimacy of the employment relationship and the status of labour as a commodity; discontent at managerial domination, which seems to underlie many disputes, is thus kept below the surface. This sublimation of workers' resistance to coercive control is, indeed, the most fundamental and persistent indication of the institutionalization of industrial conflict. So long as strikes are directed against the immediate manifestations of workers' deprivations, rather than their underlying causes, strikers will achieve only temporary relief; and they must expect to attract increasing social hostility and recurrent efforts at repression.

For the striker, then, the only real solution to the strike problem lies in a transformation of the status of labour and the whole structure of control in industry: replacing minority domination and the pursuit of profit by democratic control and the satisfaction of human needs. (By abolishing management in its present form this will, of course, also provide a radical solution to *management's* strike problem!) As was argued in the last chapter, the idea that strike activity might lead spontaneously to such a social transformation seems utopian. This is particularly true because the increasing intervention of the state on the side of employers in industrial relations means that the traditional trade union segregation of 'industrial' from 'political' activities has become largely meaningless. Every important trade union struggle over wages or conditions has today a political dimension, since it impinges directly on government economic strategy. And quite clearly, any attempt to change the organization and direction of individual enterprises or the economy as a whole would represent a highly political act – which would presuppose consciously articulated political aspirations on the part of working people.

Is such politicization of industrial conflict a serious possibility? It is important to remember that industrial disputes are only one aspect of contemporary resistance to the goals and structure of the political economy of modern capitalism. Recent years have seen the widespread questioning of all forms of established authority, a growing disillusionment with the charade of formal party politics, an increasingly articulate concern at the depredations which technology, directed only by the dictates of profit, inflicts upon the 'quality of life'. Such challenges to the logic of contemporary capitalist society have so far been isolated from the collective actions of industrial workers; so too have such movements as women's liberation, the struggle against racism, student activism, or the revolt of depressed regions. But should such movements intermesh, and should broader political questions spill over into the consciousness of workers *in their industrial actions*, the basis would exist for explicit and comprehensive demands for the democratization of industry and society as a whole.

There are already indications of such a development. Theories of workers' control, almost defunct for half a century, have in the last few years been revived and elaborated to meet the conditions of large-scale, technically sophisticated industry. In this process a small but increasing number of active trade unionists have played an important part. This is no intellectual accident: the growing demand for workers' control is a natural response to the problems which technological development, in the context of a capitalist economy, creates for organized workers. Ideas of industrial democracy articulate the experiences and aspirations which, in however confused and distorted a form, may be seen as underlying workers' day-to-day struggles on the shop floor. As Raymond Williams has argued:

'What is now called Luddism, or wildcat militancy, is very often, at root, a fight . . . to use the machines, rather than to be used by them; to impose a new social organization, where decisions are made by the men actually doing the work, as against an old organization in which decisions are invariably made elsewhere; to learn, if only in the first instance by the co-operative revolts that we call strikes, the means of a new human order.'

It should be clear that unless the educative potential of workers' struggles is realized – unless the demand for control becomes increasingly explicit – the efforts of managements and strikers to resolve their respective strike problems will continue to be mutually neutralizing. Disputes will remain a central feature of industrial relations. Managements will fail to suppress the often violent expression of workers' collective experience of deprivation. Workers will still be confronted by the *temporary* nature of whatever victories they achieve, and will continue to *react* to situations rather than exercising positive control over their industrial destinies. The crucial, and necessarily open question is whether workers themselves, in the course of their sectional conflicts, will succeed in transcending the conventional definitions of their own activity and of the industrial system which underlies it, and will thus raise their struggles to a new level of rationality.

Further Reading: Workers and Trade Unions

*v. l. ALLEN, *Trade Union Leadership*, London, Longmans, 1957.

R. M. BLACKBURN, *Union Character and Social Class*, London, Batsford, 1967.

*R. BLACKBURN and A. COCKBURN, *The Incompatibles*, London, Penguin, 1967.

P. BLUMBERG, *Industrial Democracy: the Sociology of Participation*, London, Constable, 1968.

H. A. CLEGG, *The System of Industrial Relations in Great Britain*, Oxford, Blackwell, 1970.

H. A. CLEGG, *A New Approach to Industrial Democracy*, Oxford, Blackwell, 1960.

K. COATES, *Can the Workers run Industry?* London, Sphere, 1968.

J. E. T. ELDRIDGE, *Industrial Disputes*, London, Routledge and Kegan Paul, 1968.

A. FLANDERS, *The Fawley Productivity Agreements*, London, Faber and Faber, 1964.

*R. FRASER, *Work*, London, Penguin, 1968.

*R. FRASER, *Work 2*, London, Penguin, 1969.

A. KORNHAUSER, R. DUBIN and A. M. ROSS, *Industrial Conflict*, New York, McGraw-Hill, 1954.

H. A. TURNER, G. CLACK and G. ROBERTS, *Labour Relations in the Motor Industry*, London, Allen and Unwin, 1967.

K. W. WEDDERBURN, 'Labour Law and Industrial Relations in Britain', in *British Journal of Industrial Relations*, Vol. X, 1972, pp. 270–90.

*D. WILSON, *Dockers*, London, Fontana, 1972.

* Available in paperback

Chapter Ten

The Context of Work: Leisure, Unemployment and Retirement

When a great many people are
Unable to find work —
Unemployment results.

Calvin Coolidge

. . . my task accomplished
And the long day done

W. E. Henley

In this book we have concentrated quite closely on the position of *work* in contemporary British society and on the consequences for individuals of the division of labour in their working life. We agreed in Chapter 1 that we would not constrain our subject-matter within the rigid confines of syllabus descriptions such as 'the sociology of occupations' or 'organizational analysis'. But we have restricted ourselves to work roles and have not followed too far such topics as the interconnections of work and domestic roles or the relationship of the occupational system to the class system.

But these boundaries which we have drawn around the topic of 'work' for the purpose of this present collection of readings are rather artificial ones. So one of the aims of this final chapter is to indicate some of the most important points of articulation between the system of inter-relationships based on the division of labour and other aspects of society. We need to see how an analysis of the problems of 'work' assists in illuminating the principles on which British society is organized.

Stanley Parker suggests a scheme for categorizing an individual's time and distinguishing between the many activities in which he may be involved during a day. These categories go beyond the simple distinction between 'work' and 'non-work'. When an individual is engaged on 'sold time' he is selling his labour power to the employer in return for a wage. But in order to be in a position to sell his labour power he has to prepare himself for work, to travel to work and so on. Moreover, he has to spend a certain amount of time in meeting basic psychological needs and keeping himself healthy. Some activities in which he may invest a good deal of time are not 'work' but the individual may none the less regard his participation in them as 'obligatory': they are duties rather than pleasures. Only after these four types of activity have been accounted for can we begin to talk about 'leisure' or 'free time'. The free individual in a free society of free men may have precious little time which he can call 'his own', and the scarcity of it makes it the more precious to him. This extract has been taken from one of the early chapters of Parker's book in which he goes on to use this scheme to analyse the role of work and leisure in contemporary society and to draw some implications for the future. His book is recommended for its systematic and extended analysis of the 'problem of leisure'.

In terms of Parker's typology, the poachers in Llan, the North Wales village described by Isobel Emmet, are engaged in activities which fall into Category 4. The superficially 'intermittent' and to some extent 'pointless' activities of the poachers are shown to form part of an elaborate and ritualized dance of life. They are an unconsciously co-ordinated protest against what are believed to be inherently unjust rules based on an exploitative pattern of land-holding. The English owners and the native peasants are linked by relationships of oppression and expropriation which in the eyes of the poachers legitimize their apparently illegal behaviour.

The contrast between the 'folk theory' of unemployment and the realities of the employment situation of young men in a northern city form the theme of the paper by Dianne Phillips. She shows how the simple distinction between 'employment' and 'unemployment' tends to mask the *intermittent* employment situation of both 'employed' and 'unemployed'. Moreover, the extent and distribution of the phenomenon, and therefore the dimensions of the problem which the official agencies are set up to deal with, appear to be very different depending on which estimates, and which official figures one selects.

Dorothy Wedderburn uses a study of men thrown out of work by the Rolls-Royce failure of 1971 to ask some pertinent questions about the position of work in 'an unplanned labour market'. She shows how the loss of their job often appeared to have substantial and widespread repercussions for the individuals concerned. Some were soon involved in other redundancies, and others lost their entitlement to occupational pension rights. The 'job security' which these workers had lost and to which most workers attach so much importance represents in a real sense an expression of the knowledge that in societies like ours jobs are a basic life-line *to* society. Wedderburn asks how these subjective expectations can be reconciled with the view, often expressed by social scientists and other know-alls in their more prophetic moments, that the time is approaching when technological advance will *require* individuals to be prepared to change their jobs several times during their working lives. She asks how such a credibility gap can be bridged without '. . . a fundamental revolution in technology or in power relationships'.

Tunstall's study of fishermen was undertaken over ten years ago, but we need to take care not to dismiss this account too glibly because such details as the wage rates he mentions are clearly outdated. Neither need we apologize for his apparent tendency to depart somewhat from the standards of detachment and objectivity which are held to be desirable in social scientific studies of 'workers'. Possibly the retired fishermen are still a special case in being 'one of the poorest of all groups living among us in economic as well as social terms'. But it is appropriate in a more general sense to question the moral values on which is based the assumption that poverty, or at least a substantial deterioration in one's standard of living, must *necessarily* accompany one's exit from the labour market. This fact alone emphasizes the crucial and *general* significance of the social relations based on the work system and reinforces the point that we live in a society of workers and non-workers, employers and employed, owners/controllers and wage-labourers, not yet a society of *people*.

Work and Leisure: Problems of Definition
S. Parker

Reprinted with permission from *The Future of Work and Leisure*, Granada Publishing Ltd, 1971, pp. 25–32.

Components of life space

'Life space' means the total of activities or ways of spending time that people have. In considering the various definitions of work and leisure we see that to allocate all the parts of life space either to work or to leisure would be a gross over-simplification. It is possible to use the exhaustive categories of 'work' and 'non-work', but this still does not enable us to say where the line between the two is to be drawn. Also, important differences exist *within* as well as between these two categories. A number of writers have suggested schemes for analysing the 24 hours in the average person's day into various categories. Instead of examining these schemes in detail, we may put the various categories that have been suggested into five main groups. This should make analysis easier, and it assumes that any differences among the categories in each group are fairly minor.

(1) *Work, working time, sold time, subsistence time*. Although 'work' has a wider meaning than employment, for the purpose of analysing life space it is usually identified with earning a living. If an employee is on piece rates then it is 'work', or more precisely the product of work, that he sells; if he is on time rates then he sells so much working time. However, these are both ways of measuring work *and* working time, and only differ in the way the remuneration is calculated. 'Subsistence time' lays emphasis on the *purpose* of work to the worker, that is, enabling him and his dependants to subsist.

(2) *Work-related time, work obligations*. Apart from actual working time, most people have to spend a certain amount of time in travelling to and from the place of work and in preparing or 'grooming' themselves for work. In some cases, however, at least part of the travelling time may be regarded more as a form of leisure than as work-related – for example, time spent reading newspapers or books, chatting to fellow-travellers, or

playing cards with them. Some writers regard as work-related things that would not be done if it were not for work, such as the husband doing a share of his working wife's housework. Voluntary overtime and having a second job may also be regarded as related to the main working time rather than as part of it, as may activities in the no-man's land between work and leisure such as reading on the subject of one's work when at home, attending conferences or trade union meetings which have a social as well as a work side, and so on.

(3) *Existence time, meeting physiological needs.* This is the first of three 'non-work' groups. We all have to spend a certain minimum of time on sleep and the mechanics of living – eating, washing, eliminating, etc. Beyond the minimum necessary for reasonably healthy living, extra time spent on these things may be more like a leisure activity. Eating for pleasure, taking extra care with one's appearance for a party or social occasion, sexual activity beyond the call of purely physiological need, are some examples which show that the line between the satisfaction of 'existence' needs and leisure activities is not always easy to draw.

(4) *Non-work obligations, semi-leisure.* Joffre Dumazedier, author of *Toward a Society of Leisure*, has coined the term *semi-leisure* to describe 'activities which, from the point of view of the individual, arise in the first place from leisure, but which represent in differing degrees the character of obligations'. The obligations are usually to other people, but may be to non-human objects such as pets or homes or gardens. Again, the line between obligation and leisure is not always clear and depends to a large extent on one's *attitude* to the activity. Gardening and odd-job work around the home can be a chore or an absorbing hobby, and playing with the children can be a duty or a delight.

(5) *Leisure, free time, spare time, uncommitted time, discretionary time, choosing time.* All the words after 'leisure' describe some aspect of what is meant by leisure. Residual definitions of leisure give it as time free from various commitments and obligations, and that 'free' time is best regarded as a dimension of leisure. 'Spare' time is a slightly different idea, implying that, like a spare tyre, it is not normally in use but could be put to use. 'Uncommitted' time suggests lack of obligations, of either a work or non-work character. 'Discretionary' or 'choosing' time is perhaps

the essence of leisure, because it means time that we can use at our own discretion and according to our own choice.

From a careful study of the various schemes for analysing life space three points emerge:

1. Time and activity are dimensions which are *both* present in all categories of life space, even where, for the sake of brevity, both are not always stated.

2. Between compulsory activities (in order to live or to earn a living) and freely chosen ones, some activities have the character of obligations. This applies to both work and non-work activities.

3. Leisure implies relative freedom of choice, and it is possible to work during one's 'leisure' time.

	Work time		Non-work time		
Work	Work obligations		Physiological needs	Non-work obligations	Leisure

In this scheme work may be defined as the activity involved in earning a living, plus necessary subsidiary activities such as travelling to work. Work obligations include voluntary over-time, doing things outside normal working hours associated with the job or type of work that are not strictly necessary to a minimum acceptable level of performance in the job, or having a second job. The satisfaction of physiological needs follows the conventional definition of these needs. Non-work obligations are roughly what Dumazedier calls semi-leisure, plus the domestic work part of work obligations. Leisure is time free from obliga-tions either to self or to others – time in which to do as one chooses.

Time and activity are *dimensions*, or ways of measuring some-thing. The 'something' that they measure is called a *variable*. In analysing life space the crucial *time* variable seems to be whether a given space of time is work or not, while the main *activity* variable seems to be the extent to which the activity is constrained or freely chosen. The constraint may arise from within the individual himself or may be imposed on him by the way in which he lives. The elements in the above time scheme may be re-ordered into a two-dimensional time and activity scheme:

FIGURE 1

ACTIVITY

		Constraint ◄──────────────────────────► Freedom	
Work	Work (employment)	Work obligations (connnected with employment)	'Leisure in work'
Non-work	Physiological needs	Non-work obligations	Leisure

(left axis label: TIME)

Except for leisure, particular types of activity may be fairly easily allocated to work or non-work time. Economic necessity constrains most people to have one job (work) but only if they choose to value a higher standard of living above more free time need they take a second job (work obligation). Similarly, in the non-work sphere the satisfaction of physiological needs is in its own way as necessary as work, but non-work obligations are only obligations within a framework of prior freedom to choose; for example, a man can avoid non-work obligations connected with the conjugal family by staying single.

The position of leisure is rather special. It is clearly at the 'freedom' end of the constraint-freedom scale, but it need not be restricted to non-working time. We draw attention to this paradox when we say that someone else's way of choosing to spend leisure time looks to us more like hard work. 'Work' and 'leisure in work' may consist of the same activity; the difference is that the latter is chosen for its own sake. Thus mountaineering is work for the guide but leisure in work for the amateur climber. Leisure time and employment time cannot overlap, but there is no reason why some of the time that is sold as work should not be utilized by the seller (that is, the employee) for leisure-type activities, provided that the buyer (that is, the employer or his agent) has no objection, or is ignorant of or cannot control the situation. In addition to such oases of leisure in the desert of working time, there remains the point that leisure means *choice*, and so time chosen to be spent as work activity – though not involving the constraint of employment – can be leisure just as much as more usual leisure activities.

Time is limited to the twenty-four hours in the day, but some human activities are such that two or more can take place at the same time. For example, the satisfaction of a physiological need, such as eating, can be accompanied by a leisure activity, such as listening to the radio. A chart of life space with only the time dimension has difficulty in coping with such simultaneous activities which fall into different categories. To overcome this difficulty the time-budget people have used the concepts of primary and secondary activities and have added the duration of the total of secondary activities to the twenty-four hours in the day to give a total daily time budget of up to thirty-two hours for some groups. As well as allocating primary and secondary activities to the same space of time, we may allocate primary and secondary functions to the same activity. Thus activities which are *primarily* at the constraint end of the scale, such as employment, may involve in a *secondary* way the leisure-like element of freely chosen activity, in this case, the type of work we should like to do even if we had no need of employment.

One important qualification must be made to the analysis of life space. In considering the various categories we have had in mind men in full-time employment. Certain modifications to the scheme are necessary if it is to fit the cases of other groups. In assuming that all adults work (i.e. are engaged in a full-time paid occupation) we should be right in about seventy per cent of cases. But an analysis of life space based on this majority would be incomplete if it could not be amended to take account of the minority who are not in a full-time occupation. We may consider the amendments to the scheme which seem to be necessary to account for the circumstances of four groups of 'non-workers': prisoners, housewives, the unemployed, and the 'idle rich'.

The life space of a prisoner is much more constricted than that of the average citizen on both time and activity dimensions. Although some prisoners are employed inside or outside the prison, the choice of available work is severely restricted and the financial motivation for it rather different (earning pocket-money rather than earning a living). In so far as some prison work may be more or less voluntarily undertaken to relieve boredom or satisfy a physiological or psychological need to work, it may resemble the 'work obligation' of ordinary citizens. But, by being cut off from the outside world, prisoners have virtually no non-work obligations, and even the character of leisure is different for them. The contrast between free and constrained activities which most of those in the outside world experience is largely denied to prisoners. The constraint to earn a living is removed, but so is the freedom to choose beyond a narrow range of institutional leisure activities, which must take place during hours set by the prison authorities. The concentration of the prisoner's activities in the middle range between economic constraint and personal freedom, and the unreality for him of the distinction between work and non-work, are measures of the narrowness of his life in prison.

It may seem strange to compare the life of the housewife to that of the prisoner, but a book entitled *The Captive Wife* suggests that the comparison may not be entirely unwarranted. Doing the housework is, in effect, her employment but, as compared with her husband's employment, it usually offers less scope for interest and less social contact. The life of the housewife, like that of the prisoner, tends to be restricted at both ends of the constraint-freedom scale. There is for her no real difference between work and work obligations, and the responsibilities of the household, particularly if she is a mother, must often restrict the range of her leisure activities, even though her 'free time' may be greater than that of her working sister. The proportion of her time devoted to non-work obligations is correspondingly inflated. However, it is interesting to note that time budgets collected in ten countries show that non-employed women more often combine primary and secondary activities in the same space of time than do either employed men or women. In this sense at least, the lives of housewives may be fuller than those of other people.

The unemployed constitute another category whose lives show a contraction of the normal range between constraint and freedom. Many people who are unemployed develop after a time a feeling of being useless, and may be driven to occupy themselves with trivial tasks and time-filling routines. They lose the companionship and social support of workmates. Lack of money produces a restriction on the range of leisure activities which they can engage in, thus narrowing the range of life experience from the leisure and as well as the work end. But with increases in the incomes of the unemployed through such measures as wage-related unemployment benefits, people out of work may be able to purchase a 'standard of leisure' comparable to that of those in work. The position of the retired is in some ways similar to that of the unemployed, except that absence of employment is normally planned and permanent, so that in many (though by no means all) cases adjustment in the pattern of life is not too difficult to make.

In the fourth category non-workers are in a rather different position from the other three. The idle rich are free from the necessity to earn a living but this freedom, largely for reasons connected with social status, is not used to undertake work obligations. In this respect the 'work' lives of the idle rich are even more impoverished than are those of the other three categories of non-workers we have considered. But, unlike these others, the idle rich make leisure the centre of their existence. The balance of their lives is shifted heavily towards the freedom end of the scale, just as the balance of prisoners' lives is shifted towards constraint, and for both groups the distinction between work and non-work is blurred. Another minority – those who are free from the necessity of earning a living but who do work of a kind and in circumstances of their choice – are able to separate work from non-work only on the time dimension, and sometimes not even on that. They share with the idle rich a relative lack of constraint in their lives as a whole, and demonstrate 'work in leisure'. The other side of this coin – 'leisure in work' – is apparent in those people who are able to make a living in doing what they most enjoy for its own sake. Alexander Szalai hints at the possible expansion of this group when he says that 'it is by no means a natural law that productive work or work for one's living cannot offer as much inner and external freedom, as many possibilities for self-expression and relaxation, as are to be looked for and found in most cases only in leisure spent outside the working place.'

Partisans in Peacetime: the North Wales Poachers
I. Emmet

Reprinted with permission from *A North Wales Village*, Routledge and Kegan Paul, 1964, pp. 69–76.

There is a lot of water in the mountain streams around Llan parish in November and the salmon jump up the waterfalls to spawn. No one goes on aimless strolls – they go to the bridge to see if the water is high and, finding it is, they go home to sort out gaffs, nets, hooks, torches and voluminous coats that will hide this poaching gear. Some prefer to use a large home-made net of wire, providing the water is not running so fast as to wrench it from them; some prefer to spear or spike the salmon as they swim past; some just use their hands and catch the fish when they are lying still and they say the salmon like being stroked at spawning time. Some prefer the daytime when they can see the bailiffs coming; some prefer the night when it is easy to hide and the bailiffs might be in the pub. But whatever the time, whatever the means, anyone who is Welsh (men climbing the English prestige ladder do not go poaching) goes poaching. When I say anyone, I mean men only, of course.

During the poaching season, wives are neglected, not for money-consuming beer, but for supper-helping salmon and they would rather their men came in excited from an evening's sport than lethargic or quarrelsome from an evening's drinking. This is one reason why, although it is the women whose tongues seize most sharply on any breach of the chapel code and who feel genuine shock and fear evil consequences if hay is carried on a Sunday, the women condone their husbands' 'criminality'. The other more important reason is that they do not consider poaching to be wrong.

What are the men's motives? The fish are eaten and relieve the monotony of the Welsh diet, but fresh salmon, fried, steamed, grilled and baked, itself gets monotonous very quickly over the five or six weeks of the poaching season. Further, the quality of the fish is believed to deteriorate after the first couple of weeks – larger fish come up the steams and those which have spawned and are returning to the sea have flabby flesh. On the whole the poachers are not very keen on eating the fish: they cannot sell them to hotels or fishmongers because salmon are out of season. So a large proportion of the fish a man catches, he gives away, perhaps to his foreman, perhaps to the minister, perhaps to relatives or friends living outside the district. To give gifts in this way is to store up credit of some kind, but there is a great deal of barter and gift exchange taking place all the time. So many other objects and services are used in these exchanges that I do not think that the hope of receiving a return is a major motive causing the men to catch salmon. The economic incentive is not a sufficient one in these days, though it seems to have been more important in the past, when, it is said, a much larger proportion of the fish caught was eaten in the parish.

A further attraction might seem to be the danger. But in fact the danger hardly exists: poachers are very rarely caught. The comparative safety of poaching in the area follows from the fact

that river bailiffs, like other officials, are either with the poachers
or against them. A bailiff who is part of the community wants to
drink and play darts with the men he is supposed to hunt; he
and his family depend on the co-operation of their neighbours
and their life would be impossible if he did his job well. Any
river bailiff who is not part of the Welsh community has a rather
dangerous job, especially when he is working away from home.
Poachers will not hesitate to gang up on him or take him on
singly if he traps them or catches them after a chase. A few years
ago a murderously sharp hook narrowly missed the head of one
bailiff. In the old days bailiffs were stoned and thrown in the
river and old men still carry stones in their pockets when they go
to the river. Such bitter warfare is rarely waged nowadays. But
dating back as far as the tradition that small farmers, farm-
workers and quarrymen in this poor district win few battles in
the class war, is the tradition that they usually win this kind of
battle. There is another weapon which has grown in use as
violence has lessened and this weapon provides another reason
why poaching in Llan and the district is not dangerous and also
demonstrates an interesting aspect of the social structure of rural
North Wales. This weapon is what has been called in other
environments the grapevine. The movements of the river bailiffs,
as of other officials, are known within at least a ten-mile radius
from their base. Adults and children have an amazing capacity
to remember registration numbers of cars and motor-cycles and
they notice number, colour and make so casually and invariably
that the mobile maps they carry with them seem to occupy a
dimension of their minds which I lack. London schoolboys collect
car numbers, but it is quite a different phenomenon I am discussing. I have heard a woman of over 50 who has always lived
in isolated farmsteads and who can speak no English, mentioning
car numbers as often as people's names in her conversation.
Girls of 7, teenagers, village housewives, all know the numbers or
at least can recognize at a glance, the important cars of the
district, as well as the most familiar ones. For the most important
cars are not seen every day, but when seen they are noticed.
Everyone you meet stops for a brief talk and mentions:
   'The Pentre police car passed down towards Hafoty just now.'
   'Are you sure? There's a court case on in town this morning.'
   'Well, it's XXX33, isn't it?'
Or: 'Jack saw Twm Bailiff going up by Wern at dinner-time. At
least it was his motor-bike. That red Excelsior ZZZ11.'

Young men from this district, when on a spree in London, feel nostalgia when they see a car with a home registration number. And many can recognize some particular cars and motor-bikes by their sound. Knowing vehicles is not a hobby, it is part of the business of living, generally because communications are of great importance, and particularly because the grapevine is a war weapon.

After a court case which followed a skirmish between poachers and bailiffs in 1959, the *Daily Mail* wrote about the bailiffs: 'They always talk in secret code, for they believe the poachers may have a phone-tapping source' (3rd November, 1959). I do not think the poachers are as well or as formally organized as the bailiffs implied but the report is a tribute to the efficiency of the poachers' informal warning system.

Thus the forces of officialdom, and especially the men on the law-and-order side of officialdom, are kept constantly under surveillance, although the local population is hardly aware of the watch it keeps. The North Welsh also keep a curious eye on one another's activities as do all country people, but one of the purposes most useful to themselves for which they employ their powers of observation and memory is to beat the officials. I shall not go into all the forms the anti-official war takes. Poaching is interesting for two reasons. Firstly, because on the face of it, it is so unimportant economically. And secondly, because unanimity is more easily reached against river bailiffs than against other officials. In a general way everyone is against the police, but just occasionally a farmer loses some sheep and in an effort to clear up the suspicions and fears that begin, in the hope of proving that it is a certain dog, or is not a certain dog, or in the hope of catching the culprit, some people will co-operate with the police. In a general way everybody is out to 'fiddle' from other officials, but most of these other officials are sometimes useful. No one at any time is on the side of the river bailiffs – in their role of river bailiff. People may think, in theory, and even go so far as to say, that it is a pity to catch salmon while they are breeding and thus diminish the supply, but in practice they go poaching. Being Welsh is more important than saving salmon. The fact that the work of the river bailiffs is seen as simply the preservation of game fish for the pleasure of rich English people, and not at all for the advantage of the local working population, makes it possible for people to unite against them and this makes poaching particularly suitable as an activity which unites people as Welsh;

unites them against these representatives of English rule; unites them in an anti-official war.

It is easy to understand country people trying to avoid paying taxes. It is not so obvious why they catch fish they do not eat and go to very great trouble to do so. But here almost anything banned is worth doing, to keep the war going. I suspect that if it were forbidden by the Government to grow asparagus, and the chapel were fairly indifferent to the ban, North Welsh people would grow it although few have even heard of, never mind tasted, asparagus; few know it is thought of as a luxury food and probably no one would like it. They poach partly so that they and their friends can eat salmon, partly because poaching is a sport, partly because their fathers did it when poaching provided a vital addition to the family diet, but also largely because it is forbidden by those they see as the enemy. They do not phrase all these motives in the way I have done, but it is clear from the way they speak that all these motives operate. They do not speak of a war but they speak and act as though they were engaged in one. When two boys in their teens were stopped on the road by the bailiffs and found to be carrying salmon, the feeling was widely expressed that the bailiffs were cowardly to go after such young boys and to catch them away from the river, and by a mean trick. (A bailiff had told one of the boys he would not be in Llan that night, assumed the boy would believe him, and stopped him late at night near his home.) 'We'll have to do something about those bailiffs', the men said. Next night the air was let out of the tyres of the bailiffs' van and water put in the petrol tank.

Although salmon poaching appears to be unimportant from an economic point of view, and it is certainly so in the short run, in the long run it fulfils a function which is essential to the economic life of North Wales. For what the whole poaching conspiracy does is to draw the people of North Wales very close together. There is very little class feeling inside the structure of North Wales society, as I have explained in an earlier chapter. The upper class, the owners of quarries and land, as well as the foremen in any large enterprise, have been traditionally English; power and money and property in Wales have long been in the hands of Englishmen or anglicized Welshmen – so much so that there is still a general tendency to classify all English visitors as upper class. The bloody Saxons – minus a man's particular English friends – are excluded from conversation by an insistence on the use of the Welsh language; milked for drinks in the pubs;

and foiled when they appear as officials. Hostility is extended to those Welshmen who do 'their' jobs, or adopt 'their' ways. Class antagonism is expressed through and disguised as nationalism. The anti-English feeling (which is not so much violent as all-pervading) is expressed by a group which extends far beyond the minority who vote Welsh Nationalist. It is the form which class conflict takes, and the disguise in which many social antagonisms appear. English people known to be definitely not mean, rich or snobbish, are warmly accepted into the community, although if they have jobs as officials they will be treated in one way as men and in quite another way as officials. I distinguish between two levels of anti-English feeling; that mixed feeling which is directed towards individuals; and the 'partisan' feeling which is directed towards the abstract idea of 'ruling England'.

Country people's resentment of town bureaucracy is a world-wide phenomenon. In North Wales, this antagonism, like most other social hostilities, is expressed in nationalistic terms.

Officialdom is seen as an English phenomenon, a concrete expression of English power, which can be recognized and re-sisted; and the war against it, as in the case of the poaching grapevine, cuts across village quarrels, differences in income, religion, age and sex and draws all these Welsh-speaking people together. Any mechanism which helps to do this is clearly im-portant economically, since co-operation is a must in this poor country of scattered farmsteads, where all machinery and skilled labour is shared among the farmers and all private transport (except that of officials and 'big people') is shared by everyone.

The poaching conspiracy has a significance greater than the personal motives avowed by those engaged in it. It is an annual event which strengthens ties between the inhabitants of the district. To engage in it is a sign of Welshness. It symbolizes the fellowship of people who are physically separated from one another in scattered dwellings, who have many causes to quarrel, but who need one another all the year round, and who show they are 'on the same side' every November.

As I said in the preface, I do not believe it is the work of the social anthropologist to relate people's activities to their motives. It has been suggested to me that if I say the poaching conspiracy creates solidarity among the North Welsh people then I must go further and either say that the North Welshman goes poaching with the conscious aim of creating solidarity or I must suppose that he has an unconscious desire for solidarity.

I think that a person's motives for doing most things are mixed and not easily recognized and distinguished one from the other, by himself or by outsiders, and I do not think the social anthropologist is required to try to do this sorting out. There is no reason to suppose any poacher has a conscious or unconscious desire for solidarity. Last season or the season before, though he went poaching for various reasons which may have differed from those of his colleagues, he may have shared with them a satisfactory feeling of comradeship which followed the poaching. Enemies may have forgotten quarrels and run to give him a warning, and he may then have felt that this meant he could not continue the quarrel. Nevertheless this comradeship of last season may well be forgotten when he goes poaching. He may have fresh in his mind some nuisance a neighbour has committed rather than a feeling of brotherhood with him. But the feeling of brotherhood will again follow from participation in the poaching season. In his mind he does not relate warning Sam that there is a car on the bridge with the fact that he might one day need to borrow Sam's van.

Solidarity is an outcome of the activity. In the same way, other minor satisfactions may follow on a man's participation in a poaching season. He may see a heron fishing, or a badger playing and find pleasure in it. He would not go out the next year with the intention or hope of seeing such things but they may be some of the pleasant associations with the idea of poaching which help to make it attractive to him. This would be one of the many motives a psychologist might find in some particular poacher's mind. To find it and to estimate its degree of consciousness is not for the anthropologist, who is studying a social situation and the effects on a group of its own and other groups' behaviour.

Poachers do not all have the same motives and often they may go simply because they want a fish. However, they frequently catch more than they know what to do with. My suggested explanation may stand or fall, but it does not stand or fall by my finding or failing to find satisfactory psychological links.

The chapel brought people together in the past and was the central symbol of Welshness, certainly in many parts of Wales, and, I believe, in Llan; the church being the centre for English people and those who wished for anglicization. In Llan, at least, this is no longer the case. Attendances at church and chapel are small now and although church and chapel are rallying points for opposing cliques for some purposes, members of church and chapel alike are Welsh-speaking, are 'workers' and go poaching.

At present, participation in the poaching conspiracy particularly, and in the anti-English feeling generally, is a much more important and general badge of Welshness in North Wales than is the chapel. A group of people of many conflicting interests are fused together in opposition to another group, seen as outside. The motives in the people's minds as they engage in the action which brings them together are non-economic. The result of their fusion, however, is that their mutual co-operation in economic affairs is helped and I do not think the poaching conspiracy would continue in its present strength if those involved in it needed each other's support and services less.

Young and Unemployed in a Northern City
D. Phillips

This extract has been specially prepared for this volume and has not previously been published in this form.

During the early years of the 1970s there has been a very substantial rise in unemployment in Britain. While there have been many temporary fluctuations one feature has been a worsening situation for the young, and many school leavers have found it difficult to get jobs, particularly the kinds they think of as 'desirable'.

This paper is an attempt to talk with rather more precision about what the effects of this have been on the most vulnerable group of all, those who left school at the earliest opportunity in a northern city which we will call 'Irrbridge', where the work available has traditionally been in such kinds of industry as engineering, chemicals and textiles.

Public discussion has centred around 'folk theories'. These folk theories have one theme in common but very different conclusions for policy may be drawn from them. They place particular emphasis on a vision of long-term unemployment, with children leaving school failing to get jobs, and after a while becoming dispirited about their prospects of getting jobs, and settling into a 'street-corner layabout' lifestyle. The elements of the interpretation of this lifestyle were a product of a variety of influences, some domestic, some exotic, interestingly compounded. The picture was based on the surviving images of the Depression, with its groups of furtive, listless, apathetic, half starved unemployed (occasionally getting themselves together for a Hunger March). But this time, on top of this, there was the manifest evidence of 'style' and 'aggressiveness' in the manner of the young people, based on the 'youth revolution' of the late fifties and sixties. As in most large cities, the young have always used the street as a place for play, character games and pre-courtship activities. But these 'traditional' sports take on a new dimension when they are overlain by the symbolisms of California (or home grown versions) and become worrying or, threatening. The incidence of fear, hence reported deviance, detected deviance and stabilized and repeated deviance, rises. Both the young people involved and the wider population had, in different ways, understood the stories of the American urban ghettos with their groups of alternatively apathetic or dangerously violent long-term out-of-work young, out of work because of structural unemployment probably due to technological innovation making unnecessary the 'skills' previously offered to the labour market by this most disadvantaged group.

A brief debate in the daily evening newspaper which had a high circulation locally reflects the two attitudes to the visions involved. In an article that appeared when the rate of unemployment was at a peak a sympathetic reporter put the 'tragic' aspect: 'There is little more tragic than the plight of the army of young unemployed desperately trying to make a start in life against today's almost impossible odds. . . . In a work-oriented society this idleness affects youngsters in a variety of ways. Some resign to their fate, others despair, some are angry, others indulge in anti-social behaviour.'

This attached responsibility or 'blame' to groups other than the young unemployed themselves, in doing so drawing both on the idea that they could have 'done nothing' to deserve unemployment and the broader idea that children are not in principle 'responsible'. It drew the inevitable response:

'The heartache of trying to make a start in life lies in the fact that people are only willing to accept jobs that are "suitable" or near home.

Perhaps these youngsters do not read the papers to discover if there is work available. Perhaps they do but pass jobs by because they do not suit. Perhaps it is the move, but at least they would be working for a living, inevitably earning more than supplementary benefit allowances.

There are jobs available and there are people available for these jobs. In last Friday's Gazette there were 28 junior vacancies and 175 general vacancies apart from extra specialized fields.

Someone somewhere is capable of obtaining one of these jobs. If he has no "O" levels then perhaps driving, packing, tyre fitting or any number of different trades may fit the bill.' ('A Worker')

In relation to adult unemployment, the discussion in the local newspaper has been concerned to allot responsibility in this kind of way. One of the more entertaining exchanges began with a letter proposing that the unemployed should be rounded up and conscripted into the army which would cure them of these personal characteristics that had led to their unemployment. This was countered by an indignant note pointing out that the army had done nothing to deserve a sudden enormous influx of people with layabout characteristics and on these grounds angrily rejected the proposal.

All these 'typical' views are based on the folk theory idea about long-term unemployment that the central problem is that of a group of people who are out of work for very long periods: in structural unemployment this would become permanent. For school leavers and young people, the problem would be that of failing to find a job. An examination of the statistics of the Department of Employment rapidly shows that this is *not* necessarily the most illuminating way to look at the problem.

In January 1970, of those boys who were registered as unemployed in that month, 43 per cent had been unemployed for eight weeks or less, and none had been unemployed for longer than nine weeks. By comparison, in July 1972, 43 per cent had been unemployed for one week or less but of the remainder, 14 per cent had been unemployed for nine weeks or more. Despite the trend which these statistics evidence, it is clear that the picture of 'hard core' 'long-term' unemployment is as yet much more of a threat than a reality in this city. The absolute figures of unemploy-

Table 1. Absolute number of men and boys, aged 15 to 18, registered as unemployed with the Department of Employment and Productivity and the Careers Office respectively

Date	Men	Boys
January 1970	1,515	70
June 1970	1,276	55
January 1971	1,577	75
June 1971	2,003	80
January 1972	2,856	96
June 1972	2,680	80

ment among young men published by the local office of the DEP seem less than alarming in their magnitude particularly in relation to those for adults (see Table 1).

Thus, neither in terms of the absolute number of boys unemployed nor the length of time they tended to stay unemployed does the picture given by the official statistics directly support the folk theory, or either of the 'moral judgments' arising out of it.

Some doubts about the official statistics

It is important to remember that the figures in these tables are those of *self-reported unemployment*; that is, they are produced by people walking into the employment office and declaring themselves unemployed. It has often been remarked that there may be substantial groups of people within the population who do not do so, e.g. married women, self-employed persons or marginal dropouts. If this is so, then the published unemployment figures will tend to systematically underestimate some larger population who might (on other criteria) be regarded as 'unemployed'. Are the figures for youth unemployment subject to such processes? In a small and informal survey with a sample of 105 we located 10 boys, who, though unemployed, had no contact with the careers office, which is where they should declare themselves unemployed and receive, where eligible, unemployment benefit. If this proportion is at all representative, then the official figures may be subject to a 10 per cent margin of error.

But in addition to this doubt about the number of unemployed – which was dramatically illustrated when the preliminary findings of the 1971 census showed that the number of unemployed males in Irrbridge in April of that year was 3,530, and over twice the

DEP figures[1] – the figures we have given are clearly consistent
with a number of interpretations. It may be for instance that no
boys (or at least only a few) figure in the list twice, except in the
few cases where unemployment exceeds six months. In this case,
what is happening is that an increasing number of young people
are simply changing their jobs. There is nothing *in the figures*
which would necessarily support the 'street corner lads' stereotype, of boys who have not been employed since they left school,
and who over a period of time are becoming 'unemployable',
'sinking into delinquency', 'losing their self respect', and so on.

The figures are not, in fact, consistent with the 'hard-core'
unemployed idea, at any rate in any crude form. There is no
group that stays unemployed and provides the 'backbone' of the
figures, accompanied by a fluctuating and currently increasing
number of 'temporarily' unemployed. According to the official
statistics, no boy in Irrbridge over the past three years has been
unemployed for longer than 39 weeks. But there are other ways
of interpreting the 'hard-core' idea, which seem to come closer
to what is happening. The 'crude' unemployment figures provide
no guide to these interpretations but the following picture would
again be consistent with them.

There could be a 'core' of boys, who do not stay in any job
for a long period of time, and who lose jobs frequently, returning
to the careers office for assistance in finding another. This would
mean that the unemployment figures at any one moment in time
relate to a group of boys who may be expected to get employment
shortly (i.e. in less than 39 weeks). It is important to remember
that these figures are produced as an instantaneous snapshot at
intervals of six months showing the absolute number of those
on the register at that time (with correspondingly absolute figures
for how many fall into different periods of unemployment). Then
it will be, in part, a different group of boys who figure in the next
collection of statistics. Of course, some of the group making up
the second figure will be boys who have had employment and lost
it. If we think of this process as going on all the time, then it is
apparent that the figure of 'unemployed' on the register is a sample

[1] These 'unemployment rates' are worked out in different ways and
are not therefore directly comparable. The rate which is derived from
the Census is an 'economic activity rate', obtained by relating the total
number of people in a particular census category to the proportion in
that category who claim to have been in a paid job during the week
preceding that in which the Census was taken.

of a larger (but unknown) population of boys who frequently lose and take jobs. The group of boys who make up the 'problem' is very much larger, then, than the absolute figures of unemployed youths.

The other aspect of the situation which the absolute unemployment figures cannot, as a matter of course, demonstrate, is qualitative differences between employment. For the purpose of the figures any 'job' is equal to any other 'job'. The relevance of this to 'the problem' is great.

The pattern of intermittent unemployment

Our 105 boys aged between 15 and 19 (and hence including some who had only recently left school) had held between them 248 jobs. 36 interviewed at the careers office – again including some who had left school only a month or so previously – had held 97 jobs. A group who returned postal questionnaires, sent to one in three of 1969 school leavers, had held between them an average of 2·4 jobs. It is obvious that those who would bother to return an unsolicited postal questionnaire of twelve pages with no follow-up, were, as well, a highly self-selected group.

The boys themselves do not seem to see anything very unusual in the number of jobs they have held. They do not expect to stay in any particular job very long, and we suspect that their employers do not expect them to do so either. Frequent job changing seems to be essentially accepted by both employers and employees. It would seem too, for an initial analysis, that the length of time jobs are held changes with the number of jobs held. The first job was, on the average, held for approaching six months, the second nearer four months, the third down to two to three months. An analysis of the kind of jobs held shows how much a job leading to a possible 'career', for example an apprenticeship, was a one-off chance. If it was lost, the boy would next be likely to get unskilled employment, and rarely made a 'second chance'. Those who took unskilled work to begin with did not get apprenticeships later.

It was rare that the boys mentioned durations of unemployment lasting longer than six months. The pattern was far more that of 'a month in, a month out'. But it is also true that at the time of the study in summer 1972, periods of unemployment were getting longer, jobs more difficult to get, and that for some of the boys the situation was beginning to look desperate.

Many studies have shown, and the present study tends to bear this out, that the boys are quite realistic in their ideas about the sort of job they can expect to get. There are exceptions, but on the whole they accept their 'limitations'. Apprenticeships are highly prized, and so are jobs that will teach them a trade or skill. If these are not obtainable then they will settle for unskilled work which they would prefer to be local, well paid and with 'good' hours, i.e. not finishing late at night and preferably not involving work on Saturday afternoons. Answers to questions about what sort of job they would not like usually take the form of naming one of their past jobs as one they would under no circumstances take on again, rarely naming a job that they had not tried, except in a generalized way, e.g. 'not clerical'. A major proportion of the boys interviewed had worked in unskilled jobs for small concerns, small clothing workshops, warehouse work, van boys. Such places appear to provide the main employment opportunities for the young boys in this area and of course in times of economic recession many small firms will 'feel the pinch'.

'What did you like about the job?' was one of the questions boys found difficult to answer. Some said they enjoyed the work they were doing, others that they got on well with the people they were working with – in fact, this was highly valued. Certainly *not* getting on with the people they were working with or for was one of the reasons most often given for leaving a job. Although most of the boys would have preferred to work locally, the ones that were willing to travel or move were predictably those that are rather better qualified and/or those that have moved about the country in the past – yet only one boy actually gave as a reason for liking his job that it was 'just around the corner from my house'. So answers about the attraction of jobs tended to be negative – the most usual was in fact 'I didn't' or 'nothing' and others were, 'well, it was better than not having a job' and 'just getting paid'. On the positive side, those most valued aspects were the opportunity to travel about the area, higher wages than usual and freedom from constant supervision.

Understandably, it was rather difficult to establish why the boys had left jobs. Often we were merely told that they were 'sacked' or made 'redundant' which has become a vernacular term for dismissal, for a variety of reasons. When reasons were given it seemed that being late, taking time off, arguments with the boss or foreman, not doing the work properly all figured. Obviously some felt that the employer had dismissed them unfairly – one or two mentioned that they returned after an accident or being ill to be told that they were no longer wanted. Further it was suggested that certain employers do have a policy of dismissing boys when they reach 18 years of age or before if they can find somebody younger, and therefore cheaper, to do the work. If the boys themselves took the initiative the most usual reasons were to try to earn more money or because they were bored. Dismissal appeared to be accepted philosophically, but few of the boys unemployed gave the impression that this meant that they did not want a job. This was supported by the fact that the majority had tried all possible avenues they could think of to find work. If the jobs just were not there however they would just have to wait until they reappeared. The 'blame' for the shortage of jobs was usually attributed to the government and the current economic situation. It was the government's obligation to bring more jobs into the area. Both Dave and Melvyn – two of the boys interviewed – raised this particular point.

Dave, 17 years old, had had eight jobs and was now unemployed. He had left his local secondary modern school two years previously and gone straight into a labouring job found for him by the careers office. Although he 'quite liked' the work he left after three months to get a job which paid better and tried 'pressing' in a local firm, a job suggested by a friend for its good pay. Dave however disliked the work intensely and left within a week, returning to another labouring job (again found by the local careers office) but left this in turn for another job, again in search of better pay. His four other jobs had all been short-term jobs. Dave's 'marginal' attitude to work is illustrated by response to questions on the subject of what job would he have most liked when he left school: 'don't know', or what sort of job did he fancy now: 'any', or what sort of job would he not like: 'pressing'. Yet it would be a mistake to think that Dave does not want to work; in fact he does and he has tried as many ways as he can think of to get work for he intends to marry next year and is well aware that he has to have a job.

Melvyn's first job was working on fuel injection engines which he kept for a year. Engines he liked, the block release he didn't, and it was a bad report from the local Tech. that was the reason for his being given the sack. Now he admits it was his own fault and he regrets it. However, within a month he had got a job loading boxes which he left after as short a period feeling the work was boring, and in his terms 'useless'. Further he had been told it was the firm's policy to sack boys when they reached 18 years of age and he preferred to give in his notice first. The next job was 'putting studs in overcoats' which he found equally as boring as his previous job. The time he took to go and collect his insurance cards from his previous place of employment was given as the reason for his dismissal. For three weeks he was able to work in a local garage but that employment has now finished. Now he is too old to be taken back on the mechanical engineering course. He accepts that he is not going to be able to return to working on fuel injection engines, which is what he would really like to do, and will take any job that comes along. One will, he supposes, and it is just a case of having to wait a bit for it.

If we look at the phenomenon of recent job exchange among young people in the light of very recent history, we can add another dimension. In the period of full employment for young people, when any job became unacceptable, they could change it. They need not 'progress' in such changes. And thus it made little sense to apply concepts like 'career' to this kind of sequence of job exchange. But if someone at work tried 'discipline' on them, or if they simply became bored, doing tasks that were, in the main, utterly boring, then it was possible to go on to a new situation, which, during the 'learning' period, would be less boring. They were, in other words, doing something like Simmel's description of how to operate at a party, 'playing' and 'alternating' in a 'delightful' sequence of involvement–non-involvement, controlling and varying their social interaction. (It would of course be stretching things too far to suggest that an element of this, for senior workers, was involved in strikes, which during periods of full employment were a way of taking one's leisure with heightened, rather than reduced, interaction with one's friends and work colleagues.) In a period of low employment both games turn deadly: more so for the young than for the mature workers. A high employment situation makes it possible to take pleasure, in a number of ways, from a miserable situation. A low employment situation is simply miserable.

I suspect that one of the major problems is not that of those who left school during the low employment period, but of the rather older young people who once changed jobs with facility, and who established this as a pattern for themselves, only to find that they have rendered themselves the least employable group. They have identified themselves as 'unstable' and are stigmatized by such terms as 'intermittent job record' and 'does not seem able to accept the discipline of work', by the employers and also by the formal agencies such as the careers office and the DEP.

The boundary of the problem

The problem as it exists in Irrbridge now seems to be not so much one of *unemployment* as of *employment*. To argue that any one 'employment' is equivalent to any other 'employment' is clearly untrue, as far as the perspectives of the people involved are concerned. The point holds good not only for 'jobs' which last a short while but for 'careers' too; it is arguable that 'careers' are just 'jobs' to which a boy resigns himself. There are pay-offs to such resignation for the boy; but it should not be to our purpose to encourage such resignation which has pay-offs also in entirely different directions. ('A worker' who resigns himself in this way in fact demonstrates the inevitability of such an attitude of resigned acceptance to others.) A rhetoric has grown up, that it is the duty of the government to 'bring jobs' to an area, or that a factory has provided 'so many jobs'. The boundaries of the problem are such that such measures will not solve it. If we revert to a situation of high and easily obtained employment for young people they may equally well revert to the pattern of alternation – of 'playing' with the jobs that are provided for them in the interests of 'delight'.

What has grown out of this situation is that neither side – employer as well as employee – expects employment to be a permanent thing. Both sides need to show only a minimal commitment to a particular employment. On the employer's side, adult rate insurance contributions and other contractual elements are involved in employing a young person after he is 18. The pattern has its benefits for them.

Praise, blame and the young unemployed

The idea of a 'folk theory' has at its core the notion of 'reflexivity'. That is, if enough people subscribe to it and utilize it in their interpretations of their situations, it will manifestly become true. This is hardly a new idea in sociology. It is interesting to observe, in the situation we have been looking at, the birth, emergence, origins and progress of folk theories. What is particularly striking is the possibility – which may or may not develop – of the apparently quite implausible idea that the boys themselves might be 'responsible' for their situation. There is, if my suggestion about 'alternation' in periods of high employment is correct, material available for much constructive work.

One factor that is going to be crucial here is the attitude of counter staff in careers offices, where the crucial interaction between 'unemployed young men' and the representation of the 'system' takes place. Given the very substantial increase, at time of economic cutback, of National Insurance and Social Security payments of all kinds and the way in which those who arrive to ask for them are, in the main, in disastrous personal situations, it would be very surprising if the lower echelons of concerned agencies could sustain the folk theory that holds that some un-specified group – employers, the government, 'society', 'we ourselves' are responsible. Naturally, since public money is involved, they will be required, whatever their sympathies, to adopt an attitude of distrust to applicants. Let us take it also that such white-collar workers, themselves poorly paid (some almost qualify for supplementary benefit), will have a concern to stress the differences between themselves and their clientele of which the desk or counter is a symbol. Further the consciousness of class membership, actual and aspirant, will affect this interpersonal situation. If one is instructed to be suspicious of someone, that person becomes a legitimate object of suspicion; he has done something suspicious.

If, for example, a careers officer or clerical assistant in a careers office believes that there are two basic kinds of youth that he will encounter – a large group of these unemployed who have done nothing to deserve it and hence are 'deserving' and a small group who have personal characteristics that led to their unemployment and who are seeking to subsist on state handouts but between which groups there is no clear dividing line – then the following possibility opens.

One feature of folk theories is the process by which a small number of aspects can come to stand for the 'whole' which is understood from the limited data. This process by which a small number of salient characteristics apparently justify treating an individual or a situation as in some way 'typical' of an apparently well-understood process is sometimes referred to as 'synech-dochality'. The boys the clerk meets will have characteristics in common: poorly educated, many jobs, low morale and commit-ment and a strong dislike of the situation they are in.

Given that he must in each case be 'suspicious' it is evident that the clerk or careers officer can come to realize that what he thought were the 'good' group can diminish to a point where there seem to be only a few isolated deserving cases in a welter of attempts to live off the state. But the other folk theory prevails in the press and in public. So, in the end, only the agency 'knows' what is the truth: that they are the front line troops in a battle against a gigantic and increasing conspiracy to live off public money. I am not suggesting that this attitude is general as yet although it certainly seems to colour some of the interaction in careers offices. The staff of careers offices appear to be apprehensive at the intended removal of their function of giving out unemployment pay and supplementary benefits, which should in theory set them free for their proper work. When this happens the knowledge which, in their eyes, is invaluable and irreplaceable, and their tenuous control of a situation which is getting out of hand will both be lost. In terms of some sociological analyses, the next stage should be that the boys begin to blame themselves and to see their own lives in this light. But the other theory – that it is 'someone else's' fault – is currently too readily available.

The problem of unemployment and of employment among young people is thus not one to which simple or evident solutions in such terms as 'extended provision' readily suggest themselves. For the simple, self-evident solutions are, as we have seen, based on 'folk theories' which over a period of time become built into the ways in which official and unofficial agencies organize themselves. And the data which they produce routinely will tend to be interpreted in such ways as will tend to justify the solutions which they alone are uniquely equipped to provide.

Working and Not Working
D. Wedderburn

Reprinted with permission from *The Listener*, Vol. 87, No. 2252, 25 May 1972, pp. 669–71.

There are a number of reasons for describing the Rolls-Royce crisis as a national trauma: some to do with the position of the company at the centre of British capitalism, some to do with the complex international repercussions of the crisis. Other reasons concern the growing problems of managing large-scale technology, and the blow to British pride in technological excellence. But there was also a personal trauma – for the men who lost their jobs in Derby and Glasgow in March 1971. It appears that nearly two in ten are still without work a year later and are about to exhaust their entitlement to unemployment benefit. Even those who are now in jobs again were unemployed for an average of three months before they found new work.

Rolls-Royce workers were an élite. They were highly qualified technically, had interesting work, and many who eventually lost their jobs were working on the exciting RB211 project. Employment at Rolls-Royce had epitomized security: a major reason for taking a job with the company was that it provided employment which could be depended upon. Even after November 1970 – when the first public announcement was made which indicated trouble, and the need for further government assistance for the RB211 – most Rolls-Royce men still did not believe that they were at risk and that redundancy could affect them personally.

For such men to find themselves unemployed underlines dramatically the growth of insecurity as a central feature of workers' lives in contemporary Britain. Last year two million people drew unemployment benefit at one time or another. Add to them the many women and older workers who did not claim benefit, or who decided to retire, and possibly as many as one in ten of the work-force learnt what it was like to lose a job. Not having a job is the basic insecurity, but if we also take account of the reduction in overtime working and the increase in short-time working, we are bound to accept that there has been widespread anxiety, particularly for manual workers. It is a remarkable fact that the great majority of manual workers cannot rely on knowing what will be in their wage packet from week to week. According to the Department of Employment, only two-thirds of a manual worker's income comes from his basic pay, and even that is not always guaranteed. The rest of his income depends on fluctuating items like bonus and overtime.

The loss of a job often has wider repercussions upon security in a more general sense. A sizeable number of the former Rolls-Royce workers soon became involved in other redundancies and many had lost, or suffered a serious interruption to, their occupational pension rights – which are an important aspect of the security of lifetime earning. Small wonder most workers attach considerable importance to the security aspects of a job.

Is security a more important consideration than whether or not people find their work interesting? Almost certainly it is, although little attention is paid to the implications of such a preference. On the contrary, it is still being said glibly that there must be a change in attitudes: that people must realize that in the future they will have to change occupations two or three times during their working life – technological advance will require it. Such statements accord little recognition to the fact that there are social costs attached to such changes. People are not likely to be happy with a situation where such costs appear to be randomly allocated, often to those educationally and economically least able to bear them. There is a wide credibility gap between, on the one hand, Professor Galtung's view that in the future children should go to work for a year or two to experience what it is to work, that the middle-aged man should have time to play, and that the old should go on learning, and, on the other hand, the realities of an unplanned labour market. Any radical restructuring of the traditional division of the life-span between learning, work and leisure would require a major rethinking of the way in which income is distributed, because anyone outside the traditional labour market (with the exception of those who have private means) tends to be disadvantaged.

At the moment, perhaps unconsciously, our society is busy extending the period of dependency of the young by increasing the years of full-time education, and it is also extending the period of inactivity in old age by a *de facto* lowering of the age of retirement. This extension of the period in retirement is an interesting phenomenon. It is world-wide, yet we still do not know whether it is the result of people choosing to stop work or of their being forced to do so. The proportion of men drawing their retirement pension at the earliest possible age has steadily increased in the last ten to fifteen years. This might indicate a desire to stop working if it is possible to do so without too big a drop in income. Other statistics indicate that the proportion of men in their late fifties and early sixties who are drawing sickness benefit over long periods is increasing. Unemployment of a long-term kind is a serious problem among the older age groups. Most of the Rolls-Royce men who are still without work are in their fifties or older, and they attribute their difficulty in getting work to their age. There may, therefore, be institutional changes which make it difficult for the older worker to remain in the labour market even when he wants to. Technical change may have resulted in a dearth of jobs suitable for the skills and abilities of older men. The growth of occupational pension schemes may have meant an increase in fixed retirement ages.

But if a reasonable income is available, why should people want to work at so many of the boring routine jobs of modern industry? 'I can assure you that no one works at the assembly line unless he has to. If the pension is enough to give him a decent standard of living, then he will stop': this is the way in which many car workers view the problem. The generous early retirement benefits which the United Automobile Workers' Union has negotiated in the United States have proved extremely popular. In that country a sizeable group of people is emerging who say they have retired 'because they can afford to' and 'because they want to'. If standards of living for the elderly were to rise significantly, would the same thing happen here? Is it an illusion to believe that there is an interest in work? If you ask retired people what they miss about work the majority, 56 per cent, say: nothing. A quarter say they miss the money, 10 per cent miss the people, 5 per cent the feeling of being useful, and only 4 per cent the work itself. On the other hand, 42 per cent enjoy nothing about retirement either, but 41 per cent enjoy the free time. It is possible that people who have stopped work adjust their expectations to the realities of their situation: their answers may tell us very little about the attitudes of people still in work.

The Rolls-Royce men who were skilled technicians and foremen, and also fairly young, found their work interesting, but only a fifth had chosen to work there because of the interest of the work, and only just over a quarter thought that interesting work was the most important thing about a job in general. Does this mean that the present preoccupation of many managements with questions of job enrichment and job enlargement is misplaced? Under the influence of American management consultants, a number of British companies are experimenting with such schemes. A notable example is the weekly staff agreement of ICI, which is designed to extend the scope and responsibility of the jobs of routine machine-minding manual workers. In view of the concern of manual workers with security, it must appear somewhat unfortunate, to say the least, that because of changed market conditions many of these newly enlarged jobs are disappearing in quite large-scale redundancies.

In addition to money, security and interest, there are other important features of the work situation. For many people, work is experienced as a series of constraints. Work means being in a certain place for a given period of time. It means being subject to rules about what may and may not be done. It means having to perform certain actions and to carry out certain activities. The nature of these constraints varies. It varies socially in so far as, for example, the inflexibility and anonymity of work rules is still greater for manual than for non-manual workers. There is an assumption that non-manual workers can be trusted to exercise responsibility and to share the values of management. They can be given the benefit of the doubt in discipline cases; they can be trusted to turn up on time and do not have to clock in. The nature of the constraints also varies according to the kind of work to be done. It will vary both for manual and for non-manual workers. The invoice clerk has little more opportunity for variety or for the excercise of discretion than does the man standing beside the belt of the biscuit line. The craftsman and the professional worker will be at the other end of the spectrum.

All the evidence we have, so far, suggests that workers prefer jobs which enable them to exercise some discretion in how they carry out their work, which enable them to control their pace of working and to move about physically. These are the kinds of job they describe as interesting. But it is this interest which appears to be of rather small importance for most workers when it comes to an overall assessment of work. Perhaps that is because, when compared with the overwhelming routine of the general factory, or even with office constraints, such interest is seen as a welcome windfall if it is there, but not something which is to be expected.

In all this we must take account of the physical conditions in which work is conducted. Extremes of noise, temperature, even of smell, are common for manual workers. Nearly one in five manual workers work shifts and many will be involved in night work. The miners' strike reminded us of the unpleasant conditions and physical risk which still attend much manual work. The TUC estimates that on present trends every worker can expect to be the victim of at least two serious injuries during his working life. This is an average figure, and the chances are much greater in mining or the construction industry. But perhaps most important of all is the way in which the present social organization of work involves and perpetuates certain kinds of power relationship, giving rise to what might be called the general 'alienation' of the work situation. In America there is now a phenomenon familiarly called 'blue-collar blues'. It is an expression of individual revolt against these very constraints, which takes the form of widespread absenteeism and even of sabotage of the product. It is particularly marked among the automobile workers, the very people who retire early and can see no reason why people should want to work if they have a secure income.

But we should not ignore the fact that individuals and groups do vary in what they seek from the work situation. One of the greatest differences lies between those people who, either because they have had a craft training or because they have reached a high enough level of general education, feel that their ability to do a job rests with themselves and feel that, to this extent, they are independent of a particular employer, and, on the other hand, those people who have skills which are specific to an employer or feel they have no particular skill at all. The trend in modern industry seems to be towards more and more de-skilling. Even craftsmen are less and less concerned with specific products with which they can identify, and more and more concerned with general maintenance. And among white-collar workers there is a similar trend as a result of computerization.

The Rolls-Royce men had a rude awakening. Those who were ex-craftsmen found jobs more easily, provided that they were prepared to go back onto the shop floor. Those who felt that, having become technical engineering assistants with considerable responsibility, they should therefore be able to find comparable jobs experienced difficulty because their expertise was specific to Rolls-Royce.

This is not to say that many people will not squeeze satisfaction from the most improbable work situations. The men who sit day after day in little cubicles holding up bobbins of yarn to the light are proud of their ability to detect flaws which most people cannot see. The lady wrapping ballbearings in tissue paper describes her work as 'interesting because there is always that little bit of difference, and it is good to get through the work – it makes the day go'. But are we deluding ourselves if we think that the bulk of modern employment can be made interesting without a fundamental revolution in technology or in power relationships? And if we are deluding ourselves, then the first priority is to reduce industrial accidents and to provide better working conditions, predictability of earnings and security of employment.

Fishermen on the Beach
J. Tunstall

Reprinted with permission from *The Fishermen*,
MacGibbon and Kee, 1962, pp. 259–66.

Although old women in general are poor economically they are not quite as badly off as the men, since age does not entirely take away from women their primary source of interest – their own children and relatives. For men, however, retirement brings a much more fundamental change, not only reducing their incomes, but destroying their social and working life as well. Fishermen, because of their long periods of absence have less close ties with ordinary people than do most men and thus retirement for them produces a correspondingly greater tragedy. Moreover we have shown that fishermen when at work are one of the poorest groups in our country – if the total sufferings and rewards of their life are taken into account. Consequently retired or 'beached' fishermen, as they forlornly call themselves, can be described as one of the poorest of all groups living among us in economic as well as social terms.

When they are at sea fishermen bewail the fact that no pension awaits them and that they will probably end their lives as watchmen on trawlers in the dock, earning a mere pittance. Some men leave the job around the age of forty and get themselves a low-paying but secure job on shore. But most men, fearful of going back to a labourer's job ashore, continue to go to sea as long as they can manage to get a berth on a trawler.

One group of ex-fishermen does reasonably well ashore – these are the technical men. Out of the fifty-five ex-fishermen the three highest paid men were all engineers. The top pay was that of a chief engineer on an ocean-going tug, who was making £25–£30 a week. The chief of an oil tanker operating in the Humber was getting £15–£20 a week, and a second engineer on an ocean-going tug made £17 a week.

Other engineers got secure jobs at lower pay, for instance a chief who retired at the age of fifty:

'At present I am Chief on the Fish Dock tugs. My basic wage is £9 4s 4d per week but with working wk. ends now and again and odd overtime it will average about £11 10s. Providing I prove myself satisfactory which I think I have at present I shall remain till old age says I've had enough. I would definitely go fishing again if I had my time again. It is 50 per cent easier now than it was when I started. I had 34 years at it and am more than pleased, both working conditions and working hours on deck at present have made it more pleasant for all concerned, for believe me, it was a hard life when I first started. I really have no snags about being an ex-fisherman excepting here locally if you want to apply for a job. I think the majority of bosses always had at the back of their mind one thing. Drunken fishermen. Even a recommend from a Trawler Owner always had the word sober in it, so you will see what I mean.'

Out of the 55 men, 5 were living on old age pensions, 8 were unemployed and 41 were working. The pensioners had not stopped working willingly, and filled in the question asking how long they had been out of work, indicating that they considered themselves as being unemployed and the pension as just another kind of dole. One of them said: 'It's a crime to grow old on the fish-dock' and this summed up the others' attitude.

Of the men who were working, two-thirds (27 out of 41) were making less than £10 a week. 39 gave details of what they were earning and it averaged £9 15s for the whole group. Excluding the four most highly paid men the average was £8 15s.

Three men worked as seamen on lightships. The hours in this job are long, but the wage is about average for ex-fishermen and the job has a comparatively high degree of security. A lightship-man feels himself to be quite lucky, in spite of being paid only 2s 6d an hour:

'I am now working on Lightships, my wages are £9 for a 72 hours week. Since being ashore I had six months out of work. My present work suits me fine, the money's little, but there is prospects of getting on and all the time I behave and do my work I have a job for life and a pension at 65, that is a lot to look forward to. Under no conditions would I go back fishing, although fishing is much better, there is no future in it for when you get old 90 per cent of the fishermen, deckys, mates or skippers, they all finish up as watchman or sit on park seats with only old age pensions to live on after years of exciting living.'

Sixteen of the forty-one men working were employed in some capacity on the fish-dock, or in the fishing industry. The best-off of these were those in a secure job like the tug chief engineer already quoted. But most of the men employed on the dock were employed casually or if employed regularly were paid correspondingly low wages. The fishing-industry has a policy of employing semi-disabled ex-fishermen but it does not seem to pay them much more than what their labour would fetch on the open market. A retired mate said:

'Now I am slightly disabled and at present making Fish Baskets, and I can earn approximately £9 per week. I was out of work 18 months before, I was more or less forced to take this job I am at present engaged at. Of course I had to train for 12 months at £6 10s per week. So now after 2½ years I am having to make the best of things. As far as I can see there is no other work available for such as us. To the best of my knowledge there is no other work that us beached fishermen can hope for.

I would advise any young man to take up fishing as a career, but he must set his mind on getting to the top, and of course use his head with his money. An ex-fisherman is pretty well stranded when he is beached. No employers seem to like to give work to ex-fishermen. The reason I think for this is a fisherman takes a lot of settling in a regular and sometimes monotonous shore job. The difference in his earnings forces him to try several kinds of work if the jobs are available to improve his earnings. And that in my opinion is the reason so many employers will not take fishermen on their pay roll.'

A casual worker on the fish-dock:

'I went to sea as an apprentice when I was 15 years old. My wage was 6d a week and all found. I have been casually employed on St Andrew's Dock for 6 months of each year. Casual work on dry side pays in summer £8 a week on average, but in autumn and winter it drops to £3 or £4. Prospects of other work are nil clear of watching trawlers which pays a pound for 24 hours work.

If a man has no ticket he's on the scrap heap at 40 and there is no prospect of employment anywhere as 35 is the age limit for Bobbers and this job was supposed to be for old fishermen. In my 43 years at sea I have paid 6d a week into a fund for Widows and Orphans, but now if I was to die ashore my wife would get nothing.'

Fishermen talk a great deal about ending up as watchmen but in fact since only about twenty trawlers are usually in dock at a time not many men are required for this job. It has the advantage of being connected with the industry which the man has worked in and a watchman can reckon to make some extra money in backhanders, but the hours are extremely long and a man of sixty humbly accepting a backhander from a 17-year-old deckielearner obviously has not a great deal of self-respect left:

'Since being ashore I have been out of work six months, including three months' illness. Being a trawler watchman seemed to me an automatic choice, having served forty years in the fishing industry at least I feel at home doing it and am capable for at least another five or six years. On reflection I have no regrets whatever. I enjoyed very good health and more important I felt more free than the indoor workman shut up all day in a workshop, however, having finished with the sea I take a dim view of the trawler-owners' reward for men who like myself have served a lifetime in the fishing industry. I get £5 to £6 per 7-day week as a trawler watchman. Such meagre earnings to my way of thinking are bordering serfdom.'

Few ex-fishermen worked in factories, mainly apparently because factory-employers thought them too unreliable or too slow. Seven described themselves as doing labouring jobs, while others did things like refuse-collecting. A retired bosun considered himself lucky to be in a steady labouring job:

'For labouring at the Airfield I get £8 0s 2d per 42-hour week, rely on overtime for a living wage.
Fishing is a healthy life and the money's far greater than I get at present but age getting on and wife ill. I got a shore job cause she wanted me to stop onshore on smaller wages she's been used to and there isn't many shore jobs without an age limit so I'm lucky to be working.'

Bedevilled by insecurity as fishermen, when they go back to the shore they find the old bogey even worse. Only 22 out of the 50 non-pensioners thought their job-prospects reasonably good.

24 out of 50 had been unemployed for a period of at least three months and another 6 had suffered shorter periods, meaning that three-fifths of all ex-fishermen had been unemployed though some had been ashore only two years, and none more than four. Apart from the pensioners, at the time of the survey 8 out of 41 men were actually out of work, and this was in the high employment month of June, and in 1960 a year of fairly full employment. Many men who are in their forties or early fifties and have not yet experienced unemployment must expect to do so before they reach the age of 65, and should there be an economic recession these ex-fishermen, who are frequently regarded as marginal employees, would be very much more severely hit than the general working population.

If engineers are in the best position when leaving fishing, skippers may well be in the worst (though not enough evidence has been collected to say this with certainty). A short period of illness or injury triggers off a period 'out of a ship', which continues into long-term unemployment. The skipper has grown unaccustomed to physical labour, and employers may suspect that a man who has previously had such high earnings will not settle down into a humble unskilled job. Two skippers describe being unemployed:

'At present am out of work (trying to get back fishing) I was in hospital for three months and was told to take it easy for a bit after that. I took a job in my brother's shop, so I stopped working there and have been trying to get back to sea (for a year now). I went to see the Ship Husband and he told me I was too old for mate's job. Skipper's job not much chance, they want nobody over 40, so the only thing left for me and a lot more like me is Bosun, 3rd hand, or Spare hand. After that, who knows, Watchman or N.A.B.

P.S. If you have plenty of money you give a good Back Hander to the right persons you stay in a ship, I don't suppose you want to know about that lot of corruption what goes on the dock as I could write a book myself about it. It starts from entering the dock to leaving it again.'

The second skipper:

'I have been ashore for years, out of work all that time. Get £6 10s from U.A.B. Having reached my ambition as Skipper I now think it has been a wasted life. I have applied for various jobs but have been turned down, otherwise if I had been at any other trade I may have got a light job owing to my disability.'

Even if he has a job the ex-fisherman now has too little money to go out very often, and if unemployed he must perforce spend long hours at home. Repeatedly men stress the simple benefits of home life:

'All the things that one has missed after doing 35 years at sea, such as the home comforts, value of family life.'

'I am more contented, as you have more home life and every night in bed makes the life worth living.'

'After 40 years at sea like a fish out of water, a different life altogether, but gradually adjusting oneself to it. Had family of 7, but stopped going to sea when last daughter got married. (My average money cut by half, now as Relief Engineer on dock £11 per week, £9 17s to take home.) Wife and I just getting to know one another.'

'I think the rough life on a Trawler (I mean in those days) makes a man value home-life and the love and comfort there is in the world.'

This changed attitude to home comes about not because the ex-fisherman's capacity to love his wife and home suddenly changes spontaneously, but because the circumstances of his life change, his horizons shrink. However, the wife's life, which is usually based on housework, cooking, perhaps part-time work, and social contact with the daughter and other relatives, does not change suddenly and cannot be expected to blossom forth into quite the same new-found appreciation of her fisherman husband.

Some old fishermen hang around the Hessle Road pubs and clubs, and when you go in for a drink with a group of young fishermen it's surprising how frequently you meet their fathers, uncles, fathers-in-law, or other relatives – presumably because these men intentionally go in there when they know the young men have landed. The youths gallantly buy the old men drinks, pass a backhander under the table and perhaps slap down a coin with the barman for one more drink for the old man as they move off to the waiting taxi. But other old men sit by themselves quietly eking out a pint of mild for as long as possible. One notices that, much more than with the younger fishermen, the old men's hands which clasp the pints of mild have fingers missing – a sign of the more brutal conditions of their day.

Some attend subsidized social meetings on Hessle Road to while away the hours. One such meeting was the work of a church-going woman who owned a prosperous local shop. She provided the old men with a place to meet, tables and chairs for playing games, and tea at a penny a cup. The men came every afternoon of the week in contrast to the old women who only came twice. The women chatted endlessly about their families, their grandchildren and great-grandchildren and domestic problems such as the difficulty of living in an inconveniently large house now that the children had left. The men were much more formal, playing dominoes right through the afternoon – and sadly restrained compared with the young fishermen crowded into a trawler's messdeck eagerly gambling their settlings as they steamed back from Iceland.

Those who are humble enough to accept the charity of others do so in pubs and clubs. Some wait alone for death at home, proud and defiant, while others stay indoors and thankfully accept the help of their children. One old fisherman living alone in a terrace house said:

'The bairns gave me this TV set. Without it I'd have been dead by now. Things are much better than they used to be.'

This is the way the fishermen's world ends.

Further Reading: Leisure, Unemployment and Retirement

E. W. BAKKE, *The Unemployed Man*, New York, E. P. Dutton, 1934.

J. DUMAZEDIER, *Towards a Society of Leisure*, New York, The Free Press, 1967.

J. T. DUNLOP, *Automation and Technical Change*, Engle-Wood Cliffs, New Jersey, Prentice-Hall, 1962.

I. EMMET, *Youth and Leisure in an Urban Sprawl*, Manchester, Manchester University Press, 1971.

F. HERZBERG, *Work and the Nature of Man*, London, Staples Press, 1968.

E. LARRABEE and R. MEYERSOHN, *Mass Leisure*, Glencoe, Illinois, The Free Press, 1958.

*E. J. MISHAN, *The Costs of Economic Growth*, London, Penguin, 1969.

K. ROBERTS, *Leisure*, London, Longmans, 1970.

M. SMITH, S. PARKER and C. SMITH, *Society and Leisure in Britain*, London, Penguin, 1973.

*W. H. WHYTE, *The Organization Man*, London, Penguin, 1961.

*H. L. WILENSKY, 'Labour and Leisure, Intellectual Tradition,' in *Work and Leisure in Modern Society*, Special Issue of *Industrial Relations*, Vol 1, No. 2, 1962.

* Available in paperback.

Textbook and Reader Reference

The aim of this reader is to present students and teachers with sociological work of quality relating to the key issues in the study of work. I am well aware that there does not exist a single, comprehensive textbook which one could recommend without hesitation to all. The books which we have annotated here are some of those which are widely used, or possibly should be more widely known. It is hoped that this indication of the *comparative* coverage of these texts and readers will prove useful to students and thus help to obviate the tedious chore of searching through library catalogues in the hope of finding adequate material to supplement or substitute for a recommended textbook. The categorization I have adopted is, of course, fairly rudimentary and to some extent arbitrary, as not all of these books cover the same ground.

M. ARGYLE, *The Social Psychology of Work*, London, Penguin, 1972.

*T. BURNS, *Industrial Man*, London, Penguin, 1969.

*T. CAPLOW, *The Sociology of Work*, London, McGraw-Hill, 1954.

A. ETZIONI, *A Sociological Reader on Complex Organizations*, New York, Holt, Reinhart and Winston, 1969 (2nd Edition).

*W. A. FAUNCE, *Readings in Industrial Sociology*, New York, Appleton-Century Crofts, 1967.

*A. FOX, *A Sociology of Work in Industry*, London, Collier-Macmillan, 1971.

J. KELLY, *Organizational Behaviour*, Homewood, Illinois, Irwin-Dorsey, 1969.

E. A. KRAUSE, *The Sociology of Occupations*, Boston, Little Brown, 1971.

*R. K. MERTON, A. P. GRAY, B. HOCKEY and H. SELVIN, *Reader in Bureaucracy*, Glencoe, Illinois, The Free Press, 1952.

S. NOSOW and W. H. FORM, *Man, Work and Society*, New York, Basic Books, 1962.

*S. R. PARKER, R. K. BROWN, J. CHILD and M. A. SMITH, *The Sociology of Industry*, London, Allen and Unwin, 1967.

L. TAYLOR, *Occupational Sociology*, New York, Oxford University Press, 1968.

H. M. VOLLMER and D. L. MILLS, *Professionalization*, Englewood Cliffs, New Jersey, Prentice Hall, 1966.

D. G. ZYTOWSKI, *Vocational Behaviour*, London, Holt, Reinhart and Winston, 1968.

* Available in paperback.

Textbook Reference

Men and Work	Argyle	Burns	Caplow	Etzioni	Faunce	Fox	Kelly
2. Perspective	2	1, 2, 3, 4, 5	1	1, 2	1	1	
3. Structure	1	15, 17	7	3, 7		2	1, 2
4. Entry	4		9				9, 4
5. Career	5, 6, 7	9, 13	5, 10, 11	4	3		10, 11, 12
6. Values		14	6				13, 14
7. Slavery	3	6, 9, 10, 11, 12		5	2	3	
8. Autonomy	9	16		6	4	3	
9. Unions			8		5, 6	4, 5	
10. Non-work	10				7		14

Textbook Reference

	Krause	Merton	Nosow and Form	Parker Brown, Child and Smith	Taylor	Vollmer and Mills	Zytowski
2. Perspective	1	1	1, 2	1, 15			1
3. Structure	3, 4		3, 4, 5	2	1, 2, 3	1, 2	2
4. Entry	2	5	13	3	8, 9, 10	3	4, 5, 6, 7, 8, 9
5. Career	5, 6, 7, 8, 9, 10, 11, 12, 13, 14	6	8, 9, 10, 14	4	11, 12, 13, 19	7, 10	10, 11
6. Values			12	13	7, 18	4	3
7. Slavery		2, 3, 4	11	7, 8, 9, 10	4	8	
8. Autonomy		7			20		
9. Unions			6, 7	11	5, 6	5, 7, 9	
10. Non-work	15		15	5, 6, 14			

Alternative Table of Contents

Rural occupations

Women's occupations

Unions

Index

Fontana History of Europe

Praised by academics, teachers and general readers alike, this series aims to provide an account, based on the latest research, that combines narrative and explanation. Each volume has been specifically commissioned from a leading English, American or European scholar, and is complete in itself.

The general editor of the series in J. H. Plumb, lately Professor of Modern History at Cambridge University, and Fellow of Christ's College, Cambridge.

Fontana Politics

The English Constitution Walter Bagehot
edited by R. H. S. Crossman

The Backroom Boys Noam Chomsky

For Reasons of State Noam Chomsky

Peace in the Middle East Noam Chomsky

Problems of Knowledge and Freedom Noam Chomsky

Marx and Engels: Basic Writings
edited by Lewis S. Feuer

Edmund Burke on Government, Politics and Society
edited by Brian Hill

Governing Britain A. H. Hanson and Malcolm Walles

Machiavelli: Selections
edited by John Plamenatz

Sakharov Speaks Andrei D. Sakharov

To the Finland Station Edmund Wilson

Technosphere

Technosphere is an original Fontana series that presents individual studies of particular sciences and technologies in terms of their human repercussions. The series will include original analyses of a wide variety of subjects – transport technology, drugs, computer technology, operational research and systems analysis, photography, urban planning, films, alternative medicine, and so on – with the emphasis on the present state of the science or technology in question, its social significance, and the future direction of its probable and necessary development.

Technosphere is edited by Jonathan Benthall, Director of the Royal Anthropological Institute.

Already published:

Television: Technology and Culultural Form
by Raymond Williams

Through a survey of the development of television and broadcasting institutions in Britain and America, and an analysis of the different programming forms and their scheduling by the BBC, ITV and American networks, Raymond Williams seriously questions current views on television, and maps out a critical approach to programmes as varied as 'Coronation Street' and 'News at Ten'. '. . . a powerful and reasoned attack on technological determinism.'   Stuart Hood, *Guardian*

Alternative Technology and the Politics of Technical Change
by David Dickson

David Dickson's searching analysis clearly demonstrates that, as man is forced by increasing scarcity to consume less at a time when he is compelled by economic necessity to produce more, so he must adopt fresh attitudes to technology. The characteristics of these fresh attitudes are outlined in terms that are clear and positive but reflect the tentative and experimental character of all alternative technology.

'. . . entirely convincing . . . Dickson's statement of the case for the non-neutrality of technology is by far the best I have come across.'
New Society

An Open University set book

Unended Quest: An Intellectual Autobiography

Karl Popper

Internationally hailed as one of the most outstanding philosophers writing at present – on politics, on science, on human knowledge, on society – this unique book is Sir Karl Popper's own account of his life and of the development of his ideas. In fascinating detail he traces the genesis and formulation of his major works: *The Open Society and Its Enemies*, *The Logic of Scientific Discovery*, *The Poverty of Historicism*, *Objective Knowledge*, and *Conjectures and Refutations: The Growth of Scientific Knowledge*.

'. . . a splendid introduction to the man and his ideas.'
Martin Gardner, *The New Leader*

'. . . a remarkable document of intellectual history.'   Lewis S. Feuer

'This autobiography is part discussion on method; part intellectual history of Popper's major ideas; and part a continuing discussion of his ruling preoccupations.'   Tyrrell Burgess, *New Society*

'. . . few broad areas of human thought remain unillumined by Popper's work.'   Bryan Magee

A Fontana Selection

The Sunday Gardener (*illus.*), edited by Alan Gemmell
Ideology in Social Science, edited by Robin Blackburn
Hitler: The Führer and the People, J. P. Stern
Memories, Dreams, Reflections, C. G. Jung
The Screwtape Letters, C. S. Lewis
Waiting on God, Simone Weil
Butterflies *(illus.),* E. B. Ford
Marx, David McLellan
Soft City, Jonathan Raban
Social Welfare in Modern Britain, edited by Butterworth & Holman
Europe: Hierarchy and Revolt 1320-1450, George Holmes
Black Holes, John Taylor
The First Four Georges *(illus.),* J. H. Plumb
Letters of Vincent Van Gogh (*illus.*), edited by Mark Roskill
Food for Free *(illus.),* Richard Mabey
Language Made Plain, Anthony Burgess